PERILS OF EMPIRE

PERILS OF EMPIRE

THE ROMAN REPUBLIC AND THE AMERICAN REPUBLIC

Monte L. Pearson

Algora Publishing
New York

Library of Congress Cataloging-in-Publication Data —

Pearson, Monte.
  Perils of empire: the Roman republic and the American republic / Monte Pearson.
    p. cm.
  Includes bibliographical references and index.
    ISBN 978-0-87586-612-3 (trade paper: alk. paper)—ISBN 978-0-87586-613-0 (hard
cover: alk. paper)—ISBN 978-0-87586-614-7 (ebook) 1. United States—History. 2. United
States—Territorial expansion—History. 3. Rome—History—Republic, 510-30 B.C. 4.
Imperialism—History. 5. United States—History—21st century. 6. United States—
Foreign relations—2001- 7. World politics—21st century. I. Title.

  E179.P356 2008
  973—dc22
                            2008017326

Front Cover: Statue of Emperor Trajan and Roman Wall
A statue of the Emperor Trajan stands before part of the Roman Wall.
Image: © Michael Nicholson/CORBIS
Photographer: Michael Nicholson
Date Photographed: ca. 1985-1995

Printed in the United States

For Wendy and Laura Simon-Pearson

May they live in a world without empires.

Acknowledgements

I would like to thank a number of people whose help and guidance made it possible to write this book. Let me start by acknowledging my parents, Jack and Dorothy Pearson, who spent many hours doing volunteer work while I was growing up. They are the ones who taught me that justice for all people is the fundamental basis for a good community. Along with that, every community needs good institutions, and the Cambridge Center for Adult Education plays an important role in the Boston area. I would like to thank the staff at the Center for their willingness to host my Perils of Empire class. Thanks also to the students who took the class. Their questions and enthusiasm convinced me that this comparative history project was worthy of a wider audience.

My brother, Scott, first urged me to take up my class outline and turn it into a book. Since then he has offered advice and support, most of which I took, all of which I appreciated. Finally, this book could not have reached final form without the untiring editorial work provided by my wife, Martha Simon. Her sharp eye and unfailing belief in my abilities sustained me through writer's block and other hazards.

TABLE OF CONTENTS

Introduction. Empires and Political Freedom

> History is a vast early warning system.[1]
>
> —Norman Cousins

The word Empire is back. The term first went out of fashion when the empire building competition between the European powers led to the prolonged bloodletting of World War I, and then into hiding as colony after colony achieved independence in the period after the Second World War. By 1975 the United Nations, with more than 170 sovereign members, was living, quarrelling proof that the time of empires was gone forever.

Then the Berlin Wall was toppled and the Cold War ended. Regrettably, the "peace dividend" never really developed because, even as the Russian military disintegrated and the Chinese army remained focused on maintaining domestic order, new, small-scale disturbances seemed to call for an American ability to project military power into far corners of the globe. The unwillingness of a Democratic president to reduce the American Republic's military arsenal was overshadowed by the phenomenon known as "globalization."

Symbolized by the World Wide Web, the real focus of the 1990s was on the linking of nations through the miraculous evolution of technology and the expansion of world trade. Many people saw globalization as a phenomenon that would move the world beyond empires, imperialism, and cold wars.

---

1 Cousins, Norman, *Saturday Review*, April 15, 1978

It would bring prosperity, freedom, and middle-class status to the world's people, and it would not be owned by any one nation — it would be shared. Opposition to globalization was seemingly confined to a handful of backward nations burdened with oppressive leaders vainly trying to hold back the bright new world order.

The first indication that not everyone was pleased with this new world was the massive street demonstrations during the World Trade Organization meetings in Seattle, Washington in 1999. People from an astonishing array of underdeveloped nations joined with young people, environmentalists, and trade unionists from the United States and Europe to create a week long symphony of protest against nearly every aspect of globalization. They pointed out that globalization in many countries meant shrinking wages, the loss of deeply embedded cultural practices, the flouting of ancient traditions, and a loss of national sovereignty. Protesters even claimed that globalization was not a neutral process; that its primary benefits went to American transnational corporations and financial institutions.

Then came the shock of 9/11 and opposition to the new world order suddenly took on a new and deadly face. The scattered terrorist attacks of the 1990s had somehow become a worldwide opposition movement, with a determined religious/ideological justification for opposing nearly every tenet of globalization. The horrible murder of nearly 3,000 people working in New York's World Trade Center temporarily stilled the voices of peaceful protest to globalization and swung public opinion in the United States and much of the rest of the world behind an attempt to eradicate the terrorists. The new US administration, led by a cohort of policy intellectuals known as "neoconservatives," moved quickly to exploit this opportunity to freely project American military power across the globe.

In retaliation for sheltering Osama bin Laden and al-Qaeda, the fanatical Taliban movement was forcibly evicted from power in Afghanistan; military alliances, complete with rights to develop air bases, were established in Central Asia; and the USA Patriot Act, which was the first expansion of the government's power to spy on Americans since the CIA hearings of the mid-1970s, was passed with only a handful of dissenting votes. Nations that dissented from American policies were labeled members of an "Axis of Evil." In the fall of 2002, a majority of Democrats and most of the Republicans in Congress, shown shreds of evidence that Saddam Hussein possessed weapons of mass destruction, authorized the President to use military force to eliminate this alleged new arm of the terrorist threat.

THE INVASION OF IRAQ

In January and February of 2003, the Bush administration presented its case to the United Nations that US troops should be authorized to remove Hussein from power — and the world paused. The vast majority of the world's people did not see any linkage between al-Qaeda and Hussein, between terrorist acts in New York and a secular state weakened by years of rigid sanctions. Evidence for the existence of weapons of mass destruction was flimsy, while the existence of vast oil reserves was obvious. The grand alliance against terrorism quickly unraveled, a fact punctuated by the mass rallies of February 15, 2003, when hundreds of thousands of people, in nations all over the globe, took to the streets to oppose an invasion of Iraq. When the U.N. Security Council finally, after weeks of debate, refused to authorize an invasion, the United States found itself outside the boundaries of international law. The Bush administration launched an attack upon Iraq anyway and, after the country was occupied, a new debate erupted over the power and intentions of the United States, the world's lone super-power.

Just as suddenly, the word Empire was back in public dialogue. Neo-conservative intellectuals had argued in the 1990s that the United States had the right to use military power to police the dark corners of world politics. It was time, they said, for the United States to take up the responsibilities of enforcing rules in the Empire. Human history was full of rogue nations and political movements that were tempted to upset the status quo when they felt they could get away with it.

For example, Harvard Professor Michael Ignatieff, writing in *The New York Times Magazine* in 2003, asked, "What word but empire describes the awesome thing America is becoming?"[1] He claimed that the United States has become "in a place like Iraq, the last hope for democracy and stability alike." In the fall of 2001, Max Boot, while a fellow at the Council on Foreign Relations, wrote an article in the *Weekly Standard* titled, "The Case for American Empire."[2] In it he said, "Afghanistan and other troubled lands today cry out for the sort of enlightened foreign administration once provided by self-confident Englishmen in jodhpurs and pith helmets."

Others were not so sure. In a thought provoking series of cartoons, Garry Trudeau had the infamous "Uncle Duke" prepare to become a proconsul in conquered Iraq by donning a toga, insisting his partner "Honey" speak in *Latinum* and ordering six pairs of lions. In his own special way, Trudeau had touched upon one of the intriguing aspects of Empire. The world has seen a lot of them and it is very tempting to make comparisons. Many of the Bush administration's supporters look upon the British Empire with fondness and their works are peppered with analogies to the British imperial experience.

---

1 Ignatieff, Michael, "The American Empire: The Burden," *The New York Times*, 1.5.03, available at: http://query.nytimes.com/gst/fullpage.html?res=9B03E6DA143FF936A35752C0A9659C8B63; accessed 11 December 2007

2 Boot, Max, "The Case for American Empire," *The Weekly Standard*, 10.15.01, V.7, issue 5; available at: http://www.weeklystandard.com/Utilities/printer_preview.asp?idArticle=318; accessed 11 December 2007

Like Trudeau, critics of the invasion of Iraq and other Bush administration foreign policies have been drawn to the Roman Empire for analogies and comparisons. However, after a brief foray noting the gladiators in the Coliseum, the building of roads, and images of slaves rowing ancient naval vessels, the comparisons tend to founder. Clearly, the government of the Roman Empire is not the same as the Bush Presidency. The Emperor with his Praetorian Guard and disenfranchised public is not analogous to a president who, whatever the controversy, was elected twice by voters and is subjected to intense scrutiny by the news media that may not always be intelligent but always goes for the jugular when it finds a weakness. No, the domestic politics of the American Republic bear little resemblance to the intrigues of Rome's Imperial Palace; history seems to have little to teach us in this instance.

Yet a deeper look into the far reaches of Roman history reveals a more compelling connection. For the imperial Roman Empire arose out of the ashes of the Roman Republic, one of most famous political entities in ancient history. Before the Roman Empire, a time of one-man rule and limited freedoms, there was the Roman Republic — a time of elections, civil liberties, the rule of law, public debates, and successful armies. It was a time when Caesar and Cicero would debate one another in the Senate. At first the Republic's mighty armies brought wealth and glory; then the Republican institutions began to groan under the strain of running an empire. There were feuds, then riots, then civil wars and the Republic was gone, a victim of unintended consequences.

This book is an exploration of that long-ago Republic, pointing out some startling similarities between its history and that of the American Republic and tracing the series of events leading to the Republic's collapse into civil war and eventually the dictatorship of an emperor. In some aspects the story is similar to our own: the Roman Republic began with a revolt against an unjust foreign king and the new leaders created political institutions designed to protect their newfound liberty. Many aspects are unique to that time and place, for example, the Roman practice of having priests examine the entrails of dead birds to foresee whether an army would endure defeat or celebrate victory. Along the way, there are historical parallels that give us pause as we marvel at the many ways in which the human condition remains the same.

Each historical society is unique, for each of the world's great civilizations has drawn on many roots for its strength, its knowledge, its culture, and its traditions. Each society has a specific level of technological ability and exists in a specific geographical location that provides a context for every action and belief. Every civilization is made up of unique individuals who make their own choices, based on beliefs and environmental conditions that are not the same as those that influence other individuals whose choices shape other civilizations. As a result, we should be cautious about using the events and trials of the Roman Republic as a way of making detailed predictions about the future of the American Republic.

However, we would be unwise to dismiss the fate of the Roman Republic as having no relevance to our own. For within their own context, the Roman Republic had many characteristics that were similar to those of our American Republic. Most crucially, the Romans had to balance the demands of ruling an empire with the political freedoms and Republican political institutions created at the time of independence. Eventually, the burdens of running an empire were too heavy, and the Romans lost both their electoral institutions and their freedoms. The purpose of this book is to suggest lessons Americans might draw from relevant parallels, so that when we make decisions about our empire, we have available whatever wisdom might be gained from the experience of Rome's citizens.

Stages of the Roman Republic

At every step in its evolution, the Roman Republic offers interesting parallels and comparisons to some aspect of United States history. This book will organize our exploration of that history by taking the reader through several clearly marked phases in the development of the Roman city-state's political culture and institutions. Like most historians, this author divides the story of the Roman Republic into three stages: the Early Republic, starting at the time of independence in approximately 510 BCE and lasting until about 365 BCE; the Middle Republic, which lasted until the destruction of Carthage in 146 BCE; and the Late Republic, which lasted until 31 BCE.

As you can see, the life of the Republic extended for 480 years, more than twice as long as the American Republic has been in existence. It was no fly-by-night experiment in representative government. Rather, a set of durable institutions and political practices were created that, though flawed and limited by many standards, evolved into a model of stability and representative government compared to the various authoritarian regimes imposed by kings, emperors, czars, and pharaohs in the ancient and medieval worlds. As a result, the fall of the Republic was not just another development in human history, it was a tragedy, one bemoaned by historians living during the period of the Roman Empire, by secular scholars living in the Middle Ages, and by political leaders of the American Revolutionary War era as they struggled to design a Republic that could avoid the fate of its predecessor.

The Early Roman Republic was a time of political experimentation. The city's political institutions did not emerge in full form from a constitutional convention. Instead, like England's "unwritten constitution," Rome's political system evolved as relationships between different social groups, especially the patricians and the plebeians, changed through conflict and debate, and as a result of changes in military technology and tactics. During this period Rome struggled to ward off military threats from other cities to the south and west, from marauding hill tribes to the east, and from Etruscan city-states to the north. The period ends with the Licinio-Sextian Compromise of 367 BCE when a disastrous invasion by the Gauls forced the army to adopt new tactics and the ruling patricians to grant political and economic concessions to the plebeian majority.

The Middle Republic is usually viewed as the high point of the Republic's history — the new political and social arrangements led to greater prosperity, more representative political institutions, and military success. The most important political institutions of the Republic — the Senate, the Centuriate Assembly, and the Plebeian Assembly — took on their classical forms and the electoral process, the *cursus honorum* (course of honor) became firmly established. During this time Roman citizens gained freedom from debt bondage and safeguards against arbitrary treatment by public officials. Roman armies conquered the entire Italian peninsula and overcame Carthage, the other great western Mediterranean power of the ancient era. In addition, all of Greece and large sections of the eastern Mediterranean were conquered and made into provinces of the city-state's empire. The Middle Republic came to a close in 146 BCE when Rome destroyed the great cities of Carthage and Corinth, highlighting its military dominance of the Mediterranean world and putting into question its moral authority to wield such dominance.

The Late Republic is the most well-known chapter in the Republic's story because the technology of writing and the profession of historian developed rapidly during this period. While most historians date this period from the year that Tiberius Gracchus was elected Tribune, this author believes the domestic turmoil caused by Rome's endless wars with guerilla armies in Spain mark the beginning of the period when the burdens of empire begin to crush Rome's political institutions. The Late Republic is marked by a series of failed attempts to reform the city's political and social practices. During this period violent conflicts between political factions became commonplace and generals intervened in political disputes when they were not putting down foreign rebellions. The last generation of the Republic is notable for the famous men and women who vied with one another for power and influence — Pompey the Great, Julius Caesar, Cicero, Mark Antony, Cato, and Cleopatra.

Outlines of the American Empire

This book also contains several chapters exploring the history of the American Republic and the reasons why our ancestors expanded beyond the boundaries of the American continent and gradually developed a new kind of empire. Except in a few unhappy instances, the United States has shunned the course of seizing colonies; instead the new empire is based on a complex web of unequal economic and military relationships. These relationships provide American decision makers with an unhealthy amount of power over the lives and fates of the residents of nations caught up in the web. Many people believe that without colonies there is no empire, but it is equally useful to think of an empire as a realm where one nation, the United States, uses its power to get other countries to put American interests ahead of the interests of their own populations.

A revealing way to test this thesis is to examine instances where one of the countries inside the American empire attempted to adopt economic, social, or military policies that were against the interests of the United States. For example, in 1951 a nationalist named Mohammad Mossadegh was elected Prime Minister of Iran. When he persuaded the Iranian Parliament to nationalize the British-run oil company that pumped most of the oil in the country, the American CIA sponsored a coup that threw him out of power, closed the Iranian Parliament, and imposed a dictator (known as the Shah). The Shah was a close ally of the United States and remained in power for nearly 30 years with the help of a secret police force that was trained by the CIA. (We will examine these events more thoroughly in chapter 7.)

Now, imagine that, in 1778, Lafayette had come to the United States and helped Benedict Arnold remove General Washington, shut down the Continental Congress, and set up a dictatorship that was closely allied with France for 30 years. Wouldn't it be logical to say that the US had become part of the French Empire, even though France did not actually occupy the country? If Benedict Arnold had ruled the United States with an iron hand for 30 years and then was overthrown in a revolution led by Andrew Jackson, wouldn't the people of the United States regard France as a deadly enemy and Jackson as the country's savior?

This is a brief example of how *Perils of Empire* will examine the question of America's impact on the world through the lens of empire building. The hope is that engaging in this process will encourage the reader to think "outside the box" and re-examine traditional notions about the United States' role in the world.

On the Use of Historical Dates

The Roman Republic existed in the period before the birth of Jesus Christ and the rise of Christianity. As you can imagine, they counted the years of their civilization as dating from the time of the founding of their city and moving forward through time. Therefore, it is a modern imposition to date the story of their city-state as if it were counting down, from the founding of the city to the birth of Christ. In addition, the Romans celebrated a polytheistic religion, with many gods and many religious traditions and ceremonies.

This completely different way of experiencing religious belief is, in fact, the greatest difference between the Romans and modern peoples.

For these two reasons, it seems unfair to me to date events of the Republic's story as being "before Christ." They would certainly not see it that way and, if given the chance, would probably argue that the "0" date should be located at the time when the Republic became an empire, the time when Octavian became Augustus, an occurrence that revolutionized the experience of everyone who lived in the Mediterranean world. In that spirit, I have chosen to accept the "counting backward" dating method used by all modern historians when writing about the ancient world, but I have chosen to use the alternate method of labeling each date as BCE or "Before the Common Era." This method of dating also shows respect for the other great monotheistic religions, Islam and Judaism, by labeling the period after the birth of Christ as CE, or the "Common Era." Whenever I refer to events occurring after the year "0," they will have that label.

Note that this backward style of dating can lead to confusion when one is referring to the passage of centuries. With this style, the 100 years from 500 BCE to 400 BCE is known as the 5th century BCE. In like fashion, the century from 100 BCE to the year "0" is called the 1st century BCE (even though it is actually the last century of the period before the birth of Christ).

DOMESTIC POLITICS AND FOREIGN POLICY: THE DYNAMICS OF EMPIRE

When writing the complex history of an important civilization, there is a great temptation to divide the narrative into sections. Traditionally, historians have presented information about the Roman Republic in a duel fashion, alternating between sections about domestic politics and social developments and sections describing military activities and foreign affairs. While this method is easier to present and easier to follow than other methods, it has the disadvantage of obscuring the causal dynamics that linked attitudes and events in Rome with their successes and failures in other lands. One of the arguments of this book is that, in the case of an empire, there are so many connecting threads between life in the homeland (the city-state of Rome in the case of the Roman Republic) and developments in the subjugated lands of the empire that events and trends can only be understood by viewing both at the same time, in some type of chronological order.

One of the advantages of this method of presentation is that it corresponds to the way in which people experience their lives as either residents or subjects of the empire. On any particular day, political leaders, businessmen, military personnel, citizens, slaves, and subjects will be thinking about their personal situations, events in their homelands, and developments in the territories of the empire. As a result, the occurrence of a rebellion or a famine or a terrorist attack in some part of the empire has a multitude of effects and consequences for how these individuals respond to something that, in a less imperial situation, would be viewed as primarily a domestic issue.

Modern examples from the American empire include the sharp increase in the cost of crude oil, which means a sharp increase in the cost of gasoline. This has begun to drive individuals to purchase small cars from Japanese auto makers rather than SUVs or pick-up trucks from domestic manufacturers. No analysis of the resulting lay-offs in auto factories and their suppliers would be complete without identifying the causal links in the Iraq War and the Sunni opposition to it.

The interrelationships between an imperial state and its empire compose a dense web of trends, vivid events, subtle influences, and unintended consequences. In this book we will explore how, during the Roman Republic, these interrelationships presented political leaders and citizens with dilemmas and unexpected choices. Their decisions and actions ultimately determined the tragic destiny of their beloved Republic.

In the United States, these interrelationships are rapidly drawing us into an uncertain world where the political challenges we face are riddled with dilemmas and unexpected complexities. Part of the urgency of writing this book is my belief that three dynamics: the one between our national addiction to cheap oil and terrorism, the one between terrorism and civil liberties, and the one between an endless war in the Middle East and the increasingly imperial institution of the Presidency, are dragging the American Republic into a situation where our most precious national values and liberties are at risk. If there are grave dangers ahead, then we may only be able to prosper in the next phase of our history by taking a long look at the empire we have created and the dangers it is spawning.

Chapter 1. Birth of a Republic

> If there is much about it [the Roman Republic] we can never know, then still there is much that can be brought back to life, its citizens half emerging from antique marble, their faces illuminated by a background of gold and fire, the glare of an alien yet sometimes eerily familiar world.[1]
>
> —Tom Holland, *Rubicon: The Last Years of the Roman Republic*

The village of Rome, located at a well-traveled crossing of the Tiber River, was well situated to become an important city-state in ancient times. The Tiber is one of the main rivers on the western slopes of the dominant land-form of the Italian peninsula, the Apennine Mountains. River valleys on this western slope — the gentle plains surrounding the Arno River valley (where the modern city of Florence is located), the fertile foothills along the Tiber River, and the abundant fields of the Campania region (where the modern city of Naples is located) — have long provided their inhabitants with agricultural surpluses and a mild climate. As a consequence, the people who lived in these areas played a prominent role in the history of civilization.[2] In ancient times the peninsula's other large river valley, the fertile Po River Valley in northern Italy (where modern Milan, Venice, and Bologna are located), was a rich agricultural prize, to be conquered and settled first by Celtic and German tribes from continental Europe and later by Italian peoples from the western slopes city-states.

---

1 Tom Holland, *Rubicon: The Last Years of the Roman Republic*, New York: Doubleday, 2003, p. xxi
2 Timothy Cornell & John Matthews, *Atlas of the Roman World*, Oxford: Equinox Limited,1982, p. 12

After 1,000 BCE the tribes that lived in the area around the Tiber River valley developed a common language, Latin, which was distinct from the language of the people who lived in the hills to the north, known to us as the Etruscans, and the Osco-Umbrian languages spoken by the hill peoples who lived in the rugged valleys of the Apennines to the east.[1] To the south, the tribes living in the Campania region spoke languages that were influenced by both the Etruscan and Umbrian dialects. This distinct Latin language, in turn, gave the lower Tiber River valley its ancient name of Latium.

Shared religious rituals strengthened the linguistic ties connecting the Latin tribes. Many independent communities in the area came together at regular intervals to share communal rites. The most prominent of these was the Latin Festival, or *Latiar*, which was held in honor of the most prominent of the Latin gods, Jupiter Latiaris.[2] Held each spring, this festival was attended by up to 30 distinct cities and towns, who shared great feasts on the Alban Mount. There were other sacred sites in Latium where smaller numbers of communities gathered for shared rites. For example, a cluster of tribes worshiped together in the grove of the goddess Diana at Aricia.[3] However, these shared religious experiences did not lead to political unity between the towns. We have references to a number of leagues and alliances during this early period, but no consolidation of the separate communities occurred until the 5th century BCE.

The religious and language ties did provide the basis for a variety of civil and commercial connections that were unusual in the ancient world. "In the Greek world, the ideal city-state or polis was a closed community: few outsiders became citizens, intermarriage with non-citizens was sometimes discouraged and the right to own land was restricted to citizens."[4] However, the Latins, through the growth of trade and possibly because of the movement of farmers seeking new lands or laborers migrating from one public works project to another, must have been developing closer ties than Greek cities were able to sustain. While there is no written evidence of what legal rights Latins had during this period, later developments show that intermarriage and commercial relationships became established practice between the various cities. By 493 BCE, when a group of Latin cities fought a Roman army at the battle of Lake Regillus, the resulting peace treaty stated that there would be mutually respected civil rights between Rome and thirty other Latin cities.[5] The treaty gave all Latins the right of *conubium*, allowing them

---

1 Cornell, *Atlas*, p. 22

2 Mary Boatwright, Daniel Gargola, & Richard Talbert, *The Romans: From Village to Empire*, New York, Oxford University Press, 2004, p. 45

3 H.H. Scullard, *A History of the Roman World*, New York: Routledge, 1935, p. 39

4 Boatwright, *The Romans*, p. 47

5 Scullard, *Roman World*, p. 93

to marry any resident of another Latin city. It also ratified the right of *commercium*, allowing Latins to own land in other Latin cities and to make legally enforceable contracts with citizens of other cities.

The Italian Peninsula during the period of the Republic.

The people from the village of Rome who participated in Latin religious festivals and traded in village fairs were simple farmers. The first Romans probably settled on the Palatine hill, one of the famous Seven Hills of Rome, and labored on nearby agricultural land.[1] The Romans believed that Romulus, one of the city's legendary founding brothers, first lived on the Palatine. In honor of that legend, an ancient hut, said to be one of Romulus' first dwelling places, was left standing on the hill for much of the Republican period. By the 1st century BCE the hut stood in ragged contrast to the great houses that crowded the most fashionable district in the city. After the fall

1 Philip Matyszak, *Chronicle of the Roman Republic*, London: Thames & Hudson, Ltd., 2003, p. 19

of the Republic, the emperor Augustus made his home on the Palatine hill, which eventually became the location for other imperial buildings — and the source of the word "palace."

As the population of the village of Rome grew, the other hills were also settled, with farmers building thatched huts and growing wheat, millet, and figs. They tended extensive herds of sheep, with oxen and pigs providing an early measure of a family's wealth.[1] People lived on the hills because the lowland areas of the little city, where small streams wandered through marshy areas and into the Tiber, were unhealthy, with swarms of disease-carrying insects. While the early Roman historical literature claims that Rome was "founded" by Romulus and Remus around the year 750 BCE, there is no archeological evidence for a founding event. Rather, as the population grew, the villages on each hill became more interconnected, and the people of that area began to identify themselves as Romans when they interacted with other tribes in Latium.

The growth of the city picked up its pace when the Romans began to accept large scale immigration from a tribe further up the Tiber River known as the Sabines. The lack of historical evidence about how this came about did not deter Roman historians from inventing an elaborate story about the occasion. As early historians were only a few generations removed from the time when previous events were passed on as oral stories, designed to be told around ceremonial fires, they engaged in what modern readers would consider a strange mix of facts with fancy. The result was a dramatic story that contains some elements of what might actually have happened.

The story about the Sabines coming to Rome, known as the "Rape of the Sabine Women," begins with Romulus, shortly after founding the city, inviting the Sabine King Tatius and his people to a great festival. While the Sabines were sleeping after a night of merriment and drinking, the Roman men grabbed as many unmarried Sabine women as they could and carried them off. One might note that the term "rape" in this story comes from the Latin word *rapere*, which means to seize, rather than the modern meaning of the word; the Romans were looking for wives, not just a night on the town.[2] The incident, unsurprisingly, is said to have touched off a war between the Sabines and the Romans. Surprisingly, the war ended with the two peoples becoming reconciled and King Tatius moving to Rome and becoming co-ruler of the city with Romulus. (Modern diplomats, don't try this maneuver without close supervision.)

While the story clearly has a number of invented moments, modern historians believe that an historical truth, the large-scale immigration of Sabine

1 Scullard, *Roman World*, p. 38
2 Matyszak, *Chronicle*, p. 18

individuals into Rome, is buried behind the fictionalized details. The evidence for a Sabine influence on the city includes a mixture of Sabine type words in the Latin language, words such as *bos* (ox), *scrofa* (sow), and *popina* (kitchen).[1] In addition, the next king mentioned in Roman historical stories is a person with the name of Numa Pompilius, a Sabine-type name, indicating a mixture of Roman and Sabine people sharing rule of the city. We also know that a Sabine leader named Attius Clausus migrated to Rome around 500 BCE, bringing thousands of clients and dependents. Changing his name to Appius Claudius, he was admitted to the new Republic's principal assembly, the Senate, and founded the Claudian extended family that was politically influential for the next 1,000 years.[2]

THE HISTORICAL RECORD

Written evidence of any kind for the period up until the 1st century BCE (the era of Cicero and Caesar) is scarce. Literacy was low and the technology of writing was primitive. Even in Caesar's time, people wrote on papyrus rolls, clumsy and vulnerable objects, and many documents were lost to fires and the elements. Not until after 0 CE and the era of the Imperial Empire was paper used. What was written before that time had to be transcribed onto paper or was lost forever. Later, in the period 350 CE to 700 CE, Christian mobs often burned libraries and their books because they were considered pagan documents, written by men who worshipped many gods. As a result, many invaluable historical writings and documents no longer exist.

With so much information missing, conducting research on the history of Rome is a little like using the techniques of astronomy. Scraps of evidence must be compared with other bits of information for confirmation. Archeological finds can be used to give details of how people lived and provide some confirmation that a story has a factual basis. The outlines of great events must be extrapolated from writings that clearly were meant to describe only one aspect of a larger story. Those intact writings that have come down to us from the Republican era — works by Cicero, Caesar, Sallust and a few others who lived in the 1st century BCE — must be carefully weighed against the obvious political biases of the author.

Books that were written about the Republic by historians who lived during the time of the Empire are an important source of information, because those authors had access to writings that we will never see. However, each member of this group of authors had a set of political and social biases and each had a different method for presenting history to his audience. For example, standards for professional footnotes and evaluation of evidence were not established; many books refer to manuscripts written by their predeces-

1 Cornell, *Atlas*, p. 18
2 Boatwright, *The Romans*, p. 25

sors, but do not distinguish which source of information provided which story or fact.

In addition, all ancient authors were weighed down by biases and intellectual techniques that highlighted some aspects of history and diminished others. Some biases are glaring to our modern eyes. Many groups of people — most notably women, children, and slaves — were not considered historical actors and were therefore deemed unworthy of comment in books about history. Many groups of men — small farmers, tenant farmers, laborers, shopkeepers, and craftsmen — were viewed as inferior to Rome's aristocratic political leaders and not worthy of detailed descriptions.

We now understand that, as a result of their upper class biases, the ancient authors we use for our information primarily wrote about the activities of members of the Roman political aristocracy and about wealthy, influential businessmen. For example, modern historians have come to realize that when Cicero wrote about "the mob" or "the ignorant crowds" in Rome, he wasn't talking about unemployed men and homeless beggars; rather he was talking about everyone who was not a member of either the land owning nobility or the class of wealthy businessmen. This realization has triggered a growing literature over the last forty years that is specifically designed to unearth the role that ordinary Roman citizens played in political events and activities during the life of the Republic. Not surprisingly, this new research has dramatically altered our understanding of the texture of politics in the Republic and added many layers of complexity to even the most well known of stories.[1]

Even if ancient authors had a better understanding of concepts in economics and sociology, the Romans collected very little data about society or people, making it difficult to make accurate statements about the lives and fortunes of large numbers of people. For example, the only censuses of Roman citizens during the 1st century BCE were done in 70 BCE and 28 BCE. Unfortunately, even these censuses are of limited value because they only count people, no other information was collected about them. In addition, our sources merely convey these census results as simple numbers, 900,000 in the year 70 and 4,063,000 in 28 BCE unfortunately, no explanation has survived about who is being counted.[2] Since the two numbers are incompatible with any type of modern population growth table, they must be counting different categories of people, but no one is sure whether they count just citizens, just males, or everyone in the population. This example reveals both

---

1 Examples include: Fergus Millar, *The Crowd in Rome in the Late Republic*, Ann Arbor: University of Michigan Press, 1998. Henrik Mouritsen, *Plebs and Politics in the Late Roman Republic*, Cambridge: Cambridge University Press, 2001.
2 Journal of Roman Studies, V.84, 1994, p. 25

the lack of data available to ancient historians and the limitations of the data that has come down to us.

Given these biases and limitations, what did ancient historians write about? Along with the Greeks, Roman historians believed they should tell the story of their city-state, from its creation up to the author's time. They believed that an historical account should entertain by offering vivid stories with colorful details and it should instruct by focusing on the moral qualities of leading individuals, and on their triumphs and failures. As a result of this focus on prominent individuals, histories frequently explored moral themes, with ethics rather than sociology being the joint concern of the author and his readers.[1] This is especially true of writings about pre-Republican Rome, and the early and middle eras of the Republic. Thus, Rome's early history, until the 3rd century BCE, is primarily based on historical facts teased out of stories like the "Rape of the Sabine Women" that were later confirmed by archeological research.

THE ETRUSCANS: ROME RULED BY KINGS

During the 6th and 5th centuries, that is, up until 500 BCE, Rome was greatly influenced by people to the north of the city who are now known as Etruscans. The Etruscans lived in the fertile hills and fields between the Tiber River and the Arno River. Their civilization advanced more quickly than that of the Latin tribes, perhaps reflecting the impact of sophisticated immigrants from culturally advanced areas of Asia Minor during the 8th and 7th centuries.[2] By 650 BCE there were more Etruscans than Latins, with a much larger percentage of their population concentrated in a number of urban centers. The growth of cities was stimulated by this civilization's skill at mining and metal work, providing materials for trade with other civilizations in the western Mediterranean.[3]

Like the fiercely independent city-states of Greece, Etruscan cities had tribal and language connections, but never united as one political unit. Nevertheless, many of them were large enough to support a substantial trade with the Phoenician peoples who had left their homeland in the area now known as Lebanon and had established colonies in northern Africa, Sicily, and southern Italy. Pottery remains and other cultural items also point to flourishing artistic and commercial contacts with Greek colonies established in the southern part of Italy. One tomb alone, unearthed in the ancient city of Caere, contained 150 finely crafted Greek vases.[4]

---

1 A major theme of Michael Grant in *The Ancient Historians*, New York: Barnes and Noble Books, 1970.
2 Scullard, *Roman World*, p. 27
3 Geza Alfoldy, *The Social History* of Rome, Baltimore: John Hopkins University Press, 1988, p. 3
4 Scullard, *Roman World*, p. 30

The Etruscans had a variety of religious beliefs that inspired energetic and imaginative urban construction. Their cities were carefully laid out, with secure walls marking a sacred political/religious boundary known as the *pomerian*. They were experts at draining swampy areas and paving them over to create city centers. Common people built mud-brick homes supported by wooden timbers, using stone foundations, while wealthier residents used fine cut stone to build much sturdier houses. Etruscan metal workers made beautiful bronze ornaments for temples and home decorations. The walls of still-existing Etruscan temples are covered with vivid paintings of banquets, dancing, horse racing, and fishing, as well as frightening figures from the underworld.[1] The paintings reveal the influence of Greek painting styles of the 6th century (600 BCE to 500 BCE) mixed with a distinctly Etruscan mode of expression.

Etruscan influence on Rome does not seem to have taken the form of outright conquest. In the 7th century, there are indications that trade between Etruscan merchants and Roman craftsmen grew rapidly, opening up new occupations and a chance to accumulate wealth for traders and merchants in the city.[2] Tombs and unearthed houses in Rome show a great increase in the number of Etruscan vases brought into the city, implying a vigorous trade between the regions. (Trade in items like vases was very important in the ancient world because useful liquids like olive oil and pure water from wells were stored in them. Every home would have a number of vases and, because they were used on a daily basis, they would eventually break or crack. Once a vase leaked it was still beautiful but had to be replaced by another one. This created a steady demand for new vases and thus a large market for craftsmen.)

As one would expect when a more advanced civilization has close interaction with a less advanced culture, a number of Etruscan practices became part of Rome's political culture. For example, the symbol of sovereign power in the Roman Republic, the *fasces*, a bundle of rods and axes that was always carried with a consul when he went through the streets, was borrowed from Etruscan political tradition.[3] The ceremony of the triumph, a unique event that has become one of the most remembered aspects of Roman civilization, was also taken from the Etruscans. Even the practice of gladiatorial contests was probably an adaptation from the Etruscan practice of forcing defeated enemies to kill themselves in a series of public duels.[4]

---

1 Scullard, *Roman World*, p. 30
2 Marcel LeGlay, Jean-Louis Voisin, & Yann Le Bohec, *A History of Rome*, Malden, MA: Blackwell Publishers, 1991, p. 28
3 Cornell, *Atlas*, p. 23
4 Scullard, *Roman World*, p. 31

Along with commerce came a movement into Rome of Etruscans looking for a way to improve their status by taking advantage of a culturally inferior region of Italy. Some were adventurous merchants seeking new markets and others were down on their luck aristocrats looking for new political worlds to conquer, possibly bringing with them small armies of supporters. Archeological evidence shows that Etruscans migrated into many Italian communities during this period. For example, in the 6th century BCE there were many Etruscans in the Campania region, where the Etruscan language actually predominated in several cities. In Rome there is archeological evidence of an Etruscan quarter at the foot of the Palatine hill.[1]

All of these economic and social influences made it possible for an Etruscan, a man named Lucius Tarquinius Priscus (known as Tarquinius I) to become King of Rome late in the 7th century (700 BCE to 600 BCE). There is no reliable information about how he managed to out maneuver prominent native Romans to attain the royal seat, but his reign must have at least started out with the acquiescence of the city's increasingly powerful aristocracy. By that time the wealthy landowners who dominated the city's social and political scene had organized themselves into a council of elders known as the Senate. On major policy issues the Roman–Sabine kings probably consulted this Senate, because it represented the most powerful people in the city. Since Rome did not have an inherited monarchy, the Senate also had a good deal to say in selecting who the next king would be. It is possible that the Senate consciously chose an Etruscan to be king as a way of fending off more direct rule by its powerful neighbors to the north.

The story about Priscus' selection as king throws light on how the city's social order was evolving. Archeological evidence from the 7th century shows increasingly lavish aristocratic tombs containing rich ornaments and other decorations.[2] Clearly, a small portion of the population was gathering up control of the city's wealth, probably by buying and/or seizing land from small farm owners and then renting the farmland back to tenant farmers.

One partial explanation for this evolution from the 9th century, when Rome was a village society, to the 7th century, when a small group of families began forming an aristocracy, is the superiority of cavalry in warfare during this era.[3] Those members of the community who could afford to keep horses and train youths to fight on horseback became members of the king's mounted guard. As a consequence of honors bestowed upon victorious cavalrymen, these notable families became recognized leaders and probably gained the ability to gather resources and favors from the king. This thesis is hinted at by the symbols of the new aristocracy, called the *patrician* order, which can be

---

1 LeGlay, *History of Rome*, p. 28
2 Cornell, *Atlas*, p. 20
3 Alfoldy, *Social History*, p. 7

traced to the insignia of the cavalry of early Rome.[1] The aristocracy of Greece in the 7th and 8th centuries, whose history is better known, also had its roots in the importance of cavalry and of those people who owned horses.

Roman historians addressed the question of the aristocracy's origins with several stories. The standard claim is that Romulus, after founding the city, selected one hundred "fathers" to advise him and together they formed the city's first Senate.[2] Thereafter, the families of the fathers formed the city's patrician order. While this story can clearly be seen as an honorific justification for a ruling group, another story shows that the patrician order was not always viewed in a favorable light. This second story says that Romulus was sacrificing by the river when there was a severe storm. Most people fled for cover, but the senators remained standing around Romulus.[3] After the storm, Romulus had vanished. While some believed that he had been taken directly to the heavens, others claimed that the senators had killed him and removed his body, bit by bit, under their cloaks.

Whatever the reasons for its formation, the patrician order, Rome's new aristocracy, was organized around family groupings similar to a clan (the Latin word is *gens*). Each clan or *gens* had a sacred, religious identity and celebrated its own rites.[4] Each member of the clan was known by the name of the clan as well as by a personal name. For example, an important aristocratic clan was the *gens* Fabii, whose members would have Fabian as their middle name (the nomen). By the middle Republic era many men also had a "cognomen," which occurred after the clan name, and represented their particular family branch of the *gens*.

This system is confusing and hard to understand because it is unique to the peoples of ancient Italy. The thing to remember when you see a Roman name is that the middle name, frequently of little importance in the modern United States, is the most important one. It is the family name, similar to the last name for European people who immigrated to the United States. The advantage to trying to understand the Roman naming system is that, once you have grasped the general idea, the system of Roman numerals will seem simple by comparison.

The Romans had fewer than thirty personal names (praenomens) and only ten were commonly used. While friends and family would speak to a person using their personal name, when first names were written they were normally abbreviated because everyone knew what name the abbreviation stood for:

1 Alfoldy, *Social History*, p. 7
2 Cornell, *Atlas*, p. 18
3 Matyzak, *Chronicle*, p. 20
4 Cornell, *Atlas*, p. 18

A. = Aulus	C. = Gaius	Cn. = Gnaeus
D. = Decimus	L. = Lucius	M. = Marcus
P. = Publius	Q. = Quintus	T. = Titus
Ti. = Tiberius		

The cognomen was usually a nickname that distinguished different family groups within the large number of clan members. Oddly enough, the nicknames were often unflattering descriptions of physical or personality characteristics. Examples are Brutus ("stupid"), Caesar ("hairy"), and Cicero ("chickpea"). Thus, C. Julius Caesar was addressed by his friends as Gaius, was a member of the clan Julii, and was in the Caesarian family branch of the Julii.

In Rome, the rise of the aristocracy was also marked by the increasing importance of dependent citizens known as *clientes*. The *clientela* system seems to be as old as the city, with wealthy landowners assigning portions of their land to poor Romans in need of land to farm. The *cliente* was still a free man and a Roman citizen, but owed his loyalty to the aristocrat who was his benefactor. *Clientes* had an obligation to serve their patron in political and military matters, to vote for him or his allies in city elections, and often served in his private army. This system was different than either slavery or serfdom, in that the *cliente* had voluntarily pledged to support the patron and in return that patron was morally bound to assist his *cliente* if he needed legal help or a political favor or a religious sacrifice carried out. In this uniquely Roman way, the leading families of the city were able to assemble large numbers of followers who supported that family's attempts to influence events in the city.

THE ETRUSCAN ROYALTY

After the Senate supported his ascent into power, Tarquinius I and his Etruscan successors greatly changed the city. The first impact was physical; the damp valleys between the Palatine, the Capitol, and the Velia hills were drained (an engineering feat the Etruscans had perfected) and roads were built connecting the central valley with settlements on each hill. The central valley was then paved over with flagstone.[1] In the heart of the valley, the Romans created a huge square, called the Forum, which was designated as the public center of the city. During the following century, public buildings and temples very different from the mud-brick huts of the old city were constructed around the Forum. The most impressive building project was a great temple to Jupiter Optimus Maximus, placed on the lower slope of the Capitoline hill. Larger than any known building constructed in Etruscan cities, the temple was 180 feet wide, 210 feet long, and 65 feet high, with three

---

1 LeGlay, *History of Rome*, p. 29

rows of six columns, eight feet in diameter forming a great entrance way.[1] A towering statue of Jupiter, driving a four-horse chariot greeted those who entered the temple.

Indeed, Jupiter became the "state-god" of the entire community. Jupiter's role as patron of the Roman state was manifested in his central role in the celebration of the triumph. The king, after a battlefield victory, would lead a procession through the streets, flanked by cheering crowds, to the temple of Jupiter. There he would make a splendid sacrifice in thanks to Jupiter's granting the favor of victory. In this way, military victory became its own justification, for victory showed that Jupiter, the greatest god in the heavens, favored Rome and the leader who had commanded the victorious troops. Later, in the era of the Republic, victorious consuls and generals would lead even greater parades, packed with floats gleaming with captured enemy weapons, stolen statues, and priceless art.

At the same time as Jupiter's rise to prominence, previous gods — nymphs and fairies from those rustic early days when the Latin tribes celebrated in dark woods or lofty mountains — were gradually replaced by a system of gods who took the forms of men and women. Each god had his or her temple, which added luster to some area around the Forum and had its own day of celebration and worship. For example, the magnificent temple of Saturn, built on the northern side of the Forum, was dedicated in 496 BCE with a great festival.[2]

The kings also carried out drainage projects in marshy agricultural areas around the city, greatly expanding the amount of tillable land.[3] The new farmland belonged to the state and the king probably gave it out as favors to prominent aristocrats. Rome's first really large estates began to appear in these newly irrigated areas. The Etruscan influence in agriculture included the introduction of vineyards, providing the city with a new export crop.[4]

In general, trade increased greatly during the 6th century (599 BCE to 500 BCE) leading to the formation of a wide variety of guilds in the city: bronze smiths, potters, goldsmiths, dyers, carpenters, leather-workers, tanners, and flute players.[5] As a result of its location at the lowest available crossing of the Tiber River, Rome was enriched by the growth of inter-city trade along the western coast of Italy.[6] The growing trade between Etruscan cities and the fertile plains of Campania flowed through Rome, offering bountiful opportunities for merchants and traders to exchange goods in the shops that

---

1 Scullard, *Roman World*, p. 58
2 LeGlay, *History of Rome*, p. 30
3 LeGlay, *History of Rome*, p. 28
4 Scullard, *Roman World*, p. 59
5 Scullard, *Roman World*, p. 59
6 Cornell, *Atlas*, p. 14

began to spring up around the Forum. As there was no separation of urban activities through zoning, the Forum was always a bustling center of activity with religious ceremonies, merchant caravans, royal processions, and farmers' markets all crowded into the city center.

The river crossing was also the point where sea traffic stopped and river traffic began, so docks and warehouses were built at the foot of the Aventine hill. After these facilities were constructed, goods from sea-going vessels could be safely stored until they were shipped further up the Tiber River to Etruscan cities like Veii and Falerii or taken overland to Latin cities like Albe Fucens and Praeneste.

New Social Groups and the Tyranny of Kings

With the rise of new occupations, social arrangements in the city began to change. Rome had once been primarily agricultural, with a flourishing class of land owning aristocrats, a large class of independent farmers who owned the land they farmed, and clients who rented their farmland from wealthy patrons. Now there were urban residents who did skilled labor in trades, performed day-labor on the docks, or worked in construction gangs on the public works projects sponsored by the king. These urban residents were not closely tied by the *clientela* system of the patrician order and were open to direct appeals by the king.[1] In return, the king had a variety of ways to curry favor with urban workers and merchants including sponsoring public works projects, building roads to encourage trade, or staging festivals in honor of one of the new gods. By the end of the 6th century, the sheer number of Romans meant that the old ties to villages and patrons could no longer bind the majority of the population. Rome had become a thriving community of perhaps 35,000 residents, the majority of them native-born citizens of the city-state; as a consequence, the *clientela* system was not extensive enough to prevent the king from developing a loyal following that was independent of the influence of the patrician order.[2]

The two Etruscan kings who followed Tarquinius I needed this popular support because there is evidence that they seized power through assassination of the previous king and ruled without the support of the Senate. Both of these men, first Servius Tullius and then Lucius Tarquinius Superbus (known as Tarquin the Proud), seized property from patricians who opposed them and distributed it to supporters who were not originally members of the aristocracy.[3] Servius Tullius was the more successful political leader, willing to increase the power of citizens who were not patricians in order to gain allies in his struggles with the aristocracy. He created a new assembly, called the

1 Alfoldy, *Social History*, p. 9
2 Boatwright, *The Romans*, p. 41
3 Cornell, *Atlas*, p. 21

Comitia Centuriata (referred to from now on as the Centuriate Assembly,) in which citizens were placed in voting groups called *centuries* according to the amount of property they owned. The century with the wealthiest members voted first, then the next wealthiest century and so on. Rome's economy had expanded enough and its social system had changed enough that this new assembly based on wealth gave sufficient voting power to merchants, shop-keepers, and small farmers to create some balance with the old wealth of the patrician aristocracy. Set up as a check on the influence of the Senate, the Centuriate Assembly was given the power to consider and ratify the king's decisions about war and peace.

Here we find one of the earliest parallels between Rome and the United States. Even while a king was ruling them, both peoples had significant experience with participation in a legislative assembly. Americans had legislatures, modeled after the English Parliament, soon after the official creation of each colony. Many of the leading citizens of Rome and of the American colonies had extensive involvement in legislative activities — participating in debates, lobbying other members, and communicating with an executive. As a result, when their kings were overthrown it was natural for both societies to set up political systems that included law-making assemblies to balance the power of executives.

The increasing influence of middle-income people also reflected changes in the nature of warfare. By the mid-6th century the Romans had adopted from the Etruscans new battle tactics and strategies based on armies of foot soldiers called *hoplites*.[1] These heavily armored infantry men fought in close ranks with long spears; cavalry, the military unit of aristocratic landowners, could not defeat a military unit with *hoplite* soldiers (called a *phalanx*). The *hoplites* were men who could afford to purchase body armor and spears, the same merchants, shopkeepers, and small farmers who formed a significant voting presence in the Centuriate Assembly.[2] The *hoplite phalanx* was originally developed in Greece. After the battles of Marathon and Thermopylai, when Greek soldiers defeated Persian armies that were many times their size, the *hoplite* unit became the basis for many armies in the ancient world.[3]

In addition to a new army and a new assembly, Servius Tullius changed the requirements for citizenship by dividing the Romans up into new tribes.[4] Before his reign, Romans had been divided up into tribes known as *curiae*. Each *curiae* was dominated by a handful of patrician families and the client families that had become dependent on them during the formation of the ar-

---

1 Scullard, *Roman World*, p. 72
2 Alfoldy, *Social History*, p. 14
3 John Warry, *Warfare in the Classical World*, New York: St. Martin's Press, 1980, see Ch. 24 "The Persian Wars."
4 Cornell, *Atlas*, p. 22

istocracy. New immigrants to the city and others who sought to be free of a client relationship were often excluded from the *curiae* and their citizenship status was ambiguous. King Servius created an entirely new tribal system, with everyone in the city-state assigned to tribes based on where they were living.[1] This territorial system, which initially weakened the influence of the patrician order, had the more important long-term effect of making Roman citizenship partially based on residency, rather than solely on the citizenship status of one's ancestors.

The new tribal system, while conferring citizen status upon most of the free population of Rome, also had a distinct rural bias. All residents living in the city of Rome were assigned to one of four so-called urban tribes. Servius then established 10 rural tribes, a number that increased as Rome grew until there were 31 rural tribes by the 3rd century BCE. The members of the tribes met in another new decision making body, the *Comita Tributa* (referred to from now on as the Tribal Assembly), where voting was done on a unit basis, with each tribe having one vote, with that vote decided by a majority of the tribe's members who were present at the assembly on the day of the vote. As a result, the rural tribes had 10 and later 31 votes on any issue while the urban tribes had just four. This reflected both the greater numbers of farmers than urban workers and the cultural dominance of the agricultural way of life. Creation of the Tribal Assembly also introduced the idea of the city having two legislative bodies, composed in different ways, to provide some checks on the other's powers and to balance with each other.

Like the United States in the colonial era, Rome had urban residents, but agricultural production was the lifeblood of the city's economy. Just as Thomas Jefferson lavished words of praise for the independent farmers who fought in the Continental Army and were the majority of voters in every state, so too did Roman leaders celebrate the virtues of rural life and the farmers who provided so much to the city's economy. As late as the 2nd century BCE, Cato the Elder wrote popular books on agricultural techniques and gave angry speeches denouncing the luxury and laziness of city life in contrast to the noble virtues possessed by people who made the land productive. The aristocracy, no matter how much money it later acquired through conquests, always thought of its wealth as being based in the use and ownership of land. This idea of the virtue of agricultural life, combined with the cold fact that most of the patrician order's clients lived in rural areas, led to a decided bias toward rural voters.

Like the newly formed Centuriate Assembly, the Tribal Assembly allowed every Roman citizen the opportunity to participate in the political arena. In practice, independent farmers whose votes might support the am-

---

1 LeGlay, *History of Rome*, p. 31

bitions of the patricians, the schemes of the king, or the plans of the urban merchants and tradesmen, came to be the largest voting bloc in the Tribal Assembly. For the next four centuries, Rome's growth was based on this class of independent farmers who elected the city-state's leaders through these two assemblies and marched in the city's superb legions.

The last king of Rome was Lucius Tarquinius Superbus (Tarquin the Proud), an Etruscan and the grandson of Tarquinius the First. Tarquin probably seized power through assassination, without the consent of the aristocracy, and seems to have ruled as a "tyrant," a leadership style that was common at this point in the history of Greek and Italian city-states. These tyrants relied on military strength and tried to mobilize support from members of the urban population. Like Tarquin the Proud, they frequently clashed with the aristocratic landowners who were used to having a significant influence on how the king ran the city-state.

In stories about this period, the picture we have is of a man abandoning the collaborative monarchical style of previous kings and searching for ways to establish a more authoritarian one-man rule. For example, Tarquin is said to have created a personal armed guard that bullied the public and promoted the king's interests without the restraints that other kings had been willing to accept.[1] There may have been some fear that he was trying to make the monarchy hereditary, because he was denounced for establishing personal bonds with a handful of families and ignoring the traditional consulting role that the Senate and other assemblies had once possessed. Unlike King Servius Tullius, these abuses may have meant that Tarquin the Proud found himself in conflict with the urban merchants and craftsmen who were important members of the Centuriate Assembly and with the independent farmers who formed the largest voting bloc in the Tribal Assembly. When the end eventually came, Tarquin seems to have had few defenders in the city.

In Pursuit of Liberty: The Creation of Republican Institutions

All Roman historians, from both the Republican era and from the Imperial era, tell harsh stories about Tarquin's moral lapses during his 30 or more years of rule. The most famous story in the ancient record claims that Tarquin's oppressive reign finally ended when his son raped Lucretia, daughter of a prominent patrician, who was married to Lucius Tarquinius Collatinus, one of the king's supporters.[2] According to this story, the "Rape of Lucretia" triggered an aristocratic uprising led by L. Junius Brutus (whose descendent was to lead the conspiracy to assassinate Julius Caesar).

1 LeGlay, *History of Rome*, p. 34
2 Matyzak, *Chronicle*, p. 42

Once again, this moralistic story about an important event in Rome's early history has a mythical structure based on a factual foundation. While there is no hard evidence for the existence of either Lucretia or L. Junius Brutus, we do know that Tarquin the Proud was chased out of Rome as the result of a revolution led by the patrician aristocracy. The "Lucretia" story captures the essence of the truth: in reaction to the king's arbitrary use of power, the city's patrician families took over leadership of the city and fought a series of battles with Porsenna, the king of the Etruscan city of Clusium, who tried to restore Tarquin to his throne. After their victory, they created a new government that reflected their desire for a sharing of power in the city and a wish to be free of the influence of the Etruscans.

As happened in the United States in the period before the Revolutionary War, opposition to the institution of monarchy grew in reaction to a series of arbitrary and tyrannical actions by a particular king. These actions threatened the interests of important people in the city and culminated in a rebellion that secured the city's independence, both from the king and from foreign rule. As in the United States, this combination of motives created a powerful connection between support for Republican political institutions and love of country. Republican political institutions were, in the minds of Rome's citizens, an expression of Rome's uniqueness and its independence. This pride in the city's political system is similar to what Americans feel about their republic; Americans speak fondly of the "founding fathers," believe the Constitution is a model for other countries to follow, and generally think of America as a beacon for the peoples of the world.

The moral stories about Tarquin's crimes are a reflection of the value that all Roman citizens came to place on liberty. Fed by a deep-seated anger about the arbitrary power of a monarch and reacting to more than a century of foreign dominance, the Roman aristocracy and the average Roman citizen developed a deep reverence for liberty. Indeed, as in the United States, *libertas* became the key political value of the Roman Republic. "It was central to the self-image of the Romans and at the heart of their political identity."[1]

Defending and strengthening liberty would, throughout the history of the Republic, be the proclaimed political goal of every political leader. Patricians, seeking election to high office, would routinely pledge their allegiance to the people's liberty. And this love of liberty was not confined to the educated classes. For example, in 63 BCE, when Catiline's army of rebellious farmers sent a letter of justification to the general who was seeking to crush their uprising, they proudly stated, "we, however, do not seek either power or riches, which are so often the causes of wars and dissensions among men; we seek only freedom, which no true man is willing to give up as long as he

---

1 Mouritsen, *Plebs and Politics*, p. 11

lives."[1] Later, when Clodius, leader of the plebeian neighborhood organiza-tions, forced Cicero into exile in 58 BCE, he claimed it was a triumph for the people's liberty and built a shrine to the goddess *Libertatis* on the ruins of Cicero's house.[2]

The discussions, speeches, and promises about liberty were not mere empty rhetoric. For every male citizen of the Republic, liberty meant the freedom to go his own way without arbitrary interference from an authori-tarian king or a royal bureaucracy. We need to remember that Romans of the 5th century, like Americans in the 18th century, lived in a world dominated by kings. Except for the Greek city-states, most of the earth's people were subjects of a sovereign whose power was absolute and rarely benign. Then, starting with heirs of Alexander the Great in the 3rd century, Greek liberties were restricted by the autocratic monarchies of the Hellenistic era.[3] It is no wonder that, years later, citizens of the Republic still clung proudly to the original vision of liberty that motivated the founders.

For the average male citizen, liberty also meant a degree of autonomy from rule by the aristocracy. The Republic was not a feudal society, where people in the lower classes worked for and owed tribute to members of the aristocracy. Citizens were free, within the limits of a technologically primi-tive, agricultural society, to work small farms, open shops, learn a craft, or be day laborers. They were free to participate in the complicated election process for government officials and they were free to vote in both the Tribal Assembly and the Plebeian Assembly. Only citizens who owned land or ran a prosperous shop had the wealth to be eligible to vote in the Centuriate Assembly, but that limitation was no more restrictive than similar voting requirements in the United States after the Revolutionary War.

While the members of wealthy and accomplished Roman families in the aristocracy were treated with respect, and differences in social position were considered natural, what was opposed and considered unacceptable was au-thoritarian rule by one individual with concentrated power. After Tarquin the Proud was driven out, to ensure that they would never again be sub-ject to monarchical rule, the Romans set up a Republic, literally *res publica*, government of the people. Then, to protect their liberty from the return of monarchy, the Romans created, over time, a set of political institutions and political practices that became the world's first set of checks and balances.[4]

1 Lester Hutchinson, *The Conspiracy of Catiline*, New York: Barnes and Noble, Inc.,1967, p. 106

2 W. Jeffrey Tatum, The *Patrician Tribune: Publius Clodius Pulcher*, Chapel Hill: University of North Carolina Press, 1999, p. 162

3 See Peter Green, *Alexander to Actium: The Historical Evolution of the Hellenistic Age*, Berkeley: University of California Press, 1990, Ch. 12 "Kingship and Bureaucracy: The Government of the Successor Kingdoms."

4 Tom Holland, *Rubicon: The Last Years of the Roman Republic*, New York: Doubleday, 2003, p. 3

The checks and balances were designed to prevent anyone from gaining too much power and making himself king. The two main features were: (a) election of officials, and (b) legislative assemblies made up of all citizens. Each of these features included a dazzling array of interlocking political institutions and a complex web of traditions and rituals. The elements of this densely woven political fabric are difficult to understand because each institution, tradition, and ritual evolved over the life of the Republic, so that what was prevalent in one era was overshadowed by developments in the next era. However, the observer who takes time to closely examine this fabric will discover elements of a political system that bears some striking resemblances to our own.

The connection to our own political institutions is not accidental. The founding fathers of our Revolutionary War era looked to the Roman Republic as a model for the new American republic. In George Washington's inaugural address, he claimed, "the destiny of the Republican model of government" was "deeply, perhaps...finally, staked on the experiment entrusted to the hands of the American People." He believed that the new government had the mission of restoring "the sacred fire of liberty" to the world.[1]

> The vocabulary of 18th century revolution reverberated with purposeful echoes of Republican Rome as political activists self-consciously assumed the Roman mantle. James Madison and Alexander Hamilton, the primary authors and advocates of the United States Constitution, wrote together pseudonymously as "Publius" to defend their creation, associating themselves with Publius Valerius Poplicola, founder and first consul of the Roman Republic.[2]

In 18th-century America it was customary for authors to use pseudonyms when they wrote political essays in the new country's newspapers. During the debate over ratifying the Constitution, many authors, following the example of Madison and Hamilton when they wrote the *Federalist Papers*, used names from the Roman Republic era, including Civis, Cato, Curtius, Brutus, Cincinnatus, or more directly, "a Republican."[3]

The Roman Republic's influence continued into the next generation. In 1811, when Thaddeus Stevens, later a leading Congressman during the Civil War, enrolled in the University of Vermont, the entrance exam included an examination in Latin that required the student to discuss Cicero's orations against the rebellious Roman politician Catiline.[4] When Senators Henry Clay, Daniel Webster, and John Calhoun united in opposition to President

---

1 Mortimer Sellers, "The Roman Republic and the French and American Revolutions" in Harriet Flower, ed., *The Cambridge Companion to the Roman Republic*, Cambridge: Cambridge University Press, 2004. p. 347

2 Sellers, "Roman Republic," p. 347

3 Sellers, "Roman Republic," p. 350

4 Hans L. Trefousse, *Thaddeus Stevens: Nineteenth-Century Egalitarian*, Mechanicsburg, PA: Stackpole Books, 2001, p. 4

Andrew Jackson, his supporters, looking back to the Roman Republic, labeled them the "Great Triumvirate." This was a deliberate reference to the famous alliance of Caesar, Pompey, and Crassus that was history's first Triumvirate.[1]

It should not be surprising that the Roman Republic, eighteen hundred years after its fall, still loomed large in the imagination of men who sought freedom from kings. Latin was the language used in the universities for advanced study in rhetoric, philosophy, and history. Biographies of 18th and 19th century political leaders in America and Europe make clear that the writings of Caesar, Cicero, Livy, and other Roman authors were a standard part of an educated man's library. These writings, which conveyed the strong anti-monarchical attitudes prevalent during the era of the Roman Republic, would have been inspirational to men who, in the Age of the Enlightenment, were acutely aware of the irrational nature of rule by a single person. Moreover, since the fall of the Roman Republic, kings had dominated governments in Europe and the rest of the known world. Men seeking new, more democratic forms of government were naturally attracted to the complex institutions of the Roman Republic, which had proven themselves durable for five hundred years.

---

1 Merrill D. Peterson, *The Great Triumvirate: Webster, Clay, and Calhoun*, New York: Oxford University Press, 1987, p. 5

CHAPTER 2. MILITARY GLORY AND THE COURSE OF HONOR

> The Roman constitution formed the noblest people and the greatest power that has ever existed.[1]
>
> —John Adams

POLITICAL OFFICES IN THE ROMAN REPUBLIC: THE CONSULS

In place of a monarch, the Romans decided to elect two magistrates, called consuls, who shared the leading political position in the city. The Centuriate Assembly, whose make-up we will examine more closely in the next chapter, elected the consuls and several other officials during yearly elections. The power of these leaders was limited in three ways — a one-year term of office, no provision for re-election, and the sharing of power with another official of the same rank. This cluster of limitations is unique to the Roman Republic.

The one-year term of office created an atmosphere of almost perpetual campaigning. Officials began serving their terms in March during the early years of the Republic (changed to January in 144 BCE) and elections for magistrates for the following year were held during the summer harvest festivals in July or August. Americans, who often shake their heads at the early start date for Presidential campaigns, would be stunned at the level of political campaigning in the Roman Republic.

---

1 Quoted in: Kahn, Arthur D., *The Education of Julius Caesar*, Lincoln, NE: iUniverse.com, 1986, p. ix

The founding fathers who gathered at the Constitutional Convention in 1787 turned away from the Roman model and decided to have the country run by a much stronger executive, a president, who could serve an unlimited number of four-year terms. In all likelihood, they were influenced by the extremely de-centralized nature of political authority in the country at that time. With thirteen states, each determined to go its own way if need be, the founders probably chose a single executive with a relatively long term in hopes of bringing stability to the national government and authority to its relationship with the quarreling states. Presidents certainly played that role in the early decades of the young Republic and the powers of the office were essential during Lincoln's quest to hold the country together during the Civil War.

However, in the 20th century, as the United States became an international power and the national government grew in authority, the institution of the Presidency has taken on some of the monarchical tones that the Romans feared from chief executives. By 1971, Arthur Schlesinger was writing a popular book about *The Imperial Presidency* and there has been a continuous struggle since then over the relative powers of the office. Led by Vice President Dick Cheney, the Bush administration has made a concerted effort to centralize legislative, legal, and foreign policy authority in the office of President at the expense of Congress and the courts. While these activities have not amounted to monarchy, they are enough to inspire some critics to fear for a variety of civil liberties that have, until recently, been protected by the checks and balances built into the US constitution by the founding fathers.

In spite of the limitations Rome's founders placed on their consuls, each elected consul was still a significant person because, during the months that he was the presiding officer of the Senate, he initiated all decrees and proclamations issued by the Senate. As in the other assemblies of the Roman Republic, the Senate's rules of order had no provision for members to initiate decrees or proclamations and gave no opportunity for members to offer amendments to initiatives that were under discussion. With these powers the consuls had, when they were working in harmony, considerable influence on how the Senate responded to whatever pressing issues arose during that particular year. This influence is reflected in the tradition of referring to a Roman year as "In the consulship of Publius Rutilius Rufus and Gnaeus Mallius Maximus" as the Romans would have called the year 105 BCE.

However, if the two consuls were at odds, either because of political differences or personal conflicts, then they might checkmate each other, leaving a legacy of bitterness and conflict. For example, during the year that Gaius Julius Caesar and Marcus Calpurnius Bibulus were consuls, they and their followers clashed bitterly. Bibulus, after having cow dung poured on his head when he attempted to speak to the Plebeian Assembly, finally abandoned coming to the Forum. Instead, he stayed in his house, making daily proclamations about signs from the heavens revealing divine displeasure with Caesar's legislative program. Romans responded by claiming that the year 59 BCE was therefore "In the Consulship of Julius and Caesar."

Equally important as their role as leaders of the Senate, the consuls, like American presidents, served as the commanders-in-chief of Rome's armies. Unlike American presidents, they literally acted as the city's generals, commanding Rome's armies while on military campaign. The consuls either served together during large operations or held separate commands when the city faced more than one enemy. During the 5th and 4th centuries BCE, when Romans armies primarily campaigned on the Italian peninsula during good weather, both consuls were usually out of the city from May through October, leaving only March–April and Nov–Dec for any significant legislative activity. This short law-making season is reflected in the very small number of laws passed during any Roman year. Aside from routine matters surrounding the budget or administration of the city, the historical record reveals that during many years only one or two major laws were passed.

The Roman dislike of monarchy was also reflected in the tiny number of civil servants who worked for the consuls. These men, called *lictors*, accompanied the consuls as they went about the city and served as bodyguards during military campaigns. Each consul had twelve *lictors*. These citizens were living symbols of the power of elected officials because they carried *fasces*, a set of rods that were bound together and contained an axe. The *fasces* symbolized the consuls' power to arrest citizens inside the city and to exercise the power of life and death over soldiers when on campaign outside of the city. Inside the city, the consuls could arrest individuals, but capital punishment for a citizen could only be proclaimed by a vote of the Centuriate Assembly after an open trial.

During the 5th century BCE, when Roman military victories were limited, few consuls became well known historical figures. In fact, conflict over who could be elected a consul meant that, for many years in the later part of the 5th century, no individuals were elected to the office. The problems began as soon as the king was removed in 510. The aristocratic leaders of the revolution declared that only individuals from patrician families were eligible to run for the consulship and other public offices. While the clients of aristocrats and many small farmers were willing to defer to the patrician families because they had great influence in rural areas, other residents of the city, some of whom were wealthy and accomplished in their own right, all of whom took pride in their status as free citizens, were understandably displeased with this restriction on their ability to participate in the city's government.

The non-patrician members of Roman society were called the *plebeians*, meaning "the multitude." However, the reader should step back from the image in her mind of the wretched status of the plebeians during the Roman Empire, when 600 years of unequal development had made the urban plebeians dependent on the corn dole and distracted by circuses, while rural plebeians were landless serfs, dependent upon their aristocratic masters. At the time of Roman independence, the plebeians included poor farmers who rented land, independent farmers who owned their land, and any individuals who worked in the city as craftsmen, laborers, shopkeepers, or merchants.

While some of the plebeians were poor, we have seen that a significant number of them were prosperous enough to purchase armor, to serve as *hoplite* soldiers in the Roman army, and to be voting members of the Centuriate Assembly. In addition, no matter how poor they were, every plebeian male was a voting member of the Tribal Assembly. As a result, plebeians were active citizens, and most of them believed that higher offices should be open to anyone of good status in the city who wished to become an elected leader. It was these individuals, people who were not clients of an aristocrat and who were economically independent, who came together to actively resist the ambitions of the patrician order and demand a voice in running the city.

In general, the leaders of the plebeians were men who, during the era of the Etruscan kings, made enough money to acquire some education for themselves and even more importantly, for their children. By the time of Roman independence, these educated individuals were important merchants, landlords, or shop owners in the city. As a result of their wealth and education they were probably community leaders, their opinions carried weight in meetings of the Tribal Assembly, and their sons and daughters intermarried in the age-old quest to raise a family's status through connections with other families. The patrician order's attempts to bar these accomplished members of the community from political offices meant that poorer plebeians could rely on them as natural leaders in the on-going struggle to determine who would have power and influence in the new Republic's political system.

Conflicts between the patricians and the plebeians frequently disrupted Rome during the 5th century. While the patricians were wealthy and controlled much of the land around the city, the plebeians, being the majority of the population could take the dramatic step of seceding from the city and moving to the Avantine, one of Rome's seven hills, which was outside of the settled area of the city at that time.[1] This early form of general strike not only deprived the aristocracy of workers for its fields and businesses, it left

---

1 LeGlay, *History of Rome*, p. 49

the government without many of its foot soldiers at a time when Rome's enemies were located within a few days march of the city. The first secession appears to have occurred in the year 494 BCE, following several years where the records reveal problems with the food supply and quite possibly mounting debts after a series of bad harvests.[1] We do not know what agreement was reached at this time between the two social orders to settle the dispute, but a few plebeian consuls were elected in the years following this secession.

Of equal importance, the solidarity generated by the act of secession led to the creation of a new legislative body for the city, the *Comita Plebis Tributa* (from now on referred to as the Plebeian Assembly). Only plebeians could participate in this assembly, which, like the Tribal Assembly, met and voted by tribal unit. This body elected ten 'Tribunes of the People' who were empowered to lead the Assembly and to represent the plebeians when grievances were being presented to the leading patricians in the Senate.

Political tensions in the city must have resumed shortly after these events because the records show no plebeian consuls elected between 485 and 470.[2] In addition, economic problems may have exacerbated tensions, as trade with other city-states seems to have fallen during the 5th century. One indication we have of commercial activity in the ancient world, the exchange of pottery, shows that 53 red figure vases imported from Athens have been found in Rome from the period 500-450 BCE, while only two vases have been discovered from the 450-400 period.[3] These political and economic tensions led to another general strike in 471 BCE, which ended with the patricians recognizing the tribunes as official representatives of the plebeians and perhaps granting some debt relief and other concessions.

MILITARY CAMPAIGNS OF THE LATE 5TH CENTURY

The on-going conflicts over who could be elected to the office of consul led to a typical Roman way of papering over significant conflicts — the creation of new offices with overlapping duties. To secure enough social harmony to carry out these recurring wars with hostile tribes, the patricians and plebeians shared the consular power of the Republic through an "emergency council" of military tribunes.[4] In this way, the patricians shared power with the plebeians without conceding their right to exclude them from the position of consul in "normal" times.

It was during this period, around 458 BCE, that the Aequi trapped a Roman army in a mountain valley. According to historical legend, the retired

---

1 Scullard, *Roman World*, p. 82-83
2 LeGlay, *History of Rome*, p. 49
3 Scullard, *Roman World*, p. 82
4 Boatwright, *The Romans*, p. 49

consul Lucius Quintus Cincinnatus was called from his farm and given dictatorial powers to lead a Roman rescue force. Cincinnatus saved the Roman army, inflicted a stinging defeat upon the Aequi, and then, with a grateful city ready to grant his every wish for more power, he encouraged a return to Republican government by returning to his quiet life of farming.[1] While it is unlikely that this story is correct in every detail, it is definitely based upon real events, and demonstrates the tendency of Roman historians to tell stories with moral lessons, this one a celebration of respect for Republican institutions and freedoms.

This lesson has an historical echo. Two thousand years later, when the officers of the Continental Army returned home after the War for American Independence, unpaid and given little appreciation from the Continental Congress, a band of officers advocated for a military coup to overturn the Congress and install George Washington as supreme leader of the country. In response, a majority of officers created the "Society of the Cincinnati" and became community leaders who spoke out in support of republican ideals.[2] The motto of the society, which exists to this day, is "He gave up everything to serve the republic." General Washington was elected the first president of the Society and served in that role until his death in 1799.

During the second half of the 5th century, the newly united Roman army, with plebeian soldiers led by both patrician and plebeian officers, gradually pushed the hill tribes away from the farmland in the Tiber River Valley. In alliance with other Latin city-states, they conquered territory in the foothills and established new towns populated by settlers from all of the Latin cities. Rome also began to gain the upper hand in its conflict with the Etruscan city of Veii.

Marcus Furius Camillus, a patrician who held the office of military tribune several times during this period became the most famous Roman general of the era by leading the successful siege of Veii. The city surrendered around 396 BCE and Rome was able to double the size of its territory.[3] Furius Camillus must have been perceived as a great and honorable man because the stories about him are unanimously full of praise. One story about him claims that:

> In 394 BCE Camillus was again at war, this time against Falerii. A teacher of the children of Falerii's principal citizens saw a chance to put himself on what he reckoned would be the winning side. He handed over his pupils to the Romans as they were preparing to besiege the city and told a stunned Camillus that with these child hostages, the Falerians would surrender. Camillus sent the treacherous schoolteacher back to Falerii under the guard of his students. They took with them a message that the Romans

1 Scullard, *Roman World*, p. 96

2 Sellers, *Roman Republic*, p. 358

3 Cornell, *Atlas*, p. 30

intended to win by fair rather than underhanded methods....The Falerians were so impressed by Camillus' honorable dealing that they surrendered on the spot.[1]

ROMAN POLITICAL OFFICIALS: THE PRAETOR AND LEGAL RIGHTS

The number three ranking magistrate in Rome, after the consuls, was the praetor. It is believed that this position was created in the middle of the 4th century as the city grew and its legal system became more complex. The praetor was the ranking legal official in the city, managing the courts and, for major political crimes, acting as the state's prosecutor. Demonstrating his important but subordinate role, the praetor was accompanied by six *lictors*. The Roman reluctance to place too much power in the hands of one person is evident in this office as well, for the Centuriate Assembly elected the praetor, like the consuls, to a one-year term.

The praetor can be compared to the attorney general position in many American states. Elected directly by the voters, the attorney general is usually the state's chief legal officer. This high status for Rome's top legal official reflected the value Romans placed on legal rights and their legal system. This system, like the position of consul, evolved during the 5th century as a result of conflicts between the patricians and the plebeians.

A few years after the general strike of 471 BCE a tribune of the plebeians proposed a special commission to write down the laws.[2] The nature of this proposal suggests that one of the points of dispute in the strike was over exactly what the laws said. Other historical stories suggest that patrician consuls would stretch or re-interpret laws in order to justify taking legal action against plebeians who were politically or in some other way offending the consul. Because of these abuses, the mere act of writing down community laws would be a significant advance in the struggle to create basic rights for citizens.[3] (Keep in mind that citizens were free males who lived in Roman territory and belonged to a tribe; women and slaves were not citizens.) The patricians resisted this suggestion for a number of years, but in 450 BCE a college of ten magistrates was elected to "make laws so that liberty shall be equal for all, from the highest to the lowest."[4]

The *Decemvirs*, as the group of ten were called, drew up the "Laws of the XII Tables," which became the basis of Roman law for nearly a thousand years. These laws were not a complete legal code, instead they were legal principles that were used as building blocks upon which the legal system could expand as the little city-state grew and became more complex. These

1 Matyszak, *Chronicle*, p. 67
2 Scullard, *Roman World*, p. 87
3 LeGlay, *History of Rome*, p. 51
4 LeGlay, *History of Rome*, p. 50 Quote is from Livy Book III.31.7

building blocks reflected a society where the family was "the fundamental unit of social life, and agriculture and animal rearing the primary economic activities."[1] In general, the Laws of the XII Tables spelled out legal rights that were the same for all citizens.

A central tenet of the Laws was the right of citizens to own and control property. Personal property and more significant items like land and buildings were protected from arbitrary seizure or regulations.[2] A wide variety of crimes against property were defined and a hierarchy of punishments was outlined. In addition, the Tables set up procedures for adjudicating property disputes such as conflict over property boundaries, purchases of buildings and animals, and purchases of slaves.[3]

In addition, the family unit was defined and sanctified by the law. The rights of the father, while extensive, were restricted to his immediate family, not the extended *gens* as had been the case previously, and women were given some limited legal rights, for example to own and inherit property. Women were allowed to keep their dowries, giving them a degree of financial independence unknown in other ancient societies. Rules about marriage, divorce, and inheritance were also clarified.

Access to the courts was guaranteed for all citizens and the right to a trial by a jury was given to any individual accused of a serious criminal or political crime. There were a large number of provisions about debt, how debtors could be tried, and other procedural items related to collecting debt or punishing debtors. The prominence of this topic suggests that debt problems were a major source of conflict between private individuals in the Early Republic.[4]

Only the Centuriate Assembly could vote a sentence of death for civil or political crimes. Unlike ancient and medieval kings, who could try and execute any one of their subjects, the consuls and later the praetor could only arrest and accuse people of crimes. The Romans saw this division between prosecution and judgment as a major protection against tyranny. As another protection from official tyranny, the Twelve Tables forbid the passing of a law directed at a specific individual.[5] This provision would, for example, have prevented Henry VIII from passing the law disposing of Thomas Cromwell.

Of course, it is no accident that these fundamental legal rights seem so familiar. First the English and then the American legal systems drew their inspiration from the Roman Republic's legal system. Through the centuries, the Romans built upon these legal rights by creating refinements in the rules

---

1 Boatwright, *The Romans*, p. 51
2 LeGlay, *History of Rome*, p. 51
3 Boatwright, *The Romans*, p. 51
4 Boatwright, *The Romans*, p. 51
5 Scullard, *History*, p. 123

of evidence, composition of juries, time frames for trials, permissible actions of attorneys (called advocates by the Romans) and other court issues. As still happens in the United States, Romans with money were able to get a lot more out of the legal system than regular folks, but the existence of a number of fundamental legal rights preserved the liberty of individuals most of the time.

By the time of Caesar and Cicero, the Roman legal system was very complex, with a variety of courts set up to specialize in different crimes — treason, murder, extortion, and so on. All trials took place in the open, in the public space known as the Forum. A major duty of the praetor was to manage the schedule of trials because all courts met in this same general space. The praetor would be the presiding judge at many of the trials, with a jury of prominent citizens, usually fifty or sixty men sitting together facing the open area where the advocates would present their case.[1] As all Romans loved the theatrical elements of a trial, temporary wooden bleachers were erected in a semi-circle around the proceedings and people would file in to hear advocates practice the art of oratory. If the trial involved a famous person, either from a well-known family or a person who had gained military or political triumphs, then the Forum might be filled to overflowing with people who wanted to see the show. You might envision this as a low-technology version of entertainment like Perry Mason or Ally McBeal.

Roughly the size of two football fields, more than 200 yards long and 80 yards wide, the Forum was located in the valley between the Capitoline hill and the Palatine hill.[2] On one end of the Forum, at the base of the Capitoline hill, stood the immense temple of Saturn, which also served as the National Treasury. One of the fascinating things about the Forum was the mingling of religion and the state. "Religion and daily life were not separated in the Roman mind and temples were regularly used for business and state purposes."[3]

Nearby was Rome's only prison, the *carcer* (the Latin root of "incarcerate"), a small structure with an inner chamber carved into the Capitoline hill. The Romans did not imprison people for long periods of time; instead major crimes were punishable by either execution or exile, usually to some region away from the Italian peninsula. For most Romans, death was preferable to exile, for, in the traditional culture of the Republican era, separation from the sacred city of a person's ancestors, with no hope of future interactions with family and friends was considered a slow, tormented way to die. Indeed, most of the Romans we read about being sent into exile die within a few

---

1 Anthony Everitt, *Cicero: The Life and Times of Rome's Greatest Politician*, New York: Random House, 2001, p. 32
2 Everitt, *Cicero*, p. 49
3 Everitt, *Cicero*, p. 49

years. Instead of acting as a long-term home for criminals, the *carcer* served as a symbolic political prison, housing for a few days people who had incurred the wrath of tribunes, consuls, or praetors.

Adjacent to the prison was the Comitium, or assembly ground, where the Tribal and Plebeian Assemblies gathered. At one end of the Comitium rose the Rostra, the speakers' platform for the two assemblies. The Rostra was the site of a number of physical confrontations during the late Republic, including the time when poor Calpurnius Bibulus got a load of cow manure dumped on his head. Across the Comitium from the Rostra was the Curia Hostilia, the single-chambered building where the Senate met. It was the only public building in Rome where lawmakers met under a roof. Just outside the Curia was the bench where the 10 Tribunes of the People sat, able to observe Senate meetings; they were available to any citizen who wanted to ask for help.[1]

During the first 300 years of the Republic, the long north and south sides of the Forum's rectangle were crowded with merchant stalls. Most of the retail business of this period took place in these bustling stalls. Butchers with freshly cut meat, farmers from the countryside with chickens and eggs, merchants with vases from Greece or Phoenicia, silversmiths with fine jewelry, and bakers with fresh loaves all set up shop and exchanged goods or, later on, coins with housewives looking for the evening meal, slaves purchasing goods for their masters, and men seeking household items. In the 2nd century BCE, these merchants were forced out of the Forum and relocated to nearby sections of the city. Basilicas, long shed-like buildings with double rows of colonnades, replaced the stalls.[2] The basilicas were equipped with first-floor galleries where spectators could watch the court trials that, by that century, were an everyday occurrence. The second floor of each basilica was used for law and government offices.

The Temple of Castor and Pollux, two brothers who had magically appeared before the legendary Battle of Lake Regillus in the early Republic and were thus associated with the founding of the Republic, dominated the eastern end of the Forum. The temple had a large speakers' platform in front, which was frequently used for *contios*, political meetings called by a leader who wanted to speak about a public issue. Since the Romans had no form of public address system, many meetings were relatively small gatherings of people who generally agreed with the speaker's point of view.[3] *Contios* often were used by political leaders to get a message out to supporters of a particular point of view or specific piece of legislation. In this large city without newspapers or television, political messages were spread by word of mouth;

---

1 Millar, *The Crowd in Rome*, p. 39
2 Millar, *The Crowd in Rome*, p. 41
3 Mouritsen, *Plebs & Politics*, p. 48 & 49

speakers counted on people who attended their *contio* to tell other people in the city about what they heard at the event.

The Temple of Vesta, goddess of the hearth, and the Regia, built in the time of the kings to hold sacred objects, formed the western side of the Forum. Inside the Vesta was an eternal flame, tended by six women, pledged to chastity.[1] These Vestal Virgins symbolized the purity of Rome's commitment to the gods. The *pontifex maximus*, Rome's chief religious official, supervised the Vestal Virgins as part of his role as coordinator of religious activities in the city. The *pontifex maximus* chaired the city's most august religious council, the *Collegeum Pontificum* (College of Pontiffs), and oversaw the many religious ceremonies staged each year to honor the numerous gods who had a place in Roman culture.

While the *pontifex maximus* was usually a patrician or later, a member of the political elite known as the nobility, the position was held separately from any particular state office to ensure that no one person could claim to hold supreme religious and secular power in the Republic — a merging of roles that was typical of kings. The importance of this separation for the preservation of Republican government was confirmed later, during the period of the Empire, when the emperor fortified his rule by taking the office of *pontifex maximus*. The bishop of Rome later took the title, when Christianity became the official religion of the Empire.

Most of the *quaestiones*, or jury trials, were held in the eastern half of the Forum. Roman lawyers were fond of invoking historic figures and events that might cast a favorable light on their client and were not hesitant to invoke the religious aura of the area for jurors. For example, Cicero, while defending Scaurus Metellus in 54 BCE, appealed to the fact that Scaurus' grandfather, Lucius Metellus, had once repaired the temple of Castor and Pollux: "L. Metellus himself, this man's grandfather, seems to have established these most holy gods in that *templum* before your eyes, jurors, so that they might appeal to you to save his grandson."[2] In a society that respected successful ancestors, many a verdict of *absolvo*, not guilty, was won through golden-tongued references to the exploits of a man's family.

Cicero, of course, is the most renowned of Roman advocates and a significant political leader. He created his reputation and set up his political career by making stirring speeches in high profile political trials. Perhaps his most famous speech was made in 70 BCE, during his prosecution of the corrupt governor of Sicily, Gaius Verres. Verres, one of the richest men in Rome, had framed a prominent Sicilian nobleman in order to steal his art collection.

---

1 Everitt, *Cicero*, p. 50
2 Millar, *Crowd*, p. 43

Cicero agreed to act as the advocate for a delegation from Sicily that was suing Verres on the charge of extortion.

While the evidence was overwhelming, the odds of winning the suit were not good because Roman juries at this time were susceptible to being bribed and made up entirely from members of the Senate. These Senate-juries were notorious for their unwillingness to convict fellow members of the upper class for serious crimes. On the second day of the trial, with a huge crowd hanging on his every word, Cicero faced the issue head on:

> "Today the eyes of the world are upon you," Cicero told the jurors, fearing they would allow themselves to be suborned [bribed]. "This man's case will establish whether a jury composed exclusively of Senators can possibly convict someone who is very guilty — and very rich. Let me add that because the defendant is the kind of man who is distinguished by nothing except his criminality and his wealth, the only imaginable explanation for an acquittal will be the one that brings the greatest discredit to you... if you are unable to arrive at a correct judgment in this case, the Roman People cannot expect that there will be other Senators who can. It will despair of the Senatorial Order as a whole and look around for some other type of man and some other method of administering justice."[1]

The impact was electric. Quintus Hortensius Hortalus, until that time the leading advocate in Rome, resigned from the defense team. Verres fled into exile never to return. Soon after, the law was changed so that only one third of the members of a jury could be senators.

The lure of trials in the Forum was their combination of drama and politics. As we shall see, political rivals would frequently try to get rid of one another by bringing charges of extortion or treason to a jury trial. The rough and tumble of Roman politics meant that politicians frequently walked the boundary between legal and illegal methods of raising money and inciting crowds of voters to act. This left them vulnerable to legal charges, where a jury conviction could lead to exile and a loss of their fortune. As a result, Roman politics was not for the faint of heart.

In the 3rd century BCE the office of praetor was split, with one elected official becoming the praetor *urbanus*, handling legal cases taking place in the city of Rome, and the other becoming the praetor *peregrinus*, dealing with cases where at least one of the participants was not a Roman citizen. The praetor *peregrinus* was primarily a traveling circuit judge who dispensed justice in the various Italian towns that were becoming part of the city's growing empire.

QUAESTORS AND THE ADMINISTRATION OF THE STATE

The third level of Roman official was called the quaestor. Like other officials, a quaestor was elected to a one-year term. These magistrates, the

---

1 Everitt, *Cicero*, p. 79 & 80

number gradually increasing from four in the early Republic, to eight in the Middle Republic, and then 20 during the last half-century of the Republic, handled the financial administration of a wide variety of state activities. For example, each consul acting as the general of an army had a quaestor to handle financial and administrative matters related to providing the army with supplies and weapons.

Two quaestors oversaw the work of the Treasury, making decisions about how many coins would be minted and which images would appear on them. By the end of the 2nd century BCE, they were working with the consuls to mint coins glorifying the deeds of prominent ancestors.[1] Our ability to date terms of office for officials in the early Republic and to make family connections over several centuries has been greatly aided by this unusual custom. Quaestors also collected duties at ports and, starting in the 3rd century, worked for magistrates who were governing conquered provinces.

When thinking about the varied duties of the quaestor, praetor, and consul, one can see the wide range of abilities a successful Roman politician needed. Quaestors had to have a variety of financial and administrative skills, as their work required that they be able to collect taxes from merchants selling meat in the Forum, tariffs from Egyptian ships unloading clothing in the port of Ostia, and tribute from tribes living in conquered provinces. They were also expected to manage expenditures for items as varied as new ships for the navy, blankets for an army on the march, salaries for stonemasons repairing a temple, carpenters setting up bleachers in the Forum, and per diem expenses for officials traveling to other city states. The Romans thought of civil servants as one of the more odious aspects of a monarchy and refused to create anything more than a skeleton crew of full time bureaucrats. This meant that quaestors actually did the work of counting, cajoling, and reviewing reports. During the 5th century these responsibilities were usually done on a relatively small scale, but, by the time of the Punic Wars with Carthage in the 3rd century, quaestors were in charge of supplying armies with 50,000 soldiers and fleets with 200 ships.

Praetors had to have a thorough understanding of Roman law and court procedures and were adept at playing the role of judge or prosecutor depending on the situation. They had to balance the conflicting needs of a variety of courts, each with politically important defendants and plaintiffs who, if offended by choices of timing or setting or rulings of the praetor, could make it difficult for him when he returned to the electoral arena to run for consul. Once again, as there were only a modest number of court employees, the praetor did much of the work himself.

---

1 Andrew Meadows and Jonathan Williams, "Moneta and the Monuments: Coinage and Politics in Republican Rome," *Journal Roman Studies*, V.91, 2001, p. 48

The praetor *peregrinus* had a movable court, traveling throughout Italy to hear cases — usually disputes between Roman citizens and individuals who were native to the place where the trial was being held. In each situation he would need to understand the unique status of individuals from that city, because, as Rome expanded throughout the Italian peninsula, she established unique treaty relations with conquered cities and tribes, providing citizens of these areas with carefully nuanced legal and political rights. The praetor was continually balancing the imperial rights of Roman citizens in a colonized area with the need to respect local customs and important people so that, when he ran for consul, local elites who had been given voting rights might come to Rome to support his candidacy.

Military command was the immense responsibility of a consul, which frequently meant planning and leading that season's military campaign against local opponents in Italy and, in later years, large campaigns against Carthage, the Gauls, the Greeks, and the Spanish. Each campaign offered the prospect of glory, for both the individual and his family, or defeat, a result that diminished the family's standing in the city and hampered the next generation's ability to achieve elected office.

Thus, a successful Roman politician had an amazing bundle of administrative, legal, political, personal, and military skills. Knowing the challenges their male children would face, parents in prominent political families gave their sons an intensive educational experience. There were no public schools or state-supported universities; male children usually received instruction through some combination of private tutors and lessons taught by the mother. For example, Cornelia, mother of Tiberius and Gaius Gracchus, political leaders in the 2nd century, was famous for the virtuous manner in which she brought up her two sons.[1] As the Roman elites came into contact with the sophisticated culture of Greece, more and more of their tutors were educated people from that area of the world. For example, Diophanes, a well-known Greek orator, worked for many years as Tiberius' tutor.[2]

Male children were required to memorize the Twelve Tables and other established documents of Roman law.[3] Some children of the aristocracy learned about rhetoric and mathematics in small private schools. Most important was the teaching/modeling done by the father and other adult relatives and friends. For example, Julius Caesar's father probably taught him riding, fencing and other basic military skills.[4] After Marcus Tullius Cicero reached the age of 17, his father arranged for a kind of intellectual apprentice-

---

1 Alvin Bernstein, *Tiberius Sempronius Gracchus: Tradition and Apostasy*, Ithaca: Cornell University Press, 1978, p. 43
2 Bernstein, *Tiberius*, p. 45
3 Everitt, *Cicero*, p. 28
4 Christian Meier, *Caesar: A Biography*, New York: Basic Books, 1982, p. 57

ship with Lucius Licinius Crassus, one of Rome's most prominent political leaders and a well-known orator.[1] Cicero often visited the Crassus household as a young man, listening to the great man discuss politics, the law, and the art of public speaking. It was during this time that Cicero developed his ambition to become a famous advocate, an ambition that, in the turbulent politics of the Late Republic, would lead him through the "course of honor" to the consulship.

The Cursus Honorum

The office of quaestor was the first step on what was known as the *cursus honorum*, the course of honor. To a degree unlike any other aristocracy in history, Roman nobles were deeply attached to a public, meritocratic notion of social status.[2] Ambitious members of Rome's aristocracy spent a lifetime of effort trying to be elected to the three ascending offices of quaestor, praetor, and then consul. For them, Roman liberty meant that members of the political elite were free to compete for the honor of political position.

These ambitions were based on a very public conception of what it meant to be a successful member of the Roman community. The most impressive thing a person could do was to be an elected leader, to hold public office and be known by everyone in the city.[3] This is not the same as what current American culture calls fame, which frequently is based on either shallow self-promotion or a self-absorbed flaunting of cultural rules and customs. In Rome, one was known by his deeds in the public service, his accomplishments that brought riches to the city, his exploits that showed courage and daring in the midst of danger. These adventures were often most visible in military campaigns, but could also be displayed in a court of law or during debates in an assembly.

Being elected to public office was the ultimate ratification of an aristocrat's moral worth and brought prestige and lasting honor to both him and his family. In Rome, the true measure of a noble family was the level of public office that its members had achieved over the generations. That is why the ladder of electoral positions was called the course of honor. Those elected to office were both honored and honorable, deserving of both their current position and worthy of consideration for even higher offices.

Of course, Rome was located in the real world, not some Olympian utopia, so the acquisition of honors and electoral positions was also helpful in acquiring material rewards, especially through military victories. For example, consuls who captured wealthy cities acquired enormous amounts of looted gold, silver, art, and other items. As a result, their families gained both

---

1 Everitt, *Cicero*, p. 31
2 Mouritsen, *Plebs and Politics*, p. 13
3 Holland, *Rubicon*, p. 4

political honors and material resources that could be used to educate and fund the ambitions of future generations.

The Roman aristocracy was a meritocracy however, in that success was not guaranteed. In the course of five hundred years of wars both small and great, Roman armies were frequently defeated, with their commanding officers and their families disgraced. For example, in 137 BCE the consul C. Hostilius Mancinus suffered a series of defeats at the hands of rebellious Spaniards. When he attempted to save his army from destruction by signing a peace treaty with the rebels, the Roman Senate refused to ratify the treaty. Instead, the consul was sent back to Spain, naked and in chains, to be turned over to the Spaniards for execution.

In the same way, during every election, while a few noblemen were elected to office, many others failed and were unable to claim a place of honor for their family. As a result, electoral competition was fierce, literally a struggle between each succeeding generation to maintain their family's position and regard in the city. A family whose sons were, over several generations, unable to attain election to one of the three offices on the *cursus honorum*, would fall in both esteem and wealth. Other families, blessed with talented, ambitious, or ruthless sons, would rise in the social order, claiming both victories and wealth as assets for the next generation to use in the on-going struggle for honor and glory.[1]

THE ELECTORAL CALDRON

No Roman aristocrat, no matter how wealthy or connected his family, had a chance to demonstrate his administrative, legal, and military skills unless he had the time, energy, charisma, and money to win approval at the ballot box. Getting elected to the first rung of the electoral ladder, the office of quaestor, was a key step in the process of achieving electoral glory. Only by attaining one of these official positions was a Roman nobleman able to eventually compete for the far more prestigious offices of praetor and consul. To become a quaestor, a young man needed to be one of the candidates elected by the Tribal Assembly.

There were only twelve tribes at the time of independence, but the number of tribes grew as Rome's territory expanded. By the mid-3rd century (about 240 BCE) there were 31 rural tribes, representing the variety of geographical areas that made up Rome's territory in Italy. Each new Roman settlement was assigned to a tribe so that the tribes from rural areas had roughly equal numbers of people scattered around the peninsula. The exceptions to this balancing of population rule were the people who lived in Rome itself. As a person had to be physically present to vote in a Roman election, people who

---

1 Mouritsen, *Plebs and Politics*, p. 12

The Roman Republic's Political System (2nd century BCE)

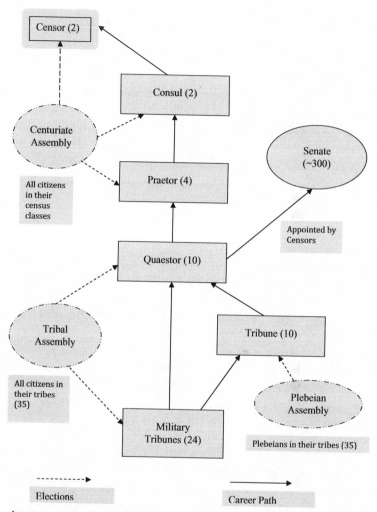

lived in Rome were much more likely to vote than farmers living in areas two, three or more days travel from the city. To restrict the impact of urban voters, the patricians continued King Tullius' policy of placing all of the voters in the city of Rome into only four urban tribes.

During the first 300 years of the Republic, citizen voters would assemble by tribe in the Forum during a festival week in July or August. Each tribe voted as a unit, with a majority of the voters present selecting the individual the tribe supported. The tribes voted in order, as chosen by lot each year, with each tribe being able to name as many candidates as there were positions open. By the 2nd century, there were too many voters to squeeze into the Forum and balloting was done on the military drill field called the *Campus Marti*, just outside the city limits. Elections in the 1st and 2nd centuries lasted all day, with votes being tallied late into the night.

As the Tribal Assembly was dominated by rural voters, usually farmers who were either independent landowners or clients of a patrician family, a candidate for political office needed to be comfortable shaking hands, visiting villages, and discussing the weather and crops. The story is told that Scipio Nasica, while campaigning for a quaestor position, "shook hands with a ploughman, and feeling his calluses, inquired if the man walked on his hands."[1] He was soundly defeated. Another key to victory was having good relations with wealthy landowners scattered throughout the Italian peninsula to ensure that they instructed their clients to vote for the candidate in the upcoming election.

THE CLIENTELA SYSTEM

As mentioned in chapter 1, every aristocrat had *clientela*, men who provided political votes and armed service when needed and in return received representation in the courts, invitations to local feasts and celebrations, and work when times were hard or crops were bad. The *clientela* system was deeply rooted in the tribal, rural nature of early Rome. It moderated social conflict by providing reciprocal supportive relationships between wealthy Romans and the rest of the rural population. These relationships would allow a family to keep their land during a summer when the husband broke his leg or find a humble position for a widow so she would not be forced to move into Rome and beg for her family. Life was full of hard work and bad fortune was a constant presence in the average person's life. Participation in the *clientela* system created a social safety net in a world where governments did not provide welfare or social security.

The support aristocrats provided their clients was not merely charity; a wealthy Roman who wanted to compete in elections or help his friends attain office needed to cultivate a devoted *clientela*, especially men who were citizens and willing to make the trip to Rome to provide votes for candidates favored by the aristocrat. Indeed, men with large *clientela* groups were considered generous and worthy citizens and their clients were proud to be associated with a prosperous and famous aristocratic family.

While some citizens who lived in the city of Rome were clients of aristocrats, probably a much smaller percentage of the population was pledged in this way than in the countryside. This was another reason for limiting the voting power of urban plebeians by placing them in only four tribes. As the

---

1 Matyszak, *Chronicle*, p. 130

city grew larger and the empire grew, political families continued to have client groups in the city, but these were more for show during public events and armed protection during disturbances rather than as an absolute number of votes.

THE INFLUENCE OF SMALL FARMERS

Even before the *clientela* system began to break down in the 2nd century, there were many small farmers who participated in elections and were not obligated to vote one way or the other unless a powerful local person was a candidate. We do not know the electoral balance between *clientela*-based voters and "independent" voters because our source materials are vague on this kind of demographic information. However, the independents must have been key voters in numerous elections because historical sources mention many instances of candidates campaigning among crowds in the Forum and in nearby villages. It was also typical for candidates to provide voters with feasts or other free handouts to influence their vote.[1] In addition, the sources tell us of a series of anti-bribery laws that testify to the existence of a pool of voters able to choose candidates based on factors other than *clientela* instructions.[2]

The available evidence about campaigning shows us that there were free, contested elections for the quaestor positions. However, there were severe limitations on who could stand for election. Since only wealthy individuals were elected to office, some historians have speculated that there was a specific property qualification that has not been discovered, but the real story is more complicated.[3] The answer lies in the well-known requirement that a person had to serve ten years in the cavalry or, in later centuries, as an officer in the army, in order to be eligible to run for the position of quaestor.[4] Only men with enough wealth to become a member of the richest census class, the *equites* (initially those members of society wealthy enough to own and care for horses), were officers or members of the cavalry in the 5th and 4th centuries. This was the basis for the tradition that only people from the *Equestrian* Order who served as officers in the army were eligible to run for office.

MILITARY GLORY AND POLITICAL ACHIEVEMENT

This connection between military service and political office brings us back to the crucial issue of electoral competition between members of the aristocracy. While only men from the *Equestrian* Order were elected to the

---

1 Alexander Yakobson, "Popular Participation in the Centuriate Assembly of the Late Republic," *Journal of Roman Studies*, V.82, 1992, p. 33

2 A.E. Astin, *Scipio Aemilianus*, Oxford: Oxbow Books Limited, 1967, p. 29

3 Holland, *Rubicon*, p. 25

4 Fergus Millar, "The Political Character of the Classical Roman Republic 200-151 B.C.," *Journal of Roman Studies*, V.74, 1984, p. 11 and Scullard, *Roman World*, p. 332

position of quaestor, not all *equites* who wanted to be quaestor were able to win election. Even in the last years of the Republic, when 20 quaestors were elected each year, there were many more who desired the office but were unable to gain enough support from voters.

How did one member of the aristocracy rise above another to win election as quaestor? Voters in Rome valued military success above all other qualifications. Junior officers who had participated in successful campaigns or better yet, officers who won distinction for bravery and military ability during battle, were clearly favored over other candidates. How did a young man become a junior officer? Each year the Tribal Assembly elected twenty-four men between the ages of 25 and 29 to be "tribunes of the military." They were assigned as middle-level officers in the legions and were thus in the thick of any battles fought.

In the elections for "tribunes of the military" the voters seemed to have a tradition of first voting for young men who were designated by one or another of the consuls as a person he wanted on his staff. Thus, the easiest way for a young man to become an officer was to have family or political ties to a consul or a consul's family. (After the 4th century, when praetors governed provinces and commanded military units, they too could nominate tribunes of the military.) The other successful candidates for tribune of the military tended to be sons from families that had a recent history of military or political success.

In this fashion, the leading political families of Rome sustained their domination by having their most promising sons compete with one another to be elected as junior officers. There were no military schools to train promising members of the middle or lower classes. Family members who had prior experience as a political/military leader provided their sons with the training needed to be an officer. Those elected tribunes of the military began a lifetime of competition with each other for military glory; glory that would bring them election to the lower rungs of the *cursus honorum*, which in turn opened the door for greater military and political responsibilities, setting the stage for election to the highest offices.

Roman militarism, the restless urge for conquest that brought first Italy and then the Mediterranean basin under Roman rule, was embedded in this meritocratic competition built into the heart of the Roman political system. The principal way to gain fame and election to higher office was to attain military victory, thus bringing glory to one's family and enhancing one's dignity.[1] There was a sense of urgency to this search for military glory because victory had to be achieved within the one-year terms that were associated with all of these offices, from "tribune of the military" to consul. As a result, a

---

1 Boatwright, *The Romans*, p. 94

dynamic cycle of conflict was created where all of the elected leaders in any campaign season had every reason to seek fame and fortune through military conquest.

The steady narrowing of opportunity for advancement as a candidate sought higher office — in 150 BCE the list went from 24 tribunes of the military to ten quaestors, from ten quaestors to six praetors, from six praetors to two consuls — combined with the very public way in which elections singled out winners from losers acted like a searing fire, purging the less talented, the less ambitious, the less connected, the less ruthless men from the *cursus honorum*. That is why the history of the Republic so often seems to be a tale of the struggles, the triumphs, the intrigues, and the tragedies of its elected leaders.

CHAPTER 3. THE STRUGGLE OF THE ORDERS AND THE RISE OF THE NOBILITY

> If it [*The History of the Peloponnesian War*] be judged useful by those inquirers who desire an exact knowledge of the past as an aid to the interpretation of the future, which in the course of human things must resemble if it does not reflect it; I shall be content.[1]
>
> —Thucydides

Once having secured a quaestor position, the ambitious Roman nobleman began courting a different political audience — the Centuriate Assembly. This assembly, in which all citizens participated, but the voting was weighted toward the wealthier individuals in the city, elected praetors and consuls. The period, usually several years, between serving as quaestor and running for praetor, was a time to create new electoral alliances with influential members of the nobility. To cement bonds of friendship (*amicitia*) and loyalty, a rising politician needed to provide other political leaders with money and client votes when they waged electoral campaigns. This ensured their support when it was his turn to seek higher office.

In addition, businessmen and advocates, people who frequently used the legal system, had to be won over if a nobleman wanted to be elected praetor. A good way to make friends was to defend an ally in court. Cicero made it a point to only defend people and seldom acted as a prosecuting advocate. His many grateful clients were the backbone of his election campaigns. Later,

1 Thucydides, *History of the Peloponnesian War*, Book 1, Chapter 1, translated by Richard Crawley, available at: http://classics.mit.edu/Thucydides/pelopwar.html; accessed on 14 Nov. 2007

to be elected consul, a rising politician also needed to hold at least one successful military command so that voters of all social classes felt comfortable entrusting the city's legions to him.

CREATING THE CENTURIATE ASSEMBLY: THE CENSUS

Competition between wealthy aristocrats began in the Centuriate Assembly long before voting occurred. Striving to attain glory through electoral victory went hand-in-hand with competition to accumulate wealth and attain elevated status in the Assembly. This competition took place through the practice known as the census. Once every five years all citizens went before two senior elected officials, the censors, in a public ceremony. Each citizen publicly presented them with a list of all his assets, including land, livestock, money, works of art, and slaves. The censors then pronounced judgment on the net worth of each person and placed him in one of six classes of the *assidui* (people who owned property). In the early days of the Republic, that placement conveyed both military and political status:

First Class — during the 5th century a man needed a minimum worth of 100,000 *asses* to belong to the wealthiest group[1]

(Note that the monetary unit known as the *as* (*asses* = plural) was not used until the 3rd century, in the 5th century wealth was measured in terms of acres of land, number of cattle, etc.)

Second Class — men in this class had a minimum worth of 75,000 *asses*

Third Class — a minimum worth of 50,000 *asses*

Fourth Class — a minimum worth of 25,000 *asses*

Fifth Class — a minimum worth of 11,000 *asses*

The Head Count (*capite censi*) — having less than 11,000 *asses* they had nothing to offer the state but their heads.[2] This significant percentage of the population was defined in Roman law as the *proletarii* (those without property).[3]

In the 5th century the wealthiest members of the First Class were further divided into 18 "centuries." (Note that the Romans did not use the word "century" to mark groups of years) These men were called *equestrians* because they already owned horses or were given horses by the state. They formed the cavalry units and officer corps of the Roman army and had a significantly higher social status than other members of the First Class. As we saw earlier, the young officers in the Roman army were selected from this *Equestrian* Order, giving the sons of wealthy aristocrats the opportunity to acquire military glory and the chance to add to the family's fortune through political success. The financial requirement for membership in the *Equestrian* Order rose

---

1 Boatwright, *The Romans*, p. 69
2 LeGlay, *History of Rome*, p. 32
3 Alfoldy, *Social History*, p. 17

greatly as the riches of empire flowed into the hands of leading aristocrats and businessmen. By the time of Julius Caesar, a man had to have a minimum net worth of 400,000 sesterces, 10 times the minimum for the First Class, to be counted as a member of the *Equestrian* Order.[1]

The remaining members of the First Class were divided into 80 centuries of heavily armored soldiers. Until the middle of the 4th century, soldiers had to purchase and maintain their own weapons and protective armor, so there was a practical argument for wealthier citizens taking on the role of heavily armored members of the infantry or being given the responsibility to feed and care for cavalry horses. The cost of a 5th century soldiers' armaments — his shield made of wood, leather, and bronze; his body armor of bronze and canvas; a bronze helmet with horsehair or feathered crest; bronze leg guards; an 8- to 10-foot spear with iron head and sharpened bronze butt; and a sword made of iron — was comparable to the cost of a modern car.[2]

As in the electoral process, there was a competitive, meritocratic dynamic in the census count. As new sources and forms of wealth developed over the decades, successful business men and land owners from the First Class were able to rise into the *Equestrian* Order and secure opportunities for their sons to become officers in the military. Downward mobility was also a constant in Roman society. A family whose sons were killed in battle, died from disease at an early age, or were inept farmers or businessmen might see its wealth decline and its good public name fade in glory.

Julius Caesar's family faced just such a fate in 108 BCE. Caesar's grandfather, Gaius Julius Caesar, realized that he could not afford to help his sons take on the expense of being military officers and then running for office. To rescue the family's fortunes, he arranged for his oldest daughter Julia to marry Gaius Marius, a successful general and wealthy newcomer to Roman politics. (This connection is so important that Colleen McCullough's epic series of books about Caesar begins with the marriage negotiations between his grandfather and Marius.)[3] Because of this marriage alliance, Marius financed Caesar's father's rise to the praetorship, while he gained prestige and social connections from becoming a member of an old patrician family. Without this marriage arrangement Julius Caesar would never have had the wealth or status to become a quaestor, let alone a consul and a general.

In the 5th century, the Second, Third, and Fourth Classes were each divided into 20 centuries of lightly armed foot soldiers, while the Fifth Class had 30 centuries of men armed with slings. As the population of the Roman Republic increased, the number of centuries remained the same, quickly break-

1 Mary Beard and Michael Crawford, *Rome in the Late Republic*, Ithaca: Cornell University Press, 1978, p. 45
2 Warry, *Warfare*, p. 34 & 35
3 Colleen McCullough, *The First Man in Rome*, New York: Avon, 1990, p. 15

ing any connection between the term century and the number of people in those units. Census categories lost their military significance in the middle of the 4th century, when military units began to be organized according to a person's ability as a soldier and the state provided soldiers with their weapons. However, until the end of the Republic, each man continued to vote according to his census ranking.

The final grouping of Roman citizens, the men of the Head Count, were not eligible to serve because men were expected to provide their own equipment in the 5th century. Men in the Head Count lived from day-to-day as tenant farmers or laborers in the countryside or city — as men without property they were not considered honorable enough to participate in the military.

The property-based census system for military service allowed the Roman Republic to field a genuine citizens' army. Unlike many city-states and unlike any of the ancient kingdoms, the Roman army marched without mercenaries, manned entirely by citizens who desired to protect their city. As property holders and respected citizens, men in the Roman legions were fighting to protect their family's future and their way of life, a powerful incentive against desertion or running away in the heat of battle. The Greek historian Polybius claimed that it was the élan of Rome's citizen army that made it the greatest fighting unit of the Mediterranean World.[1]

The census system also established membership in one of the city's principal decision-making bodies, the Centuriate Assembly. This assembly had 193 voting units, also called centuries. As in other Roman assemblies, balloting was done by unit voting, with each century polling its members and then casting one vote for the candidate getting a majority or plurality of the vote inside the unit. In the early Republic, with 18 centuries of *equestrians* and 80 centuries for other members of the First Class, the two groups had an absolute majority of unit votes. Later, in the middle of the 3rd century, this was changed to 18 and 70, giving more weight to the Second and Third Classes, populated primarily by loyal, hardworking people with small farms who, by that time, served as the main body of infantry in the Roman army.[2]

In addition to the First Class possessing a majority of voting units in the 5th and 4th centuries, voting was further skewed in favor of the wealthy by the vote counting system. Voting was done by order of wealth, with the 18 *equestrian* centuries voting and announcing results first, then the First Class centuries, and finally the rest of the centuries. Voting stopped when enough candidates to fill the available positions received a majority of votes. In this weighted system, the Third Class frequently did not vote and the Fourth and Fifth Classes almost never voted.

1 LeGlay, *History of Rome*, p. 70
2 Alfody, *Social History*, p. 38

During periods of political stability, this wealth-oriented vote counting system ensured that candidates for praetor and consul spent most of their time campaigning among members of the First and Second Classes. However, this voting system could not be dominated by the wealthy when the First Class was split between the candidacies of several popular leaders. As we will see, public opinion in the city was volatile, and during crises the Centuriate Assembly would elect reform candidates or popular military figures who were at odds with leaders of the aristocracy.

Patricians versus Plebeians

As we saw in chapter 2, wealthy and accomplished plebeians felt that they and their families deserved more *dignitas* in the new state. This upper crust of plebeians, usually members of the First Class, resented the aristocracy's decision to exclude plebeians from elected offices. We know that the patrician order was a relatively small percentage of the Roman population; Roman antiquarians have calculated that there were only 136 patrician extended families in existence in 509 BCE.[1] Thus, these families were clearly outnumbered by plebeians even in the First Class of the Centuriate Assembly, which had 80 votes while the patrician-dominated *Equestrian* Class had just 18. Dissatisfaction with their exclusion from the *cursus honorum* would repeatedly place the plebeians in conflict with the patricians.

Along with their arbitrary monopoly on electoral offices, the ruling patricians seldom exhibited any concern about the economic interests of people who did not own large tracts of land. This was especially true regarding the issue of debt. At the beginning of the Republic, many plebeians were farmers, struggling to make a living from the small farms that surrounded the city. Like small farmers in other times and other civilizations, poor seasons with poor crops forced these hard working citizens to take on debt.[2] Other plebeians worked as day laborers in the fields or in shops in the city and faced many days when no work was available. As a result, they too ended up taking loans, loans that were hard to repay when work was erratic.

In Rome, during the early days of the Republic, debtors guaranteed their loans with their personal liberty. The Twelve Tables laid out in great detail the procedures a creditor could use to get a debt paid off.[3] Once judgment had been rendered in court, debtors had thirty days to pay off a debt that was due. After that the creditor could seize and hold the debtor. If no one paid off his debt in three days, then the debtor could be sold into slavery or be forced to work for the creditor.

---

1 Conell, *Atlas*, p. 26
2 Boatwright, *The Romans*, p.53
3 Boatwright, *The Romans*, p. 51

The parallel with debt in the United States during the Revolutionary War era is interesting. Bankruptcy in colonial America was seen as a moral sin, with preachers regularly thundering about paying up debts and the rewards of frugal living. As moral outcasts, debtors were often thrown into prison, with little thought about how they might pay their creditors from that position.[1] By comparison, the creditor in Rome, through sale of debtors into slavery, at least had some prospect of recovering his losses. The illogical paradox of the American debtors' prison led many poor individuals to clamor for changes in American debt laws.

By the late 18th century individual debtors were joined in agitation for bankruptcy laws by members of the rising merchant class, who had to take many financial risks as part of the normal course of business. In the 1790s, some of the most important merchants in the United States were locked into debtors' prisons, including William Duer and John Pintard, both of whom were prominent patriots during the Revolutionary War. Finally, in 1800, the US Congress passed bankruptcy legislation, but it applied only to merchants, bankers, and insurers who owed a minimum of $1,000 — a large sum at that time.[2] The law was attacked by those who felt debt was a sin and by those who disdained the class bias of the relief and it was repealed in 1803. The US Congress did not pass national bankruptcy legislation until 1898, after most of the states had revised their laws.

The Plebeian Assembly

As was noted in chapter 2, conflict between the patricians and the plebeians led to the creation of the Plebeian Assembly, which elected ten leaders called tribunes of the plebeians. As with other Roman magistrates, each tribune was elected to serve a one-year term. During the Early Republic, the position of tribune was not on the *cursus honorum* because only plebeians could be elected to the position and they were not eligible for other offices. The tribunes never ran together as a ticket or articulated a common program when they campaigned. In fact, they usually were divided between a majority of members who had only minor ambitions for their term of office and one or two genuinely forceful leaders who either quarreled bitterly or worked together, allowing them to have tremendous influence in the Assembly and the city.

The Plebeian Assembly functioned under the same rules as other Roman legislative bodies — only a tribune could convene the group, only a tribune could offer motions for the members to vote on, and there was no opportunity to offer amendments or for members to speak on the issue. The Assembly

---

1 Mann, Bruce H., *Republic of Debtors: Bankruptcy in the Age of American Independence*, Cambridge: Harvard University Press, 2002.

2 Mann, *Debtors*, p. 222

was organized on the same tribal basis as the Tribal Assembly, even down to placing the multitude of urban plebs in four voting tribes while the number of rural tribes continued to increase as Rome expanded over the centuries.

Even with all of their powers, tribunes were not always in control of events in the Assembly because Roman citizens were seldom passive participants in political meetings. "In practice, however, despite this official control of both the agenda and the speakers, citizens could still register dissatisfaction with the proceedings informally, through demonstrations, heckling, and occasionally even by destroying an official's insignia of office, such as his fasces or his official chair."[1] The Assembly's most important role was to act as a forum for those who wanted to articulate economic and political grievances against the patrician rulers of Rome.

This uncomfortable duality of power inside the Roman political system led to frequent conflicts that are known as "The Struggle of the Orders." The plebeians developed a powerful weapon for this struggle when in the 5th century tribunes were given the right to veto actions of the consuls, other magistrates, other tribunes, and even the Senate. This power extended to actions both large and small. For example, when Cicero attempted to give a farewell oration after his term as consul, a tribune, embittered by the executions he had ordered during that term, vetoed his right to give the speech. Tribunes did not suffer physical harm when they exercised a veto because they were "inviolable." Anyone who struck a tribune was cursed, exiled from the city, and his possessions were sold to benefit plebeian temples.[2] However, the use of the veto was tempered by the fact that, after the expiration of his yearlong term of office, the tribune would continue to live in the city, exposed to retribution by those people that his vetoes offended.[3]

THE SACK OF ROME

After the long campaign to capture Veii that was discussed in the previous chapter, Rome became the largest city-state in Latium and immediately began constructing a series of favorable trade and military agreements with the smaller Latin communities. When negotiating with these small cities, Rome's influence was enhanced because it formed a connected landmass, while the Latin communities were often separated from each other by Roman territory.[4] However, before these gains could be consolidated, an invading army of Gauls devastated the Roman city-state.

By the end of the Iron Age, Celtic tribes dominated a wide swath of northern Europe, including the areas we now know as England, France, Germany,

---

1 Boatwright, *The Romans*, p. 67
2 LeGlay, *History of Rome*, p. 53
3 Matyszak, *Chronicles*, p. 13
4 Scullard, *Roman World*, p. 101

and the Balkans. While they made magnificent iron tools, they usually did not live in settled cities and were regarded as barbarians by the peoples of Greece and Italy. They were attracted to the warmer climates, fertile soils, and wealthy cities of those more advanced civilizations and Celts from the area known as Gaul (modern France) began crossing the Alps and moving into the Po River Valley at the beginning of the 5[1] century.[1] The Etruscan cities to the north of Rome bore the brunt of this combination migration/invasion and by the beginning of the 4th century had lost all of the Po Valley, except for the area known as Veneti (modern Venice).

Sometime between 390 and 380 (the date is disputed) warriors from the Senones tribe from Gaul began raiding the upper Tiber River area and confronted the small Etruscan city of Clusium. (The year 390 is the traditional date given for the Gaelic attack, the date named by Livy, our principal source for this time period. However, there are more recent claims of a 381 date based on an analysis of ancient lists of consuls and the year they were elected to office, a method that is known to be accurate.[2] I believe these new claims are supported by archeological research which pinpoints the date for the building of a new, larger wall around the city as 378 BCE.[3] In the context of uprisings by Rome's Latin rivals and the hill tribes after the sack of Rome, it seems unlikely that the Romans would have waited 12 years to re-build the city's principal defensive structure.)

While the exact nature of Rome's involvement is not clear, it seems likely that the city sent a delegation to Clusium to participate in negotiations. Perhaps predictably, the delegation quarreled with the aggressive barbarians, killing several of their leaders and then retreating back to Rome with a throng of Gauls close behind.[4] To stop them, the Romans put together an army of 10 to 15,000 soldiers, including some Latin allies. They met on the banks of a stream called the Allia, where the Roman ranks were quickly outflanked and routed. The Gauls poured into the defenseless city, looting and burning as they moved through the deserted streets. The speed of the Gaelic advance meant that civilians in the city had to flee with little more than what they could carry on their backs, losing everything else to the invaders.

Livy tells us that the Gauls stayed for several months, raiding settlements near the city and using the captured city as shelter for the winter.[5] Living in temporary shelters until the Gauls left, the Romans were overwhelmed with fear and humiliation. The fear was deep-seated — of taller stature than Mediterranean peoples, Gaelic warriors raced into battle naked; wielding

1 Cornell, *Atlas*, p. 30
2 LeGlay, *History of Rome*, p. 55
3 Both Cornell, *Atlas*, p. 34 and Scullard, *Roman World*, p. 105, agree on this date for the wall.
4 Scullard, *Roman World*, p. 103
5 LeGlay, *History of Rome*, p. 55

nasty iron weapons, uttering strange war cries, and trailing streaming hair.[1] They raided central Italy and northern Greece repeatedly during the 4th century and rumors of a possible Gaelic invasion were enough to send Romans into a panic. "Greeks and Romans would long continue to regard Gauls as uncivilized, warlike, predatory, and expansionistic."[2]

DEFENSIVE IMPERIALISM AND THE BUSH DOCTRINE

There is a parallel between the reaction of the Romans to this terrible loss and the American response to the horrors of 9/11. In both cases this defeat at the hands of a barbarian enemy came as a lightning bolt, smashing cherished ideas about security and comfort in the homeland. In both cases the political elite and the general public became obsessed with obtaining "security." In both cases security came to be defined as eliminating potential enemies before they had a chance to attack.

The sack of Rome by the Gauls made the Romans deeply fearful of invasion. They began seeking security by capturing and setting up "buffer states." Thereafter their foreign policy can be described as "Defensive Imperialism." The army concentrated on capturing nearby city-states or tribal areas in Italy in order to create a defensive buffer between the city of Rome and possible invaders. A century later, the security mission was to protect the Italian core of the Roman state from possible invaders from other parts of the Mediterranean. This involved conquering areas like Sicily and Greece that were in close sailing distance to Italy.

In both situations, the newly conquered area would, in turn, have on its border an unfriendly city-state or national group, which threatened the security of the buffer area. To protect the buffer area, the Romans thought it necessary to conqueror the unfriendly border state, which would, in turn, have borders with yet another unfriendly state, creating an endless cycle of new enemies and new conquests. As we shall see, there were a number of cases when the threat from an unfriendly border state was exaggerated in order to justify an attack that was actually designed to win glory and plunder for the officials leading the invasion.

The destruction of the twin towers in New York understandably made Americans deeply fearful of terrorist attacks. The Bush administration sought security by identifying "rogue states" with weapons of mass destruction that were allied to terrorist organizations. The "Bush Doctrine," established in 2002, claimed that the danger of sneak attack from terrorist organizations called for a US policy of "pre-emptive strikes" on rogue states. Rogue states were attacked because they might have or might develop weapons of mass destruction and give them to terrorist groups. The invasion of Iraq in 2003

1 Scullard, *Roman World*, p. 102
2 Boatwright, *The Romans*, p. 59

was justified as a pre-emptive strike on a hated dictator who was on the verge of giving weapons of mass destruction to al-Qaeda. In spite of the false premises and disastrous results of that action, the same type of arguments about the danger of nuclear weapons and their possible use by a terrorist organization led to calls in 2007 for a pre-emptive strike on Iran. It remains to be seen whether the new president elected in 2008 will continue the pre-emptive strike strategy.

The Struggle of the Orders

There were good reasons for Romans to feel embarrassment and anger about the sack of their city. Etruscan cities were known to have held off Gaelic assaults for years, or to quickly retake captured towns before the invaders could loot them.[1] The ease with which one of the largest Roman armies put into the field up to that time had been overrun by the barbarians must have led to a good deal of debate in the city about how to improve the military. As we will discuss in chapter 4, the eventual result was a thorough revamping of the army — its armaments, its organization, and its tactics.

The sack of Rome may also have undermined the patrician claim to exclusive leadership of the city. While a council of military tribunes that included plebeian members governed the city, military officers were patrician cavalrymen and the patrician Senate clearly dominated policy making in the city. While we have no written evidence of a specific decline in the legitimacy of the patrician monopoly of power, this colossal military failure may have made plebeians less deferential to patrician rule and more likely advocate for their own rights when tensions over other issues brought the Struggle of the Orders to new levels of intensity.

Stories about disorder and conflict related to the problems of debt and debt slavery are extensive during the period after the sack of Rome. As we have seen, in extreme cases the Laws of the XII Tables allowed a lender to sell a person who defaulted on a loan into slavery. More typical was *nexum*, the Roman version of debt-bondage.[2] If a person failed to repay his loan, his ability to work was the collateral. As the collateral, the debtor could be forced to work off the loan under conditions determined by the person who made the loan.[3] Opposition to *nexum* was widespread among the plebeians because a person in debt-bondage had great difficulty earning enough money to work off the debt. In the rush to re-build Rome after the Gauls had burned and looted the city, many plebeians incurred heavy debts that they could not

---

1 Scullard, *Roman World*, p. 102
2 Cornell, *Atlas*, p. 26
3 Cornell, *Atlas*, p. 26

re-pay, leading to a significant increase in the number of people trapped in *nexum*.[1]

The other source of discontent was the unfair distribution of new lands. It has been estimated that the average size of a peasant farm in the 5th and 4th centuries was about seven *iugera* (1 *iugerum* is approximately 2/3 of an acre).[2] Since this amount is half the amount of land a family needed to live on, peasants must have had access to other land, probably to public land, the *ager publicus*. This land was owned by the state after it was seized from another town or tribe. Rather than have it sit idle, the state would allow peasants to farm or graze on portions for free as a way to supplement their incomes. However, wealthy patricians (who were officers in the Roman army and got the first look at a new area) frequently took over the better parts of new *ager publicus* shortly after a conquest.[3] They then would place clients on the land or force small farmers to pay some type of rental in return for using it. The defeat of Veii, which might have been an opportunity to relieve social tensions over land issues, probably aggravated tensions because of the unequal distribution of large swaths of the newly acquired *ager publicus*. This injustice, combined with the pressure of rising debts, rallied plebeian support behind those who would alter the distribution of power in the city.

Troubles in the city are reflected in the stories/legends told about this period. Livy went into great detail about the story of M. Manlius Capitolinus, the first patrician on record as breaking with his class and becoming an advocate for the plebeian cause. Manlius was a hero in the defense of the Capitoline hill from the Gauls and was a leading citizen in the city. Livy claims that he was jealous of the honors given to M. Furius Camillus when he defeated the Aequi and Volsci tribes.

> "With his head full of these notions and being unfortunately a man of headstrong and passionate nature, he found that his influence was not so powerful with the patricians as he thought it ought to be, so he went over to the plebs — the first to do so and adopted the political methods of their magistrates."[4] [That is, methods used by the tribunes.]

Livy also claims that Manlius was "impelled by the breeze of popular favor more than by conviction or judgment" and he "preferred notoriety to respectability."[5] These arguments may or may not be a true portrait of his motives; the point to remember is that all future Roman reformers faced similar accusations that they were merely seeking public acclaim and did not have sincere convictions about the desirability of their reform proposals.

---

1 Alfoldy, *Social History*, p. 21

2 Cornell, *Atlas*, p. 27

3 Alfoldy, *Social History*, p. 21

4 Titus Livy, *History of Rome*, Book 6.11 available from livius.org/rome/; text translated at: http://mcadams.posc.mu.edu/txt/ah/livy/livey06.html; accessed 22 July 2007

5 Livy, *History of Rome*, Book 6.11

The reformer, in this twist, becomes a threat to plebeian liberty. Livy lets us know that this was indeed the Senate's strategy by having a senator give this speech:

> It is our intention to fix a day for his trial. Nothing is less desired by the people than kingly power. As soon as that body of plebeians become aware that the quarrel is not with them, and find that from being his supporters they have become his judges; as soon as they see a patrician on his trial, and learn that the charge before them is one of aiming at monarchy, they will not show favor to any man more than to their own liberty.[1]

While Livy disapproves of Manlius' populist methods (as would any upper class Roman living in the 1st century of the imperial empire), he also helps us understand why Manlius was popular and why the plebeians supported him:

> Not content with the agrarian laws which had hitherto always served the tribunes of the plebs as the material for their agitation, he began to undermine the whole system of credit, for he saw that the laws of debt caused more irritation than the others; they not only threatened poverty and disgrace, but they terrified the freeman with the prospect of fetters and imprisonment.[2]

In fact, Livy's description of Manlius' actions can inspire a good deal of admiration:

> When he saw a centurion, a distinguished soldier, led away as an adjudged debtor, he ran into the middle of the Forum with his crowd of supporters and laid his hand on him. After declaiming against the tyranny of patricians and the brutality of usurers and the wretched condition of the plebs he said, "It was then in vain that I with this right hand saved the Capitol and Citadel if I have to see a fellow-citizen and a comrade in arms carried off to chains and slavery just as though he had been captured by the victorious Gauls." Then before all the people, he paid the sum due to the creditors, and after thus freeing the man by "copper and scales," sent him home. The released debtor appealed to gods and men to reward Manlius, his deliverer and the beneficial protector of the Roman plebs.[3]

Manlius aroused the plebeians against the debt laws, but did not hold a magistrate position that would have allowed him to offer legislative proposals. Frightened by this push for reform outside the established political system and by the large crowds of people who came to hear Manlius' speeches in the Forum, the military tribunes had the Centuriate Assembly try and convict him for treason. His punishment was to be hurled from the Tarpeian Rock, a steep cliff on the west side of the Capitoline hill where people convicted of treason were thrown to their death. As with other legends, there may be much in this dramatic story that is made up, but some ele-

1 Livy, *History of Rome*, Book 6.19
2 Livy, *History of Rome*, Book 6.11
3 Livy, *History of Rome*, Book 6.14

ment of truth about the problem of debts and Manlius' rise and fall probably remains.

Suppression of Manlius and his debt reform movement did not ease the plight of plebeian workers. In this extremely tense atmosphere, two plebeians decided to move a reform legislative program through the Plebeian Assembly. In 376 BCE, just a few years after the city was sacked, the newly elected tribunes, C. Licinius Stolo and L. Sextius Lateranus proposed that no individual could hold more than 500 *iuger* (about 300 acres) of *ager publicus* (a law that would open up many *iugers* of public land for use by poorer farmers), that the interest paid on any current loans be deducted from the principal and the rest of the loan paid off over three years, and that the dual consulship be restored, with one position reserved for a plebeian and one for a patrician.[1] The patricians mobilized support from the other eight tribunes and had them veto the entire package.

In response, Licinius and Sextius paralyzed the Roman government by vetoing acts of the Senate and even the election of new military tribunes.[2] For 10 years Licinius and Sextius managed to win re-election and re-introduced their reform proposals; for ten years supporters of the patricians also were elected tribunes and vetoed the legislation. For 10 years Licinius and Sextius vetoed all significant actions attempted by the Senate or military tribunes. In desperation, the Senate had to appoint Dictators at least twice to defend the city from hill tribes (the actions of a Dictator, who was usually elected for a six-month term to respond to a military emergency, could not be vetoed by a tribune).

The deadlock, an enormous test of wills between a powerful elite and a desperate majority, was waged without shedding blood or any significant attempts to violently remove the tribunes. Eventually a peaceful resolution was achieved through the intervention of M. Furius Camillus, hero of Veii and conqueror of the Aequi and Volsci. Appointed Dictator once again in 367 BCE, he used his influence to get the Senate to acquiesce to the tribune's reform package.[3] The Licinio-Sextian Compromise of 367 initiated a flood of reform legislation and social change over the next 70 years that swept away many vestiges of patrician rule.

L. Sextius Lateranus was elected to one of the two consul positions the very next year and C. Licinius Stolo was elected consul two years later. As part of the Compromise of 367, the patricians had won the creation of a new office reserved only for patricians, the praetor, who was empowered to serve as the chief magistrate of the judicial system (discussed in chapter 2). Elected by the Centuriate Assembly in the same manner as consuls, the of-

1 Scullard, *Roman World*, p. 116
2 LeGlay, *History of Rome*, p. 59
3 Boatwright, *The Romans*, p. 60

fice was opened to plebeians in 356.[1] In 356, plebeians became eligible to be appointed Dictator and in 351 it was legislated that plebeian consuls could be elected to the censorship. Finally, in 300 BCE the position of *pontifex maximus*, the head of the city's college of priests, was opened to plebeians.[2]

CREATION OF THE NOBILITY

This rapid opening of all offices to plebeians meant that the Senate, too, became a joint patrician-plebeian institution. As wealthy plebeians, already members of the First Class, were elected to posts on the *cursus honorum*, they became members of the Senate and social equals to their counterparts in the patrician aristocracy. Over time, the mingling of these two groups led to the custom that anyone whose ancestor had held an office, especially the consulship, was called a "noble." This comes from the Latin term *nobilis* meaning "one who is well known." By the end of the 4th century a new political governing class, called the nobility, had come into being.

This unique social grouping consisted of families, both patrician and plebeian, that had an ancestor who had been elected by the Centuriate Assembly to a senior magistracy (praetor and consul). The prestige of gaining a senior office enhanced the family's social standing in Rome's tradition-bound society and made it much more likely that the most competent and energetic sons of these families would be selected as military officers and later elected to political office. In effect, this created an electoral/military aristocracy, where sons rose to leadership position through a combination of birth, military accomplishment, and electoral success.

While this nobility was a social, economic, and political elite, it was still based upon the meritocratic notions inherited from the original patrician aristocracy — competition for electoral office and competition through the census for positions in one of the 18 *Equestrian* centuries in the Centuriate Assembly. As a result, when Rome expanded throughout Italy during the next century, new elite families became members of the nobility as soon as they were able to successfully compete for offices or accumulate enough wealth to achieve *Equestrian* status. In this way, by 267 BCE more and more elite families from Latin city-states, Campania, and other conquered territory in central Italy became members of the "Roman" nobility.

DEFERENCE AND THE ROMAN POLITICAL CULTURE

The vast majority of the Roman population accepted the nobility's rise to power and deferred to members of the nobility who competed for political office. The key to this acceptance was the nobility's success in reforming the military, conquering Rome's rivals, and providing better economic condi-

---

1 LeGlay, *History of Rome*, p. 60
2 LeGlay, *History of Rome*, p. 60

tions for the plebeians. We will explore those successes in the next chapter. Another dimension of Roman acceptance was that, once the new noble families led the city to success and glory, they were able to pass their elevated status down, through the generations, to their descendants.

Rome's political culture was based on a reverence for the past and the people who made the past glorious. There were extensive oral traditions about the noble actions of the leaders who founded the Republic (primarily members of the patrician order). Stories of past glories and triumphs inevitably were threaded with mythology about the virtues of these leaders, which current leaders were urged to emulate and soldiers and voters were expected to reward with obedience and electoral endorsement. In Rome's family-oriented culture, individuals were seen as possessing the merits and virtues of their illustrious family ancestors, and therefore deserving of the right to become leaders themselves.

By eventually giving way and allowing wealthy plebeians to become part of this cycle of virtue, the patrician aristocracy co-opted the only potential source of rival leaders in Rome and created a new, expanded ruling group, the nobility. As time passed and plebeian political and military leaders achieved great honors, they too developed a mythological status. As a result, the sons of successful plebeian families were able, with sons of the remaining patrician families, to monopolize elections to the quaestor, praetor, and consul positions.

Inequality, Dignitas, and Liberty

The social changes that allowed the nobility to develop, while originating from intense political conflicts, were settled in the period after the Great Compromise without bloodshed and in a spirit of compromise. Of course, the rise of the nobility meant that Rome was still not a full democracy. There were great inequalities of wealth, status, and education that restricted what one could become. These inequalities also limited who might run for political office. However, as is the case in the United States, inequalities of wealth were viewed as natural and generally accepted if the person and his ancestors had a good reputation. Romans believed that differences in wealth and position reflected the high moral character, the *dignitas*, with which superior individuals led their lives. While it was important for a man to act with high moral character, one did not achieve *dignitas* merely through one's own efforts; it was a status handed down through inherited blood, the accumulated accomplishments of a person's family.

The pairing of *libertas* with *dignitas* explains many of the mysteries of the Roman Republic's political system. As we shall see, many political practices were based on a uniquely Roman interpretation of the interplay between individual liberty for every citizen and deferential treatment for those whose ancestors were wealthy and accomplished. Every citizen understood the importance of *dignitas* and recognized it in the Republic's prominent citizens. *Dignitas* was passed down from father to son in a generational chain of achievement and service. Deference for *dignitas* almost always led to men from distinguished families being elected to political office.

A brief contrast with the United States will give the reader a better understanding of the interrelated notions of *dignitas* and deference. In the modern United States, people are not judged so much by what their parents did, as by what they have accomplished. People who have gained wealth, fame, or position are given some level of deference in respect to their personal accomplishments. In our forward looking culture, individuals are not seen as building upon the wealth, fame, and accomplishments of their parents or grandparents; because we cling to the notion that the United States is a society where everyone starts out with a roughly equal opportunity, everyone has the opportunity to be rich or the chance to be President. Therefore, an individual's effort and talents are seen as the principal reasons for their prominent position in the world. Americans accept inequality of wealth and position because they believe it is the inevitable reflection of the inequality of effort and talent that each individual brings to the scramble of modern life.

In a smaller, more transparent society like the Roman Republic, where people had a more realistic idea of how people inherited either assets or debits from their families, people saw prominent individuals as having status because of the influence and position of their family. People believed that those individuals who grew up in families that gave their children access to educational resources like tutoring, the chance to travel, networks of followers, and ready access to money were cultured and accomplished people who could be counted on to act with great moral character when active in public affairs. As such, they possessed *dignitas* and were treated with deference by citizens who were not from similarly blessed families.

THE ROMAN SENATE

The social changes that led to the creation of the nobility reinforced the role of the Senate as the dominant political institution in Rome. While election to the offices of quaestor, praetor, and consul resulted in relatively brief one-year terms, by the 4th century BCE, they were doorways into lifetime membership in Rome's most prestigious political body, the Roman Senate. It is unclear exactly how members of the Senate were chosen before the 4th century; however by 325 BCE it had become customary for any individual, patrician or plebeian, elected to the position of quaestor to be appointed to a lifetime membership in the Senate by the censors. As a result, unlike other legislative assemblies in the city, and unlike other legislative assemblies in world history, by the Middle Republic, the Senate was a deliberative body of former magistrates, thereby embodying the political wisdom and skills of a whole generation of successful elected leaders.

In a traditional society like Rome, decrees issued by this gathering of about 300 distinguished, older men, were respected and obeyed by both serving magistrates and ordinary citizens. Members of the Senate were noteworthy for their white tunics decorated with a broad purple stripe, once a symbol of royal authority, now signifying the solidarity of a collective authority. They were known as "the fathers" and addressed one another as *Patre* (father).

The Senate made most decisions related to foreign policy, including the waging of war, authorization of treaties, and negotiations with foreign ambassadors. In the Middle and Late Republic senators would be sent on missions to other countries to bargain over trade rights or to mediate disputes. The Senate decided on military assignments for the consuls and later determined which provinces newly elected praetors would govern. The Senate also controlled expenditures by the Treasury, deciding how much would be raised in taxes and through which types of tax. Oddly enough, the Senate did not enact laws, instead it issued decrees, *senatus consulta*, that served as advice to magistrates and provided authority for them to act.

Given that political leaders spent most of their lives as senators and spent only brief periods of time as magistrates, the will of the Senate was generally followed; an independent official who ignored the Senate would, in the course of a few months, find himself an ineffective senator with little support for gaining election to a higher office. In general, "Senators had a strong sense of belonging to a well-defined and honored group in society, and, on occasion, they could be quite willing to assert the Senate's power and prestige against magistrates and assemblies."[1] Later in the history of the Republic, when the Plebeian Assembly gained the right to pass laws, that body seldom approved measures that were not first approved by a *senatus consulta*.

The Senate usually met in the Curia, the ornate building located at one end of the Roman forum. Sessions were called and presided over by the consuls, with the first senator being invited to speak being the *princeps senatus*, the senior or leading senator. The rest of the senators then spoke in rank order according to their age and the level of office they had attained — former consuls speaking before former praetors, etc.[2] Senators who had not gained the office of praetor seldom spoke during debates. Voting was done through a division of the house; those voting yes moving to the right half of the Senate chamber, while those voting no went to the left side.

---

1 Boatwright, *The Romans*, p. 64
2 LeGlay, *History of Rome*, p. 66

It was in the Senate, more than anywhere else, where the use of rhetoric was prized and made a difference. The Romans did not have political parties with platforms and a set of basic beliefs that would unite a large number of senators. Instead, each senator acted on his own, evaluating each issue as it came up, with no party loyalty or ideology to determine his vote. His loyalties were to a much more diverse cast of family ties, political and personal friendships, and business relationships.[1] While these loyalties were often useful for deciding which candidates to support in elections, they usually did not provide a stable guide for how to approach larger issues of state policy — whether of war and peace, or of taxes and expenditures. In these situations, those senators who could present their case most eloquently frequently swayed votes.

Unfortunately, few records of Senate debates have survived. The few accounts that do survive give us some hint at the high drama that must have been a regular occurrence. The debate between Julius Caesar and Marcus Cato in 62 BCE is perhaps one of the most striking moments in the history of the Republic. Cicero, the senior consul that year, had arrested a group of prominent citizens and charged them with supporting a rebel army in Etruria. The Senate had already passed a measure known as the "ultimate decree" which gave Cicero the right to execute anyone who supported the rebellion. However, the decree clashed with the right of Roman citizens to a jury trial in cases where the state sought the death penalty. Cicero came to ask the senators for their opinion.

A huge crowd had gathered in the Forum and they shouted and chanted as the senators came into the Curia. At first the senators, caught up in rumors about the city on the verge of being burned down, spoke in turn for the death penalty. Then, Caesar, recently elected praetor and friends with several of the accused men, rose and a hush fell over the body. While acknowledging the Senate's authority to sentence citizens to death in extreme emergencies, he pointed out how angry people would be:

> He reminded them how unpopular severe sentences were and how much the people were attached to its most important civil liberty; he also hinted at the agitation — perhaps even accusations — that the consul and the Senate would have to fear if they passed and executed this resolution...according to (the Roman historian) Sallust, Caesar invoked the ancestors, who had abolished the death penalty. They were after all superior in ability and wisdom to anyone present, "for from small beginnings they created so great an empire that we can sustain it only with difficulty, after it was won with such energy." Moreover, the death penalty, though wholly justified in this case, would serve as a precedent for others who were not faced with such an emergency.[2]

---

1 Lily Ross Taylor, *Party Politics in the Age of Caesar*, Berkeley: University of California Press, 1949, p. 7
2 Meier, *Caesar*, p. 171

Caesar then proposed that the men be placed under permanent house arrest and their property confiscated. Now opinion in the Senate swung completely around and senator after senator announced they had changed their minds and supported Caesar's proposal. Then Marcus Cato rose and spoke:

> Caesar was trying to subvert the state. He wanted to frighten the Senate about a situation from which he had a good deal to fear himself..."If we could afford to risk the consequences of making a mistake," Cato said (according to Sallust), "I would be quite willing to let experience convince you of your folly, since you scorn advice. But we are completely encircled. Catilina and his army are ready to grip us by the throat, and there are other foes within the walls, in the very heart of our city."[1]

Now the climate of opinion swayed again and senators rushed to agree with Cato. The death warrant was passed and Cicero had a group of armed guards carry out the sentence at once. As a result of this exchange, Cato became the leader of the conservative faction in the Senate and he and Caesar were to clash repeatedly in the future.

Unlike modern legislative bodies, the Senate (as was the case with the other Roman legislative assemblies) had no standing committees. The work of drafting legislation, discussing political alternatives, and gathering support for one idea or another was done informally, through personal contacts between groups of influential senators. In a small city-state like Rome, everyone in the political elite knew everyone else and had a long family history of interactions over matters of state, business, and social ties. This system was workable because the Senate and the other Assemblies only considered a small number of legislative proposals in any particular year. When Publius Clodius Pulcher was elected as one of the ten tribunes in 58 BCE, it was considered remarkable when he was able to push through a legislative package with four separate laws.

For many years modern historians believed that the great issues in the Roman Republic were almost always dealt with through coalitions of families, with voting blocks determined by ties of marriage and mutual business interests. However, while such voting blocks can occasionally be identified for a particular policy or a vote, recent research has failed to show any enduring family factions that could be said to vote together over significant periods of time.[2] This especially holds true over generations, as individual great leaders, from leading noble families, were unable to ensure that their sons continued to wield significant influence. During the more fully documented decades of the late Republic, conflict between rival factions led by Pompey, Caesar, Crassus, and Cato led to splits in noble families, with brothers and cousins at odds with one another in a series of votes and elections. In earlier

---

1 Everitt, *Cicero*, p. 109

2 P.A. Brunt, *The Fall of the Roman Republic and Related Essays*, Oxford: Oxford University Press, 1988, p. 470.

periods of social peace there probably were brief periods where family ties served to guide policy decisions, but in times of great conflict and division, every nobleman had to make choices on his own.

Chapter 4. The New Roman Legion and the Conquest of Italy

History doesn't repeat itself, but it often rhymes.[1]

—Mark Twain

The Compromise of 367 was a watershed event in the evolution of the Roman Republic. Although the Struggle of the Orders was not over, the balance of power between the plebeians and the patricians was redrawn in a way that made it easier to enact further reforms in the future. Freed for the moment from draining conflicts over debt and liberated by a sudden increase in social mobility, the Romans invested a great deal of energy in revising their military system. The new social harmony was the basis for the tremendous military successes that occurred in the second half of the 4th century.

Burdened with internal divisions, the Roman *hoplite* army, with its phalanxes of plebeian soldiers commanded by patrician officers, had proven itself inadequate to the task of protecting Rome from Gaelic raiding parties. In addition, except for the capture of Veii, a town only ten miles away, the army had been unable to secure the city from occasional attacks by Latin or Etruscan city-states. Perhaps most frustrating of all, the army had trouble inflicting long-lasting defeats on the hostile tribes living in the nearby Apennine Mountains. The repetitive nature of the ancient descriptions of Rome's conflicts with the Volsci, Aequi, and Hernici reflect the indecisive outcome of battles that were gloriously "won" or "lost." It was not because Rome was

---

1 Quoted in, Kenneth Baer & Andrei Cherny, "Editors Note," *DemocracyJournal*, available at: www.democracyjournal.org/article.php?ID=6577; accessed on 19 December 2007

a small community; at the time of independence in 510 BCE the city had 30 to 35,000 residents, with at least 6,000 men making up two legions of *hoplite* soldiers.[1] By the end of the century, during the struggle to capture Veii, the city had grown and might have been able to muster an additional legion of soldiers. By comparison, during this period Sparta had an army of approximately 8,000 men, while Athens could muster perhaps 10,000.[2] So the problem was not in the size of the army but in how it fought.

Between 380 and 340 BCE a series of changes were made in the Roman army's weaponry and tactics. While M. Furius Camillus is often given most of the credit for these changes, they were probably the work of a significant number of officers working together. Interestingly enough, they must have put some effort into examining the evolution of warfare in Greece, because the changes they adopted mirrored some of the new tactics and weapons that had emerged in the Greek world after the Peloponnesian War. In addition to adopting some of these new tactics, the Romans came up with several innovations of their own that would eventually make the Roman legion the dominant military unit in the ancient world.

The Greeks were the first people to fight with *hoplite* armies in the 7th century BCE Greek *hoplite* soldiers, massed in the formation called the phalanx, successfully defended their homeland from vastly larger armies mobilized by the Persian Empire. At the core of the *hoplite* army were heavily armored soldiers. Protected by bronze armor and shields and holding a long, heavy spear, these soldiers would march upon their opponents shoulder to shoulder. With each man locking his shield into the shield of his comrades and with four or more lines of soldiers behind the front line thrusting their spears out in front of the formation, a *hoplite* army phalanx must have looked like an angry porcupine waddling slowly into battle.[3] A cavalry unit could not attack the porcupine because horses, quite sensibly, would not approach it. Unarmored masses of barbarian warriors were swept away, just as the lightly armored Persian infantry died by the thousands when confronted with highly disciplined hoplite units from Sparta, Corinth, and Athens.

On the other hand, when the phalanxes of two *hoplite* armies met, the contest quickly become a matter of weight bearing on weight; with spears glancing off of heavily armored men and their shields, the two porcupines would become locked in a shoving match.[4] Battles like these would come to a sudden end when one or more units in the formations broke down through exhaustion or attrition. At that point an opposing hoplite unit could wedge into the middle of the enemy formation and begin a flanking attack on the

1 Cornell, *Atlas*, p. 28
2 Potter, "Roman Army," p. 67
3 Warry, *Warfare*, p. 34
4 Warry, *Warfare*, p. 37

rest of the *hoplite* lines. Inevitably, the phalanx would disintegrate, with men throwing down their heavy shields and running away. The word *ripsaspis*, literally "one who throws away his shield," is still the term for a deserter in modern Greek.[1] Most of the casualties in hoplite battles occurred when the cavalry cut down men as they tried to flee from the battlefield.

By the end of the Peloponnesian War (404 BCE), as opposing armies adjusted to the phalanx concept, the Romans and the Greeks discovered three problems with *hoplite* infantry as their main battlefield unit. First, because the soldiers were weighted down with bronze armor, they could not chase a defeated enemy. Disciplined soldiers were often able to rally and hold off the cavalry that attempted to pursue them. This meant that *hoplite* victories were frequently tactical, battlefield-localized victories that did not destroy the enemy's army or his will to fight.[2] Second, *hoplites* could repulse tribal enemies like the Volsci, but often could not inflict heavy casualties because their opponents would simply fade back into the hills, ready to resume raids on cities and farms when the army moved or was disbanded for winter. Finally, the phalanx was cumbersome and only capable of moving forward. When attacked in the flank or rear by cavalry or lightly armed troops, the units were unable to adjust and defend themselves. For example, against the numerically superior Gaelic raiding party at the battle of Allia, the Roman right wing was quickly outflanked and the whole army just fell apart and ran away.[3]

In addition to these tactical difficulties, the 5th century Roman army was hobbled by the social and financial differences between its citizen-soldiers. When it prepared for battle, the army was drawn up in three lines, with younger soldiers from the First and Second Classes brandishing their long spears in the first line (the *hastatis*, "men with spears") and older, more experienced soldiers (the *principes*, "leaders") from those classes providing backup in the second line. They too, were armed with *hoplite* spears.[4] The more poorly armed members of the 3rd, 4th, and 5th classes were drawn up behind them in a third, last line of defense.[5] These soldiers (the *triarii*, "third-liners") could also be used to escort supply trains and to protect the army's camp. In effect, the financial differences between members of the citizens' army meant that one-half or more of the soldiers were not fully equipped for the *hoplite* style of fighting. As a result, older men who could afford the hoplite's expensive equipment fought in front of younger, more vigorous men who

---

1 Warry, *Warfare*, p. 37

2 Potter, "Roman Army," p. 68

3 Scullard, *Roman World*, p. 103

4 Warry, *Warfare*, p. 112

5 Anna Maria Liberati and Fabio Bourbon, *Ancient Rome*, New York: Barnes and Noble Publishing, 2004, p. 92

were not as well equipped because of their lower economic status in civilian society.

During the 4th century, the army changed its weapons, tactics, and social make-up. One of the key changes was to have the first and second line of troops hurl javelins, instead of carrying spears. Javelins were used effectively by Thebean troops to defeat Sparta's elite *hoplite* phalanxes at the battle of Leuctra in 371 BCE.[1] Thebean javelin throwers worked in partnership with Thebean *hoplites*. Armed with three or four javelins, they ran up to the Spartan phalanxes and created holes in the solid ranks by hurtling their iron-headed javelins with deadly accuracy, using a leather thong to generate a powerful sling-shot motion. The javelins killed or wounded numerous soldiers in the first and second ranks, causing confusion and leaving holes in the formation. In effect, the porcupine temporarily had vulnerable bare spots. The Thebean phalanxes then charged the Spartans, taking advantage of holes in the once solid front to break through the lines and begin the process of attacking from the flank.

The Romans adopted the new weapon wholeheartedly, with both the *hastati* and the *principes* dropping the heavy spear of the hoplite formation in favor of two or three javelins, called *pila*, and a short, straight, iron sword called the *gladius*.[2] Soldiers also switched to shields and armor made with wood and iron, making it less expensive to equip a soldier and allowing their formations to be faster and more maneuverable.

An enormous social change accompanied this change in equipment. After the great compromise of 367, men who served in the army on a year-around basis received a salary. With this payment, men in the Second, Third, Fourth, and Fifth Classes could afford the less expensive iron fighting weapons the army began to use. In a short time there was a standardization of equipment, and the need to place athletic young men from the less wealthy classes in the third-line disappeared.[3] These younger men, formerly the *triarii*, moved up and became part of the *principes* or *hastati* lines, while the older men moved back and became the last line of defense.

The *triarii* did not participate in the initial rounds of combat. If the first two lines were defeated or overrun, the *triarii* provided a porcupine line of spears for the others to rally behind. "Long after they had ceased to exist as a unit in the Roman army, the expression 'it has come to the *triarii*' was used by Romans to describe a desperate situation."[4] This re-organization of lines led, over time, to a blurring of social status in the ranks. Units were gradually established and populated with soldiers based on military ability

---

1 Warry, *Warfare*, p. 50 & 60
2 Scullard, *Roman World*, p. 346
3 Warry, *Warfare*, p. 113
4 Matyszak, *Chronicle*, p. 80

and function rather than wealth or family.[1] In another change, units were recruited from their tribes, providing a local identity to each unit that was not based on economic class.[2] This is similar to the American practice in the Civil War, adopted by both the Union and the Confederacy, of basing military unit membership upon the state where the regiment was formed. Army units were officially named after states, for example, the 110th Massachusetts or the 3rd Virginia.

With the new weapons came a new battle structure that increased the maneuverability of units. The *hastati* and *principes* began the battle in checkerboard formations so as to allow each man enough room to throw his two *pila*, "Once the front two ranks have hurled their *pila*, the second rank closes up with the front rank and swords are drawn. The third and fourth ranks then throw *pila*, close up, and draw swords."[3] With the formation now drawn up into tight lines, the *hastati* charged the enemy lines, hoping to take advantage of the confusion and gaps caused by the shower of deadly *pila*.

Notice how the image of the formation has changed. Now, the porcupine is launching deadly showers of quills upon his enemy and then running at him, thrusting with short, sharp quills. Thus, unlike *hoplite* armies, the new Roman army was designed to rapidly overrun its opponent with its main battle line.[4] If the first shock of swordsmen hitting the enemy lines did not break their formations, the *hastati* withdrew and the *principes* moved up and attacked the enemy's main line with javelins and then a sword charge. The combination of deadly showers of javelins and aggressive sword charges made the new Roman army a nasty opponent.

During the rest of the Republic, a Roman legion consisted of 60 centuries, about 3,600 infantrymen, along with approximately 300 cavalrymen and scouts. Arraigned in battle formation, a legion's frontage would stretch from 200 to 250 yards, more than two football fields.[5] Each legion was led by an officer, or *legatus*, who was usually a political leader from the Senate. His staff consisted of six military tribunes, elected by the Tribal Assembly (a total of 24 were elected each year as the army usually had at least four legions in the field after 367 BCE).

The Conquest of Campania and the Defeat of the Latin League

The Romans had plenty of opportunities to perfect their new weapons and tactics because in 362 BCE they entered a period of nearly constant war-

---

1 Scullard, *Roman World*, p. 345
2 Warry, *Warfare*, p. 113
3 Warry, *Classical Warfare*, p. 112
4 Potter, "Roman Army," p. 75
5 Warry, *Warfare*, p. 112

fare (during the summer campaign seasons) that lasted until 270 BCE. Whatever the ups and downs of Rome's fortunes during these wars, the city itself
was now secure behind the re-built Servian Wall (named after the Etruscan
king who first built a wall around the city). The wall was made from solid
stone, stacked some twelve feet thick and 24 feet high, and extended around
the entire city, a distance of 5 ½ miles.[1] The city imported Greek contrac-
tors to supervise the hard work of cutting and stacking stones, which was
probably done by soldiers. The work was done so well that no foreign army
was able to penetrate this wall and invade the city for 775 years, until the
Visigoths sacked Rome in 410 CE.

The impressive new city wall and the re-organized Roman military were
very successful in protecting the city from Gaelic invasions. The historical records speak of battles with Gaelic raiding parties in 360 and at least
two other occasions in the 4th century. The Gauls had no ability to capture
strongly-defended walled cities and were badly defeated by the revived
Roman legions when they stopped and committed themselves to a full-scale
battle. We have a brief excerpt from Appian of Alexandria's book, *Roman
History*, where he describes one of the first instances of Rome's new battle
tactics being used in a battle with the Gauls:

> Afterwards the Boii, the most savage of the Gallic tribes, attacked the Ro-
> mans. Caius Sulpicius, the dictator, marched against them, and is said to
> have used the following stratagem. He commanded those who were in the
> front line to discharge their javelins, and immediately crouch low; then the
> second, third, and fourth lines to discharge theirs, each crouching in turn...
> then when the last line had hurled their javelins, all were to rush forward
> suddenly with a shout and join battle at close quarters. The hurling of so
> many missiles, followed by an immediate charge, would throw the enemy
> into confusion...In this way the army of the Boii was completely destroyed
> by the Romans.[2]

The small cities of the Latin League were similarly overwhelmed; Rome
was a bigger city with a large army that now fought in a style that the tiny
hoplite armies of the Latin towns could not match. Within a few years, members of the Latin League had entered into new, unequal military and economic treaties with Rome, relationships that confirmed Rome's dominance
of Latium.[3]

Rome's strengthened position in Latium now placed its legions on the
border of the Campania region. An area of fertile farms, where crops were
harvested twice a year, Campania was dominated by the flourishing cities
of Capua and Neapolis (now Naples). Their wealth proved a great tempta-

---

1 Scullard, *Roman World*, p. 105
2 Appian of Alexandria, *Roman History*, Epit.1, 358 VC; available from www.livius.org/ap-ark/
appian/appian_gallic_1.html
3 Cornell, *Atlas*, p. 34

tion to raiding parties from the Samnite tribes that occupied the Apennine Mountains to the east of Campania. In 343 BCE, hard pressed to defend their

Latium and Campania were absorbed into the Roman political community in the 4th century.

lands, Capua and its allies requested assistance from Rome.[1] During a short, obscure period historians call the First Samnite War, Rome was able to solidify its relationship with leaders of cities in the region.

About this time, many Latin cities became tired of playing second fiddle to Rome in commercial and military matters and resolved to restore the Rome — Latin League relationship to the equal balance of power that held sway in the 5th century. Determined to win better terms than their current unequal treaties, they formed an alliance with several cities in Campania that were disturbed by signs that the Romans were planning a long stay in their region (a common problem when a small power invites a big power in for protection) and attacked Roman garrisons in 342 BCE. In retaliation, the consul Titus Manlius Imperiosus led an army down the Liris River Valley into the heart of Campania and defeated the Latin League/Campanian army at the battle of Trifanum. The tribes of Campania signed new treaties with the Romans and the Latins, after further losses, also signed peace treaties.

In the midst of this rebellion by the Latin League and Campania, Roman leaders were preoccupied with social conflicts in the city over debt policies and continuing agitation by urban plebeians for farmland. The new treaties between Rome and her defeated neighbors can only be understood in the

---

1 Boatwright, *The Romans*, p. 79

context of Rome's leaders trying to solve their pressing domestic problems by establishing entirely new types of relationships with the rest of central Italy. These new relationships were essential for the stability of the Republic because the on-going problem of indebtedness reached a crisis point in 342 BCE. In that year there was a wide-spread mutiny in the army, just before the war with the Latin League. Indeed, one historian, H.H. Scullard, argues that the Latin League revolted at this time because of Rome's preoccupation with the mutiny.[1] If that was the sequence of events, then the need for domestic harmony and prosperity was surely driven home for the emerging nobility by this instance of a domestic disturbance sparking foreign uprisings.

The mutiny seems to have its roots in the initial occupation of Campania. The military guard in Campania envied the riches of the people in this region. They became bitter because they were poor and owed overwhelming debts in Rome. As the discontent spread, the Roman commander in the area heard about their plotting and tried to crush any attempt at mutiny. Appian of Alexandria tells the story this way:

> Concealing his intentions, he disarmed some of them and dismissed them, as soldiers entitled to discharge for long service. The more villainous ones he ordered to Rome on the pretense of important business, and he sent with them a military tribune with orders to keep a secret watch over them. Both parties of soldiers suspected that their design had leaked out, and they broke away from the tribune near the town of Terracina. They set free all those who were working under sentence in the fields, armed them as well as they could, and marched to Rome to the number of about 20,000.[2]

Clearly there is more to the story than Appian is telling us. 20,000 men is the equivalent of five Roman legions, and the "more villainous" soldiers by this account must have numbered in the thousands. However, the story probably is correct in highlighting the impact on ordinary Roman soldiers of the visions of abundance they saw when they patrolled Campanian farms and cities. This was 25 years, a full generation, after the Compromise of 367 had wiped away the debt burden of many plebeian families. Since then, while wealthy plebeians were moving up the social ladder by securing election to offices on the course of honor, the average plebeian was piling up new debts as a result of the same economic forces that plagued poor people in the city before the political settlement. Once there, the illogical debt laws that made up the practice of *nexum* kept them trapped in debt, unable to work their way out.

Thus, in spite of the great changes in the social position of plebeians, for the average citizen the city was often not a fruitful place to live. Appius continues with his story about the debt march on Rome:

---

1 Scullard, *Roman World*, p. 118
2 Appian of Alexandria, *Roman History*, From the Peiresc manuscript: #1, 342 VC; available from www.livius.org/ap-ark/appian/appian_samnite_1.html

> About one day's march from the city they were met by [M. Valerius] Corvus who went into camp near them on the Alban mount. He remained quietly in his camp while investigating what the matter was, and did not consider it wise to attack these desperadoes. The men [from the two armed groups] mingled with each other privately, the guards acknowledging with groans and tears, as among relatives and friends, [the city was still small enough where everyone knew everyone else or was related] that they were to blame, but declaring that the cause of it all was the debts they owed at Rome.
>
> When Corvus understood this he shrank from the responsibility of so much civil bloodshed and advised the Senate to release these men from debt. He exaggerated the difficulty of the war if it should be necessary to put down such a large body of men, who would fight with the energy of despair. He had strong suspicions also of the result of the meetings and conferences, lest his own army, who were relatives of these men and not less oppressed with debt, should be to some extent lacking in fidelity. The Senate was moved by his arguments and decreed a cancellation of debts to all Romans, and immunity also to these revolters. The latter laid down their arms and returned to the city.[1]

It is telling that Corvus felt the men in his army were as burdened with debt as the mutinous soldiers, another way of acknowledging how widespread the problem was. While Corvus was confronting the mutineers, the Senate was hearing reports of the Latin League growing restless and gathering their soldiers. These dual challenges threatened the city with disaster. One can easily imagine the Senate being eager to work out some sort of compromise as suggested by a man whose judgment they trusted.

Rome and the soldiers were fortunate in the man they encountered outside the gates of the city. Valerius Maximus had first come to prominence in a campaign against the Gauls. As with other Romans who were viewed as heroic figures by 1st and 2nd century authors, his biography includes a distinctly mythical story. When

> a gigantic Gaul stepped forward and challenged the Romans to single combat...Valerius volunteered to take on this Goliath. In the fight, he was apparently assisted by a raven (*corvus* in Latin) which repeatedly struck the Gaul in the face. Aided by this distraction, Valerius slew his opponent, and took the name Corvus in recognition of his unexpected ally.[2]

M. Valerius Corvus was consul in 348 and 346, winning military glory by defeating the troublesome Volscian tribe. He was an easy going and popular general who took part in athletic contests that the soldiers held when they were not in combat.[3] It is probably this ability to empathize with his soldiers' lot in life that led him to recognize the truth in their cry for justice.

With social harmony restored by these debt reductions, Rome's legions were victorious and Rome's domination of Latium and Campania was firmly

---

1 Appian of Alexandria, *Roman History*, From the Peiresc manuscript: #2; available from www. livius.org/ap-ark/appian/appian_samnite_1.html

2 Matyszak, *Chronicle*, p. 69

3 Matyszak, *Chronicle*, p. 69

established. The lessons of the debt mutiny seem to have deeply affected the treaties established with the defeated enemy; each was written with an eye toward the domestic audience that had so recently been driven to rebellion.

The peace settlements became the cornerstones of the new, expanding Republic. Instead of treating the rebellious tribes as conquered peoples, Rome incorporated all of these areas into the Roman political community, using a spectrum of treaties that laid out a menu of rights and obligations. Most of the smaller cities in Latium were absorbed directly into the Roman state. Their residents became full citizens of Rome and could vote in Roman assemblies and elections if they traveled to the city. These communities were called *municipia*; they retained their local government institutions, elected local officials, and carried out traditional local religious ceremonies.[1] In the event of war, their residents were drafted into the Roman army just like people living in Rome. Significant sections of land in these communities became Roman *auger publicus* and plebeian citizens from Rome were invited to settle in many of these areas.[2]

Some of the colony cities created jointly with the Latin League during the 5th century and a few large Latin cities, especially Tibur and Praeneste, were given the special status known as "allies of the Latin name" (*socii nomiis Latini*). Their ties of *commercium* and *conubium* with other Latin cities were dissolved; they could exercise these rights only with Roman citizens.[3] Their residents were not Roman citizens and could not vote in Roman elections. Both the Latin colonies and Latin cities were required to contribute military units to any Roman army that was raised for campaigns.

Finally, non-Latin cities and towns in Campania and in the Volsci, Hernici, and Aequi tribal areas, were given the status of nonvoting municipalities (*municipia sine suffragio*). These municipalities were expected to contribute military units when Rome went to war. Ties of *commercium* and *conubium* could only be established with Roman citizens, once again, precluding political and economic alliances with other cities.[4] As in other conquered areas, large amounts of land were seized for use by plebeian settlers or became Roman public land.

By giving the residents a limited form of citizenship that encouraged trade and personal interaction with Roman citizens, they were encouraged to gradually develop commercial, family, and religious ties that eventually pulled them into the Roman community. On a day-to-day basis Rome ruled with a relatively light hand — none of the allied communities had to pay financial tribute to Rome and all of the non-citizen communities were able

1 Boatwright, *The Romans*, p. 80
2 Cornell, *Atlas*, p. 39
3 Boatwright, *The Romans*, p. 80
4 Cornell, *Atlas*, p. 34

to maintain their existing civic orders, usually a social system with a few leading aristocratic families and a mass of semi-enfranchised residents. The nobility in Rome rapidly developed close ties with the aristocratic elites in many Italian towns and on a number of occasions Roman legions intervened on behalf of these elites to put down popular rebellions.[1]

As part of its Republican tradition, Rome did not possess a bureaucracy that could run captured city-states without the cooperation of local elites and it did not have a full-time army that could garrison a hostile region and constantly be on guard against revolts.[2] The complicated system of full and limited rights given to the towns in the new confederacy allowed Rome to control large areas of central Italy, have ready access to manpower for future conflicts, and to gain farmland for her plebeian families. As a result, Rome was able to expand its territory without undermining its Republican institutions. An oppressive bureaucracy and a standing army of occupation are institutions most comfortably located in a monarchical state. Bringing them into existence in 335 BCE would probably have rapidly compromised Roman liberties.[3]

Rome also established more than 50 colonies of Roman citizens at strategic locations, ensuring the loyalty of regions that had recently been overrun. They were placed "at locations open to enemy attack, in recently subjugated regions liable to revolt, at strategic river crossings and road junctions, and on vulnerable sections of coastline."[4] Most of the colonies were quite large, with 2,500 to 6,000 adult males.[5] The settlers held the rights of *commercium* and *conubium* with Rome, allowing them to maintain economic and social ties to Rome and preserving their loyalty and sense of identity with the mother city. As most of the people interested in founding a colony were poor, urban plebeians, colonies were an excellent way for Rome to satisfy the "land hunger" of its plebeian citizens.

Before the Great Compromise of 367 and the mutiny of 342, patrician military officers had the first chance to occupy new *auger publicus* and the number of settlers placed in colonies did not have a significant impact on debt and poverty in the city. In the new Roman social order, the benefits of war were thrown open to plebeians, creating a great deal of social mobility and allowing those urban residents who preferred a rural life to return to farming. The prosperity created by these opportunities to acquire productive farmland led to a rapid decline in social conflict in the city.[6]

1 Cornell, *Atlas*, p. 40
2 Boatwright, *The Romans*, p. 84
3 Cornell, *Atlas*, p. 34
4 Boatwright, *The Romans*, p. 82
5 Boatwright, *The Romans*, p. 82
6 Cornell, *Atlas*, p. 36

Even the worst aspects of the debt problem were finally eliminated. The tangle of issues created by the debt laws, the *nexum*, was resolved near the end of the century by the *Lex Petelia*. The historian H.H. Scullard claims that the legislation "stands out like an ancient Magna Carta."[1] The major breakthrough was the concept that loans were to be secured by the property of the borrower, not by his person. Debt could still rob a person of his prosperity, but not his freedom. The Roman historian Livy wrote, "In that year, the liberty of the Roman plebs had, as it were, a new beginning; for men ceased to be imprisoned for debt."[2]

The most pressing social problems between rich and poor in the city were resolved by the wealth, in land and plunder, generated by expansion and war.[3] There is a close connection between domestic politics and foreign policy at this point. While many historians present these two dimensions of Roman history as separate, parallel trends, in truth they were causally linked, with the domestic political situation just as often pulling the military expansion cart.

> The reason for these wars of conquest was not some irrational Roman push for expansion. Rather, it was the need to solve the internal problems of Roman society through the expansion of the sphere of Roman dominance... reform was organically and inseparably connected with the process of expansion."[4]

The Roman Republic began expanding rapidly because, in this particular historical situation, social reforms also improved the city's military effectiveness.

> Perhaps the most important feature of the developments of the late fifth to mid-fourth centuries was that they gave tangible rewards for fighting to the classes that would make up the bulk of the Roman army, both as officers and men, rewards that took the form of either enhanced status or of access to new lands.[5]

The political deference of other social classes to the city's patrician elite in 5th century elections was based on deference for families that were leaders of agricultural communities. However, as the Republic, in the 4th and 3rd centuries BCE fought a series of successful wars, this political deference became more firmly rooted in the tangible successes of the new ruling group.[6] Successful wars generated deep bonds of loyalty and encouraged deference to leadership groups, allowing the nobility that rose out of the Great Compromise of 367 to gradually become the unchallenged leaders of the city.

---

1 Scullard, *Roman World*, p. 117
2 Livy as quoted in: Scullard, *Roman World*, p. 117
3 Boatwright, *The Romans*, p. 95
4 Alfoldy, *Social History*, p. 26
5 Potter, "The Roman Army," p. 70
6 Andrew J.E. Bell, "Cicero and the Spectacle of Power," *Journal of Roman Studies*, V.87, 1997, p. 1

The Second and Third Wars with the Samnites

The dynamics of what was earlier described as "defensive imperialism" can be seen at work in the next round of wars in Italy. The Roman conquest of northern Campania placed the city in close proximity with the Samnites, a diverse group of tribes that dominated the Apennines Mountains in central Italy. The Samnites lived in small, scattered villages and were not able to accumulate much wealth because of the poor nature of the soil in their valleys. They maintained a loose confederation, which came together quickly when a conflict arose, but made it difficult to successfully coordinate and wage a long war.[1] Their main interest was in southern Italy, where they engaged in an on-again, off-again conflict with Tarentum, the principal Greek city in southern Italy.

With Rome unified and prosperous and the legions reinforced by military units contributed by Latin and allied cities, the Republic decided to aggressively secure its borders with the Samnites. In 328, Rome established a Latin colony at the river crossing known as Fregellae in the strategically important Liris River Valley. This was viewed as an unwarranted intrusion by the Samnites and The Second Samnite War broke out in the following year. Rome had an early success when the Greek city of Naples decided to evict their Samnite garrison and became a Roman ally.[2] The city's experienced mariners became the nucleus of Rome's first naval fleets and control of Naples gave Rome a secure foothold in southern Campania.

Encouraged by this and other successful skirmishes, the Romans brushed aside a Samnite peace proposal in 321 and sent a large army, commanded by both consuls, into the heart of the Samnite's mountain territory. Theodore Mommsen, the greatest classical historian of the 19th century, tells the story:

> The Romans, who had entered the valley unopposed, found its outlet obstructed by abattis [Note: a means of defense consisting of a barrier of felled trees, the ends of whose branches are sharpened and directed outwards, against the enemy] and strongly occupied; on marching back they saw that the entrance was similarly closed, while at the same time the crests of the surrounding mountains were crowned by Samnite cohorts. They perceived, when it was too late, that they had suffered themselves to be misled by a stratagem, and that the Samnites awaited them, not at Luceria, but in the fatal pass of Caudium. They fought, but without hope of success and without earnest aim; the Roman army was totally unable to maneuver and was completely vanquished without a struggle. The Roman generals offered to capitulate.
>
> ... The terms laid down were moderate enough; Rome was to raze the fortresses which she had constructed in defiance of the treaty — Cales and Fregellae — and to renew her equal alliance with Samnium. After the

1 Scullard, *Roman World*, p. 110
2 Cornell, *Atlas*, p. 37

Roman generals had agreed to these terms and had given six hundred hostages chosen from the cavalry for their faithful execution — besides pledging their own word and that of all their staff-officers on oath to the same effect — the Roman army was dismissed uninjured, but disgraced; for the Samnite army, drunk with victory, could not resist the desire to subject their hated enemies to the disgraceful formality of laying down their arms and passing under the yoke.[1]

The Senate agreed to a five-year peace and gave up the fortified colony of Fregellae, but the Samnites missed their one opportunity to stop the expanding Roman Republic and the war resumed as soon as the five years elapsed.

Passing under the yoke was a ritual performed to humiliate a defeated army. Cincinnatus, who rescued a Roman army around 450 BCE, made the defeated Aequis army pass under a yoke made by two spears fixed upright in the ground and a third fastened across the top between them. Each soldier had to lay down his weapons and pass under this yoke, bending his head as he did so. To complete the humiliation, Cincinnatus' soldiers lined up on either side of the yoke to jeer as they passed. For a soldier to pass under the yoke was a tremendous disgrace for it reflected an unmanly willingness to lose honor instead of dying gloriously. The practice has given to our language the word subjugate, meaning to subdue or conquer, from the Latin words *sub*, under, and *jugum*, a yoke for an ox or horse.

In 315 BCE, while the main army of Roman soldiers was founding a Latin colony on the Adriatic Sea, the Samnites surprised Rome by launching the invasion of Campania that they should have attempted in 321. They crossed the Lirus River and won a victory against a hastily formed legion, but bogged down trying to advance up the coast to the port of Ostia. Rome was threatened, but the Latin allies did not waiver in their loyalty, confirming the wisdom of Rome creating a confederacy rather than posing as an occupying power.[2] The next year the main body of the army defeated the Samnites near Tarracina on the southern coast. Fregellae was then re-captured and made into a fortress town again, and the Romans solidified their hold on Campania by capturing Nola, a town protected by steep cliffs and high walls, which dominated the land to the east of Neapolis.

After a five-year period of peace, the third and final war with the Samnites led to their defeat and the creation of the same kind of alliance and colony system that Rome had used to secure Latium. In 290, the entire Sabine population, closely connected to Rome for generations, was given full citizenship, greatly expanding the citizen base for recruitment into the legions. Over the next two decades the Romans gradually conquered all of Etruria, up to the

---

1 Mommsen, Theodore, *History of Rome*, 1855, Book II, Chapter VI, "Struggle of the Italians Against Rome," p. 53; available from www.Italian.classic-literature.co.uk/history-of-rome/; accessed 22 July 2007

2 Scullard, *Roman World*, p. 134

edge of Cisalpine Gaul, and made these communities members of the Roman confederacy with grants of Latin status. Rome was the leading city-state on the peninsula.

RAPID GROWTH AND SOCIAL CHANGE

As in previous decades, Roman victories at the end of the 4th century brought more wealth into the city and made land available to citizens looking for farms. The new wealth made it possible to continue the process of social change in the city and, in a virtuous cycle, these changes strengthened the Roman state, making more victories possible. The granting of Latin status, with its emphasis on economic and social ties between Rome and its many allies and confederates made Rome the most dynamic city in Italy. Wealth poured into the state's treasury, making it possible for a new round of public work projects that rivaled the efforts of King Servius. The censor for 312, Appius Claudius Caecus began two of the enormous public works projects that would mark Roman civilization. The first was the construction of an aqueduct, the *aqua Appia*, to bring water from the Apennine Mountains to the city. This strongly suggests that, even during a period of constant warfare and frequent establishment of colonies, the city's population had grown to the point where local sources of water were inadequate.[1]

It is estimated that Rome was one of the largest cities in the Mediterranean by 300 BCE, with a population of 150,000 persons.[2] Wealth brought into the city through conquest must have provided large amounts of work in the service sector and in construction. In addition, the city was a manufacturing center for fine pottery; remains have been found at many places around the western Mediterranean, especially southern Gaul and the area around Carthage in northern Africa.[3] In fact, by 272 another aqueduct had to be constructed to meet the needs of the city's booming population.

Many tradesmen and merchants with Latin rights moved to Rome, where they had rights of *commercium* and intermarriage. By residing in the city until the next census (held generally every five years) they were able to gain full citizenship and become participants in the political process.[4] Another growing part of the city's population was freedmen, slaves who had been released from their bonds by their masters. Freedmen (*libertus*) could not be enfranchised, but their sons (*libertines*) could be.[5] Freedmen usually worked in urban occupations and the most ambitious and talented ones were eventually able to rise to positions of wealth and influence. While freedmen initially

---

1 Boatwright, *The Romans*, p. 84
2 Cornell, *Atlas*, p. 42
3 Cornell, *Atlas*, p. 39
4 Scullard, *Roman World*, p. 120
5 Scullard, *Roman World*, p. 121

had service ties to their masters, and often took their master's family name, the next generation did not have the same obligations.

The term for the act of freeing an individual slave, manumission, is from the Latin *manumittere*, literally to send off by hand, which refers to the Roman ceremony where the master liberates the slave with a symbolic slap. Manumission is an individual act, taken by a private slave owner, as opposed to emancipation, which is the freeing of an entire group of people through government decree. For many slave owners, at this stage in Roman history, slavery was viewed as a temporary condition because most slaves were Italians with close cultural and ethnic ties to Latins.[1] These ties prevented the full-fledged development of an ideology claiming that slaves were inferior and thus somehow deserving of their lowly status. As a result, manumission was a frequent occurrence.

Later, in the 2nd and 1st centuries, as Rome expanded into other regions of the Mediterranean and captured slaves from other ethnic, racial, and cultural groups, slaves came to be seen as "others," not really human, and were forced to labor in appalling conditions. Another aspect of this change was that 4th century slaves were usually owned individually to work in a shop, kitchen, or farm. It was not until the 2nd century that the Romans fully developed large-scale slave labor sites — huge mine complexes, plantations, rowers on ships, and household staffs for large mansions. As the scale of slave holding increased, the social/personal distance between the owner and the slave increased. The slave became an asset to be exploited, rather than a person to work with.

A vital legal right was achieved in 300 BCE when the *lex Valeria de provocatione* mandated that a citizen accused of a capital crime could not be flogged or executed before he had the opportunity to appeal his case to the Centuriate Assembly, which would act as the jury.[2] While the general right to *provocatio* had been mentioned before in the Twelve Tables and Livy claims some type of *provocatione* law was passed by the Centuriate Assembly shortly after the beginning of the Republic, there must have been many instances of officials acting without regard to this right. The *lex Valeria* set out in clear language the process by which a citizen could exercise the right and how officials were limited in their use of force.

The *lex Valeria* was somewhat restricted in that it only gave the right of appeal to citizens who were within the boundaries of Rome. However, in the 2nd century, the "right to provocatio" was extended to all citizens anywhere as long as they were not enrolled in the army.[3] This right became one of the principal inducements for people who were in allied cities in Italy and later

1 Scullard, *Roman World*, p. 358
2 Alfoldy, *Social History*, p. 23
3 Scullard, *Roman World*, p. 322

residents of Roman provinces to attain citizenship. As Roman citizens, individuals had legal rights that protected them from official abuses of power and ensured the right of trial by some type of jury.

An incident in the New Testament demonstrates the impact of this right. The Apostle Paul, who was a Roman citizen, got into a dispute with some residents of Philippe in Greece. They dragged him and a friend to their local officials who beat them and then threw them into prison. When the officials discovered he was a Roman citizen they feared reprisals and asked him to quietly leave the prison and the city. His reply is telling, "They have beaten us in public, uncondemned, men who are Roman citizens, and have thrown us into prison; and now are they going to discharge us in secret? Certainly not! Let them come and take us out themselves." (Acts 16.38) Note how the local officials were responsible for administering their city, but feared the intervention of Roman officials if they violated specific laws regulating their powers to run the city.

Once his aqueduct was built, Appius Claudius began a second enormous construction project; a paved road, the *Via Appia*, running 152 miles from Rome to Capua, a project that was initially designed to rapidly move troops into the contested Campania region, but in the long run also supported a booming trade between that region and Latium.[1] In 306, the *Via Valeria* was built directly east into the Apennines to connect Rome with the large city of Tibur, the new colony Alba Fucens, and Corfinium, the principal city of the Marrucini tribe. These road and aqueduct projects employed hundreds of engineers and laborers, bringing prosperity to day laborers who built the roads and steady business for other urban residents who supplied the tools and raw materials for the building process.[2] They also created enduring trade and cultural ties between Rome and communities along the road, reinforcing the connections established by the Latin rights system of alliances. As you can see by the names of the roads, there was an enormous incentive for men elected to the censor position to initiate these projects — their names were immortalized by the sheer scope and grandeur of the work being accomplished.

TAMING THE PLEBEIAN ASSEMBLY

During the period of the Second and Third Samnite Wars, the merging of the old patrician aristocracy and wealthy members of the plebeian order continued at a rapid pace. The yearly campaigns against the Samnites, the Etrurians, the Aequi, and the Latins provided many opportunities for the sons of wealthy plebeians to be appointed military tribunes, gain military experience, develop reputations for bravery and leadership, and secure elec-

1 Matyszak, *Chronicle*, p. 73
2 Matyszak, *Chronicle*, p. 73

tion to the office of quaestor. Those of exceptional ability were elected to serve as praetors and consuls, leading armies into battle and returning to Rome victorious. As these consuls' families became well known, they were accepted as part of the nobility and their sons, after extensive training at home, were appointed or elected as military tribunes, beginning the cycle again.

Their willingness to vote for members of the new nobility demonstrates that the plebeians, in general, held traditional views about who ought to serve as leaders of the Republic. Even in the early part of the 4th century, when the Struggle of the Orders was at its height, the question was not about the legitimacy of Rome being ruled by economic and social elites. Rather, it was a matter of creating a balance, where elite rule would be limited by the preservation of plebeian liberties and political leaders were obliged to address plebeian economic needs. Throughout most of the history of the Republic this duality of fierce opposition to particular policies in contrast with a general acceptance of rule by first the patricians and then the nobility was a hallmark of Roman politics.

As a result, conflict between the Plebeian Assembly and the rest of Rome's political order began to decline. The sons of wealthy plebeians were still elected to serve as tribunes, but it was no longer in the interests of these individuals to mobilize unhappy members of the lower classes to legislate against the interests of the wealthy. They were now eager to use the office to demonstrate to voters in the Tribal Assembly why they should be elected to the position of quaestor in a future electoral cycle.[1] As a result, by the beginning of the 3rd century the Plebeian Assembly no longer functioned as the angry voice of the lower classes demanding change.[2] With this development, the nobility solidified its hold on the political system and the Senate became the dominant political body in the city.

ROME AND AMERICA: EXPANSION AND SOCIAL REFORM

The era of the "Early Republic" is synonymous with the Struggle of the Orders because this conflict so deeply shaped Rome's political institutions, its social order, and its ability to effectively wage war against its neighbors. Once the Struggle of the Orders was resolved there followed what historians call the classical period of the "Middle Republic," a time when relations between social groups were relatively harmonious. Taken together, the reforms of this period made Rome a more prosperous, a more just, and a more united community.

---

1 Cornell, *Atlas*, p. 37
2 Rachel Feig Vishnia, *State, Society, and Popular Leaders in Mid-Republican Rome 241-167 B.C.*, New York: Taylor & Francis, Inc. p. 114

While wealthy plebeians gained access to the nobility, the plebeian order as a whole gained as well. Political reforms improved life for every plebeian by expanding their *libertas*, arming them with rights that gave them some measure of autonomy from the ruling elite. The right to appeal judgments involving flogging or the death penalty — *provocatio*, knowledge of the details of legal procedures — *legis actiones*, and the opportunity for the sons of freedmen, the *libertine*, to become citizens, were enormous advances over the meager civil liberties granted to people living in kingdoms and other types of ancient regimes.

Ending the practice of *nexum* and gaining the opportunity to acquire land by joining a colony or receiving a grant of *ager publius* gave Roman plebeians the opportunity to make a decent living for themselves and their families. In addition, the granting of Latin rights to dozens of communities put thousands of individuals in Italy on track to becoming citizens in the expanding Roman commonwealth.

In a society where the bulk of the population was illiterate — there were no public schools during this era — we should not judge plebeians harshly if they were more interested in free land and freedom from prosecution than in exercising daily control over the city's political institutions. The plebeian public was willing to cede status and honor to the ruling nobility as long as that group was energetic about meeting the social and economic needs of the whole population.

While the situation in the United States was different in many ways from Rome, the new American Republic did go through an evolutionary process of reform. We often forget that the "founding fathers" were unrepresentative of the population of the young Republic. White men who were merchants, lawyers, or aristocrats dominated political offices in the US when the Constitution was ratified in 1789. The voting public consisted of men who met some form of property requirement, as determined by each state. Members of the US Senate were elected by their state legislatures and women did not vote or participate in the political process. Most egregiously, the Constitution itself stated that black individuals only counted as 2/3 of a person when allocating Congressional seats to the various states, thus confirming the enslaved Negro's diminished position in society.

Since then, the political history of the United States has been a slow, but steady process of granting excluded groups full citizenship status and greater access to economic prosperity. As in Rome, many of these steps involved giving public lands to poor citizens. In 1787, Congress passed the Northwest Ordinance, specifying the process by which any citizen could stake a claim to farm on public lands owned by the United States in the vast region now known as the upper Mid-West (Ohio, Indiana, Michigan, Illinois, and Wisconsin). The Ordinance prohibited the practice of slavery in this area, thus making the Ohio River the boundary between slave and free states. In the early 19th century agitation in state legislatures led to white men without property being given the right to vote. Then, at the end of the Civil War, slavery was abolished and the 14th Amendment gave black men the right to vote.

After the Civil War, an array of public lands was opened up to settlers through the Homestead Act and other measures. (Tragically, a significant amount of this land was occupied by Native American tribes who received scant compensation for losing their entire way of life). In the most dramatic instance of land distribution to the poor, in 1888, Congress authorized a land rush in the Oklahoma territory. On April 22, 1889, an estimated 50,000 people raced into the area to claim approximately two million acres of good farmland.

By 1898, all of the states had abolished imprisonment for debt.[1] In 1913, the 17th Amendment to the Constitution stated that Senators were to be elected directly by citizens. In 1920, seventy-two years after the first women's rights convention in Seneca Falls, the 19th Amendment gave women the right to vote. In 1935, the Wagner Act (named after the Democratic Senator from New York, Robert F. Wagner, who introduced the legislation) gave workers the right to organize unions. The GI Bill, created for veterans of the Second World War, provided the means for working class individuals to gain access to college and a ticket into the great American middle class of the late 20th century.

The civil rights movement of the late 1950s and 1960s eliminated many restrictions on voting rights and took steps toward eliminating racial bias in hiring for jobs and the selling of homes. Finally, the women's movement unleashed social changes that eventually flooded the universities and the workforce with women who were no longer consigned to the home. While the Equal Rights Amendment to the Constitution was never ratified, the social and political impacts of this change continue to revise the American landscape.

While the Roman Republic and the American Republic are not identical, in both societies there were tendencies for political and economic institutions to evolve in positive ways. That is, both Republics were becoming more democratic and providing more economic opportunities for the average citizen. Perhaps this is the inevitable result when political institutions involve large numbers of people in deciding the fate of their country.

---

1 Bradley Hansen, "Bankruptcy Law in the United States," *EH.Net*; available from http://eh.net/encyclopedia/article/Hansen.bankruptcy.law.us; accessed 22 July 2007

Chapter 5. The Republic Acquires an Empire

> Prudent men are wont to say — and this not rashly or without good ground
> — that he who would foresee what has to be should reflect on what has
> been, for everything that happens in the world at any time has a genuine
> resemblance to what happened in ancient times.[1]

—Niccolo Machiavelli, *Discourses on Livy*

Agathocles, ruler of Syracuse, the largest city on Sicily, had established control over much of the island and formed alliances with many of the Greek cities on the Italian mainland at the end of the 4th century. (Syracuse was founded by the Greek city of Corinth in 734 BCE.)[2] When he died in 289, the region quickly descended into turmoil. In 284, the Greek city of Thurii (founded by Athenians in 443 BCE) was put under siege by a hill tribe army. The oligarchic faction in the city promptly requested assistance from Rome. A Roman consul broke the siege and left a Roman garrison there to protect the city.

In rapid succession the Greek cities Locri, Regium, and Croton also sought Roman protection. In addition to protecting them from the hill tribes, the Romans began to meddle in each city's internal feuds. As it had in central Italy, Rome consistently supported the oligarchic factions, creating friction with Tarentum, the largest and wealthiest Greek city in Italy (founded by settlers from Sparta). When the democratic faction in Thurii asked for as-

---

1 Niccolo Machiavelli, *Discourses on the First Decade of Livy*, 3.43; as quoted in: Holland, *Rubicon*, p. xviii

2 Robert Morkot, *The Penguin Historical Atlas of Ancient Greece*, London: Penguin Books 1996, p. 54

sistance, Tarentum sent an army to expel the Roman garrison.[1] Rome responded by sending a consul and two legions to raid the countryside around Tarentum, which led the Greeks to call for assistance from King Pyrrhus of Epirus, a small country on the western coast of Greece.

Pyrrhic Victories and the Conquest of Southern Italy

An able monarch whose military ambitions on the Greek peninsula were thwarted by Epirus' limited resources, Pyrrhus landed in southern Italy with 25,000 well-trained, professional soldiers and 20 elephants.[2] With this invasion, he initiated a new period in Roman history, a time when the new military and political institutions of the Republic would be tested by some of the leading nations of the ancient world. Alexander the Great had recently used the Greek phalanx to conquer the Persian Empire and Pyrrhus, one of Alexander's cousins, was adept at using this fearsome military force.

L. Aemilius Barbula, consul in 281, commanded the two legions that confronted Pyrrhus. In this first encounter, Pyrrhus was fortunate in the place of battle, for it was a broad, flat plain and his rows of hoplite spearmen were able to maintain their dense lines, the porcupine of the phalanx not offering the sword wielding Romans any opportunities to split them up and attack their flanks. However, the Romans inflicted many casualties on the Greek mercenaries with their javelins and were able to hold the phalanx back by swiftly rotating lines, first the *hastati* throwing javelins and doing a sword charge, then retreating and the *principes* taking their turn. The Greeks won the battle when their elephants charged the Roman cavalry on the flanks, for the horses were terrified of the huge, noisy elephants and, quite sensibly, refused to fight them.[3] The legions were outflanked by the Greek elephants and were forced to leave the field.

While Pyrrhus won this battle and the Romans suffered greater casualties than he did, the Greek king could ill afford such costly victories because he had no trained troops to replace his lost officers and infantrymen. There is a story that Pyrrhus, when congratulated on his success by leaders from Tarentum, exclaimed, "One more such victory and I am undone!" From this comes the famous phrase "Pyrrhic victory" meaning a triumph that brings ruin to the victor.

For the moment, Pyrrhus was the master of southern Italy; the defeated Roman army retreated back toward Rome and the Samnites, Bruttii, and Lucanians sent warriors to assist him in an invasion of central Italy. However, he received another surprise in Campania when the towns of Capua and Neapolis refused to abandon the Roman cause and closed their gates to

---

1 LeGlay, *History of Rome*, p. 71
2 Scullard, *Roman World*, p. 141
3 Scullard, *Roman World*, p. 142

him.[1] Pyrrhus had no siege equipment with which to attack a fortified city, so he left Campania and marched toward Rome. There, two Roman legions blocked his approach to the city. Deprived of a decisive victory, Pyrrhus offered to leave Italy if the Romans would sign a treaty guaranteeing the independence of Tarentum and returning captured lands to the Samnites and Lucanians.[2] By this time the Romans were determined to control southern Italy and, after a lengthy debate in the Senate, refused his offer.

The war resumed in 279. Pyrrhus imposed heavy taxes on his Greek allies in Italy, hired more mercenaries from Greece, and bought new elephants to replace those that had been killed or wounded. The taxes must have drained many resources from the cities — bronze tablets discovered at the temple of Zeus Olympius in the city of Locri record the payment of 300 tons of silver "to the king."[3] Pyrrhus attacked the Romans near the town of Ausculum. This time the phalanxes developed spaces between their lines as they marched through the woods and hills.[4] The more agile legions launched sword wielding attacks into these spaces, driving the Greeks back and creating confusion up and down their lines. The next day, Pyrrhus found more level ground for his phalanxes to advance and an elephant charge once again swept away the Roman cavalry and crumpled the Roman flank. As before, the Greek army suffered too many casualties to advance and had to return to Tarentum.

Two years later Pyrrhus made one last throw of the dice, marching back into Campania hoping for a quick victory. Instead, he was decisively defeated at Beneventum. The Roman army had finally devised an effective defense against the elephants, using infantry to attack their legs. Without them, the phalanx could not overcome the legion. The victorious consul, Manius Curius Dentatus, was able to build another aqueduct for Rome with the gold and silver he captured in Pyrrhus' camp.[5]

Out of options for his expensive mercenary army, Pyrrhus left Italy. His defeat and departure left southern Italy open to Roman conquest. They moved quickly to besiege the city of Tarentum, capturing it in 272 BCE. The only city large enough to be a rival in southern Italy was now in Roman hands. While the city was allowed to keep its independence, a Roman garrison was left in its citadel to ensure that there would be no interventions from nearby Greece.[6] (Tarentum is closer to Greece than any point in Sicily is to North Africa.) The triumph of the two consuls who had captured the

---

1 Cornell, *Atlas*, p. 39
2 Boatwright, *The Romans*, p. 93
3 Boatwright, *The Romans*, p. 93
4 Scullard, *Roman World*, p. 143
5 Boatwright, *The Romans*, p. 93
6 LeGlay, *History of Rome*, p. 73

city "featured a parade of all the statues, paintings, and other marvels seized from the town."[1]

The Roman Republic was still a simple, rural culture at this time and the ornate beauty of the items from the south had an enduring impact on Roman art, literature, and religion. The parade, where all the citizens of the city could watch in awe as the wealth of the ancient western world's most highly developed culture passed by, was the first large-scale interaction of Roman society with Greek cultural items. From now on, Rome would have a "closer engagement" with the Greek world and the marvelous culture that the Greeks had developed over the previous 250 years.[2] The cultural exchange between this robust, but unsophisticated Republic and Greek poetry, architecture, mythology, literature, and art gradually initiated a process of "Hellenization" that would lead to the creation of a *Greco-Roman* culture, a culture that would form the basis of "Western Civilization."

EXPANDING REPUBLICS: AMERICA AND ROME

Both of the Republics in our study were bursting with expansionist energy. Over the course of 100 years, the Roman Republic recovered from the Gallic sack of Rome and became master of the Italian peninsula. The American Republic conquered and settled the entire North American continent in less than 120 years. As part of the peace treaty that ended the Revolutionary War against Great Britain, the 13 colonies acquired the area between the Appalachian Mountains and the Mississippi River; a significant extension of the Republic's territory. After that, the United States only had to engage in two major wars that threatened its march across the continent. The British defeat at New Orleans in 1814 prevented the loss of the newly acquired Louisiana territory and the unprovoked war against Mexico in 1848 led to the annexation of Texas, the Southwest, and California. With these two exceptions, the United States was able to acquire legal rights to the rest of its mainland territory through purchases and/or negotiations with European nations.

The key transaction was President Jefferson's purchase of the Louisiana Territory from Napoleon in 1803. For $15 million the young Republic acquired almost one-quarter of the territory of the modern United States. Florida was purchased for $5 million from the fading Spanish empire in 1819. The slogan "54-40 or Fight" allowed James Polk to edge out the more restrained Henry Clay in the presidential election of 1844, but Polk then proceeded to peacefully negotiate with the British to create a boundary for the Pacific Northwest at the 49th parallel.

---

1 LeGlay, *History of Rome*, p. 73
2 Boatwright, *The Romans*, p. 94

The other side of the story is the Native American people who "owned" the whole continent before 1500. Except for the French and Indian War, when a coalition of tribes entered into an alliance with the French government, the English settlers and later the United State government had clear military superiority over Native American tribes whenever there was a dispute over territory. As a result, the story of Native American peoples after 1600 is a long history of war, defeat, and displacement. This started as soon as the late 17th century when King Phillips' War led to the almost total eradication of Native Americans from New England.

The Romans felt that the Latin peoples and most of the other tribes in Italy were from a similar ethnic group and strove to involve them in a Roman confederacy through treaties that gave the defeated communities rights and responsibilities. Most Anglo-Americans had no such feelings of kinship with Native Americans; they were generally seen as savages or barbarians, dangerous and uncivilized people who could not be trusted. Even Eastern tribes that attempted to assimilate and adopt European customs, like the Cherokee Nation, were forced to migrate to the Great Plains when advancing settlers desired their lands. For example, the Indian Removal Act of 1830 (supported by President Andrew Jackson and opposed by Davy Crockett, Daniel Webster, and Henry Clay) condemned the Cherokee to a thousand mile exile along the "trail of tears."

The "cowboy and Indian" wars of the second half of the 19th century pushed the plains peoples into reservations and opened up the western part of the continent to settlement by European peoples who were ethnically similar to 19th century white Americans. The Naturalization Act of 1795 made it clear who was welcome to become part of the new Republic. The Act declared that citizenship in the United States was restricted to "free white persons."[1] While a relatively modest number of individuals immigrated to the United States before 1840, in the next decade political unrest and crop failures in Germany and Ireland sparked a dramatic increase in the number of people coming to the American Republic. In the 1840s, more than 1,713,000 immigrants made the difficult passage and another 2,598,000 came in the 1850s.

The Homestead Act of 1862, which promised 160 acres to any citizen willing to farm the land for five years, provided an incentive for land hungry farmers from Europe to come to the new world. During the 1880s, an astounding 5,246,000 people immigrated to the US, including more than one million Germans. In 1882 the ethnic identity of the country was reaffirmed when the Chinese Exclusion Act barred almost all immigration from Asian countries. Then, during the decade from 1901 to 1910, a record 8,795,000 peo-

---

1 *Open Collections Program*, Harvard University Library, available from http://ocp.hul.harvard.edu/immigration/dates.html; accessed 22 July 2007.

ple immigrated to the US, including two million Italians. This influx led to the creation of the Dillingham Commission, which reported that immigration from eastern and southern Europe threatened the cohesion of American society. The report and the emotional reaction against foreigners associated with the Red Scare of 1919 and 1920, led to the Immigration Act of 1924. Immigration from any nation in one year was limited to 2% of that nationality's percentage of the US population in the 1890 census — a requirement that essentially shut down immigration from "undesirable" parts of Europe. The Oriental Exclusion Act of 1924 then prohibited immigration from Asia. The new laws had a dramatic effect in the decade of the 1930s: only 532,400 people immigrated to the United States.

While the expansion process was quite different in many ways, the end results were similar. During its conquest of Italy, the Roman Republic fought a series of wars against many different tribal groups on the Italian peninsula. After many bloody conflicts and occasional massacres, a confederation was created by 265 BCE, which included the defeated peoples intermingled with colonies of Roman and Latin citizens. During its period of expansion, the American Republic fought a series of small wars against the many Native American tribes on the North American continent. Through bloody conflicts and removal to reservations, the Native Americans were cleared away to make room for white settlers who immigrated to the United States from Europe. This led to the creation, by 1898, of a united group of states that were relatively homogeneous, with the exception of African slaves who were brought to the US in the early days of the Republic. For both Republics, the initial process of expansion over contiguous land areas, the Italian peninsula and the American continent, set the stage for more difficult imperial adventures. The real empire building process began with the establishment of colonies overseas.

THE FIRST PUNIC WAR

Rome's expansion into southern Italy inevitably involved her in relationships with the island of Sicily. While Rome was very much a land-oriented society, with almost no navy and few maritime linkages, its new allies in Neapolis and southern Italy had extensive trading relations with Greece, North Africa, and Sicily. As mentioned above, when Agathocles of Syracuse died in 289 BCE, politics in southern Italy and in Sicily became very unstable. The wealthy trading city of Carthage, located in North Africa across from Sicily, had many interests and allies on the island and began to overshadow Syracuse. In 264 BCE, the young King Hiero II of Syracuse tried to strengthen his kingdom by besieging the strategic town of Messina in northeastern Sicily, directly across the straits from the toe of Italy.[1] Messina had been occupied

---

1 Cornell, *Atlas*, p. 43

for twenty-five years by Italian mercenaries known as the Mamertines. They accepted help from Carthage to fend off Hiero II and, when Carthage's naval units showed no inclination to leave, they decided to appeal to their fellow Italians in Rome for assistance.

Here we have a good example of defensive imperialism. Rome and Carthage had signed a treaty in 306 where each had pledged to not interfere in the other's presumed area of influence — Rome was not to meddle in Sicily and Carthage would not get involved in Italian affairs.[1] Carthage was willing to sign this treaty because her imperial strategy was to gradually acquire territories and then incorporate them into a closed trading block. Founded in the 9th century by Phoenician traders (Punic is from *punicus*, the Latin word for Phoenician), the city had gradually gained control of coastal northern Africa, Sardinia, and coastal Spain, including the Straits of Gibraltar. (Ancient history note: Phoenicia, a great seafaring nation, was located in the area we now know as Lebanon.) Acquiring Sicily would give Carthage a near monopoly on trade in the western Mediterranean. However, Rome in 306 was not interested in the fate of islands away from the Italian mainland.

Forty years later, Rome's new allies in Neapolis and southern Italy faced a sharp loss of income if Carthage shut off their commerce with Sicily and saw the call for assistance from the Mamertines as a perfect opportunity for Rome to block Carthage's attempt to dominate the island. The issue was put before the Senate by leaders of the Claudii family, which had begun investing in overseas trade expeditions in partnership with merchants in southern Italy.[2] The dynamic of defensive imperialism is clearly visible here — Rome's conquest of southern Italy led to concerns about that area's relationship with its nearest neighbor, Sicily. In this way, involvement in the affairs of Sicily, which had been of no interest to Rome in 306, became an urgent foreign policy issue in 264 BCE. When the Senate balked at breaking the treaty, the consuls convinced the Plebeian Assembly to authorize sending an army to the island.

The intervention went well at first. The old consul Appius Claudius successfully crossed the Strait of Messina and routed the Carthaginian garrison in Messina. Hiero II of Syracuse became a loyal Roman ally and the Roman army captured the city of Agrigentum, Carthage's largest base in central Sicily. To secure the entire island, the Republic built a fleet of 100 large warships called *quinqueremes*. These large, clumsy ships had 50 or 60 enormous oars, with five men pulling on each oar. Only one of these men had to be a skilled oarsman, allowing the Romans to recruit farmers and other non-seafaring people to operate their warships.[3] This new fleet surprisingly won two sig-

---

1 Scullard, *Roman World*, p. 164
2 LeGlay, *History of Rome*, p. 81
3 Potter, "Roman Army," p. 77

nificant naval engagements off the coast of Sicily. The key to these victories was Rome's decision to use her ships as platforms for land troops, with the decisive moment in an engagement being when the captain brought his ship up alongside an opponent.[1] To prevent an opposing ship from breaking away, the Roman developed the *corvus* (raven) a heavy, spiked plank that could be

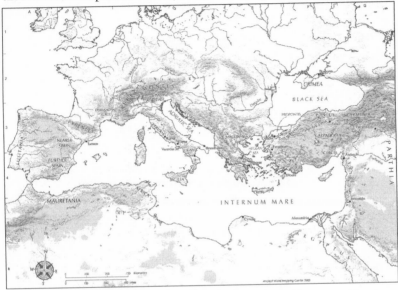

Within a century of the capture of Sicily, the Republic came to dominate the rich lands around the Mediterranean Sea.

impaled on a Carthaginian ship and then act as a walkway for soldiers to race across.

With victories on land and sea, Rome was ready to invade Carthage's home territory and bring the war to a conclusion. M. Atilius Regulus, the consul in 256, led a Roman army to North Africa, captured the coastal town of Aspis, and camped for the winter on the outskirts of Carthage. However, the next spring Carthage counter-attacked with 100 elephants and a large cavalry force; while the elephants trampled the Roman center, the cavalry swept around the flanks and surrounded Regulus' two legions — fewer than 2,000 Romans escaped back to the shore.[2] A horrible fate awaited them; a Roman fleet of 264 ships picked them up, but the inexperienced consul M. Aemilius Paullus blundered into a huge storm off the southern tip of Italy and 184 ships sank.[3] With crews of 250 sailors, plus their soldier passengers, it is possible that more than 40,000 men drowned in that tragic storm.

1 Matyszak, *Chronicle*, p. 88

2 Scullard, *Roman World*, p. 172

3 Matyszak, *Chronicles*, p. 82

After another round of boat building, the consul Appius Claudius Pulcher (Pulcher means good-looking) took command of another fleet in 249 and decided to try a surprise attack on the Carthaginian fleet moored in the small harbor at Drepanum. Before the attack he consulted the gods, using sacred chickens. If the birds ate birdseed scattered on the deck, then the gods were favorable to an attack (one might detect a certain bias in this decision-making system). This time, however, the chickens refused to eat. Impatient for his chance at victory, Claudius roared, "Well, let them drink!" and had them thrown overboard.[1] Perhaps predictably, Carthage's fleet escaped from the harbor and attacked Claudius from the rear. In the resulting confusion, the Romans lost 93 of their 120 ships, with the crews being forced to abandon them and crawl ashore. "A modern naval expert has remarked 'those chickens knew their consul'."[2]

Exhausted from its losses at sea, Rome concentrated on blockading Carthage's two remaining bases on Sicily, Drepanum and Lilybaeum. The fighting dragged on for six years, until 242 when a group of aristocrats loaned the city enough money to build 200 warships that sailed out to blockade Drepanum.[3] To save its base, Carthage pulled together a fleet of 170 ships and, loaded with supplies, attempted to run the blockade during heavy seas. The consul C. Lutaius Catulus had been vigorously drilling his green crews to be ready for this moment. The overloaded Carthaginian warships were completely overwhelmed, with 50 ships sunk and another 70 captured. The war was over at last.

In the resulting peace treaty Rome acquired Sicily and received 3,200 *talents* of silver over 10 years. (A talent was as much silver as a man could carry, about 50 to 55 pounds.) The island became the city's breadbasket, reliably supplying large quantities of corn and wheat for many centuries. In a break with the Commonwealth pattern of government used in Italy, the Romans made Sicily a province, ruled by a praetor.[4] Towns and residents paid taxes to Rome, but were not required to mobilize military units to participate in Roman wars. In this way, the first overseas part of the Roman Republic's empire came into existence. Another province came soon afterward. When Carthage was pre-occupied with a rebellion by its mercenary army in 238 BCE, Rome took over the islands of Sardinia and Corsica. A fourth praetor position was created to administer these islands. Carthage's reaction to this land grab would eventually have a significant impact on Rome. In 237 BCE, the Carthaginian general Hamilcar Barca was sent to Spain to expand the city's coastal trading outposts into a full province. He was very successful

1 Scullard, *Roman World*, p. 175
2 Matyszak, *Chronicles*, p. 85
3 Scullard, *Roman World*, p. 177
4 Cornell, *Atlas*, p. 44

and, after his death in 222, his son Hannibal became Carthage's leading general on the peninsula.

As we will see, the First Punic War was as significant for Rome as the Spanish American War of 1898 was for the United States. The conquest of Cuba, Puerto Rico, and the Philippines was the American Republic's first major war outside of the continental United States. The new territories did not become part of the US political system, but were governed as colonies. Cuba was a colony until 1903 and an informal protectorate until 1958, the Philippines was a colony until 1946 and an informal protectorate until 1985, and Puerto Rico was a colony until 1950, when it evolved to its current status of commonwealth.

THE SOCIAL ORDER OF THE MIDDLE REPUBLIC

Shortly after the end of the First Punic War, the Centuriate Assembly was modified to reflect the growing importance of farmers with relatively small amounts of land. The re-distribution of *auger publicus* to poor citizens and the granting of citizenship to nearby tribes like the Sabines had greatly expanded the number of economically secure and politically conservative voters in the Second and Third Classes of the Assembly.[1] To reflect the importance of these individuals who made up a crucial percentage of the rank and file in the legions and who rowed the oars of the navy, ten centuries were transferred out of the First Class (reducing its numbers from 80 to 70) and distributed in an unknown fashion throughout the other Classes.[2]

With this re-distribution, the 18 centuries of the *Equestrian* Order and the 70 centuries of the First Class no longer had a majority of voting units in the 193-unit Centuriate Assembly. Candidates for the offices of praetor, consul, and censor needed to find votes amongst the farmers in the Second Class in order to win election. In closely contested races, especially when the votes were split between four candidates for consul or eight candidates for praetor, the smallholders in the Third Class might turn out to be deciding votes. Recognizing their importance to society, the nobility cultivated its relationship with these small farmers and sought to support their interests.[3]

This diffusion of voting power meant that there were several distinct social groups that individuals who ran for office in the Middle Republic needed to sway. They had to create bonds of friendship with other members of the nobility, who, like their patrician predecessors, maintained clientele groups willing to vote for the people they favored. Candidates also spent time with the wealthy members of the *Equestrian* Order. Those whose income came from cultivating large landholdings also had rural clientele groups whose

---

1 Vishnia, *State, Society, Leaders*, p. 46
2 Scullard, *Roman World*, p. 187
3 Vishnia, *State, Society, Leaders*, p. 142 and 158

votes they could count on, while the growing number of merchants in the *Equestrian* Order had business connections in many towns where new Italian citizens lived. The First Class in the Centuriate Assembly had become a diverse mixture of urban merchants, landowners who were able to create farms larger than the average smallholding, and the scattering of lawyers and craftsmen who were able to maintain an independent financial existence. Small farmers made up the bulk of voters in the Second and Third Classes of the Centuriate Assembly and probably formed the largest bloc of voters in the Tribal Assembly, an important consideration when running for the position of quaestor.

The class of small farmers was the pivotal group in the electoral system. They were the people who most identified with the families of the nobility because the leading members of the nobility were their officers in battle. Bonds of blood and comradeship were created, bonds that resulted in votes when the small farmers and their descendents went to the polls.[1] A similar process occurred in the northern United States after the Civil War, when the thousands of white farmers who made up the rank and file of the Army of the Republic came home to vote for President Lincoln's Republican Party.[2] This initial instinct was cemented when the general who won the war, Ulysses S. Grant, became the standard bearer for the Republican Party in the Presidential elections of 1868 and 1872. These Republican voting habits were maintained through the 1870s and 1880s; Republican candidates who campaigned on a platform of northern superiority and veterans rights were said to be "waving the bloody shirt."[3]

Roman candidates in the 4th, 3rd, and 2nd centuries campaigned by reminding voters of the good works of their fathers and other ancestors, offering an entertaining array of stories about their battlefield exploits. They would then discuss their own accomplishments, demonstrating that they were worthy inheritors of the mantle of leadership. Campaigning was face-to-face, with a good deal of personal interaction between the candidate and the voters and between supporters of the candidate and their friends. Given the almost permanent nature of campaigning, with more than two dozen officials elected every year during the 3rd century for example, there was plenty of opportunity for vote trading, both in any one year and between years as prominent individuals would begin campaigning for their next campaign at least two years in advance. Surprisingly, candidates almost never spoke about important political issues; elections were about status, military accomplishments, friendships, and ancestors. An ancient tract about election tactics, supposedly written by Cicero's brother, specifically warns against "expressing himself on public affairs during the campaign."[4]

1 Alfoldy, *Social History*, p. 37
2 Lawrence Goodwyn, *The Populist Moment*, Oxford: Oxford University Press, 1978, pp. 5-6
3 Goodwyn, *Populist Moment*, p. 6
4 Taylor, *Party Politics*, p. 64

The triumph was the most elaborate of a variety of public ceremonies and celebrations that placed a public spotlight on the deeds of successful members of the nobility.[1] Remember that the very term nobility comes from "one who is well known" and political leaders intent on climbing the *cursus honorum* had to take every opportunity to let the public see them. Once elite status was no longer merely connected to aristocratic birth, but also required a record of public accomplishment, then political leaders who became quaestors, praetors, and consuls sought to shine in the same way American presidential candidates work day and night for years to attract attention to themselves.[2] The triumph of Scipio Africanus, after his defeat of Hannibal, was typical. Try to imagine this parade as Appian described it, winding through the city and stopping at the Temple of Jupiter, the god of war:

> Everyone in the procession wore crowns. Trumpeters led the advance, and wagons laded with spoils. Towers were borne along representing the captured cities, and pictures illustrating the campaigns; then gold and silver coin and bullion . . . White oxen came next, and after them elephants and the captive Carthaginian and Numidian leaders. Lictors wearing purple tunics preceded the general; also a chorus of harpists and pipers — in imitation of an Etruscan procession — wearing belts and golden crowns, and marching in regular order, keeping step with song and dance. . . . Next came a number of incense-bearers, and after them the general himself in a richly decorated chariot.
>
> He wore a crown of gold and precious stones, and was dressed, in traditional fashion, in a purple toga woven with golden stars. He carried a scepter of ivory, and a laurel branch, which is invariably the Roman symbol of victory. Riding in the same chariot with him were boys and girls, and — on the trace-horses either side of him — young men, his own relatives. . . . After these came the army itself; marshaled in squadrons and cohorts, all of them crowned and carrying laurel branches, the bravest of them bearing their military prizes.[3]

Note how the general's glory was shared with younger men in his family. His glory was their first step in seeking political office. There were many examples of sons and close relatives of consuls also reaching the consulate, carried along by the success of their father or uncle.

Another way in which the patricians and later the nobility enhanced their prestige was to demonstrate elaborate connections to illustrious ancestors. The funeral of a member of the nobility was a great spectacle.[4] The casket was carried through the streets of the city with actors wearing masks of the dead man and his illustrious ancestors. Each actor was clothed in robes appropriate for the highest office each man had obtained during his lifetime.

---

1 Boatwright, *The Romans*, p. 99

2 Flower, "Spectacle and Political Culture," in Flower, Harriet I, *The Cambridge Companion to the Roman Republic*, Cambridge: Cambridge University Press, 2004, p. 323

3 Boatwright, *The Romans*, p. 101

4 Bernstein, *Tiberius Sempronius Gracchus*, p. 21

If one or more ancestors had celebrated a triumph, then other actors wore weapons and military attire from that period.

With clients marching and musicians playing, the entire procession would go to the Forum, the public heart of Rome, where the deceased man's oldest son would mount the Rostrum and eulogize his father and his ancestors.[1] The speech would list their achievements, extol their virtues, and assure the public that the current generation was equally worthy of election to high office and military command. Later, the masks were placed in an elaborate wooden shrine in the atrium of the family mansion, so all who entered would be reminded of the distinguished nature of the family that lived there. For the average Roman, funerals served as a kind of history lesson, with the battles and exploits of high-ranking individuals dramatically woven into the history of the community as a whole.[2] Given that there was no public education system, no systematic history of the city taught to the young, these were the primary stories people heard about the past and it may have been difficult for ordinary people to imagine life in the community without these leaders from the nobility.

RELIGION AND THE STATE

Roman religion as passed down through myths and stories was primarily a shared, public religion, bringing the community together to pray for the success of the state. As with the Greeks, it was a form of polytheism, but Roman gods did not exist in a unified pantheon as in Greece.[3] Instead, there were a variety of gods taking on different roles, each with his or her special functions, festivals, holidays, and cult activities. The principal deities in the early Republic were the triad of Jupiter, the supreme god and protector of the Roman people; Mars, the god of agriculture (and only later of war); and Quirinus, who was at that time the god of war. In the late Republic, coinciding with a greater involvement of women in religious activities, there were significant shifts in religious sentiment regarding the importance and role of various gods. Mars and Quirinus continued to be worshiped, but were replaced in the official triad by two goddesses, Juno, who was worshipped as Jupiter's wife, and Minerva, a goddess of wisdom, crafts, and martial arts.

Beneath this shifting triad of official deities was an extremely diverse collection of lesser gods imported from other parts of the new empire, especially from the Greek world. Mixed in with these imported gods were a variety of indigenous deities honored as local or community gods by neighborhoods, towns, crafts, or other groups of people. In general, worship of these deities

---

1 Boatwright, *The Romans*, p. 103

2 Flower, "Spectacle & Political Culture," p. 335

3 Rupke, Jorg, "Roman Religion," in Flower, Harriet, *The Cambridge Companion to the Roman Republic*, Cambridge: Cambridge University Press, 2004, p. 193

allowed the groups' members to express and reinforce their sense of connection to one another.[1] Each of the localized deities had their own temples, rituals, holidays, and priests.

This plethora of religious practices is obviously different from modern monotheistic religions in terms of the numbers of gods, but there are other differences that reveal something about the mindset of ancient peoples. Ancient people had very little control over their health compared to modern people. With almost no ability to treat medical conditions, people got sick or injured and died or recovered in ways that seemed random. People also knew far less about how the world worked, why it rained, why wood burned, and other questions that have since been answered by science. In this very uncertain environment, people saw their lives as heavily dependent on fate or luck, *fortuna*. For individuals, worship of the gods frequently consisted of ritualized practices, inherited from childhood, pleas for assistance that may or may not lead to positive results because gods in the Roman world were not thought to have a personal relationship with the individual worshiper.[2] As a result, the experience of religion was quite different for a Roman citizen than for a modern Christian, Jew, or Moslem.

Rather than serving as personal deities, concerned about the lives and souls of their flock, most gods, especially the city's official gods — Jupiter, Mars, Quirinus, Juno, Minerva and a handful of others — were concerned with the growth and success of the city. Prominent people in the city, originally patricians and then leaders of the nobility, claimed that, as leaders of the Roman Republic, they were the appropriate people to take on the role of communicating with and interpreting the will of the gods. As a result, the men who served as official religious leaders had dual roles; in addition to their part-time role as priests, they were usually prominent members of the Senate.[3]

An elaborate hierarchy of religious offices and procedures developed to cultivate the Roman Republic's relationship with the gods. The most important body of religious leaders was the college of pontiffs, led by the *pontifex maximus*, which supervised a wide range of religious ceremonies and holidays and influenced the activities of other religious bodies.[4] Priests known as *flamens* oversaw specific temples and cults, with the priest of Jupiter, the *flamen Dialis* being the most prestigious. There was also a college of *augers*, who interpreted the *auspices* in order to divine the approval or disapproval of the gods for actions planned by magistrates or political assemblies.[5] Like the

1 Boatwright, *The Romans*, p. 71
2 Beard and Crawford, *Rome in the Late Republic*, p.24
3 Rupke, "Roman Religion," p. 189
4 Boatwright, *The Romans*, p. 72
5 Boatwright, *The Romans*, p. 74

college of pontiffs, the college of *augers* was divided equally between patrician and plebeian members.

This mixing of politics and religion led to a range of religious practices that were primarily devoted to ensuring that public activities — the passing of a law, the launching of a war, the staging of elections — met with the favor of the gods. Consulting of the *auspices,* for example, was seldom done to decide an issue of personal morality; the *auspices* were indications of how the gods felt about a proposed public action.[1] While there were debates over the meaning of any particular event, a flash of lightning or a bird soaring over a meeting, there was a general sense that Jupiter and his circle of gods favored Rome and were pleased by her conquests and accomplishments.[2] Rome's military successes in the 4th and 3rd centuries reinforced this self-justifying notion.

POLICING AND THE CITY OF ROME

One of the unique aspects of the social harmony created by this mix of religious approval, ancestor worship, military success, and aggressive land reform was the astonishing level of social order in Rome. The city was very different than any modern city because it had no police force. The use of specialized police forces for urban area is a product of the 18th and 19th centuries; earlier societies did not have independent police departments.[3] Before the industrial revolution, kings, emperors, pharaohs, and other rulers used soldiers from the regular army to maintain public order. The troops were used to prevent large-scale incidents of disorder or political unrest.

Rome was different. One of the unique aspects of Republican Rome was the sacred border around the city, the *pomerium* (a concept borrowed from the Etruscans), which excluded Roman military units from the city. While this religious prohibition made it difficult for a would-be-king to stage a military coup, it also meant that soldiers could not be called in to restore public order. This unusual situation demonstrates the Roman willingness to make sacrifices and accommodations to ensure that their liberties could not be stolen. This desire to prevent a take-over by a would-be-king went so far as the prohibition against a serving general from entering the city. If he wanted to consult with the Senate, that body would leave the city and meet with him at a special site on the Campus Marti — outside the *pomerium*.

In place of police, Roman magistrates (consuls and praetors) enforced order through the legitimate power of their office — that is, citizens of the Early and Middle Republican eras readily acknowledged their authority and obeyed their commands. While praetors and consuls had *lictors* that carried

---

1 Boatwright, *The Romans*, p. 74
2 Beard & Crawford, *Rome in the Late Republic*, p. 31
3 Wilfred Nippel, "Policing Rome," *Journal of Roman Studies*, V.74, 1984, p. 20

the "fasces," which included sticks and axes, these were merely symbols of the legitimate power that magistrates had been granted by the community. The *lictors* never attacked wrongdoers with their axes. "The capability of *lictors* to quell serious disturbances depended on the authority of the magistrate being positively accepted."[1]

A telling example of this authority occurred in 213 BCE. At that time, leading senators saw foreign cults as a growing problem that undermined the state religion. One day a group of senators attempted to physically remove a group of cult members who were practicing their religion in the Forum. The crowd in the Forum became angry and attacked the senators, driving them off. The Senate then requested that the praetor *urbanus* suppress the activities of the cults. That magistrate held a *contio* (public meeting) and proclaimed that cult books must be turned in to his office and there would be no more practicing in public.[2] As far as the historical evidence shows, all of the citizens obeyed this command and there were no more incidents of people performing cult rituals in public.

This extraordinary authority and obedience reflects a conservative, deferential society, where the authority of traditional leaders is greatly respected. The patricians and later the nobility were very aware of the value of this deference to authority and were very concerned about conspiracies that might embolden plebeians to ignore the commands of magistrates and act against the established order. For example, the Twelve Tables banned night meetings in the city.[3] The magistrates were not the only representatives of order in the city. There was a group of individuals known as the "*tresviri capitals*" that watched for fires at night and had the power to arrest run away slaves and obvious criminals.[4] However, they did not involve themselves in political or civil disputes between groups of citizens.

While people usually obeyed the commands of high officials, the Romans also had a high tolerance for physical conflict in the practice of politics. There was no police force to rush in and break up an angry crowd in the Forum. As a result, many political differences were played out in angry pushing and shoving matches that would shock a modern citizen. The alternative would have been to give someone or some group the power to wield a police force against individuals or political groups — in Roman eyes the actions of a king or tyrant.[5] The danger of keeping a permanent police force in the city was demonstrated by the crimes of the Praetorian Guard, which was created by the Emperor Augustus to act as a permanent police force to secure his

---

1 Nippel, "Policing Rome," p. 23
2 Nippel, "Policing Rome," p. 21
3 Nippel, "Policing Rome," p. 24
4 Nippel, "Policing Rome," p. 21
5 Nippel, "Policing Rome," p. 25

control in Rome. Within 50 years of its creation, the leaders of the Praetorian Guard were heavily involved in the politics of overthrowing emperors and picking new ones.

HANNIBAL AND THE SECOND PUNIC WAR

The immediate cause of the Second Punic War with Carthage was Hannibal Barca's successful siege of the large, independent city of Saguntine in Spain. Rome, while neglecting to send assistance to the city, sent a delegation to Carthage after its fall in 219 BCE, demanding that Hannibal be turned over to Rome for punishment. When the city's leaders refused, the Senate declared war on Carthage. Rome, which by this time had a far stronger navy than Carthage, prepared to attack Spain and North Africa simultaneously, but Hannibal surprised everyone by successfully moving an army of 20,000 infantrymen and 6,000 cavalry across the Alps in 218. His plan was to defeat the Roman army in Italy, triggering a general uprising of all the people who had been conquered and forced to join the Roman Commonwealth.[1]

At the Trebia River in the Po River Valley, Hannibal met the consul Ti. Sempronius Longus and routed his army. At this, the Gauls in the Po Valley went into revolt and the area slid out of Roman control. The consul Gaius Flaminius then marched up the highway he built, the *Via Flaminia*, and entered Etruria. There, along the shores of Lake Trasimene, he was ambushed and killed along with 15,000 of his soldiers.[2] After a year's pause to train new legions, the consuls of 216, C. Terentius Varro and L. Aemilius Paullus, marched against Hannibal with a combined Roman and allied army of at least 75,000 men. In one of the great disasters in military history, Hannibal surrounded and butchered this army, with up to 50,000 men dying in just one afternoon at Cannae. Paullus was killed, as were an estimated 80 senators.

After this defeat, a number of tribes and cities declared their independence or actually joined Hannibal's army. The Latin allies and cities to the north and west of Rome remained loyal, but the hill tribes of the Samnites, Lucanians, and Brutti all supported Hannibal. Worst of all, two of the largest cities in Italy, Syracuse and Capua declared for Hannibal and he captured the large port city of Tarentum in 212. However, Hannibal could not capture Rome, protected by its sturdy walls, and the Romans would not surrender or negotiate. During this dark period, the strong sense of social harmony in the city kept it united and defiant in the face of repeated defeats.

Rome was able to strike back because Hannibal was unable to get reinforcements from Carthage and his army was too small to defend all of the Italian towns that had come to his side. Even with southern Italy in rebellion,

---

1 Boatwright, *The Romans*, p. 114
2 Matyszak, *Chronicle*, p. 92

Rome still had much greater reserves of trained manpower than Hannibal and was gradually able to capture and sack the rebellious cities. With all of southern Italy devastated by the war and many cities destroyed, the war turned into a grim test of wills.

Rome was able to break out of this stalemate by shattering Carthage's hold on Spain. In 209, a remarkable soldier named Publius Cornelius Scipio captured Carthago Nova, one of the largest cities in Spain and invaded the fertile Baetis River valley in southwestern Spain. Scipio defeated Hannibal's brother, Hasdrubal, who then marched his army across the Alps in an attempt to reinforce his brother's dwindling army. However, he was killed and his army captured in northern Italy. Hannibal's last hope of defeating Rome died with him.

Rome was now strong enough to contain Hannibal in southern Italy while Scipio invaded North Africa. He won several victories and threatened Carthage's food supply. Desperate, Carthage brought Hannibal back to defend the city. The two great generals met at the Battle of Zama in 202 and Scipio won decisively. He returned to Rome, celebrated a great triumph, and added Africanus to his name. Rome imposed a harsh peace upon Carthage. She lost all of her territory except for the land around the city, gave up her naval fleet, and agreed to pay an indemnity of 100 *talents* of silver a year for 50 years. In addition, Rome took the resource-rich land of Spain as another colony.

Defensive Imperialism in Greece

In 200, with their ears still ringing from Scipio Africanus' triumphant parade through Rome, the Senate agreed to help several Greek city-states resist King Philip of Macedonia, who had gained Rome's hatred by signing a treaty with Hannibal.[1] This resort to war so soon after the exhausting struggle with Hannibal has caused much discussion. Some historians believe that the kingdoms of Rhodes and Pergamum, hard pressed by Philip's navy, exaggerated Philip's power by telling the Senate he was allied with Antiochus the Great, the little known, almost mythical king of the Seleucid Empire.[2] Based in Syria, Mesopotamia, and Persia, the Seleucid Empire was one of the largest and most powerful Hellenistic kingdoms created after the death of Alexander the Great. Antiochus had recently returned from a successful campaign against kingdoms in India and was believed to be a great warrior. However, the idea that he and Philip were allies was a deception because the Macedonian kings and the Seleucid kings had been bitter rivals for over a century and Macedonia would never have allowed a Seleucid army into Greece.

---

1 Boatwright, *The Romans*, p. 128
2 Maurice Holleaux, "Preventive Warfare," in Gruen, ed. *Imperialism in the Roman Republic*, New York: holt, Rinehart, Winston, 1970, p. 42

The Roman debates around the declaration of war offers a revealing insight on the role of religion and the central role of defensive imperialism in the city's foreign policy. When the Senate began discussing the question, an *auger* was brought in to interpret how the gods felt about the prospect of a new war. After consulting the *auspices* he reported that there would be "an extension of territory, victory, and a triumph" as a result of the war. This extremely secular message from the gods is a stark example of the political role religion played in the Roman Republic. The Senate, duly impressed by the sentiments of the gods, voted for war, but the citizenry, through a vote in the Centuriate Assembly rejected the motion.[1]

Shortly after this rejection, Philip attacked Athens, an ally of Rome and a city much beloved by those Romans who had come to appreciate the accomplishments of Greek culture. This aggression by Philip gave the consuls a new reason to call a session of the Centuriate Assembly. At this assembly, they argued that if Philip, supported by Antiochus, was to conquer Athens and Pergamum, he would dominate the Aegean Sea and become a dangerous opponent. Given his assistance to Hannibal, Rome might then expect him to cross the narrow seas between Greece and Italy, just as Pyrrhus had eighty years before.[2] The image of Philip following in Pyrrhus' footsteps was a frightening one for Roman citizens and the assembly voted for war.

Rome sent an army of several legions to Greece, led by the ambitious young consul T. Quinctius Flamininus, a descendent of Quinctius Cincinnatus, the man who had returned to his farm after winning a great victory in the 5th century.[3] Flamininus successfully ousted Philip from his strongholds in Greece and inspired many of Philips' Greek allies to change sides. Desperate, Philip attacked Flamininus with 30,000 men aligned in the traditional Greek phalanx. In a hilly area called Cynoscephalae (the dog's head) the more flexible formation of the legions enabled part of Flamininus' army to fall upon the rear of Philips' right wing and destroy it.[4] Flamininus then negotiated a peace that left Macedonia intact, but forced Philip to withdraw from Greece and Asia Minor.

In the power vacuum created by Philip's defeat and the rapid withdrawal of the Roman army from Greece, Antiochus the Great saw an opportunity to replace Philip as the principal power in the Aegean Sea. He marched through Asia Minor, overran the Greek cities around Pergamum, and seized Thrace, the European region on the north side of the Hellespont (the water passage to the Black Sea that separates Asia from Europe). Hoping to rival Rome and Macedonia for influence in Greece, Antiochus played with fire by asking for a peace treaty with Rome, but refusing to leave Thrace. Following the logic

---

1 Scullard, *Roman World*, p. 247

2 Vishnia, *State, Society, Leaders*, p. 161

3 Matyszak, *Chronicle*, p. 107

4 Garrett G. Fagan, *Great Battles of the Ancient World*, Chantilly, VA: The Teaching Company, 2005, p. 30

---

of defensive imperialism, Rome could not allow Antiochus to threaten her new sphere of influence in Greece and refused to bargain with the king unless he withdrew from Europe.

At this delicate point, the Aetolian League attacked their old enemy Sparta and invited Antiochus to send an army to assist them. Seeking to cement his relationships with these Greek cities, Antiochus made a fatal error and sent a small army of about 10,000 men.[1] Rome immediately sent several legions to Greece and defeated the Syrians and the Aetolian League at Thermopylae, forcing the Seleucid king to evacuate Greece and Thrace. Antiochus was now willing to give up his claim to Thrace, but it was too late. The aroused Romans sent an army commanded by L. Cornelius Scipio, the brother of Scipio Africanus, into Asia Minor and, at Magnesia in 189 BCE, the Romans crushed a huge Seleucid army.[2] To prevent a Roman invasion of Syria and the destruction of his dynasty, Antiochus was forced to give up all of his claims to Asia Minor and Greece, surrender his ships and war elephants, and pay an enormous indemnity of 15,000 *talents* of silver over 15 years.

As the dominant military power in the region, Rome at first treated the cities of Greece and Asia Minor as independent client states. Roman *equites* poured into the rich cities of the Hellenistic world while the Senate sent envoys to Greek cities to meddle in their internal political squabbles. Then, nationalists in Macedonia and several Greek city-states tried to escape from Rome's grasp and the legions had to be used to crush a series of revolts. By 151 BCE, Macedonia was a Roman province and the rest of Greece was closely supervised by Roman officials.

* * *

Over the course of 100 years the Roman Republic acquired an overseas empire with colonial administrations ruling Spain, Sicily, Corsica, Sardinia, Macedonia. The small states of Pergamum, Rhodes, Carthage, and Numibia, eager to avoid the complete loss of their independence, adjusted their foreign and domestic policies according to Rome's desires. In the long run, a policy of defensive imperialism, when you are the strongest military power in the world, is a policy of conquest, one border dispute at a time. The new empire would soon generate dramatic changes in Roman society and Roman politics. However, before we examine those changes, it is time for us to take a longer look at the American Republic and the overseas empire it began to develop at the close of the 19th century. Like its ancient counterpart, the new American Republic was bursting with energy and expansionist fever. Like the Roman Republic, it went from being a minor nation to a world colossus in a mere 100 years.

---

1 Scullard, *Roman World*, p. 263
2 Boatwright, *The Romans*, p. 130

Chapter 6. Origins of the American Empire

A new consciousness seems to have come upon us — the consciousness of strength — and with it a new appetite, the yearning to show our strength …. Ambition, interest, land hunger, pride, the mere joy of fighting, whatever it may be, we are animated by a new sensation. We are face to face with a strange destiny. The taste of Empire is in the mouth of the people even as the taste of blood in the jungle….[1]

> — Editorial in the Washington DC newspaper, *The Post*, on the eve of war, 1898

John Milton Hay was smart, he was good looking, and he was witty, but most of all he was lucky. Drifting after graduating from Brown University in the spring of 1858, he finally decided to clerk in his uncle's law office in Springfield, Illinois in 1859. There, he became friends with John G. Nicolay, personal secretary for Springfield's most famous lawyer, Abraham Lincoln. When they moved to the White House, Nicolay convinced the new President that Hay would be a useful assistant.[2]

Cheerful and outgoing, able to mix easily with all types of people, Hay became a friend and confidant of the President. Lincoln treated him like a son and Hay, who looked younger than his early 20s, viewed him with intense admiration. He wrote a letter to John Nicolay in September of 1863, "The old man sits here and wields like a backwoods Jupiter the bolts of war

---

1 Zinn, *20th Century*, p. 3
2 Available from www.mrlincolnswhitehouse.org, "Relatives and Residents: John Hay"; accessed 22 July 2007

and the machinery of government with a hand especially steady and equally firm."[1] As someone perceived as having great influence with the President, politicians, businessmen, and generals were happy to dine with Hay. This made him an importance source of information for the President and a person who could be trusted to deliver messages discretely. A good conversationalist who also knew how to listen, Hay made friendships that would serve him well over the course of his life.

Hay also came to appreciate and share Lincoln's dislike of the costs of war:

> One of the most tender and compassionate of men, he was forced to give orders which cost thousands of lives; by nature a man of order and thrift, he saw the daily spectacle of unutterable waste and destruction which he could not prevent. The cry of the widow and the orphan was always in his ears; the awful responsibility resting upon him as the protector of an imperiled republic kept him true to his duty, but could not make him unmindful of the intimate details of that vast sum of human misery involved in civil war.[2]

Just weeks before being assassinated, Lincoln appointed him secretary to the diplomatic mission in Paris. This launched him on an on-again, off-again diplomatic career that spanned the rest of the century. A few years later, as a diplomat in Spain, Hay conveyed the American government's unhappiness with the Spanish government's brutal treatment of a rebellion on the island of Cuba.[3] Hay then came home and for several years was one of the most accomplished editorial page writers for Horace Greeley's influential *New York Tribune*. His luck held out again when he married a wealthy businessman's daughter and moved to Cleveland. When his father-in law died, Hay inherited his fortune, increased it through shrewd investments, and became a major donor to Republican candidates in Ohio. When Hay was appointed Assistant Secretary of State for President Rutherford Hayes, he moved to Washington D.C. and became close friends with the era's leading American intellectual, Henry Adams. Through Adams, Hay came to know a wide range of politicians and intellectuals, including Theodore Roosevelt and Henry Cabot Lodge (who would soon be elected to represent Massachusetts in the US Senate).

Ohio was the training ground for presidents in the late 19th century; five of the seven presidents in that period — Grant, Hayes, Garfield, Harrison, and McKinley were from Ohio. Hay was especially close to William McKinley, paying off a bad loan to help him avoid bankruptcy just before the former

---

1 Available from www.mrlincolnswhitehouse.org, "Relatives and Residents: John Hay"; accessed 22 July 2007
2 Warren Zimmermann, *First Great Triumph: How Five Americans Made their Country a World Power*, New York: Farrar, Straus, and Giroux, 2002, p. 47
3 Zimmermann, *First Triumph*, p. 56

major in the Union army won election as governor of Ohio.[1] When McKinley won the presidential election of 1896, he asked Hay to be his ambassador to England. The former presidential assistant presented his credentials to the King in the spring of 1897.

THE DESIRE FOR MARKETS

The year 1897 proved to be pivotal. In that year, a number of social, political, military, and economic trends converged to create the conditions for a totally new type of expansion overseas. The first of these trends was the closing of the American frontier. For a century, the American Republic had put much of its energy into expanding across the vast North American continent. Then, in 1890, the Bureau of the Census announced that the frontier was closed; the continent was now a settled area. Shortly after that, in 1893, the failure of the Philadelphia and Reading Railroad set off a financial panic and the country collapsed into a frightening economic slump.

> "Never before," judged the *Commercial and Financial Chronicle* in August of 1893, "has there been such a sudden and striking cessation of industrial activity . . . Mills, factories, furnaces, mines nearly everywhere shut down in large numbers . . . and hundreds of thousands of men [were] thrown out of employment."[2]

During previous economic downturns the impact of poor economic conditions was softened by the self-sufficient nature of most of the work done in the United States. In the first half of the 19th century, most of the country's citizens were farmers who grew their own food and made many of the products they used. Towns were primarily populated with craftsmen who sold goods and services that local people needed no matter what the general economic climate. However, after the Civil War more and more workers and farmers produced for markets in other parts of the country. The furious building of railroads in the US linked the farms of the mid-West to markets in the east and vice versa, creating a much greater level of interdependence. In addition, a much larger percentage of workers labored for large corporations producing goods for markets all over the country.

As a result, in the 1890s, a significant percentage of the population depended for its livelihood on being able to sell what they produced in markets that were far away from where they lived and worked. With the Depression, farmers could not sell their wheat and the factories had no market for the shiny products of the industrial age. To prevent their factories and mines from going bankrupt, the owners resorted to slashing wages, a desperate measure that frequently led to strikes by angry workers. In Pullman, Illi-

---

1 Zimmermann, *First Triumph*, p. 81
2 William A. Williams, *The Tragedy of American Diplomacy*, New York: W.W. Norton and Company,1959, p. 29

nois, George Pullman reduced the number of men he had building Pullman sleeping cars for the railroads and cut the remaining workers' wages by 33 to 50 percent.[1] The workers walked out and asked Eugene Debs to have his American Railways Union support a boycott of Pullman sleeping cars. More than 100,000 men went on strike. Over the protests of the governor of Illinois, Democratic President Grover Cleveland sent federal troops to occupy Chicago, crush the strike, and imprison Debs. While this enormous struggle was going on, there were 30 other major strikes in workplaces all across the country.[2]

To preserve social peace and pull the economy out of its stagnant condition, businessmen, farmers, and politicians began to talk about the need to find new markets for American goods. With crops rotting in the field and factories idle, the immediate assumption was that Americans were producing too many goods for the domestic market to absorb. In 1897, Senator Albert Beveridge of Indiana summed up many people's thoughts, "American factories are making more than the American people can use; American soil is producing more than they can consume. Fate has written our policy for us; the trade of the world must and shall be ours."[3] The agitation for political action to open markets for American goods came from two types of people. The first group consisted of trade associations, people who said they needed more markets for a particular product, be it steel or shoes or wheat or beef. Editorials in *Scientific American*, *Iron Age*, and *Engineering Magazine* made the case for manufacturers of the products they wrote about needing more foreign markets.[4]

American intellectuals produced more general reasons why the Republic, as a whole, needed to find new markets and outlets for its energies. Frederick Jackson Turner, a professor at the University of Wisconsin, was the most prominent of these theorists. Turner claimed that the essence of America was its drive to develop the continental frontier. He then linked the closing of the frontier with the economic downturn and forecast a new future for the Republic:

> That these energies of expansion will no longer operate would be a rash prediction; and the demands for a vigorous foreign policy, for an interoceanic canal, for a revival of our power upon the seas, and for the extension of American influence to outlying islands and adjoining countries, are indications that the movement will continue.[5]

1 James Chace, *1912: Wilson, Roosevelt, Taft, & Debs, The Election that Changed the Country*, New York: Simon & Schuster, 2004, p. 76

2 Williams, *Tragedy*, p. 29

3 Howard Zinn, *The Twentieth Century: A People's History*, Cambridge: Harper and Row, Publishers, 1984, p. 3

4 Williams, *Tragedy*, p. 31

5 Zimmermann, *First Triumph*, p. 24

Another intellectual who supported expansion was Brooks Adams, grandson of John Quincy Adams, and the brother of Henry Adams. He was a friend of men like Theodore Roosevelt, Senator Henry Cabot Lodge, and John Hay, so his ideas were probably more influential than others. He theorized that expansion was the key for any society to continue to be wealthy and warned that the US would "stagnate" if it did not firmly take hold of Latin American and exploit the riches of Asia.[1]

The somewhat belligerent tone of these remarks is more understandable in the context of 19th century international trade. Most of the world that anxious Americans looked to for markets had already been carved up into colonies and "spheres of influence" by the European powers. Great Britain alone had colonies and protectorates covering one-quarter of the earth's surface and fully monopolized trade with those areas. France, Germany, Portugal, and Russia also had colonial holdings with markets that were closed to American commerce. Merchants from the United States could, of course, trade with France, Russia, Japan, and other industrial countries, but these countries used tariffs on industrial goods and food products to protect their own domestic producers.[2] As a result, only Latin America, China, some islands in the Pacific, and a few places in Asia and the Middle East were, in fact, open to a significant expansion of American trade.

NAVAL POWER AND TRADE

At this point the developments we identified earlier — the closing of the American frontier, a nasty economic slump, and demands for an expansion of foreign trade — combined with a new trend in military thinking. All of the European colonial powers were placing a growing emphasis on naval power in the mad scramble to increase a nation's wealth through international trade. Before the mid-19th century, writings about naval warfare emphasized the ability to control the seas and send armies to conquer a desired territory. Captain A.T. Mahan of the US Navy updated naval theory by emphasizing how command of the seas would facilitate trade and make a nation wealthy and powerful. Of course, nations like Britain and France were following this strategy as early as the 18th century, but Mahan was the first writer to bring together many partial ideas and present them as a cohesive, persuasive theory. In the process Mahan gave special force to the idea that sea power is the principal way for nations to develop wealth and power through foreign trade:

> The due use and control of the sea is but one link in the chain of exchange by which wealth accumulates; but it is the central link, which lays under

---

1 Williams, *Tragedy*, p. 33

2 Stephen Kinzer, *Overthrow: America's Century of Regime Change from Hawaii to Iraq*, New York: Henry Holt and Company, 2004, p 34

contribution [sic] other nations for the benefit of the one holding it, and which, history seems to assert, most surely of all gathers riches.[1]

We need not concern ourselves here with Mahan's debates with other military scholars about the relative value of sea power versus military units on land; rather the interesting point is that in the 1890s "journalists, admirals, and statesmen hung upon his predictions and accepted his teachings as a virtually complete doctrine of power-politics."[2]

Mahan was celebrated in Britain, but his main impact was on the United States, where those who wanted to capture overseas markets seized on his work. In 1886, Mahan was teaching at the new Naval War College and needed a guest lecturer on the War of 1812. He brought in a young politician who had written a well-regarded book on naval combat in the War of 1812 during his undergraduate years at Harvard. Theodore Roosevelt's lectures were a big hit on campus and he and Mahan struck up a life-long friendship.[3] By 1890 he was corresponding with Senator Henry Cabot Lodge, a good friend of Roosevelt's, and they managed to get him transferred to the Naval Department in Washington so he could talk about his ideas with other leaders in the capital.[4] Shortly after this, Lodge wrote in a popular magazine:

> In the interests of our commerce . . . we should build the Nicaragua canal [on the isthmus of Panama] and for the protection of that canal and for the sake of our commercial supremacy in the Pacific we should control the Hawaiian islands and maintain our influence in Samoa . . . and when the Nicaraguan canal is built, the island of Cuba . . . will become a necessity.[5]

The most immediate outcome of this type of sentiment was a large increase in expenditures for the navy. In 1890 federal spending on the navy amounted to just seven percent of the budget, but by 1914 the $139 million for naval expenses amounted to 19 percent of the federal budget.[6]

One practical aspect of naval power will be of growing importance as we examine the new American empire. Naval fleets in the late 19th century burned coal and had to be constantly re-fueled in order to maintain their swift movement around the world's oceans. As a consequence, the acquisition of friendly ports for naval bases and coaling stations was a pre-requisite for any self-respecting naval power.[7] One is struck, when glancing at a map charting British naval bases and colonies, by the intricate web of coaling stations and friendly ports that were the backbone of the British Empire.[8] American leaders, eager to develop their own naval presence, must have care-

---

1 Paul M. Kennedy, *The Rise and Fall of British Naval Mastery*, London: Ashfield Press, 1976, p. 7
2 Kennedy, *British Mastery*, p. 183
3 Zimmermann, *First Triumph*, p. 92
4 Zinn, *20th Century*, p. 3
5 Zinn, *20th Century*, p. 2
6 Paul M. Kennedy, *The Rise and Fall of the Great Powers*, New York: Random House, 1987, p. 247
7 Kennedy, *British Mastery*, p. 182
8 Kennedy, *British Mastery*, p. 207

fully studied maps of the British Empire because they imitated the British example wherever possible. For example, Robert M. La Follette (who later became a critic of empire) began his political career in 1897, one year before the Spanish American War, by calling for a larger navy and by suggesting "Spain's island possessions throughout the world would provide excellent bases for the fleet."[1]

The growing clamor for overseas markets and the rising desire for naval power came together to create a near obsession with China. The United States had already prospered from trade with China; the speedy clipper ships that raced from New England around the Strait of Magellan to China and back had made ports like Salem and Marblehead as wealthy as New York and Philadelphia in the antebellum period. In April of 1898, the State Department published a "Review of the World's Commerce" claiming that the key to increasing foreign trade was preventing other powers from excluding US companies and products from China. That vast underdeveloped nation, "has, for many years been one of the most promising fields for American enterprise, industry, and capital."[2]

When the report was issued, the door to the last promising market for American exports was rapidly closing. In 1894, the Japanese easily defeated China in a brief war and established a protectorate over Korea and Taiwan. In 1897, Germany seized the important port of Kiao-chao and was given extensive trade rights in the surrounding area by the weakening Chinese government. France had already taken control of French Indo-China (now Vietnam and Laos) and Britain had grabbed Hong Kong and other trading cities along the Yangtze River. American leaders grew more and more alarmed as the newly crowned queen of trade was gradually closed to American merchants.

Well before the 1890s, the United States had made a number of efforts to create a "bridge" across the Pacific in order to be a bigger player in the China trade game. In 1853 Commodore Matthew Perry sailed into Tokyo harbor and bullied the Japanese into signing a commercial treaty. That had not resulted in significant amounts of trade or the acquisition of a naval base because the Japanese reacted quickly to this humiliation and initiated what is called the Meiji Restoration, a nation-wide modernization effort that led to the Japanese industrializing in less than 50 years. In 1871, five US navy warships attacked and captured forts at the mouth of the River Han in Korea. They hoped to force the Koreans into opening their markets and perhaps

1 Williams, *Tragedy*, p. 34
2 Williams, *Tragedy*, p. 49

provide the US with a naval base close to China.[1] The Koreans, however, fought back fiercely and the navy had to retreat empty-handed.

The biggest imperial success was in Hawaii. American businessmen flooded those islands during the second half of the 19th century, creating sugar plantations, warehouses, and docks. They soon dominated the islands' economy and the country's unsophisticated legislature. During the 1880s native Hawaiians, the Kanaka, began to resent foreign domination and called for "Hawaii for Hawaiians."[2] When Queen Liliuokalani assumed the throne, after the death of her brother, she sided with the native Hawaiians. This outraged American residents and an armed band took over the government building and abolished the Hawaiian monarchy. When Hawaiians loyal to the Queen tried to take back the building, they found that the US minister to Hawaii, John L. Stevens, had sent marines from the nearby cruiser Boston to protect the new government.[3]

To his credit, President Cleveland refused to approve a treaty annexing Hawaii and even attempted to restore the Queen. However, Americans on the island refused to yield and instead, made Hawaii an independent country. Congress supported the usurpers and Cleveland decided not to press the issue. Theodore Roosevelt called Cleveland's lack of support for the rebels "a crime against white civilization."[4] In 1898, after the US victory in the Spanish-American War, Republican President William McKinley, approved a treaty annexing Hawaii and securing the Pearl Harbor naval base.

AMERICA'S DESTINY

Mixing with the desire for new foreign markets and the ambition to build fleets and secure naval bases was a potent social brew of ideas about white America's duty and destiny. During the 19th century, expansion across the American continent was widely seen as the young Republic's "manifest destiny." As with the young Roman Republic, there was sense that Republican government, in which every citizen was a participant in the nation's destiny, was unleashing a primal human energy. Many writers thought that this burst of energy and creativity was making the United States a beacon for other people. For example, the first journalist to use the phrase manifest destiny was John O'Sullivan who wrote about the country's "boundless future" and said:

---

1 James A. Field Jr., *History of U.S. Naval Operations: Korea*, Dept. of the Navy, Naval Historical Center, available from www.history.navy.mil/books/field/chla.htm; accessed 25 March 2007
2 Small Planet Communications, Expansion in the Pacific, available from www.smplanet.com/imperialism/hawaii.html; accessed 25 March 2007
3 Small Planet Communications, *Expansion in the Pacific*, available from www.smplanet.com/imperialism/hawaii.html; accessed 25 March 2007
4 Zinn, *20th Century*, p. 4

For this blessed mission to the nations of the world, which are shut out from the life-giving light of truth, has America been chosen; and her high example shall smite unto death the tyranny of kings, hierarchs, and oligarchs, and carry the glad tidings of peace and good will where myriads now endure an existence scarcely more enviable than that of beasts of the field.[1]

O'Sullivan's poetic vision shows that this notion was not merely a crass attempt to expand the nation's power and influence. The spread of Republican institutions across the continent was, for many people, a moral crusade, providing an example to the world of how people could and should live. Then, as the century went on, America became more than an example; people from other lands immigrated to the United States eager to participate in the opening up of the continent. The rising tide of immigration into the United States, with people quite visibly voting with their feet in favor of participating in the new society, reinforced the idea that the world's people preferred the American way of life. America became the world's melting pot and a beacon of liberty — recall the words carved on the Statue of Liberty in the 1880s; they evoke a remarkable vision of the United States and its place in the world:

> Give me your tired, your poor,
> Your huddled masses, yearning to breathe free,
> The wretched refuse of your teeming shores.
> Send these, the homeless, tempest-tossed to me.
> I lift my lamp beside the golden door.

It is a marvelous vision, one that still inspires immigrants from every nation, more than a century after the statue was dedicated in New York's harbor. However, in the process of marveling at the country's accomplishments and place in world opinion, 19th century political and intellectual leaders began to confuse the phenomenon of individuals voluntarily coming to the United States to seek liberty with the quite different notion of the US imposing liberty on individuals living in their native lands. This confusion is evident in a statement by the progressive reformer Robert M. La Follette, who supported the annexation of the Philippines and claimed that the American Republic had always sought to expand, which was a good thing, because "it has made men free."[2]

As was pointed out in chapter 5, the westward expansion made it possible for white immigrants to be free of old world ties and despotism, but it certainly did not make Native Americans free. Liberty does not exist in a vacuum. A crucial dimension of liberty is the freedom to choose how to live,

1 Quoted in Zimmermann, *First Triumph*, p. 33
2 Williams, *Tragedy*, p. 62

to decide what values and social norms and political institutions one wants to embrace. If the freedom to choose is to be real, then the choices too, must be real, that is, there must be more than one. As a consequence of living in different parts of this diverse planet for hundreds of generations, humans have created a variety of cultural and social experiences. Within those different experiences individuals may decide to improve or reform various dimensions of the experience, but they seldom reject the entire way of life. Thus, for it to be genuine, liberty must find its place within the old way of life. For this reason, liberty cannot be imposed on a people if, in the process, the rest of the way of life is overturned. This American confusion about liberty and choice continues today in Iraq, as Democrats and Republicans remain perplexed by the failure of Sunnis and Shiites to embrace the liberties the Bush administration has so generously imposed on them.

Unfortunately, the underside of Manifest Destiny was a racial contempt for non-white people who supposedly did not possess the character needed to fully live the American way of life. Perhaps most shocking of all was the dominance of racist ideas in the elite universities of 19th century America. For example, at Harvard University, Nathaniel Southgate Shaler, who was one of the leading professors on campus, taught about white supremacy stemming from the racial heritage of England.[1] Professor James Hosmer of John Hopkins University said "The primacy of the world lies with us. English institutions, English speech, English thought, are to become the main features of the political, social, and intellectual life of mankind."[2] Darwin's ideas about natural selection lent a scientific aura to racial ideas claiming that individuals or nations that were successful, as Great Britain clearly was in the 19th century, were superior to other people and societies. Since many of the country's political leaders attended these institutions of higher learning, and because they set a tone for other colleges and for magazines and other media, the American political elite of the 1890s believed that their racial prejudices were based on widely acknowledged, sound, scientific, intellectual principles.

As a result, ideas about the white race's superiority were openly expressed in the 1890s. Senator Albert Beveridge of Indiana thought the expansion of American rule was a step forward in human history because it meant "the disappearance of debased civilizations and decaying races before the higher civilization of the nobler and more virile types of man."[3] When Representative Charles Cochrane of Mississippi predicted "the conquest of the world by the Aryan races," the House of Representatives burst into applause.[4]

---

1 Zimmermann, *First Triumph*, p. 35
2 Zimmermann, *First Triumph*, p. 36
3 Kinzer, *Overthrow*, p. 84
4 Kinzer, *Overthrow*, p. 84

By 1897 then, the need for more markets to pull the country out of severe economic conditions, the desire to expand the nation's power by constructing a fleet and acquiring naval bases, and the idea that conquest brought liberty and civilization to barbarian peoples, all combined to lead the United States to ignore President Washington's warning against "foreign entanglements." All that was needed was an opportunity to jump into the imperial arena. That opportunity came just 90 miles from the Florida coast.

THE SPANISH AMERICAN WAR

The vast Spanish Empire of the 17th and 18th centuries had shrunk to just Cuba, Puerto Rico, the Philippine Islands, and a few islands in the Pacific by the middle of the nineteenth century. While US ambassador John Hay had urged Spain to grant Cuban independence, elements of the Spanish ruling elites were determined to hang on to their last colonial possessions. In 1895, with the *grito de Baire*, a call to arms, Jose Marti returned to Cuba and ignited another round of guerrilla war.[1] In 1896 in the Philippines, Andres Bonifacio, leader of the group called Katipunan, issued the *grito de Balintawak* and began a guerrilla war in that Spanish colony. Marti and Bonifacio were both killed at early stages in the fighting, but their movements continued the struggle for independence.

Americans were keenly interested in the Cuban conflict. US agricultural companies had invested more than $50 million on the island and a thriving trade was being disrupted by the guerrilla war.[2] Naval and political planners had already identified Cuba as a fine location for naval bases that would facilitate control of the Caribbean. Finally, public opinion, which had always favored the anti-colonial flavor of the rebellion, was inflamed by the Spanish anti-guerrilla policy of *Reconcentration*. *Reconcentration* involved moving most of the Cuban population to camps controlled by the Spanish army and putting the rest of the island under martial law.[3] The policy was disastrous; an estimated 30% of the individuals in the camps died from unsanitary conditions and inadequate food supplies, a well-reported fact in the American "yellow press." With tensions growing, President McKinley decided to put pressure on the Spanish by sending the battleship USS Maine to Havana. When the Maine mysteriously blew up on February 15, 1898, war became inevitable.

The public rallied to the war, dazzled by the shining promise of Cuban independence. When the US Senate declared war in April of 1898, Senator

---

1 Library of Congress; *The World of 1898: The Spanish American War*, available from www.loc.gov/rr/hispanic/1898/intro.html; accessed 22 March 2007

2 Zimmermann, *First Triumph*, p. 250

3 Library of Congress; *The World of 1898: The Spanish American War*, "Reconcentration," available from www.loc.gov/rr/hispanic/1898/intro.html; accessed 22 March 2007

Henry M. Teller of Colorado had an amendment attached to the declaration stating that the United States:

> hereby disclaims any disposition of intention to exercise sovereignty, jurisdiction, or control over said island except for pacification thereof, and asserts its determination, when that is accomplished, to leave the government and control of the island to its people.[1]

With the declaration of war, Commodore George Dewey, who had been put in command of the Pacific fleet at the urging of Roosevelt, immediately left from Hong Kong with the Filipino leader Emilio Aguinaldo on board his flagship. Just six days after the declaration of war he destroyed the Spanish fleet in Manila Bay and re-united Aguinaldo with his rebel soldiers. While Dewey blockaded the harbor, the guerrillas harassed the Spanish garrison until US troops could arrive and storm the city. Meanwhile, a small army of American soldiers landed near Santiago, Cuba, the island's capital and second largest city in mid-June of 1898. They successfully stormed the fort on the San Juan heights while Lt. Colonel Theodore Roosevelt led the Rough Riders to victory on nearby Kettle Hill. With his ships in danger from shore-based artillery, the Spanish admiral had to sail his fleet out of the harbor where it was defeated and captured by a superior American force. With no fleet, the Spanish army was blockaded on the island and the war was effectively over in mid-July of 1898.

The Peace Treaty of Paris was signed in December of 1898. The treaty gave Cuba, Puerto Rico, and Guam to the United States, and arranged for Spain to sell the Philippines to the US for $20 million. In one stroke, the American Republic established US naval dominance of the Caribbean and, with bases on Midway, Samoa, and Hawaii, projected American power across the Pacific to the gates of China.

At first it had not been certain that the US would annex the Philippines. While the Senate was debating the new treaty in February of 1899, Rudyard Kipling published a famous poem encouraging America to annex the islands. The first verse went like this:

Take up the White Man's burden
Send forth the best ye breed,
Go; bind your sons to exile
To serve your captives' need;
To wait, in heavy harness,
On fluttered folk and wild,
Your new-caught sullen peoples,
Half-devil and half-child.[2]

---

1 Library of Congress; *The World of 1898: The Spanish American War,* "Teller and Platt Amendments," available from www.loc.gov/rr/hispanic/1898/teller.html; accessed 25 March 2007.
2 Kinzer, *Overthrow,* p. 83

After the Treaty of Paris was signed and the Philippines became an American colony, Emilio Aguinaldo, leader of the rebel army in the island, led a guerrilla war against the United States that lasted four years. Aguinaldo was defeated only after between 100,000 and 200,000 Filipinos had died from starvation, disease, and battlefield massacres. Mark Twain, Vice-President of the Anti-Imperialist League which opposed the occupation, said the American flag should be changed with "the white stripes painted black and the stars replaced by skull and crossbones."[1]

In addition, all was not well in Cuba. While Cuban freedom was a rallying cry during the war, interest in Cuban independence was actually quite low in ruling circles in the United States. Whitelaw Reid, the publisher of the *New York Tribune* wrote about "the absolute necessity of controlling Cuba for our own defense."[2] While the American people had supported the war to free Cuba from Spanish rule, political and economic leaders were leery of the rebels' program of land reform and controlling natural resources.[3] In addition, after years of rebellion, the Cubans were unlikely to allow foreign naval bases on their shores so soon after independence. To give notice about who was really in charge on the island, no Cubans were allowed to participate in the Paris Peace Conference, the rebel army was not allowed to march in the victory parade through Santiago, and a US military governor ruled the island in place of the promised Cuban-led government.[4]

The abrupt change of attitude in US political circles was articulated clearly by the *New York Times*, which said in an editorial that the United States should become "permanent possessors of Cuba if the Cubans prove to be altogether incapable of self-government."[5] Given the racial differences between Cubans and the white majority in the United States, deciding the answer to this question turned out to be not that difficult for US policy makers. Two out of five of people on the island were black, while another significant percentage was of mixed racial heritage.[6] It was easy for American leaders to compare the Cubans to other peoples who were not considered capable of self-government. Senator Beveridge of Indiana told an audience "Self-government only applies to those who are capable of self-government. We govern the Indians without their consent. We govern the territories without their consent. We govern our children without their consent."[7] Senior US officers had contempt for the ragged rebel army, especially for the many black

1 Kinzer, *Overthrow*, p. 54

2 Kinzer, *Overthrow*, p. 40

3 Kinzer, *Overthrow*, p. 36

4 Zimmermann, *First Triumph*, p. 294

5 Kinzer, *Overthrow*, p. 40

6 Zinn, *20th Century*, p. 7

7 William Loren Katz, *Current Essays*, "Imperialism and Race: Iraq (2006) and the Philippines (1906)," available from www.williamlkatz.com; accessed 22 March 2007.

soldiers in its ranks. Brigadier General Samuel Young dismissed the Cuban army as "a lot of degenerates, absolutely devoid of honor or gratitude . . . no more capable of self-government that the savages of Africa."[1]

In practice, General John Brook and later General Leonard Wood ran a military occupation of the island. Unlike the Philippines, there was no guerilla war because General Maximo Gomes, commander of the Cuban army and a respected war hero, decided that armed resistance would only create more suffering in a country exhausted from four years of bloody fighting.[2] With peace, business followed the flag: United Fruit bought 1,900,000 acres of land at 20 cents per acre, Bethlehem Steel bought mineral rights all over the island, and other companies built and owned Cuba's railroads.[3] That the Cubans resented the American occupation astonished correspondents from the United States. They told their American audiences that this resentment was proof of the Cubans' "ignorance and immaturity."[4]

Given the pre-war promises that the United States would grant Cuba its independence in the near future, US leaders were caught in a dilemma. As Secretary of War Elihu Root put it "The trouble with Cuba is that, although technically a foreign country, practically and morally it occupies an intermediate position, since we have required it to become a part of our political and military system, and to form a part of our lines of exterior defense."[5] Conflict was inevitable because the American idea of what the Cuban government should be like clashed dramatically with the social reform visions held by Cuban leaders. The island's military governor, Leonard Wood, wrote to President McKinley "When people ask me what I mean by stable government, I tell them, 'Money at six percent.'"[6]

To ensure that Cuba had money at six percent and remained part of the United States' "lines of exterior defense," Secretary of War Elihu Root and Senator Orville Platt of Connecticut proposed a law that came to be known as the Platt Amendment. The Amendment stipulated that the United States would end its military occupation of Cuba if the Cubans adopted a constitution that gave the United States the right to have military bases on the island, to veto treaties between Cuba and other nations, and to supervise the Cuban treasury. The final blow came in a fourth provision, which gave the United States "the right to intervene for the preservation of Cuban independence [or] the maintenance of a government adequate for the protection of life, property, and individual liberty."[7]

---

1 Zimmermann, *First Triumph*, p. 294
2 Zimmermann, *First Triumph*, p. 372
3 Zinn, *20th Century*, p 14
4 Kinzer, *Overthrow*, p. 42
5 Zimmermann, *First Triumph*, p. 374
6 Kinzer, *Overthrow*, p 42
7 Kinzer, *Overthrow*, p. 43

When it was passed in the Republican-controlled Senate by a vote of 43-20, the reaction in Cuba was stormy, but non-violent. A huge crowd marched through Santiago in a torchlight procession to protest the Senate's high-handed action. Municipal governments flooded the capital with protest resolutions and calls for the Cuban constitutional convention to reject the US demands.[1] A committee established to consider the country's options called the demand for military bases "a mutilation of the fatherland."[2] Not surprisingly, the convention rejected the Platt Amendment. The US response was to insist that the island would remain under military rule until the amendment was accepted. So, with few options, the convention, after three months of haggling, voted to include the Platt Amendment in the Cuban constitution by a vote of 16-11.

The United State immediately began building a permanent naval base on the eastern end of the island at Guantanamo Bay — the lease contained no termination date. The threat of intervention was not an idle one; in 1906 a political crisis over a rigged election brought US marines and a military governor back to the island for two years. US marines would later use the right of intervention to take over the island and the Cuban government in 1912, 1917, and 1920.[3] While the Platt Amendment was removed from the Cuban constitution in 1934, the ill will it fostered lasted into the 1950s when another revolutionary movement overthrew the US-backed dictator Fulgencio Batista. When the movement's leader made his first speech to the people of Santiago, Fidel Castro said, "This time the revolution will not be frustrated! This time, fortunately for Cuba, the revolution will achieve its true objective. It will not be like 1898, when the Americans came and made themselves masters of the country."[4]

THE OPEN DOOR POLICY

Even as it struggled to put down the rebellion in the Philippines, the American Republic began the process of cracking open the Chinese market for American merchants. This market was rapidly closing as Russia, Britain, France, Japan, Germany, and Italy claimed "spheres of influence" in the ancient kingdom. With a greatly enlarged fleet, naval bases all through the Pacific, and a crushing defeat of former European power Spain under its belt, the McKinley administration would try to preserve free trade in China.

To pull together his post-war foreign policy, President McKinley asked John Hay to become Secretary of State. Hay was reluctant because his health

---

1 Kinzer, *Overthrow*, p. 43

2 Zinn, *20th Century*, p. 15

3 Chalmers Johnson, *Sorrows of Empire: Militarism, Secrecy, and the End of the Republic*, New York: Metropolitan Books, 2004, p. 41

4 Kinzer, *Overthrow*, p. 90

was not good, but his friend Henry Adams urged him to serve the nation, so he took up office in the fall of 1898. Hay proved to be a vital counter-balance to the military ambitions of other members of the Republican Party like Roosevelt, Lodge, and Secretary of Defense Elihu Root. His understanding of the human costs of war, nurtured during his service with Lincoln, led him instinctually to see war as a last resort. In addition, he did not "accept the primacy of the military and strategic factors that energized Mahan, Roosevelt, and Lodge."[1] For Hay, a business leader and intellectual from Ohio, the main goal of American foreign policy was to secure a level playing field for the highly efficient corporations that dominated the country's economy. In this he was reflecting the views of Republican industrialists.[2]

When Germany and Britain reached a vague agreement about German rights to exploit the Chinese port of Kiao-chao in the summer of 1899, Hay sent out the first set of "Open Door" Notes to the Kaiser's foreign minister. After saying that he was "Earnestly desirous to remove any cause of irritation...," he gently pointed out to the German government that the US government wanted (read this slowly to catch the subtle diplomatic phrasing):

> to insure at the same time to the commerce of all nations in China the undoubted benefits which should accrue from a formal recognition by the various powers claiming "spheres of interest" that they [all nations active in China] shall enjoy perfect equality of treatment for their commerce and navigation within such "spheres,"[3]

That is, Hay wanted assurances from all of the colonial powers in China that, within their spheres of influence, they would not charge special tariffs on goods being landed from ships of other nationalities or charge special fees when railroads they controlled were used to ship these products to other markets in China. This, of course, would negate much of the benefit of having a "sphere of influence." Similar notes were sent to all of the other governments occupying parts of China. Unwilling to offend the new American power, they all politely expressed interest in such a concept, but quietly declined to officially agree. Hay then boldly announced in March of 1900 that all of the powers had agreed to fair trade rules in China.[4] It was the beginning of the "Open Door" Policy.

The Boxer Rebellion, which began in late 1899 and reached its peak when the Boxers besieged foreign diplomats and military personnel in Beijing in the summer of 1900, showed that western pressure on China was precipitating the break down of the tottering Ch'ing Dynasty (until recently it was

1 Zimmermann, *First Triumph*, p. 426

2 Williams, Tragedy, p. 50

3 *From Revolution to Reconstruction: An .HTML Project,* "Documents: The First Open Door Note 1899,"; available from www.odur.let.rug.nl/~usa/D/1876-1900/foreignpolicy/opendr.htm; accessed 26 March 2007

4 Zimmermann, *First Triumph*, p. 447

known as the Manchu Dynasty). In the aftermath of the rebellion's collapse, John Hay sought to preserve the Chinese market by shielding the crumbling dynasty from the nations that had teamed up to crush the Boxers. That fall he issued the second set of Open Door Notes. In a world dominated by the scramble for colonies, these notes struck a new tone:

> The policy of the Government of the United States is to seek a solution which may bring about permanent safety and peace to China, preserve Chinese territorial and administrative entity, protect all rights guaranteed to friendly powers by treaty and international law, and safeguard for the world the principle of equal and impartial trade with all parts of the Chinese Empire.[1]

The Open Door Notes did not, by themselves, restore China's territorial integrity. Just a few years later, Russia and Japan went to war to decide who could gobble up the province of Manchuria. However, they did cause Britain, France, Italy, and Germany to pause in their rush to grab Chinese territory, a pause that helped prevent China from being completely divided up into colonies as Africa had been. The continuing existence of the core of the Chinese nation made it possible for Chinese nationalists, led by Sun Yixian, to overthrow the Ch'ing Dynasty in 1911 and begin the first steps toward national renewal.

In a nation torn by debate over the bloody guerrilla war in the Philippines and unhappy about its occupation of Cuba, the Open Door Notes seemed high-minded by comparison. Hay became a celebrated figure in the United States, a man who was able to link the anti-colonial legacy of the founding fathers with the business imperatives of the 20th century.[2] On the one hand, the Notes were a practical effort to ensure that American businesses had access to Chinese markets. The Boston *Transcript* laid out the underlying logic, "We have an infinitely wider scope in the Chinese markets than we should have had with a 'sphere of influence' in competition with half a dozen other spheres."[3] As it turned out, the policy Hay developed for China worked equally well when applied to disputes in other parts of the world. The colonial empires created in the 19th century would be challenged in the 20th century and the Open Door Policy served as a consistent guide for American attempts to take advantage of anti-colonial movements by prying open previously closed markets for American products.

On the other hand, the Open Door Policy allowed the United States to rise above the costly and divisive colonial strategy being pursued in the Philippines. To call for an open door, for the freedom of trade for all, did not,

---

1 *The Fieldstone School U.S. History Survey*, Unit Nine The Nation Enters the World Stage, "The Open Door Notes (1899-1900)"; available from www.pinzler.com/ushistory/opendoorsupp. html; accessed 25 March 2007

2 Zimmermann, *First Triumph*, p. 447

3 Williams, *Tragedy*, p. 52

at least on the surface, appear to be self-serving. Instead, it appealed to the American sense of fair play and sympathy with political movements seeking independence and self-sufficiency. Hay had managed to articulate a policy that resonated with both the entrepreneurial dynamic and with the democratic self-image of the American people in the early 20th century. "Bundled into the concept of openness were several other values. [Americans believed that] a world open to American enterprise and influence was a world conducive not only to economic opportunity but also to political liberty."[1]

This connection between political freedom and free markets allowed Americans to see the spirit of the Statue of Liberty once again reflected in US foreign policy. Unlike other world powers, after the Philippines, the United States disdained the acquisition of colonies and spoke in favor of advocates for liberty. American diplomats and politicians invariably called for European colonial powers to open up markets in the Middle East, in Africa, and in Asia — an act, they said, that would sooner or later lead to political freedoms. Americans came to believe that, after a brief detour during the Spanish-American War period, US foreign policy once again reflected the ideals of the founding fathers.

However, while all actions were taken in the name of liberty and free markets, the US became more and more involved in the domestic affairs of other nations, something distinctly unlike the ideals of the founding fathers. In 1904, when the Dominican Republic went bankrupt, Secretary of State Hay and President Roosevelt prevented European governments from intervening to collect money owed to their banks by devising a scheme where the US oversaw the country's customs office and redistributed funds to debtors and to the new Dominican government. To justify this US takeover of one function of the Dominican government Roosevelt announced the "Roosevelt Corollary" to the Monroe Doctrine. In it he said that:

> If a nation . . . keeps order and pays its obligations, it need fear no interference from the United States. Chronic wrongdoing, or an impotence which results in a general loosening of the ties of civilized society may . . . ultimately require intervention by some civilized nation.[2]

In the Western Hemisphere, the "civilized nation" was the United States. With the Roosevelt Corollary the United States extended its right of intervention beyond Cuba to all of Latin America. The Roosevelt Corollary "also illustrated the increasing influence of economic interests on US policy in Latin America. American business, which had been ambivalent about getting into war over Cuba, was now behind much of the pressure to enforce

---

1 Andrew J. Bacevich, *American Empire: The Realities and Consequences of U.S. Diplomacy*, Cambridge: Harvard University Press, 2002, p. 26
2 *U.S. Dept of State*, "Roosevelt Corollary," available from www.state.gov/r/pa/ho/time/gp/17660. htm; accessed 17 March 2007

stability in the hemisphere."[1] The power to enforce stability was wielded by the US Marine Corp. Between 1900 and 1934 the United States sent marines to Honduras seven time, Haiti twice, Mexico three times, Columbia four times, and Nicaragua five times.

> The country that had proclaimed the Monroe Doctrine to protect the independence of Spanish-speaking countries on the New World mainland now found itself in the anomalous position of replacing Spain as a colonial ruler and repressing national independence movements.[2]

THE BI-PARTISAN EMPIRE

The Roosevelt Corollary continued during the administration of Republican President Taft. His policy, known as "Dollar Diplomacy," led to interventions in several countries to ensure that US businesses could operate without restrictions. However, the next stage in the creation of an American empire was the eagerness with which a Democratic President and Secretary of State put on imperial robes. To be sure, Democrats in Congress had voted against many Republican initiatives, but this was out of reluctance to become entangled in colonial adventures rather than from a principled anti-imperialism. The new president, Woodrow Wilson, was happy to embrace the notion of the United States as a world power. While he was a professor at and then President of Princeton University, Wilson supported the Spanish-American War and the occupation of the Philippines, and spoke in favor of President Roosevelt's seizure of land to build the Panama Canal.[3]

The new president also agreed with the idea that the United States should be prepared to use military muscle to ensure foreign markets were open to American trade. In a lecture at Columbia University in 1907, he said:

> Since trade ignores national boundaries and the manufacturer insists on having the world as a market, the flag of his nation must follow him, and the doors of the nations which are closed must be battered down . . . Concessions obtained by financiers [large banks] must be safeguarded, by ministers of state, even if the sovereignty of unwilling nations be outraged in the process.[4]

Wilson's thinking about trade and expansion was influenced by his agreement with Frederick Jackson Turner about the significance of the closing of the American Frontier. In 1896 he explained how to interpret Turner in this way, "The days of glad expansion are gone, our life grows tense and difficult."[5] Wilson's Secretary of State, William Jennings Bryan, the party's presidential nominee in 1896 and 1900, pronounced himself eager to enforce

1 Zimmermann, *First Triumph*, p. 441
2 Abernethy, David B., *The Dynamics of Global Dominance: European Overseas Empires, 1415-1980*, (New Haven: Yale Univ. Press, 2000) quoted in Johnson, *Sorrows*, p. 192
3 Zimmermann, *First Triumph*, p. 476
4 Williams, *Tragedy*, p. 72
5 Williams, *Tragedy*, p. 71

the Roosevelt Corollary by intervening in the domestic affairs of Latin American nations. In 1913, he said that the United States should continue to be the "paramount influence in the Western Hemisphere," and this dominance would "give our country such increased influence . . . that we would prevent revolutions, promote education, and advance stable and just government . . . we would in the end profit negatively, by not having to incur expense in guarding our own and foreign interests there, and, positively, by the increase of trade."[1]

There were two differences between the new Democratic government and the previous Republican administrations. First, Wilson and Bryan were energetic domestic reformers; they initiated the 16th Amendment creating a progressive income tax, persuaded Congress to enact a federal child labor law, created the Federal Reserve System to regulate banks, and established an estate tax.[2] (While Theodore Roosevelt advocated for progressive reforms, progressives were a minority in the Republican Party. Roosevelt attained the presidency through McKinley's assassination and, when he ran against the unpopular Taft in 1912, he was unable to win the Republican nomination.)[3] This was the first instance where a Democratic administration juggled the dual role of domestic reformer and enthusiastic supporter of the empire. Democratic initiatives at home were primarily designed to distribute the riches of empire and industrialization more equitably. Playing this dual role would come to characterize the Democratic Party after the Wilson presidency.

The second difference was the moralistic tone the Democrats gave to the Open Door Policy. Wilson updated Manifest Destiny by saying that the United States would be "the justest [sic], the most progressive, the most honorable, and the most enlightened nation in the world."[4] For Wilson, a devoted Presbyterian, this meant that the United States had a moral, Christian duty to compel other countries to be as good as America. For example, this moral attitude led him to say that the United States had to train Filipinos to govern themselves, even if the Filipinos had to be forced to endure their training. "When men take up arms to set other men free," he said, "there is something sacred and holy in the warfare. I will not cry peace as long as there is sin and wrong in the world."[5]

Wilson and Bryan intervened repeatedly in Latin America. To protect the sea routes to the Panama Canal from Germany, they sent marines to occupy

---

1 Williams, *Tragedy*, p. 68
2 Johnson, *Sorrows*, p. 46
3 Chace, *1912*, see Chapters 5, 6, & 7
4 Williams, *Tragedy*, p. 69
5 Williams, *Tragedy*, p. 69

Haiti; the leathernecks stayed for nineteen years.[1] Later they sent marines into the Dominican Republic, an occupation that lasted until 1924. With Mexico in turmoil because of a prolonged revolution, Wilson sent troops into Mexico several times; the US navy occupied the key port of Veracruz in 1914 and General John "Black Jack" Pershing invaded Mexico in 1916 in an attempt to capture the rebel leader Pancho Villa.[2] Each time he sent troops to Mexico, Wilson justified his actions by saying the United States was supporting democracy and the rule of law in the bitterly divided nation.

Wilson's contradictory combination of a moral passion for democracy and staunch opposition to any political movement that did not advocate free market principles collided in the tangled negotiations at Versailles after the end of the First World War. Nine months before the end of the war, Wilson laid out a post-war program in his famous Fourteen Points. In the spirit of the Open Door Policy, Point Three called for "The removal, so far as possible, of all economic barriers and the establishment of equality of trade conditions among all the nations consenting to the peace . . ."[3] Point Four called for "adjustment of all colonial claims based upon a strict observance of the principle that in determining all such questions of sovereignty, the interests of the populations concerned must have equal weight with the equitable claims of the government whose title is to be determined."[4] Most of the remaining points specified territorial adjustments in Europe based on Point Four.

At the peace conference, Wilson negotiated away most his other ideals in order to get the British and French to agree to a League of Nations. "The freest opportunity to autonomous development" ended up not applying to British India, French Indo-China, Japanese Manchuria, or even the Philippines.[5] Perhaps most relevant to the 21st century, Point Twelve about the Ottoman Empire, which declared "the other nationalities which are now under Turkish rule should be assured an undoubted security of life and an absolutely unmolested opportunity of autonomous development . . ." was not followed. Instead, the French and the British used the break-up of the Ottoman/Turkish Empire as an opportunity to divide the area up into weak new nations dominated by the two European powers. For example, the British protectorate of Iraq was created during the conference.

Why were the "interests of the populations concerned" abandoned? The Bolshevik Revolution in Russia appalled Wilson and made him suspicious of independence movements in Eastern Europe and the colonial world. As

1 Zimmermann, *First Triumph*, p. 476

2 Johnson, *Sorrows*, p. 47

3 *U.S. Department of State*, "Basic Readings in U.S. Democracy," Woodrow Wilson, Fourteen Points Speech (1918); available from http://usinfo.state.gov/usa/infousa/facts/demo.htm; accessed 30 March 2007

4 U.S. Department of State, "Fourteen Points,"

5 Johnson, *Sorrows*, p. 50

conference participant Herbert Hoover remarked, "Communist Russia was a specter which wandered into the Peace Conference almost daily."[1] The problem of preventing further communist revolutions (which would firmly close doors to American business and business practices) overshadowed the principle of self-determination. For believers in the Open Door Policy, it did no good to free colonial peoples if they then chose to cut themselves off from the international free market by taking the communist path to development. Already, at the time of the peace conference, there was a new communist government in Hungary and revolutionary uprisings in Germany. Thus, Wilson supported the colonial plans of the French and British, sent American troops to support the White Russians in the civil war against the Bolsheviks, and consoled himself with the League of Nations, an organization that he believed would preserve national boundaries and allow for a slow evolution into a world of free market states.

Wilson's abandonment of most of the principles of self-determination and his acceptance of the vengeful policies that crippled the post-war German economy did not change his rhetoric. When he sent the peace treaty to the Senate he proclaimed, "The stage is set, the destiny disclosed. It has come about by no plan of our conceiving, but by the hand of God, who led us in this way."[2] The Senate, unconvinced of God's role in the treaty, rejected it by a solid majority. This was not an isolationist vote, as is commonly portrayed. Instead, the newly elected majority of Republican Senators, led by long-time expansionist Henry Cabot Lodge, feared that the League of Nations would restrict the United States' ability to intervene in Latin America or to seize opportunities to extend American influence into previously closed economies. The "no" vote, Wilson's crippling stroke, and the Republican victory in the 1920 presidential election, returned control of US foreign policy to men like Herbert Hoover who were more interested in opening markets for American corporations than they were in moralizing about political systems.

THE STRATEGY OF OPENNESS

What were the key characteristics of this new kind of empire that emerged at the beginning of the 20th century? Unlike previous empires, the United States moved away from acquiring colonies. Instead, the US government adopted a "strategy of openness," first articulated in the Open Door Policy, a strategy that focused on pressuring all nations to open their markets to trade and investment by American corporations.[3] The "strategy of openness" included the right to intervene with military force whenever a country

---

1 Williams, *Tragedy*, p. 113
2 Chase, *1912*, p. 269
3 Bacevich, *American Empire*, p. 6; the term "strategy of openness" is borrowed from Professor Bacevich's pioneering work.

wavered from the free market path by restricting the activities of American businesses. The Open Door Policy and later versions of the "strategy of openness" were popular with the American public because of the widely held belief that the United States was selflessly striving to help other nations achieve the mixture of political liberty and free markets that had made the United States a great nation. Finally, American political and military leaders believed that possessing a network of military bases would make it easier to pressure reluctant nations to open their doors to American businesses.

Leaders from both political parties supported the "strategy of openness" and accepted the new American empire as a logical consequence of the country's growing power. While the 1920s marked a period where American policy makers concentrated on enhancing prosperity at home and the 1930s was very focused on domestic issues, the devastation wrought by World War II and the United States' leading role in winning that war set the stage for a new expansion of the emerging American empire.

Chapter 7. The Open Empire

> I don't know why we need to stand by and watch a country go Communist
> due to the irresponsibility of its own people.[1]

—Henry Kissinger

Henry Kissinger is a model Cold Warrior. Most of his life has been devoted to waging the Cold War and then handling the peace in ways that would maximize America's ability to contain other major powers and preserve its influence over the rest of the world. Born in Germany in 1923, he and his Jewish parents were forced to flee from Nazi persecution in 1938. After serving as an interpreter for the US Army in World War II, he went to Harvard and became an expert on 19th century European diplomacy.

In 1957, he published *Nuclear War and Foreign Policy*, which argued that it was possible for the United States to win a war against the Soviet Union using tactical nuclear weapons and conventional ground armies.[2] The book captured the attention of General Maxwell Taylor, then Army Chief of Staff, Nelson Rockefeller, who became the Republican Governor of New York in 1959, and Senator John F. Kennedy of Massachusetts. These men felt constrained by then Secretary of State John Foster Dulles' strategy of threatening "massive retaliation" with nuclear weapons to deter the Soviet Union from invading Western Europe. It also caught the attention of people who

---

1 Kinzer, *Overthrow*, p. 180

2 *British Broadcasting Company*, "The Trials of Henry Kissinger," available from www.bbc.co.uk/bbcfour/documentaries/features/feature_kissinger_profile.shtml; accessed 24 May 2007.

believed that the idea of "limited" nuclear war was insanity; Kissinger's ideas (and German accent) were bitingly satirized in the 1964 hit movie *Dr. Strangelove.*

In addition to his position as Director of the Harvard Defense Studies Program, Dr. Kissinger served as Director of the Special Studies Project for the Rockefeller Brothers Fund, giving him access to leading political leaders and military officials.[1] During the 1960s he served as an advisor to the Kennedy administration and make three trips to Vietnam behalf of the Johnson administration.[2] He spent 1968 working on Nelson Rockefeller's presidential campaign, but when former vice-president Richard Nixon won the Presidency, he took Rockefeller's advice and agreed to serve as Assistant to the President for National Security Affairs.

For eight years, Dr. Kissinger was at the center of American foreign policy, helping to create détente with Russia and China, and approving of a series of violent responses to communist, socialist, and nationalist movements in the non-aligned world. The work on détente made him an international celebrity, with his picture on the covers of *Time* and *Newsweek*, and led to his promotion to Secretary of State in 1973. However, his sponsorship of violent governments in the non-aligned world gained him a different type of attention, with a number of groups campaigning to have him punished as an accomplice to torture and political murder. As we will see, his was a pivotal role in shaping the new American empire and the Cold War world.

The Cold War

With Britain, France, and Germany devastated by World War II, the United States vaulted into a new role as the world's most powerful capitalist nation. In addition to having the largest economy in the world (the US produced more than half of the entire world's industrial output in 1946), the US had built or captured military bases in more than a dozen countries and had more naval warships and long range bombers than the rest of the world combined.[3] From this position of economic and military dominance, American policy makers moved aggressively to implement the "strategy of openness" on a world scale. As early as July 4, 1947, Democratic President Harry Truman presented an ambitious post-war agenda to an Independence Day crowd. Truman told the gathering that, in the modern era, the nations of the world are interdependent and continuing prosperity called for "economic and financial policies to support a world economy rather than separate

---

1 *Nobel Prize Committee,* "Henry Kissinger: Biography," Nobel Peace Prize 1973, available from www.nobelprize.org/cgi-bin/nobel_prizes/peace/laureates/1973/kissinger-bio.html; accessed 17 May 2007.

2 *Time Magazine,* "New Man for the Situation Room," 12.03.68, available from www.time.com/time/08816839639,00.html; accessed 24 May 2007.

3 Kennedy, Paul, *Rise and Fall of the Great Powers,* New York, NY: Random House, 1987, p. 358

nationalistic economies."[1] The unspoken presumption behind these words was that American officials would serve as the final arbiters in determining what rules governed world trade and investment.[2] While there were partisan disagreements about specific activities to reach those goals, we will see that Presidents from both parties have consistently implemented this general strategy.[3]

Over the course of the Cold War, the United States carried out a two-pronged strategy to preserve and enhance the emerging American empire. The core element was "containment" of the Soviet Union, China, and communism in general. Communist countries insisted on public control of natural resources and currencies, strict controls over investment activities of domestic and foreign corporations, and rejected allowing foreign bases on their home soil. All of these basic elements of communist rule were rejections of the central principles of the strategy of openness.

To understand the US ability during this era to influence events all over the world, the threat of communist military aggression needs to be kept in perspective — while the Soviet Union was a nuclear power with a large economy and a powerful army, the Soviets never sent soldiers outside of the Soviet bloc until the war in Afghanistan in 1979 and had no military bases outside of its territory and Eastern Europe. In addition, the face-off between thousands of American and Soviet soldiers in Europe raised the specter of nuclear war during the 1950s, but tensions relaxed after the Cuban Missile Crisis of 1962 showed that neither power wanted to push the other into a full-scale nuclear conflict.

In the non-aligned world, there was little chance that the sterile "Soviet model" of communism would be attractive to a significant number of the world's less developed nations.[4] The USSR's three major Cold War leaders — the murderous, tyrant Stalin, the bombastic Khrushchev, and the bureaucratic gray Leonid Brezhnev — were vivid symbols of a rigid, authoritarian elite whose misrule led to an epic national breakdown at the end of the 1980s. While China's Maoist developmental model had more appeal to some non-aligned countries, China itself was a military midget, with almost no air force or navy, and the country's inward looking leadership group devoted most of its energy to quarreling over domestic political and economic issues.

As a result, containment of Soviet-style communism was primarily a military and diplomatic strategy involving the creation of a network of military bases and alliances that encircled the Eastern Europe/ Soviet Union/ China land bloc. The Soviets readily entered into this race to build bases as an ex-

1 Bacevich, *American Empire*, p. 5
2 Bacevich, *American Empire*, p. 6
3 Ivan Eland, *The Empire has no Clothes*, Oakland, CA: The Independent Institute, 2004, p. 11
4 Eland, *No Clothes*, p. 14

cuse to keep their thumb on restless Eastern European colonies and Central Asian provinces. "The initial effect of the Cold War was to justify the grip of both super-powers on numerous territories each had defended or liberated during World War II."[1] On the American side, the US built large army bases and military airfields in defeated Germany, with nearly 285,000 soldiers and airmen confronting 380,000 Soviet forces occupying East Germany. From 1945 until 1972, the US Defense Department ruled the 1.3 million residents of the island of Okinawa, with much of the island covered with Marine Corps and air bases.

The list of countries that had or continue to have US military bases is very long. While some bases were important elements of the containment ring around the communist bloc, many others were established with an eye toward maintaining US influence in the host country. In 2001, twelve years after the fall of the Berlin Wall, there were still 22 countries with bases holding 500 or more soldiers, sailors, or airmen, including Greenland, Iceland, England, Germany, Italy, Bosnia, Serbia, Turkey, Saudi Arabia, Bahrain, Kuwait, Oman, Korea, and Australia.[2] More than fifty years after the armistice negotiated by President Eisenhower, there are still 37,000 military personnel on the Korean peninsula. All together, counting smaller military installations, radar spy stations, and naval support bases, in 2001 the US had 725 bases in thirty-eight countries with 251,098 military personnel.[3] Since 9/11 many more bases have been added to this network because the Defense Department has built bases in former provinces of Soviet Central Asia, in Afghanistan, and, of course, a dozen enormous bases in Iraq.

Henry Kissinger's greatest successes with President Nixon came in managing this containment strategy with the two main Communist nations. He had highly developed ideas on this topic as he had written a well-regarded book about the Austrian diplomat Metternich and the balance of power he maintained in post-Napoleonic Europe.[4] With relationships in a period of relative calm after the Cuban Missile Crisis, Kissinger persuaded the president not to destabilize the balance of power by trying to gain nuclear superiority over the Soviet Union. Instead, he advocated a policy of détente, which led to the Strategic Arms Limitation Talks and a break-through treaty limiting the nuclear arsenals of the two great nuclear powers. Later, he made two secret trips to China to clear the way for Nixon's trip to China in the spring of 1972, one of the great shocks of the Cold War and a great leap forward toward improving US relations with that communist country.

---

1 Johnson, *Sorrows*, p. 34

2 Johnson, *Sorrows*, pp. 156-160

3 Johnson, *Sorrows*, p. 154

4 *Time Magazine*, "New Man," 12.03.68

IMPOSING THE STRATEGY OF OPENNESS

The strategy of containment, in concert with the generous Marshall Plan, succeeded in preserving democratic, capitalist societies in Western Europe and created the foundations for a democratic, capitalist post-war Japan. However, the strategy of openness had a less benign impact on the non-aligned countries. In addition to creating networks of trade agreements with nations that wanted to open their economies, American presidents used four general tactics to force reluctant nations to remain or become open to American trade and influence. First, the US engaged in two "hot wars," direct military conflicts with small communist countries to prevent them from expanding. Second, US presidents provided aid and political support for unsavory military and authoritarian governments in return for permission to build or use military bases. Third, US presidents provided assistance to military and civilian dictatorships willing to crush socialist or nationalist movements that advocated restrictions on foreign capital or the closing of US military bases. Finally, the US used a variety of undercover methods to overthrow legitimate governments that restrained, taxed, or nationalized American businesses.

The US, with the support of the United Nations, was the main western country that protected South Korea when North Korea's communist government invaded in 1950. The bloody stalemate that occurred when communist China came to North Korea's aid was a major factor in Dwight Eisenhower's election as president in 1952. Eisenhower rapidly negotiated a truce and focused much of his administration on enhancing the American nuclear weapons arsenal.

The administration of Democratic President John F. Kennedy continued Eisenhower's nuclear build-up, but Robert McNamara and his "wiz kids" in the Pentagon were also enthusiastic about using the nation's military power in a proactive way to extend the open empire. President Kennedy described a military policy with few limits to Congress in March of 1961:

> Our defense posture must be both flexible and determined. Any potential aggressor contemplating an attack on any part of the free world with any kind of weapons . . . must know that our response will be suitable, selective, swift, and effective . . . We must be able to make deliberate choices in weapons and strategy, shift the tempo of our productions, and alter the direction of our forces to meet rapidly changing conditions or objectives at very short notice and under any circumstances.[1]

It is important to note that, during the Cold War, when American leaders talked about the "free world," they meant any place that was not part of

---

1 Quoted in Lt. Colonel Laurel A. Mayer & Dr. Ronald J. Stupak, "The evolution of Flexible Response in the Post-Vietnam Era," *Air University Review*, Nov-Dec. 1975, available from www.airpowr.maxwell.af.mil/airchronicles/aureview/1975/nov-dec/mayer.html; accessed May 24 2007.

the Soviet bloc. Thus, all of the non-aligned nations were placed under the American military umbrella whether they wanted to be there or not.

The Kennedy administration's first opportunity to use its new, flexible weapons came in Vietnam, where President Eisenhower had supported the temporary South Vietnamese government when it refused to hold reunification elections in 1956. Eisenhower later wrote that if the elections had been held, "80% of the population would have voted for the communist Ho Chi Minh."[1] South Vietnam's leader, President Ngo Dinh Diem, was unpopular and a guerrilla war supported by North Vietnam grew rapidly. With the new emphasis on small-scale warfare, as typified by creation of the Green Berets, the Kennedy administration responded by sending 16,000 military "advisors" to South Vietnam. Later, convinced that Diem's government was collapsing in spite of American assistance, Kennedy approved a military coup that led to Diem's overthrow and murder in 1963.[2] The Johnson administration eventually was forced to deploy more than 500,000 American soldiers to prop up the revolving cast of warlords who succeeded Diem.

When discontent with the war in Vietnam forced Lyndon Johnson to decline to run for re-election in 1968, Richard Nixon was able to capture the office he had just missed being elected to in 1960. With the Paris Peace Talks in stalemate Nixon and Kissinger tried to intimidate the Vietnamese through a series of bloody escalations. These included the invasion of Cambodia in 1970, an act that triggered that fragile nation's breakdown and eventually led to the genocidal Khmer Rouge regime; the massive escalation of the air war in South Vietnam during 1971, which greatly increased the number of civilian casualties; and finally, the bombing of Hanoi and other cities during the Christmas holidays in 1972, a negotiating tactic that led to the deaths of thousands of Vietnamese civilians. However, the North Vietnamese refused to give up their goal of a united Vietnam and public opposition to the war in the United States finally compelled the complete withdrawal of American combat units in 1973. For their work negotiating the cease-fire, Kissinger and his Vietnamese counterpart, Le Duc Tho, won the Nobel Prize that the same year. By 1975, the South Vietnamese government collapsed and the country was unified under a communist government.

Most US interventions were more successful. During the Cold War every American president was willing to locate military bases in countries with brutal military or personal dictatorships because their leaders were "anti-communist" and left their economies open to American businesses. For example, one of most glaring instances of this policy was in Spain, where the US maintained ties with Francisco Franco, a Fascist who came to power

---

1 Dwight Eisenhower, *Mandate for Change*, New York: Doubleday, 1963, p. 372
2 Kinzer, *Overthrow*, p. 169

in the 1930s using guns and "volunteer units" sent by his friends Hitler and Mussolini. The US gave Franco political and military support for many years in return for the right to operate naval and air bases near the Straits of Gibraltar. The comedy show *Saturday Night Live* reflected the glee many people felt after the infamous dictator's death in 1975 by announcing in weekly news bulletins, "Franco is still dead!"

The United States also used the "communist threat" to justify support of military and civilian dictatorships that allowed free reign to American businesses while crushing socialist or nationalist movements that favored economic policies unfavorable to American business interests. The most controversial instance was in South Africa, where for many years the US supported a white minority government that imposed openly racist controls over the black majority. The Reagan administration was infamous for dubbing its support for this apartheid regime "constructive engagement."

Another example of this policy came to light in 2002, when documents released by the State Department showed that, when he was Secretary of State in 1976, Dr. Kissinger gave the green light to Argentina's new military junta when it wanted to unleash paramilitary death squads on suspected socialists and labor union activists.[1] The death squads kidnapped between 10,000 and 30,000 individuals over the next three years, with most of them never being heard from again. The question of the "missing" still haunts Argentina's politics. Similar stories can be told about free market, military dictatorships that were US allies in Brazil, South Korea, El Salvador, Indonesia, Greece, Zaire, Portugal, Nicaragua, and Egypt.

The most aggressive tactic used to further the strategy of openness was to overthrow governments that threatened to restrict the operations of US corporations or to nationalize critical national industries. For example, when the socialist leader Salvador Allende was elected President of Chile in 1970, Henry Kissinger had the CIA launch a campaign to de-stabilize the country. Allende had angered American businesses operating in Chile by campaigning on a promise to nationalize the wildly profitable Chilean copper industry and the country's American-owned telephone system. General Rene Schneider, the commander-in-chief of the Chilean army, refused to participate in a coup plot and was murdered with CIA assistance in the fall of 1970.[2] Then, on November 6, 1970, President Nixon met with the National Security Council to discuss how to eliminate Allende's government. At the meeting Nixon said, "Latin America is not gone, and we want to keep it . . . No impression should be permitted in Latin America that they can get away with this, that it's safe to go this way."[3]

---

1 Tim Johnson, "Argentina's 'Dirty War' Hounding Kissinger," *Miami Herald*, 8.30.02
2 Kinzer, *Overthrow*, p. 183
3 Kinzer, *Overthrow*, p. 185

When Allende came to the United Nations in December of 1972, he carefully laid out what was at stake in the struggle to nationalize his country's most valuable resource.

> These same firms exploited Chilean copper for many years, made more than four billion dollars in profit in the last forty-two years alone, while their initial investments were less than thirty million. . . . My country, Chile, would have been totally transformed by that four billion dollars.[1]

The CIA spent about $8 million in a campaign to disrupt the Chilean economy and win the support of right-wing military officers. In Chile, the numbers 9/11 stand for the day in 1973 that General Augusto Pinochet led a coup against the President. Allende barricaded himself into the Presidential Palace and died in a hail of rockets and bombs. To intimidate the President's most active supporters, the army rounded up thousands of students from the University of Chile and put them in the city of Santiago's soccer stadium. All day and through the night, soldiers took turns firing machine guns into the crowds of helpless students. *Newsweek* Magazine published a cover picture of the Presidential Palace being fired upon and titled it, "Death of a Dream."

The Cold War overthrow of a democratically elected government in the Middle East continues to haunt the United States. In 1951 a nationalist named Mohammad Mossadegh was elected Prime Minister of Iran. He immediately placed before the Iranian Parliament a bill calling for the nationalization of the Anglo-Iranian Oil Company, a firm owned by the British government, which paid Iran just 16 cents for every dollar it earned pumping and selling Iran's oil.[2] The bill was passed unanimously, but the British refused to negotiate compensation for their company. In January of 1952, *Time* Magazine named Mossadegh "Man of the Year" and called him the "Iranian George Washington."[3]

However, John Foster Dulles, the new Secretary of State for Dwight Eisenhower convinced the President that the communist party in Iran was very powerful and was ready to take over the country in the event that Mossadegh was assassinated or fell from power.[4] Dulles, a successful corporate lawyer before becoming Secretary of State, was obsessed with protecting the rights of multinational corporations and took a dim view of any government that would infringe on the property rights of a company.[5] After several abortive coup attempts, the CIA paid a retired general named Zahedi to lead a decisive military coup that placed Mossadegh under house arrest until his death.[6]

1 Kinzer, *Overthrow*, p. 189
2 Kinzer, *Overthrow*, p. 117
3 Kinzer, *Overthrow*, p. 120
4 Eland, *No Clothes*, p. 63
5 Kinzer, *Overthrow*, p. 122
6 Johnson, *Sorrows*, p. 220

The coup restored Mohammad Reza Shah to the royal throne. He immediately consolidated his power by asking the CIA to help him create a secret police force.[1] In a world full of secret police, Savak became notorious for its brutality. The Shah suppressed opposition political parties, trade unions, and newspapers. However, dissidents found sanctuary in mosques and religious schools because Muslim clerics also opposed the Shah's secular regime. The United States became the Shah's very public ally, providing his government with millions of dollars worth of military aid. Democratic President Jimmy Carter hosted the Shah at the White House and said in a banquet toast, "If ever there was a country which has blossomed forth under enlightened leadership, it would be the ancient empire of Persia."[2] These open ties to the hated Shah encouraged a deep set anti-Americanism in the population.[3] When a broad coalition of religious and secular groups combined to overthrow the Shah in 1979, huge crowds marched through the streets chanting against the nation they regarded as, "the great Satan." Later that year, the American embassy was stormed and its staff taken hostage to ensure that the United States could not plan a second coup.[4]

THE RISE OF OIL IN THE POLITICS OF EMPIRE

The case of Iran demonstrates the growing importance of oil in the calculus of American empire. The United States entered the 20th century as one of the leading oil producing nations in the world. By 1935 eight of the top sixteen American companies ranked by assets were oil companies — Standard Oil of New Jersey (Esso, later Exxon, #1), Standard Oil of New York (Socony, later Mobil, #4), Standard Oil of Indiana (later Amoco, #5), Standard Oil of California (later Chevron, #10), Texaco (based in Texas, #11), Gulf (based in Pennsylvania, #12), Shell (15), and Sinclair (16).[5] Five of the other eight largest companies manufactured gasoline-powered vehicles or the steel for their frames.

Fueling the wealth being generated by the oil/automobile juggernaut was a national embrace of travel using the automobile. In 1929, the United States had about two-thirds of the world's cars. In 1950 the United States consumed half of the oil produced in the entire world, with two-thirds of that being used by automobiles and the other third by industry and electric power generators.[6] The great migration to the suburbs and beyond that has re-made the American landscape since the 1940s was based on cheap gaso-

---

1 Kinzer, *Overthrow*, p. 200
2 Kinzer, *Overthrow*, p. 201
3 Eland, *No Clothes*, p. 87
4 Kinzer, *Overthrow*, p. 203
5 Kevin Phillips, *American Theocracy: The Peril and Politics of Radical Religion, Oil, and Borrowed Money in the 21st Century*, London: Viking Penguin, 2006, p. 37
6 Phillips, *American Theocracy*, p. 20

line and little has changed since then. In the first decade of the 21st century, "Americans enjoyed a lifestyle roughly twice as energy intensive as those in Europe and Japan, some ten times the global average. Of the world's 520 million automobiles, unsurprisingly, more than 200 million were driven in the United States . . ."[1]

However, oil is a finite resource and as early as the 1950s geologists were predicting that oil production in the United States would peak by 1970.[2] Knowledge that the gushers would not last forever in the United States led to growing attention to supplies in other countries. As early as the Treaty of Paris, after World War I, Britain and France had solidified their colonial hold on the Middle East's oil producing lands, but the United States also began improving its relations with key nations in that region. In 1933, Standard Oil of California received the rights to extract oil in Saudi Arabia's eastern region.[3] In 1927, Gulf Oil purchased oil concessions in Kuwait and SoCal purchased the rights to drill oil in Bahrain, a tiny sheikdom along the Persian Gulf.[4] With the end of World War II, the European powers slowly relinquished their colonial rule and the US became the leading power in the region.

In the 1970s Middle Eastern oil became both more valuable and more insecure as a series of events de-stabilized the Middle East and ran up the price of oil. Even as US oil production was peaking, a number of leading oil producers nationalized their oil industries — Iraq in 1972, Libya in 1975, Iran in 1979, and Saudi Arabia in 1981. In addition, the Organization of Petroleum Exporting Countries (OPEC) had an influx of new members and became strong enough to double the price of oil in the winter of 1973-74.[5] Americans suffered through miles-long lines and service stations closing at 5:00 p.m. during that long winter. It was a shock to realize that American oil companies no longer had full control of the liquid that had become the country's lifeblood.

When Henry Kissinger became Secretary of State in the fall of 1973, these events compelled him to be very involved in attempts to create a more peaceful environment in the Middle East. Egypt's surprise invasion of Israel in October of 1973 led to the OPEC oil embargo against nations that supported Israel, especially the United States. The embargo and resulting sharp increase in oil prices led to disruptive inflation in the United States. To give Arab nations the impression that the US had adopted a more balanced policy between Israel and it Arab rivals, Kissinger employed "shuttle diplo-

---

1 Phillips, *American Theocracy*, p. 33

2 Phillips, *American Theocracy*, p. 21

3 Johnson, *Sorrows*, p. 217

4 Phillips, *American Theocracy*, p. 50

5 Phillips, *American Theocracy*, p. 41

macy," playing the middleman in negotiations between the two sides.[1] This personal effort eventually led to the end of the oil embargo and encouraged Saudi Arabia, Iran, and other countries with strong ties to the US to moderate OPEC price increases.

Oil prices jumped again after the Iranian Revolution, sparking double-digit interest rates in the United States and sinking Jimmy Carter's presidency. Oil prices then declined in the 1980s as a result of vigorous energy conservation efforts in all of the world's industrialized nations. Even in the United States oil consumption declined by 15% between 1977 and 1985 and gasoline prices fell sharply.[2] However, a new cloud rose over the world's oil economy in 1989 when Saddam Hussein occupied Kuwait and threatened Saudi Arabia. A multinational army kicked Saddam's army out of Kuwait with heavy losses, but he remained in power. The United States responded by expanding its network of airfields and army bases in the Persian Gulf region. From bases in Kuwait, Saudi Arabia, and Turkey the US maintained no-fly zones over the Kurdish areas of northern Iraq and the Shi'ia areas of southern Iraq for the rest of the decade. Combined with strict sanctions on his government, these efforts led to a drastic reduction in Iraq's oil production, but reassured producers in Saudi Arabia and the Persian Gulf states.

THE MUSCLE BEHIND THE DRIVE FOR OPENNESS

With the fall of the Berlin Wall and the break-up of the Soviet Union in 1989, the Cold War came to an end, but the drive to create a world open to American corporations continued. As in previous decades, an enormous military establishment was maintained to intimidate any nation that resisted the call for openness. In 2001, before the attack on 9/11, eleven years after the fall of the Berlin War, there were still about 90,000 US military personnel based in Germany.[3] Fifty-six years after the surrender ceremony on the battleship Missouri, 40,000 US soldiers, sailors, and marines were still based on Okinawa.[4] In the FY'2002 budget, passed by Congress before the events of 9/11, the Pentagon was authorized to spend $348.5 billion on military activities, about equal to what the next 13 countries spent for defense.[5]

Under President Clinton, the US fought no major wars, but the definition of national security was stretched to include a variety of global ills like terrorism, drug trafficking, ethnic conflicts, the price of oil, and biological warfare.[6] Security analysts warned of the danger from dictators in Iraq, China,

---

1 *Oxford University Press*, "Political Biography of Henry Kissinger," available from www.answers.com/topic/henry-kissinger; accessed 4 June 2007.
2 Phillips, *American Theocracy*, p. 55
3 Johnson, *Sorrows*, p. 198
4 Johnson, *Sorrows*, p. 202
5 Eland, *No Clothes*, p. 27
6 Bacevich, *American Empire*, p. 118 & 121

North Korea, Iran, and in multiple states in Africa.[1] In the shadow of the public debate over these multiple, vague, mostly second-level fears, the long hoped for "peace dividend" at the end of the Cold War quietly disappeared.

The Cold War had changed much in the American political culture. Before World War II, the end of a war or military emergency had meant full-scale demobilization of the armed forces. For example, the US Army at the time of Lee's surrender in 1865 numbered more than one million men. Within a year it had shrunk to only 57,000 soldiers.[2] In contrast, there were few reductions in the American military after the fall of the Berlin Wall and almost no debate over the role of the armed forces in a world where there were no significant military threats to the United States. Instead, there was a general consensus in both political parties and the public that the US should retain a position of "military supremacy."[3]

This continuing emphasis on military power fits perfectly with the notion that the "strategy of openness" remains the principal guide for American foreign policy. As Ivan Eland remarks, "If the main goal of post-World War II US foreign policy had been to fight communism, the Pax Americana that spanned the globe would have been dismantled after the Soviet empire fell."[4] Instead the American military umbrella was maintained and even extended to cover Eastern Europe, the Persian Gulf, and Central Asia. In fact, the whole world was now open to American military operations. Anthony Lake, President Clinton's National Security Advisor, gave a speech in 1993 calling for American foreign policy to move "From Containment to Enlargement."[5] Lake believed, now that the US was the world's sole superpower, it was time to ensure that free markets dominated every part of the globe. Significantly, Lake did not mention two long-standing liberal internationalist goals that a Democratic President might have been expected to pursue — worldwide disarmament and the strengthening of the United Nations.[6] Movement toward either of those goals would mean reducing the size of the US military establishment and restraining US ability to launch military interventions in its newly enlarged sphere of influence.

One example of the Clinton administration's militarized foreign policy was the pursuit of military supremacy in the Persian Gulf. The no-fly zones and occasional rocket attacks on Saddam Hussein's Iraq proved useful because they justified keeping US aircraft and naval units in large bases around the Persian Gulf. After the Gulf War, US forces in Saudi Arabia moved into

---

1 Eland, *No Clothes*, p. 226
2 Bacevich, *American Empire*, p. 124
3 Bacevich, *American Empire*, p. 126
4 Eland, *No Clothes*, p. 12
5 Bacevich, *American Empire*, p. 98
6 Bacevich, *American Empire*, p. 100

the Prince Sultan Air Base, which is approximately the same size as the country of Bahrain and has a 15,000 foot-long runway.[1] 6,000 US soldiers and airmen were based there, along with fighter squadrons, AWAC surveillance aircraft, and U-2 spy planes to keep a close eye on Saddam's movements. A new $200 million base, Camp Arifjan, was built in Kuwait in 1999.[2] Arifjan has space for 10,000 soldiers and has weapons storage facilities for an entire combat brigade that might be airlifted in for emergency operations. In 1995, the US Fifth Fleet set up its headquarters in Bahrain, which is south of Kuwait on the Persian Gulf. About 4,500 navy personnel were stationed there in a base that was once operated by Great Britain.[3]

Attention also turned to the relatively untapped oil reserves of Central Asia around the Caspian Sea. To increase the US presence in that region, the Clinton administration sent paratroopers from the 82nd Airborne Division to train Kazakhstani soldiers and tough troops from the 10th Mountain Division to train Uzbekistani soldiers. After that, National Guard soldiers from Montana, Arizona, and Louisiana spent time in these remote areas training native soldiers and developing useful contacts.

The turmoil in Afghanistan after the Soviet withdrawal in 1989 made it dangerous to run natural gas pipelines from the Caspian Sea area through that country to ports in Pakistan, a staunch US ally. To solidify control over these gas and oil routes, the United States and Pakistan decided, in the mid 1990s, to assist a small Afghanistan organization calling itself 'Students of Islam' in its bid to establish a strong central government.[4] The Taliban, as the organization came to be known, captured the nation's capital, Kabul, in September of 1996. US oil companies tried to convince the new government to grant approvals for the pipeline, but the radical group went with the advice it received from one of the leaders of the anti-Soviet resistance movement, Osama bin Laden, who did not want them to cooperate with American companies.[5] This was the murky situation when the Bush administration took office.

GLOBALIZATION: THE NEXT STAGE OF THE OPEN DOOR POLICY

While the US military establishment was expanding its mission for the new era, Clinton administration officials told Congress that their principal foreign policy emphasis was to foster economic growth through international trade.[6] Democrat Bill Clinton was able to defeat the incumbent, Repub-

---

1 Johnson, *Sorrows*, p. 239
2 Johnson, *Sorrows*, p. 243
3 Johnson, *Sorrows*, p. 245
4 Johnson, *Sorrows*, p. 177
5 Johnson, *Sorrows*, p. 179
6 Bacevich, *American Empire*, p. 41

lican George H.W. Bush in 1992, because the country, after a boom fueled by Ronald Reagan's deficit spending policies, had slipped into a period of economic stagnation. From a rate of 5.2% in June of 1990, the US unemployment rate climbed slowly but steadily to 7.8% in June of 1992 and stubbornly sat at 7.4% as voters went to the polls in November.[1] Clinton's campaign manager's mantra, "It's the Economy, Stupid," remained as a warning that Clinton's re-election hopes rested on his ability to bring that unemployment rate down.

The President set the tone for his foreign policy priorities, stating bluntly, "Growth at home depends on growth abroad."[2] The policy of openness was essential for this strategy. Samuel R. Berger, the President's National Security Advisor put it this way, "We have to continue to open markets . . . because that's where the customers are . . . We have a mature market — we have to expand, we have to grow."[3] Secretary of State Madeleine Albright saw the world in the same way, "Our own prosperity depends on having partners that are open to our exports, investments, and ideas." As in 1898, trade and investment were national security issues because American political leaders feared the political repercussions of an extended period of poor economic growth.

These leaders continued to have faith, as William McKinley and John Hay did, that American businesses, on an open playing field, would dominate trade and investment in every part of the world. President Clinton assured a student audience, "You know, we're going to do very, very well, as the world becomes more interdependent."[4] In the 1990s it was clear that the information revolution was transforming the way economic activity was carried out in every industry. With Japan mired in a colossal real estate crash and Germany staggering under the enormous expense of integrating East Germany into western society, the United States was uniquely positioned to use the information revolution to gain a competitive edge in communications, manufacturing, and financial services. Bill Gates, Chairman of Microsoft, wrote that the US would lead the worldwide information revolution because American companies were the leaders "in almost every technology that will be a part of building the broadband infrastructure: microprocessors, software, entertainment, personal computers, set-top boxes, and network-switching equipment."[5]

The sweeping economic, social, and cultural changes driven by the information revolution came to be called "globalization." The idea of globalization was popular with many people because of its universal appeal. Rather

---

1 *U.S. Dept of Labor*, "Civilian Unemployment Rate," available at http://research.stlouisfed.org/fred2/data/UNRATE.txt; accessed 7 June 2007.

2 Bacevich, *American Empire*, p. 86

3 Bacevich, *American Empire*, p. 85

4 Bacevich, *American Empire*, p. 38

5 Bacevich, *American Empire*, p. 40

than a conscious policy of setting global trade and investment rules to favor American interests, it was viewed by many people as the next wave of technological development, an inevitable leap forward in the march of progress.[1] President Clinton and many other officials encouraged this sense of the inevitability of globalization. For example, in 1999 the President said, "Today we must embrace the inexorable logic of globalization — that everything from the strength of our economy to the safety of our cities, to the health of our people, depends on events not only within our borders, but half a world away."[2]

Many visionaries wrote about globalization as a process that would bring together the diverse people of the earth. One advocate of globalization, Theodore Levitt, predicted that globalization would lead to "homogenization" of the world. He wrote:

> Nothing confirms this as much as the success of McDonald's from the Champs Elysees to the Ginza, of Coca-Cola in Bahrain and Pepsi-Cola in Moscow, and of rock music, Greek salad, Hollywood movies, Revlon cosmetics, Sony televisions, and Levi's jeans everywhere.[3]

This list highlights the almost unconscious assumption that "homogenization meant Americanization."[4] The inclusion of Hollywood movies and rock music also highlights the extent to which American cultural products are now important components of the US export industry. In fact, cultural products are frequently the first wave in the invasion of American commercial supremacy. People who watch American movies and television shows, listen to American rock and roll, and visit American web sites are more likely to buy a Coke and wear Levi's jeans. Consider, for example, the difficulties posed for American corporations if French or Spanish were the language of the Internet rather than English.

So important did President Clinton rank his globalization agenda that he postponed Congressional action in the fall of 1993 on his major campaign priority, a massive overhaul of the costly and inefficient American health care system, to press for ratification of the North American Free Trade Agreement (NAFTA). NAFTA was negotiated by the Bush administration with Canada and Mexico and contained many provisions that "opened up" trade and investment between the three countries. Since many Democrats refused to support a treaty lacking meaningful guarantees that workers would have the right to unionize or that the environment would be protected, the President was forced to cobble together an unlikely coalition of conservative Democrats and free trade Republicans to get the treaty approved (in the House

---

1 Johnson, *Sorrows*, p. 260
2 Johnson, *Sorrows*, p. 261
3 As quoted in, Bacevich, *American Empire*, p. 40
4 Bacevich, *American Empire*, p. 40

of Representatives: 132 Republicans and 102 Democrats voted in favor, 43 Republicans and 156 Democrats and one independent voted against).

The United States also pushed for greater openness through two international organizations, the International Monetary Fund (IMF) and the World Trade Organization (WTO). The IMF was created in 1944, to prevent the breakdowns in international trade that had deepened the depression of the 1930s. Member nations donated money to the IMF, which then provided loans to nations that were having difficulty paying their debts to foreign creditors.

As the largest contributor to the fund, the US heavily influences IMF policies because voting power on the IMF governing board is based on the amount of money each nation donates. While the IMF's emergency loans have occasionally been valuable, under United States direction the IMF has consistently used its power over debtor nations to promote the strategy of openness.[1] As a prerequisite to making a loan, the IMF imposes a "structural adjustment" agreement requiring the loan recipient to both eliminate laws that restrict the actions of transnational corporations and financial institutions and to reduce the role of the public sector in the nation's economy. It is as if the Fire Department, in return for putting out a fire in your house, requires you to allow the Police Department to station a radio dispatcher and a gun rack in your living room. Standard IMF requirements include lowering tariffs on foreign goods entering the country; removing legal restrictions on transnational corporations purchasing the debtor country's businesses and banks; giving transnational corporations the right to purchase mines, oil fields or other natural resources that had previously been protected from foreign ownership; placing limits on the right to strike; and cutting government budget deficits by reducing food subsidies, slashing expenditures on public health, and dramatically raising fees on services like public transportation.

IMF economists promoted these changes as 'tough medicine' that would restore financial confidence in the debtor nation and inspire transnational banks and corporations to resume investing in the country. Dozens of countries, ranging from the poorly managed to the unlucky to the extremely poor, ran into debt problems during the Cold War or the 1990s and were forced to swallow the IMF's debt medicine. Frequently, the social and economic consequences of these policies were so unpopular that only authoritarian regimes were able impose a full package of reforms. Less authoritarian governments were often able to get away with fewer changes by making the plea that larger cutbacks would trigger unrest that would de-stabilize the country's currency even further.

---

1 Arthur MacEwan, "Economic Debacle in Argentina: The IMF Strikes Again," January, 2002, *International Development Economics Associates*, available from www.networkideas.org/featart/ jan2002/prnt100102_Economic_Debacle.htm; accessed 10 May 2007.

To complement the IMF's efforts, the Clinton administration pushed for the creation of the World Trade Organization in 1995. Its stated goal was to remove barriers to expansions in international trade. As its actual effect was to open up more markets for American products, Clinton hailed its accomplishments, telling Americans, "Since the United States has the most productive and competitive economy in the world, that is good news for our workers and our future."[1]

The trade off to hardships imposed on less developed counties by these policies is the claim that openness will spur trade and the creation of wealth. Unfortunately, in most countries the result is a small number of people who prosper and a much larger number whose standard of living declines. That has been Mexico's experience under NAFTA. NAFTA went into effect on January 1, 1994 and by 2001 real wages were lower than in 1994 and unemployment was rising.[2] In 2001, 75% of Mexico's population lived in poverty, up from 49% in 1981. This is the seldom mentioned source of the wave of illegal immigration coming into the United States. In 1990, there were 2 million undocumented Mexicans working in the US, by 2004, there were 6 million.[3] As Laura Carlsen, Director of the International Relations Center's Americas Program recently wrote, "Mexico is not producing enough decent jobs for its people — and the United States is hiring."[4] Mexico's story has been repeated again and again in the less developed world.

We should not be surprised at these results. In general, newly opened markets are dominated by efficient transnational corporations, which are no longer restrained by community rules and expectations. Joseph Stiglitz, formerly an economist at the World Bank, has become a leading critic of free trade and openness. He says:

> It is now a commonplace that the international trade agreements about which the United States spoke so proudly only a few years ago were grossly unfair to countries in the Third World . . . The problem [with globalists is] . . . their fundamentalist market ideology, a faith in free, unfettered markets that is supported by neither modern theory nor historical experience.[5]

The actual historical record is that all of the highly developed countries in the world got that way by imposing high tariffs on foreign products and using many other social and cultural regulations to protect their domestic businesses from foreign competition.[6] England began practicing protection-

---

1 Bacevich, *American Empire*, p. 97

2 Klein, *Fences*, p. 50

3 American Friends Service Committee, "North American Free Trade Agreement," available from www.afsc.org/trade-matters/trade-agreements/NAFTA.htm; accessed 11 May 2007.

4 Laura Carlsen, "Migrants: Globalization's Junk Mail," *International Relations Center Americas Program*, available from www.irc-online.org/americaspolicy/am/4211; accessed 8 May 2007.

5 As quoted in, Johnson, *Sorrows*, p. 262

6 MacEwan, "Economic Debacle in Argentina," Jan, 2002

ist policies in the 15th century, when Henry VII taxed wool imports from the world's leading wool manufacturers in the Netherlands and Belgium in order to drive up their costs and make them less competitive with English woolens.[1]

Between 1790 and 1940, the United States protected its financial and manufacturing corporations with very high tariffs. Senator Henry Clay, the leader of the Whig Party in the antebellum era, successfully advocated for an "American System," which emphasized government investment in infrastructure and high tariff rates.[2] Reacting to British preaching about the virtues of free trade (they were the most efficient and competitive manufacturing economy in the 19th century), President Ulysses S. Grant replied that, "within 200 years, when the US has gotten out of protection all it can offer, then it too will adopt free trade."[3]

The contrasting results between those nations who manage their economic relationships with the world and those who adopt the openness policies advocated by the United States, the IMF, and the WTO became very stark during the financial collapses of the 1990s. For example, between 1993 and early 1997, international investors poured $100 billion into real estate and stock speculation in the booming Asian countries of Korea, Thailand, Indonesia, and Malaysia.[4] Then, in the summer of 1997, foreign investors suddenly panicked and pulled their money out of financial markets in eastern Asia. While Korea took an IMF loan package and wages in the country fell 15% in one year, Malaysian Prime Minister Mahathir Mohamad defied the IMF and placed strict controls on money flowing in and out of his country. He even stated that Western speculators were irresponsibly harming healthy Asian economies.[5] His willingness to defy the trend toward openness infuriated western economists and policy makers, who predicted that hyperinflation and economic collapse would soon follow. Thomas Friedman, a columnist at the *New York Times* who sings the praises of globalization at every opportunity, wrote:

> Excuse me, Mahathir, but what planet are you living on? You talk about participating in globalization as if it were a choice you had. Globalization isn't a choice. It's a reality . . . And the most basic truth about globalization is this: *No one is in charge* . . . the global marketplace today is an Electronic

---

1 Ha-Joon Chang, "Kicking Away the Ladder," *Post-Autistic Economics Review*, issue no. 15, September 4, 2002, article 3, available from www.paecon.net/PAEtexts/Chang1.htm; accessed 12 May 2007.

2 Peterson, "The Great Triumvirate," p. 68-84

3 Chang, "Kicking Away the Ladder," 9.4.02

4 Walden Bello, "Globalization in Asia and China," Sept. 2004, *Transnational Institute*, available from www.tni.org/detail_page.phtml?page=archives_bello_chinaglob; accessed 19 May 2007.

5 Paul Krugman, "Capital Control Freaks," 9.27.99, available from www.slate.com/id=35534; accessed 17 May 2007.

Herd of often anonymous stock, bond, and currency traders and multinational investors.[1]

However, Mahathir, who led Malaysia for two decades while it attracted more capital than any other emerging market, had the last word.[2] The controls imposed on September 14, 1998 required that all investment funds placed in Malaysian stocks had to remain in the country for a year. Then, rather than raising interest rates and cutting government spending, as the IMF requires, the government cut rates and spent more money to prevent a recession.[3] Ethan Kaplan and Dani Rodrik at the Kennedy School of Government have done a time-lapsed economic study which shows that, contrary to the dire warnings from Friedman and mainstream economists, the Malaysian economy actually suffered fewer losses and recovered much faster than Korea, Thailand, or Indonesia, nations in similar situations who had followed the IMF's traditional advice and suffered huge declines in living standards.[4]

Malaysia's successful defiance of the IMF and international speculators paved the way for Argentina to default on IMF and private loans during its prolonged economic crisis in 2002 and 2003. The statement of the Argentine government's spokesperson captured the emerging view of less developed countries about globalization and the US strategy of openness:

> We are not saying the blame for what is wrong should be pinned on the fund, we assume the responsibility as a country ... but what we are saying is the bureaucracy at the Fund has promoted the policies that put us in this situation.[5]

By borrowing money at low interest rates from oil-rich Venezuela, Argentina was able to pay off its IMF debt and re-schedule its foreign debt at lower interest rates without following the dreaded IMF strategy of high interest rates, budget cuts, and concessions to international corporations. The result — the Argentine economy has grown 45% over the last five years.[6]

Globalization as a tactic in the US strategy of openness was being openly resisted on a number of fronts by the end of the 1990s. Many less developed and newly industrializing countries were searching for ways to regulate foreign investments and the flow of capital into and out of their countries. Political activists from every corner of the globe contradicted Thomas Fried-

1 Johnson, *Sorrows*, p. 274

2 John A. Miller, "Malaysia and the Myth of Self-Regulating Markets," *International Development Economics Association*, available from www.networkideas.org/book/jan2003/bk30_Jomo.htm; accessed 14 May 2007

3 Rodrik and Kaplan, "Malaysian Capital Controls," February 2001

4 Rodrik and Kaplan, "Malaysian Capital Controls," February 2001

5 BBCNews, "Argentina in $1 bn. Loan Default," available from http://news.bbc.co.uk/2/hi/business/2573183.stm; accessed 11 May 2007

6 Dean Baker, "The IMF: A Sandbox to Play In," *Truthout*, 4.10.07; available from http://www.truthout.org/docs_2006/041007A.shtml; accessed 12 April 2007

man, pointing out that the policies prescribed by the WTO, the IMF, and the United States were not the only ways to respond to the information revolution and that the people who ran those institutions were creating the rules for a game where only transnational corporations won and nearly everyone else ended up losing.[1]

Tensions over US, IMF, and WTO practices exploded into the public arena in November of 1999 when the WTO held its annual meeting in Seattle, Washington. For a full week, 50,000 protesters from every part of the globe joined American trade unionists, environmentalists, globalization idealists, and anarchists in a series of carefully planned demonstrations that disrupted the WTO's meetings and made parts of downtown Seattle look like a war zone. These protests were followed by similar protest gatherings during international conferences in Rome, London, Barcelona, and Buenos Aires. These "counter summits" began publicizing other forms of development — all of them standing in stark contrast to the strategy of openness. After these embarrassing protests the IMF, the WTO, and other international business meetings began to be held in far-off, inaccessible places — the WTO meeting in 2001 took place in the repressive Persian Gulf state of Qatar, where political protest is strictly forbidden.[2]

* * *

During the Presidential election of 2000, foreign policy played almost no role in either of the candidates' programs, nor did it figure prominently in the electorate's calculations about whom to vote for. Leaders from both parties generally endorsed the Clinton administration's unprecedented expansion of the American empire:

> Comparing the actual views of Bush and Gore, or more generally comparing the views of Democratic foreign policy experts with those of their Republican counterparts during the campaign was akin to comparing the prime time programming of competing television networks. Some differences exist . . . But enumerating those differences doesn't go very far toward identifying the true nature of the enterprise known as commercial television.[3]

While the strategy of openness was becoming more and more controversial in other countries, Americans and their political leaders still believed that globalization was a natural and inevitable step in the history of progress. There was no sense that resistance to the American empire amounted to anything more than the complaints of a few isolated activists. During the next decade, these beliefs turned out to be wildly, disastrously wrong, with the world of 2008 looking far more ominous than any American could have imagined during that long ago election campaign.

1 Johnson, *Sorrows*, p. 274
2 Klein, *Fences*, p. xxiv
3 Bacevich, *American Empire*, p. 201

Chapter 8. The Price of Empire

> Because the past repeats only in general resemblance, there is always something different, something new. This truth, together with the usual effects of the passage of time, makes it easy for later generations to dismiss any awkward precedents...[1]
> —Kevin Phillips, *American Theology*

A dazzling torrent of riches poured into Rome. Treasure stolen from fabulously wealthy cities like Carthage, Corinth, and Pella filled up the Roman treasury and supported the families of Roman generals for generations. After his victory at the battle of Pydna in 168 BCE, L. Aemilius Paullus looted the royal Macedonian palace at Pella and removed the art, gold, jewelry, and precious stones that had been accumulated there since Alexander the Great's conquest of Persia. When he returned to Rome, his triumphant parade through the streets of the city took several days, with the first day taken up by 250 wagons filled with art objects and giant paintings glorifying his victorious campaign in Greece.[2] On the second day 3,000 men carried silver coins in jars, gleaming weapons, and captured armor.

The proceeds of Paullus' victory were so enormous that the Senate ended all regular taxation on Roman citizens and future conquests meant that taxes were not reinstated until the civil wars after Caesar's assassination.[3] Paullus himself is said to have refrained from taking money or treasure — already wealthy, he confined his reward to the royal library of Macedonia, which

---

1 Phillips, "American Theocracy," p. 298
2 Flower, "Spectacle," p. 328
3 Green, *Alexander to Actium*, p. 415

he used to educate his sons.[1] When Paullus died, his estate was valued at 370,000 *denarii*, almost four times the minimum required for entry into the *Equestrian* Order.[2] By the middle of the 2nd century, this was not considered to be an especially great fortune.

THE RICHES OF EMPIRE

Defeated states that maintained their independence were usually forced to send large indemnities to the Roman government. For example, after his defeat at Cynoscephalae in 197 BCE, Phillip II of Macedonia had to send the Roman treasury 1,000 silver *talents* over a period of 20 years. A *talent* was considered to be the load a man can carry and was somewhere between 50 and 55 pounds. After the battle of Magnesia in Asia Minor, the Seleucid king Antiochus III was forced to pay an indemnity of 15,000 *talents* over 15 years.[3] This works out to roughly 50,000 pounds of silver shipped to the Republican government each year.

The sale of slaves when a city or region was conquered also brought enormous riches to the Roman treasury. During the First Punic War, the Republic seized an estimated 75,000 captives who were sold as slaves, netting the state some 15 million *denarii* to assist with war expenditures.[4] Even small wars to suppress rebellions in just one province of the new empire could lead to large numbers of individuals being sold into slavery. For example, Tiberius Sempronius Gracchus crushed a rebellion in Sardinia in 177 BCE and sold so many Sardinians into slavery that the market in Rome was temporarily saturated. The expression *Sardi venales* (Sardinians for sale) entered the Roman idiom as a way of talking about cheap items available at the market.[5]

For members of the nobility, a reliable source of new wealth was election to serve as governor of a newly acquired province of the empire. After taking Sicily, Sardinia, and Corsica from Carthage, the Plebeian Assembly created two new praetor positions to manage the big islands of Sicily and Sardinia. When Spain became a Roman possession after the Second Punic War, two more praetor positions were created to manage that vast province. New quaestor positions were also created to help these provincial governors manage their finances.

This system of electing praetors to one-year terms as provincial governors created a dynamic similar to the one created by the practice of electing consuls to one-year terms. Just as consuls were driven, by their brief chance to serve as commander of an army, to seek military victories that would bring

---

1 Green, *Alexander to Actium*, p. 415

2 Alfoldy, *Social History*, p. 46

3 Green, *Alexander to Actium*, p. 421

4 Scullard, *Roman World*, p. 358

5 Matyszak, *Chronicle*, p. 122

luster to their reputations and plunder for their family, so too, newly elected praetors were determined to make as much money as possible during their brief chance to hold autocratic control of a region. While the one-year term may have prevented any Roman governor from accumulating enough power to become a threat to the city, it also meant that provinces were not so much ruled as ravaged.

A 1st century example we know about is Gaius Caesar, Julius Caesar's father. The Julii family was of noble blood, but relatively poor, before Gaius Marius married Julius Caesar's Aunt Julia. With the riches and connections Marius had accumulated as a result of his military victories, Gaius Caesar was able to win election as a praetor and was appointed governor of the province of Asia in Asia Minor. It was clear what he was expected to accomplish:

> Few Senators advanced to provincial governorships, and rare was the fam-
> ily that attained more than one such post in a generation. The fortunate
> appointee expected to amass sufficient wealth to enrich his family for
> generations...The Julians had failed to obtain a generous share of the vast
> plunder of the previous century; now, as a result of their connections to
> Marius, they had an opportunity to catch up with their wealthier rivals in
> the nobility.[1]

Once he arrived in his province, a new governor was likely to meet with other prominent Romans who were deeply invested in the area. These were Roman businessmen, members of the *Equestrian* Order, who moved into captured provinces and seized upon the dozens of opportunities to engage in profitable commerce that came naturally to citizens of the occupying power. The most powerful of these international businessmen were known as *publicani*. While many members of the *Equestrian* Order were businessmen, the *publicani* were distinct in their role of carrying out administrative and manufacturing activities in close partnership with the state.

The *publicani* were essential members of the state system because, as one dimension of their belief in limiting the power of government, the Romans privatized many government functions. The *publicani* formed joint stock companies that bid for contracts to work for the state. "They provided public works (such as roads and aqueducts), supplies (such as horses and armor), and services (particularly tax collection), in return for a cash payment from the state."[2] The *publicani* became the richest businessmen in the *Equestrian* Order because their contracts with the state were very large, with guaranteed profits. (They were similar to the "cost-plus" contracts awarded by the Pentagon.)

---

1 Kahn, *Education of Caesar*, p. 23
2 Matyszak, *Chronicle*, p. 137

The *publicani's* activities in the provinces were mostly unrestricted by any Roman authority other than the provincial governor. The opportunities for mutual enrichment were plentiful:

> As governor of Asia Gaius [Caesar] had promoted the interests of the entrepreneurs, Marius' partisans, as an inscription erected by oil men (olive) in Gaius' honor on the Aegean island of Delos attests.[1]

The *publicani* made great fortunes through state contracts to operate silver mines in Spain, manufacture armor for garrisons, build roads in Greece, and collect tariffs at the great ports of the Mediterranean. Other businessmen and aristocrats in the *Equestrian* Order, more commonly known as *equites,* also became wealthy dealing in slaves, growing wheat in Sicily, and harvesting olive oil in northern Africa. Like the aristocrats in the nobility, they poured their profits into the purchase of large estates in Campania, Etruria, and southern Italy. By the middle of the 2nd century, there was little difference in the wealth held by the nobility and the wealth possessed by the *equites* — both social groups in the *Equestrian* Order were rich beyond the wildest imaginations of their ancestors.

Consequences of Wealth

The great riches enjoyed by the nobility and the *equites* led to many changes in Roman society. The very use and enjoyment of their newly obtained wealth was a violation of some of the most fundamental public Roman virtues, as celebrated in the *mos maiorum* (literally, the way of our ancestors). The *mos maiorum* consisted of the social customs, cultural traditions, and religious practices that were followed by the Romans' highly successful ancestors. These customs incorporated a number of virtues, including *pietas* — devotion, a willingness to do one's duty for the gods, the family and the Republic; *frugalitas* — frugality or simplicity of living; *diligentia* — discipline, diligence; *virtus*, strength, courage, manliness; and *gravitas* — seriousness of purpose, sense of dignity.[2]

In Rome, the possession of these virtues by prominent families was one of the principal justifications for the nobility's monopoly on political office. However, in the 2nd century members of the nobility began living "an ostentatious and luxurious life-style."[3] One example is the construction of enormous, elaborate homes on the Palatine hill and on rural estates. The "House of the Faun" uncovered at Pompeii in Campania is a startling example of this

---

1 Kahn, *Education of Caesar*, p. 37
2 Scullard, *Roman World*, p. 361 and available from www.Everything2.com; search: "Roman Virtues," accessed 25 July 2007.
3 Cornell, *Atlas*, p. 54

trend. The house covers 31,000 square feet, a size that is comparable to royal palaces in the Hellenistic monarchies.[1]

This is an oversized example of what one historian has called "the Villa Phenomenon." Many members of the nobility invested their new wealth in "mansions combining the amenities of city life with the charms of the country."[2] This phenomenon was most visible along the coast of what is now the Gulf of Naples. During the 2nd and 1st centuries, wealthy Romans built large villas overlooking the sea and held sumptuous banquets to be sure everyone could come and see their new toys. Anyone who has toured the mansions along the "gold coast" of Newport, Rhode Island, where 19th century robber barons built mansions by copying the best designs from Italy, will have an idea of what it must have felt like.

This lifestyle offended many Romans and undermined the moral authority of the nobility. Several laws passed during this period give us insight into the lifestyles of wealthy Romans. In 181 BCE, a law was passed limiting the number of guests a person could have at a banquet in the home.[3] In 81, to resurrect *frugalitas* and *gravitas*, the Dictator Sulla passed a law imposing maximum prices on food served at dinner parties in an attempt to limit competition between aristocrats for holding the most lavish parties.[4] However, these laws could not hold back the tide of social change.

This lavish lifestyle, and the elitist culture that sprang from it, created a new kind of separation of the wealthy members of society from ordinary Romans. Earlier patricians and nobles believed they were better that the average Roman, but that distinction was based on possession of a pure character created by breeding and ancestry. It was also moderated by a strong sense of *pietas* for all members of the *res publica*. The nobility in the 2nd century believed it was simply superior to ordinary Romans. The plebeians knew of this attitude and resented the rich in a way that had not been present even during the Struggle of the Orders.[5]

CRISIS ON THE LAND

The most destructive aspect of this new wealth was the rush to invest it in agricultural land. There was a lot of land for sale in the 2nd century BCE, because the wars of empire were devastating for the small farmers who made up the ranks of the city's legions. Before the Second Punic War, Rome's wars were summertime affairs on the Italian peninsula. The small farmers who

1 Boatwright, *The Romans*, p. 147

2 Jean-Jacques Aubert, "The Republican Economy and Roman Law," in Flower, Harriet, ed., *The Cambridge Companion to the Roman Republic*, Cambridge: Cambridge University Press, 2004. p. 169

3 Vishnia, *State, Society, Leaders*, p. 165

4 Aubert, "The Republican Economy," p. 169

5 Holland, *Rubicon*, p. 18

were members of the Second, Third, Fourth, and Fifth Classes in the Centuriate Assembly had time to tend their crops before being mustered into service
and were usually able to come back from combat to bring in the harvest.

The war against Hannibal was on a completely different scale. Between
217 and 203 BCE, Rome usually had 28 legions, about 120,000 men, in service
on a year-round basis.[1] About an equal number of soldiers were provided
by the Italian allies. Many of the men who fought in this period never came
home again. Whole armies were lost in the battles against Hannibal — between 40,000 and 50,000 were killed at Cannae in just one day. The presence of Hannibal's army in Italy for almost 15 years led to great hardship for
farmers in southern Italy. Their land was plundered for supplies, livestock
was driven off for consumption by his army, and buildings were destroyed
in battles.[2]

The problems for the Italian peasantry continued after the war. The rapid
expansion of the empire led to a series of engagements away from Italy — in
Spain, Macedonia, Greece, and Asia Minor. To successfully wage these wars
it is estimated that the Republic maintained a combined Roman-Italian
army of 130,000 men for the 35 years after the beginning of the 2nd century; as
a result, half the adult males on the peninsula served, year-round, in the army
for at least seven of the 20 years between age 20 and age 40.[3]

> Such a level of involvement in warfare was disastrous for the class of peas-
> ant smallholders. Many peasant families were thus deprived of essential
> manpower for long periods, or permanently, if their menfolk were killed in
> battle. Farms were neglected, debts were incurred and dispossession fol-
> lowed through sale or eviction.[4]

Remember that problems with indebtedness had plagued the average
Roman even in the best of times; if there were bad harvests or periods when
the women and children were unable to bring in a good crop, then debts
piled up quickly and sale of the farm was the only recourse.[5] In this period
of weakness and distress, small farms were rapidly bought out and added
to the estates of fabulously wealthy members of the nobility and by *equites*
who wished to acquire land and gain agricultural respectability. As landholdings grew larger the Roman ruling classes began creating large estates
called *latifundia*.[6]

The old solution to land problems for the plebeians was to establish colonies, and initially a large number of colonies were established for soldiers
returning from service. Between 197 and 177, twenty colonies were estab-

---

1 LeGlay, *History of Rome*, p. 89
2 Alfoldy, *Social History*, p. 52
3 Cornell, *Atlas*, p. 55
4 Cornell, *Atlas*, p. 55
5 Meier, *Caesar*, p. 29
6 Bernstein, *Tiberius Sempronius Gracchus*, p. 84

lished with an estimated 60,000 families re-settled.[1] However, their new farms were subject to the same economic stresses that were driving thousands of families off the land each year.[2] Some displaced farmers moved to the prosperous cities along the western coast, but it is unclear how many jobs were available for them. Slaves were brought in to work on large-scale public works projects and manufacturing activities. In addition, the growing class of freedmen frequently had craft and retailing skills that people who had worked on the land their whole lives could not match.

Many small farmers who lost their land probably stayed on as tenant farmers, no longer *assidui*, property owners, but still citizens and able to participate in Plebeian and Tribal Assembly deliberations.[3] Tenant farmers were more efficient at growing and harvesting grain than slave gangs, so there continued to be an economic reason not to replace them with slaves.[4] Other displaced small farm owners worked small plots and took temporary jobs at harvest and planting time on the big *latifundias* or when work was available in nearby cities.[5]

The rapid demographic changes in the countryside meant that the gap between rich and poor grew steadily during the 2nd century. While we do not have any systematic income data, one measure of the gap is that a legionnaire was paid 480 *sesterces* per year while Scipio Africanus left each of his daughters a dowry of 300,000 *sesterces* when he died.[6]

The deterioration of rural life on the Italian peninsula began to break down the social and political bonds that had connected small farmers to the nobility in the 4th and 3rd centuries. These farmers had voted for members of the traditional leading families in the Centuriate Assembly and supported their sons in the Tribal Assembly, but by the middle of the 2nd century, this alliance was breaking up.[7] The nobility's nervousness about rural unhappiness is reflected in a law designed to minimize the influence of the rural poor. The *lex Aelia et Fufia* made it illegal to propose and pass a law around the time of elections.[8] The purpose was to prevent popular reform laws from being proposed in the Plebeian Assembly when Rome was crowded with country people who had come to the city to support their patron's candidates in the Tribal and Centuriate Assemblies. Another sign of discontent was the wide-

---

1 Vishnia, *State, Society, Leaders*, p. 142 & 158
2 Lily Ross Taylor, "Forerunners of the Gracchi," *Journal of Roman Studies*, #52, 1962, p. 21
3 Bernstein, *Tiberius Sempronius Gracchus*, p. 91
4 Bernstein, *Tiberius Sempronius Gracchus*, p. 95
5 David Stockton, *The Gracchi*, Oxford: Oxford University Press, 1979, p. 18
6 Stockton, *The Gracchi*, p. 7
7 Alfoldy, *Social History*, p. 61
8 Bernstein, *Tiberius*, p. 97

spread avoidance of the draft, known as the *levy*, for the Macedonian War in 160 BCE.[1]

ROME: THE GROWTH OF AN UNDERCLASS

The instability brewing in the countryside compounded the chaotic growth of Rome, the political capital and economic hub of Italy. A significant number of displaced farmers moved to Rome where they lived on handouts and part-time jobs. Former soldiers took up residence in the city, as did thousands of freed slaves. Those slaves who had practiced a trade in their homeland became craftsmen, traders, and shopkeepers (*tabernarii*). The rich, who mainly lived on the Palatine hill, were heavy consumers of all types of consumer goods and services, many of which could be satisfied by workers in the city. The city was known for manufacturing a variety of products including clothing, jars and bowls, locks, keys, heavy ploughs, yokes, and baskets.[2]

In spite of this bustling economic activity, there was not enough work for the people who poured into the city; in this period before the industrial revolution, there were no large factories to absorb the labor of thousands of unskilled migrant workers. Vast slum neighborhoods sprang up to house the new urban poor.[3] The city had no urban planning or publicly provided housing, so the poor were crammed into dirty, unhealthy tenement buildings called *insulae* (literally: islands) that frequently fell down or burned.[4] Marcus Crassus, one of the wealthiest men in Rome in the 1st century, enhanced his wealth by creating a private fire department. When an *insula* caught fire, his fire wagons would show up and, for a significant fee, put out the fire. If the owner could not pay for the service, Crassus offered to buy the site from the hapless owner at a price that steadily declined as more and more of the building was consumed in the flames.

A large, unemployed underclass developed that made the city dangerous and created an unruly social world. Many people in the city struggled to pay for food on a daily basis; when there was a bad harvest in Sicily or an economic downturn, hunger became a burning political issue. We have one demographic gauge for the scale of the problem. In 58 BCE, Rome had grown to somewhere between 750,000 and one million people. That year more than 320,000 hungry people, 32 to 40 per cent of the population depending on which total is used, participated in the free corn ration implemented by the radical Tribune Publius Clodius Pulcher.[5] In a city with 500,000 residents

1 Vishnia, *State, Society, Leaders*, p. 150
2 Scullard, *Roman World*, p. 352
3 Meier, *Caesar*, p. 30
4 Holland, *Rubicon*, p. 16
5 Fergus Millar, "A Critique of the Cambridge History of the Roman Republic," in *Journal of Roman Studies*, V.85, 1995, p. 240

in 140 BCE, a similar ratio of hungry people would mean 150,000 to 200,000 individuals living on the edge of starvation. There were no social services or public programs for the poor. In general, a new phenomenon in the ancient world was forming: a proletariat.

INEQUALITY IN AMERICA

It would be foolish to think of inequality in America today as being comparable to the situation that developed in Republican Rome. The standard of living is much higher for the average person in the United States and there is a social safety net that takes care of many people. However, an interesting parallel is occurring in the distribution of wealth as the American empire grows and becomes a more dominant aspect of American life.

The first period of the American empire, from the Spanish American War up through the Vietnam War, brought rising prosperity for the average citizen. This mirrors the experience of the Roman Republic during the 4th and 3rd centuries. The Progressive Era and then the Roaring Twenties gradually increased the income of many sectors of the urban population. The Great Depression was an enormous setback, but after World War II, there was a 25-year period of growth that lifted incomes at every level of society.[1] The spread of unions, the growth of Social Security and later Medicare and Medicaid, the use of policies like the minimum wage to ensure the bottom fifth of the population shared in economic growth, the rapid increase in professional jobs, and the slow improvement in civil rights for African-Americans all created an unprecedented level of material prosperity for the average person. The most visible feature of this economic expansion was the explosive growth of suburban America where millions of people were able to own their own homes for the first time.

Economic growth was stimulated by a combination of factors. The low gas prices secured by American oil corporations made it inexpensive to operate the millions of autos being produced by thousands of well-paid union workers and mid-level auto executives. The rise of the automobile made it possible to build those new suburbs and stimulated public investment in highways, streets, and bridges.[2] Government spending for a permanent military establishment operated as an engine of growth; research, production, and deployment of thousands of nuclear missiles, airplanes, and submarines provided good jobs for thousands of well-paid workers in California, Texas, and other Sunbelt states. Consumers outside of the Soviet-Chinese bloc were eager to buy sophisticated products from American factories. This was

---

1 Teresa Tritch, "The Rise of the Super Rich," *The New York Times*, 7.19.06; available from http://www.truthout.org/cgi-bin/artman/exec/view.cgi/62/21309; accessed 25 July 2007

2 Paul Baran and Paul Sweezy, *Monopoly Capital*, New York: Monthly Review Press, 1966, pp. 218-224

the era when "Made in Japan" was shorthand for cheap, flimsy products, a political and cultural put-down as rooted in imperial dominance as *Sardi venales* in Rome.

The economics of the American empire began to change in the late 1960s. Military spending during the Vietnam War, combined with increased social spending on the "Great Society," touched off a steady rise in inflation. The resurgence of industrial economies in Western Europe and Japan posed greater competition for American exporters and led to a rapid decline in the US trade surplus. Then, in 1974, came the first oil price shocks and the creation of OPEC. During President Carter's term "stagflation," a combination of inflation and stagnant growth entered our vocabulary. Auto makers grappled with lagging auto sales as a result of high gasoline prices and inexpensive, high quality Japanese cars. Elected in reaction to Carter's economic failures, President Reagan reversed earlier trends by curtailing social service spending, cracking down on unions, opposing civil rights measures, cutting taxes on the wealthy, and blocking increases in the minimum wage.

Since the early 1970s, inequality has grown slowly but surely, accelerating during periods of recession, with the entire population's real income growing only during the boom years of the late 1990s.[1] This income stagnation has affected even affluent white-collar professionals and managers. Between 1972 and 2001, the real wage and salary income of Americans at the 90th percentile of income distribution only rose 34 percent, barely one percent per year.[2] By contrast, households at the 99th percentile of income distribution (in 2005 this corresponded to an income of $402,306) enjoyed an increase of 87 percent between 1972 and 2001; households with incomes in the 99.99th percentile (over $6 million) had a rise in income of 497 percent between 1972 and 2001.

Since 2001, the gap between the top one percent of the population and everyone else continued to grow. For example, between 2003 and 2004, real average income for the top one percent of households grew by nearly 17% while the remaining 99% of the population averaged a gain of less than three percent before inflation.[3] Much of this startling gain was due to the unprecedented salaries, bonuses, and stock options collected by top corporate executives. In a related statistic, the top one percent of households received 57.5 percent of all income from dividends and capital gains in 2003, a significant increase from 53.4 percent just a year earlier. An interesting historical

---

1 Tritch, "Super Rich," 7.19.06
2 Paul Krugman, "Graduates versus Oligarchs," *The New York Times*, 2.27.06; available from http://www.truthout.org/cgi-bin/artman/exec/view.cgi/48/17995; accessed 25 July 2007
3 Tritch, "Super Rich," 7.19.06

note is that, in 2004, "the top one percent [of households] held a bigger share of total income than at any time since 1929."[1]

There is also a stark echo of statistics quoted earlier about the Roman Republic. In 2006, the average US army private made $25,000 a year while the average CEO of a defense firm made $7.7 million.[2] David Lesar, CEO of Halliburton, was paid a total of $79.8 million, about $16 million per year, from 2002 to 2006.[3]

The growth of a new group of super rich people would not be notable if the rest of America was also prospering. However, the cumulative effect of decades of income stagnation is beginning to place painful stresses on American families. At the bottom of the income pyramid, the number of Americans without health coverage went up by 1.3 million in 2005, with a record 46.6 million people facing financial disaster whenever a major illness or injury occurred.[4] One measure of the impact of not having health coverage is that almost half of all personal bankruptcies in the US are now the result of medical debts. In the area of wages, the federal minimum wage, which directly benefits 6.5 million workers, was increased in 1997 (to $5.15 per hour) and then lost about 20 percent of its value until it was increased by the new Democratic Congress in 2007. By way of contrast, the top rate for the estate tax (affecting only 8,200 very large estates) has been reduced every year since 2002.[5]

The stress on middle-income families in the United States is also increasing. The struggle to maintain living standards in a period of stagnating incomes meant that in 2006 the savings rate for the entire country was a negative one percent.[6] The savings rate has been negative for an entire year only four times since 1900 — in 1932 and 1933, and in 2005 and 2006. A major reason people are having trouble saving is the rising cost of goods and services that form the basis of a middle class lifestyle. While the cost of personal music players and other electronic gadgets has gone down, the price of essential big-ticket items like housing, health care, and college has risen dramatically. For example, the total cost of tuition, fees, room and board at four-year public colleges and universities jumped 44 percent between 2002

1 Tritch, "Super Rich," 7.19.06

2 Derrick Jackson, "Soldiers die, CEOs prosper," *Boston Globe*, 8.30.06

3 Michael Brush, "War Means a Windfall for CEOs," MSN Money, 9.19.07; available from http://article.moneycentral.msn.com/Investing/CompanyFocus/WarMeansAWindfallForCEOs.aspx; accessed 20 September 2007

4 Lou Dobbs, "Are You a Casualty of the Class War?," CNN, 10.4.06; available from http://www.cnn.com/2006/US/10/03/Dobbs.Oct4/index.html; accessed 25 July 2007

5 Aviva Aron-Dine, "Since Last Minimum Wage Increase, Congress has Reduced Estate Tax Burdens Eight Times," *Center on Budget and Policy Priorities*, 8.30.06; available from http://www.cbpp.org/8-2-06tax2.pdf; accessed 25 July 2007

6 *Associated Press*, "Personal Savings Drop to a 74-year Low," 2.1.07; available from http://www.msnbc.msn.com/id/16922582/; accessed 25 July 2007

and 2006.[1] Housing costs are also rising; more than one-third of homeowners with a mortgage in 2005 had housing costs higher than 30% of their income, while in 1999 the percentage of homeowners with excessive housing expenses was 26.7 percent.

The political response to growing inequality in the United States has, up to this point, been tepid. If you ask the average American about super rich people he or she will bring up the names of movie stars and professional athletes. Discussions about stagnating wages will usually lead to denunciations of illegal immigrants and criticism of the fringe benefits enjoyed by government employees. In a perceptive book, *Class Inequality and Political Order*, Frank Parkin states that one of the roles of social democratic or left-of-center political parties in a capitalist society is to provide the average citizen with an alternative explanation of how and why inequality occurs.[2] To counteract feelings of individual blame and guilt, the party's candidates and elected office holders should both denounce inequality and advocate for new policies to address the problem. However, since the beginning of the new era of inequality in the 1970s, the Democratic Party's principal response is to point out that the problem exists when seeking votes during election campaigns.

It is interesting to reflect on recent social and cultural trends in the United States when thinking about Parkin's implicit criticism of the Democrats. In the absence of a political party willing to campaign on a platform advocating remedies to problems related to inequality, Parkin says:

> One likely consequence of such an occurrence is that the subordinate value system would increasingly provide the framework of social meaning among the working class. That is, interpretations of and responses to class inequalities would probably be weighted more heavily in the direction of adaptation and accommodation.[3]

If present income distribution trends continue, it will be instructive to see what political consequences might emerge in the coming decade or during a severe recession.

THE RISE OF THE PUBLICANI

The *publicani*, rich men who formed joint stock companies and bid for government contracts were, as we saw earlier, essential partners in the work of imperial government. The growing influence of this group of international businessmen was demonstrated in 215 BCE. Two *publicani* firms deliberately sank their cargo ships, which were bound for Spain to supply the army, and demanded compensation from the Senate, which had insured all ships working for the state during the war.[4] The Senate agreed, but two tribunes

---

1 Dobbs, "Are You a Casualty of the Class War?" 10.4.06
2 Frank Parkin, *Class Inequality and Social Order*, New York: Praeger Publishers, 1971, pp. 97-99
3 Parkin, *Class Inequality*, p. 100
4 Scullard, *Roman World*, p. 318

brought capital charges for treason against the owners. During the trial, a large crowd of *equites* gathered and started a riot in the Forum, with the result being an acquittal for the guilty *publicani*.

This incident highlights how the *publicani* were altering Roman politics. First, the *publicani*'s principal customer was the state, so the companies and individuals who made up this group had much in common. Because of their common interests, they were able to coordinate their activities and become a pressure group in the political system.[1] Second, the *publicani*, given their ability to form a unified position on an issue, were occasionally able to mobilize other *equites*. Third, the rising cost of running for office meant that political candidates needed the financial support of *publicani* in order to pay for their election campaigns.

For two centuries after the Great Compromise of 367 BCE, the steady expansion of the Roman Republic was driven by three mutually reinforcing dynamics. The first was the policy of "defensive imperialism," in which Rome acquired buffer states and then became involved in further conflicts. In tandem ran a domestic political dynamic, in which the leading men of the city, seeking honors for themselves and their families, were elected to be consuls and generals for only a year, giving them every incentive to seek immediate opportunities for military conquest. The third dynamic was the social pressure to provide land for the plebeians through the conquest of new territories. The combination of these dynamics led to the conquest of Italy and the creation of a confederacy on the Italian peninsula, where most of the conquered communities achieved the status of partial citizenship or became treaty allies of Rome.

The dynamics of expansion changed in Rome after the Second Punic War. The newly acquired overseas empire — Sicily, Spain, and North Africa — did not become part of the Roman confederacy and, instead, were heavily exploited for their wealth. When new areas became Roman provinces — Macedonia in 148, Greece in 146, and Asia Minor in 132 — they were treated like Spain and Sicily, places where provincial governors and the *publicani* could make fabulous fortunes. In every province, Romans dominated economic life, making great fortunes off the resources of other peoples. Cicero tells us that in 74 BCE, "Gaul is packed with traders, crammed with Roman citizens. No Gaul does business independently of a citizen of Rome; not a penny changes hands without the transaction being recorded in the books of Roman citizens."[2] Economic imperialism thus replaced defensive imperialism as one of the dynamics fueling Roman expansion.[3]

---

1 Cornell, *Atlas*, p. 56
2 Cornell, *Atlas*, p. 63
3 LeGlay, *History of Rome*, p. 96

We have already seen how another dynamic of early Roman expansion, the acquisition of land for the plebeians, was actually reversed by the wars and economic changes that came with conquering an overseas empire. Along with the shift to economic imperialism there was a change in the dynamics of the domestic political cycle. In the 2nd century the leading men of the city were elected to be praetors and consuls for only a year, giving them powerful incentives to seek opportunities for plunder while they governed a province or conquered a new region. In this process, they formed alliances with the *publicani*. For a Roman governor, "it would increase his future electioneering prospects if he adopted a lenient attitude toward the Italian merchants and businessmen who invaded the provinces."[1]

Over time, more and more praetors, consuls, and censors owed much of their success to their commercial and political ties with members of the *publicani*. They understood that "the one needed the other if they were both to end up rich. [As a result,] Roman government increasingly began to mutate into what can perhaps best be described as a military–fiscal complex."[2] These cross ties between the two groups led to a strong bias toward policies of conquest and exploitation around the Mediterranean.

THE MILITARY–INDUSTRIAL COMPLEX

The development of corrupting connections between businessmen and political leaders, one of the consequences of the Roman Republic acquiring an empire, has a clear parallel in the United States. In his Farewell Address to the nation, in January of 1961, President Dwight D. Eisenhower warned of a similar problem:

> My fellow Americans... We have been compelled to create a permanent armament industry of vast proportions. Three-and-a-half million men and women are directly engaged in the defense establishment. . . .

> This conjunction of an immense military establishment and a large arms industry is new in the American experience. The total influence, economic, political, even spiritual, is felt in every city, every state house, every office of the federal government. We recognize the imperative need for this development, yet we must not fail to comprehend its grave implications. . . .

> In the councils of government, we must guard against the acquisition of unwarranted influence, whether sought or unsought, by the military industrial complex. The potential for the disastrous rise of misplaced power exists and will persist.[3]

The war in Iraq has, once again, highlighted the continuing influence of transnational defense corporations in the making of foreign and military pol-

1 Scullard, *Roman World*, p. 328

2 Holland, *Rubicon*, p. 42

3 Dwight D. Eisenhower, "Farewell Address," 1.19.1961; available from http://mcadams.posc. mu.edu/ike.htm; accessed 25 July 2007

icies. Until 2000, Vice President Dick Cheney was Chief Executive Officer of Halliburton, a giant transnational company. In April of 2003, Halliburton received a $7 billion, no-bid contract for repairing Iraq's oil industry and then had it revoked because of Congressional outrage. However, it later got the contract back in a questionable competitive bidding process.[1] Kellogg, Brown, & Root, a subsidiary of Halliburton, received $16 billion in contracts for projects in Iraq and Afghanistan from 2004 through 2006 — billions more than any other company.[2]

Another example of transnational corporations using political influence to gain lucrative contracts is the case of Bechtel Corporation. At the time of the invasion of Iraq, Riley Bechtel, a senior member of the family that owns the company, was a member of President Bush's Export Council and Jack Sheehan, a senior Vice President at Bechtel was a member of the Defense Policy Board, a group established to give advice to then Secretary of Defense Donald Rumsfeld.[3] Meanwhile, George Shultz, a Bechtel board member and former Secretary of State under President Reagan, penned an op-ed in the Washington Post in September of 2002 where he said, "A strong foundation exists for immediate military action against Hussein and for a multilateral effort to re-build Iraq after he is gone."[4] Shultz must have been pleased when the Defense Department gave Bechtel a huge contract in 2003 to re-build Iraq's oil infrastructure.

These are just a few examples of the problem inherent in business and government partnerships that develop when a republic tries to manage an empire by contracting with private companies. The military-industrial complex continues to have undue influence on US foreign policy, 48 years after President Eisenhower's warning.

ELECTORAL CORRUPTION AND ROMAN POLITICS

After the Second Punic War, the Senate was eager to resume the routines of the election process because it wanted the honor and fortune associated with the praetor and consul positions to once more be spread throughout the families of the nobility. A law was passed that formalized the requirement that no one could run for a quaestor position without serving for 10 years as an officer and that men had to run for office in the traditional order of quaestor, praetor, and consul. However, the Republic now controlled an empire, and the dynamics created by its existence made it impossible to re-

---

1 *HalliburtonWatch.org.* "Iraqi Oil Infrastructure Contracts," available from http://www.halliburtonwatch.org/about_hal/oilinfra.html; accessed 25 July 2007

2 Bill Buzenberg, "Baghdad Bonanza," The Center for Public Integrity, 11.4.07; available from http://www.truthout.org/docs_2006/112007T.shtml; accessed 21 November 2007

3 Pratapp Chatterjee, "Bechtel Wins Iraq War Contracts," *Corpwatch.org*, 4.24.03; available from http://www.corpwatch.org/article.php?id=6532&printsafe=1; accessed 25 July 2007

4 Chatterjee, "Bechtel," 4.24.03

turn to the old ways. For example, every year there were now six wealthy, successful praetors, from noble families, with proven vote-getting ability in the Centuriate Assembly, each with military accomplishments and prominent ancestors, seeking election to just two consul positions each year.

Second, in addition to heightened competition for a limited number of positions, the financial rewards for victory became much greater in the 2nd century.[1] Consuls who won great victories in the East came home with enormous amounts of treasure. Praetors too, as governors of new provinces had the opportunity to amass great fortunes. This made the praetor position a tempting office for those quaestors who, in earlier times, would have been content with reaching that office and becoming a senator. After the Second Punic War there were twelve quaestors to take care of the financial affairs of provinces, ports, temples, and standing armies and all of these tasks required close interaction with helpful *publicani*. So they entered into fierce and expensive competition for the six prized praetor positions. Elections in the Tribal Assembly were effected in the same way, since the quaestors were elected in this body and the stakes for attaining that office became much higher as it became a stepping stone to unrivaled riches.

Finally, the complexion of the Tribal Assembly was changed by the crisis on the land. Farmers who lost their land dropped out of the Centuriate Assembly but they were still citizens and could participate in the Tribal Assembly elections, as well as in the Plebeian Assembly. As far as we know, farmers who lost their land and moved to Rome were not automatically switched out of their rural tribe and into one of the four urban tribes.[2] Therefore, they remained an important percentage of the vote, a significant group who were not part of a nobleman's clientele and were no longer emotionally tied to the military glories of the 3rd century. Those farmers who continued to own their land were economically pinched by competition with foreign commodities and farms maintained with slave labor. They must have frequently joined the landless voters in supporting those candidates who offered them immediate benefits.

For all these reasons, the growth of an overseas empire led to a much more intense, more expensive electoral competition at each stage of the *cursus honorum*. Desperate candidates, those with significant financial resources, but not blessed with military glory or glittering ancestors, began bribing voters. While our sources speak mainly of bribery in the elections for consul, that is because, by and large, we have few accounts of specific election campaigns for quaestor or praetor. However, since there were significant amounts of bribery in the Centuriate Assembly, which was dominated by

---

1 Beard & Crawford, *Late Republic*, p. 69
2 Taylor, *Party Politics*, p. 53

wealthier voters, then there must have been extensive amounts of bribery of poorer citizens in the Tribal Assembly. By 181 BCE, a bribery law was needed to prevent the flagrant buying of votes.[1] That law was ineffective and in 159 a more stringent measure made bribery a capital offense.

The bribery law of 159 made it very difficult for candidates to openly distribute money to voters. Instead, politicians developed a variety of indirect ways to distribute bribes. Cicero claimed in one of his speeches that an extremely common method for distributing bribes was to have friends, associates, and relatives of the candidate hold large dinner parties and pass out cash to those who attended.[2] However, in a city with 500,000 residents and with another 500,000 potential voters living in traveling distance of Rome it was impossible to distribute bribes merely through supporters. To fill the gap, distributing money on behalf of candidates emerged as a profession.

The *divisores* or bribery-agents had regular connections with officials from each tribal unit and distributed cash on behalf of any candidate who wanted to give out significant sums of money.[3] There was a ready-made network for this form of bribery because each Tribe had a headquarters in the area around the forum.[4] The tribal agents were well known figures and the *divisores* probably cultivated relationship with them and had established methods for handing out money. *Divisores* were important people in the late Republic and possessed considerable influence. This was demonstrated in 67 BCE, when the consul C. Calpurnius Piso proposed a law against bribery that included penalties against the *divisores.* When he went to the Plebeian Assembly to speak about his motion, he was attacked by a mob and chased from the Forum. Only after the Senate provided a bodyguard was he able to go to the Assembly and get the law passed.[5]

The really expensive way to legally impress voters was to sponsor games, festivals, or feasts. Candidates and officials wishing to accumulate good will with the mass of people would make enormous expenditures to do things that would be talked about for years. For example, while he was serving as consul in 70 BCE, M. Licinius Crassus, the richest man in Rome (the one with the fire department), tried to upstage his rival and fellow consul Pompey the Great. Pompey had staged elaborate games with elephants in celebration of his victories in Spain that summer, so Crassus arranged to supply free grain to the entire population of Rome for three months. In addition, he held a

---

1 Astin, *Scipio,* p. 29

2 Taylor, *Party Politics,* p. 63

3 Erich S. Gruen, *The Last Generation of the Roman Republic,* Berkeley: University of California Press, 1974, p. 214

4 Yakobson, "Popular Participation in the Centuriate Assembly," p. 42

5 Gruen, *Last Generation,* p. 215

feast for the entire population of the city, setting up hundreds of tables and filling them with rich foods that the average Roman could never afford.[1]

Many and varied were the ways officials spent money to impress the population with their generous spirit. In 67, Cicero, through the gratitude of legal clients from Sicily, was able to flood the markets with Sicilian wheat, thus lowering the price of grain in the city and winning him much praise.[2] Many nobles put on gladiatorial games, a traditional way of honoring a family member who died, but also a way of attracting positive attention.[3] We know that these were standard ways of influencing voters because Cicero, while acting as the defense advocate for a former consul on trial for bribery, talked about the "splendor" of the games and the "magnificence" of the spectacles that Murena gave while he was a praetor.[4] They delighted "the people" and he concluded by saying, "This is enough for our case: elections are a question of numbers and a crowd."[5]

To bribe voters, to stage feasts, to put on games and other public festivals, and to travel around Italy campaigning for office took huge sums of money. While some candidates were famous military commanders or had family names that won votes no matter whom their opponents were, most candidates had to work very hard to win office. Even very rich men could not produce enough ready cash to conduct a campaign or stage a festival. As a result, most candidates had to take out loans from wealthy merchants, especially the *publicani*, who had large amounts of cash on hand. Members of the nobility understood their need for large election loans when they began their political careers and most of them sought to cultivate friendships and alliances with the *publicani* they encountered while serving in state positions. By the middle of the 2nd century, the commercial interests of the *publicani* and the electoral ambitions of the nobility combined to weigh heavily on every aspect of government, from decisions about land reform to the administration of provinces.

Money and American Politics

It has always been helpful to have money if you wanted to be elected to office in the United States. However, activist civic associations, veterans groups, political parties, reform movements, and labor unions frequently challenged the influence of wealthy people in elections. Unfortunately, the growing impact of television and the decline of political parties, civic groups, and unions in the 1960s and 70s began to change this political diversity.

---

1 Matyszak, *Chronicle*, p. 178
2 Everitt, *Cicero*, p. 81
3 Taylor, *Party Politics*, p. 30
4 Yakobson, "Popular Participation in the Centuriate Assembly," p. 35
5 Yakobson, "Popular Participation in the Centuriate Assembly," p. 37

Growing concern about the role of money in shaping elections led to the Federal Election Campaign Act of 1974, which limits the amount individuals, political parties, and political action committees (PACs) can contribute to political campaigns. However, just as the bribery laws in the Roman Republic could not keep a flood of money from pouring into politics, so too, in the American Republic, people found ways to get around the laws and contribute growing amounts of money to candidates they favored.

The sums involved have grown exponentially. In the 1987–88 federal election cycle, Democratic Party candidates raised a total of $114 million and Republican Party candidates raised $251 million. Fifteen years later, in the 2003–2004 federal election cycle, the Democrats raised $679 million and the Republicans brought in $782 million.[1] Note that these figures do not include the amount spent on state and local political campaigns.

These enormous sums reflect the large sums of money a candidate needs to raise in order to win election to a single House or Senate seat. In 2004, the average Republican in the House of Representatives spent $1.5 million defending his seat while the average Democrat spent $1.1 million.[2] In contested races, the cost goes way up. In 2004, there were ten contested House races where the two candidates combined spent more than $5 million. Three were in Texas, and there was one each in South Dakota, Pennsylvania, New Mexico, Louisiana, Nevada, Illinois and Missouri.[3] The numbers for the Senate are many times greater. In 2004, there were ten closely contested Senate races where the two candidates combined to spend more than $16 million.

These figures show that a person who wants to run for a seat in the House or the Senate has to wage two campaigns: one to persuade donors to contribute to her campaign and the second to persuade citizens to vote for her. If she does not do well in the first campaign, then she is unlikely to win the second one. The difference is that the campaign for donations is carried out with a tiny percentage of American citizens. The non-partisan Center for Responsive Politics did a study of donations in the 2001–2002 federal election cycle and found that 236,552 people (one-tenth of one percent of American adults) donated $1,000 or more to a candidate, party, or political action committee. Their total donations of $728.6 million amounted to 63% of the total funds used by Republican and Democratic candidates.[4]

---

1 *Opensecrets.org*, "The Big Picture: Fundraising Totals by Cycle," available from http://www.opensecrets.org/bigpicture/index.asp; accessed 25 July 2007

2 *Opensecrets.org*, "The Big Picture: The Price of Admission," available from http://www.opensecrets.org/bigpicture/stats.asp?cycle=2004; accessed 25 July 2007

3 *Opensecrets.org*, "The Big Picture: Most Expensive Races," available from http://www.opensecrets.org/bigpicture/topraces.asp?cycle=2004; accessed 25 July 2007

4 *Opensecrets.org*, "The Big Picture: Donor Demographics," available from http://www.opensecrets.org/bigpicture/donordemographics.asp?cycle=2004; accessed 25 July 2007

Politicians at all levels must directly court these 236,500 people if they want to wage a competitive race. In addition to directly donating two thirds of the money used in elections, this tiny minority of the population includes many of the decision makers in large businesses, in political action committees, and in some labor unions. Thus, they also control most of the other large sources of money that are invested in political campaigns.

Since 2004, there has been a great deal of discussion about how Internet fundraising makes political fundraising more democratic; however, wealthy donors still dominate campaign finances. This influence extends into Presidential primary campaigns as well as congressional elections. For example, in the first three months of 2007, Hillary Clinton and Barack Obama each raised more than $25 million and John Edwards raised $14 million. Of these amounts, 80% came in the form of donations of $1,000 or more.[1] Spending these large sums of money on television is an essential part of any campaign. It is estimated that candidates will spend $800 million on television advertising alone in the 2008 presidential election season.[2]

Major donors do not caucus and discuss what politicians must say to receive their donations. They are diverse in terms of being liberal, moderate, or conservative and usually they do not get together and consciously unite behind particular candidates. However, they do set limits on political discussion, that is, they have a major impact on what kinds of issues get discussed and what issues get ignored. They do this by giving money to candidates who say things they support and by not giving money to candidates that displease them. This is especially relevant in each party's primary campaigns, rather than in general elections when donors have only two choices.

In the party primaries, there is usually a wider ideological range between the candidates than in a general election, where the tendency is for candidates to push their policy positions into the center of the political spectrum. In the Democratic party, for example, there are many people who believe in the need for significant changes in public policies — they support ideas like increasing taxes on the rich, legislation making it easier to create unions, and stiff taxes on oil company profits — all issues that have significant support from Democratic voters in public opinion polls. However, candidates who support ideas like these too specifically or enthusiastically are branded as too liberal or radical and receive little financial support from the upper level of Democratic donors. Wealthy donors view such candidates as unrealistic, not sophisticated enough to understand the limits of the real world, and unlikely to get elected — too far outside of the mainstream. As a result, po-

---

1 Dan Balz, "Fundraising Challenges Campaign Ideas," *The Washington Post*, 4.17.07; available from www.msnbc.msn.com/id/18145687/; accessed 24 July 2007
2 Joanna Weiss, "In high tech world, candidates still turn to TV," *Boston Globe*, 12.6.07

tential candidates with these views seldom are in a position to raise enough money to seriously campaign for office.

This is especially true of policy ideas that involve changing the economic status quo; that is, shaking things up by seriously addressing the trend toward growing inequality. People who are at the top of the income hierarchy have generally benefited from recent economic trends and oppose significant changes in tax and regulatory policies. For example, wealthy individuals are frequently involved in businesses or professions that embrace globalization and the American empire. These people are "free trade" Democrats and as soon as potential candidates propose serious limitations on the "free" exchange of goods, services, and investments that are part of the globalization package, large contributions, both in the form of individual and corporate donations, go to other candidates.

In the American Republic of the 21st century, candidates are unable to compete if they cannot raise millions of dollars from a small number of rich individuals — and these Americans are generally opposed to major shifts in policies related to the distribution of wealth. Perversely, many of the social and economic trends that are squeezing the incomes of average Americans are the sources of new wealth for the 250,000 individuals who donate most of the money during election campaigns. While the Democratic Party of the New Deal enacted reforms that changed the distribution of income during the middle of the 20th century, reliance on wealthy donors has limited the party's ability to advocate for significant changes since that time. One highly visible way of measuring the importance of high-end donors to the party will be to see how a Democratic President handles President Bush's tax cuts for the wealthy when they expire in 2009 and 2010.

* * *

In the late Roman Republic, the nobility and their supporters in the *publicani* became more and more resistant to reforms that might address the growing disparities between the rich and the poor created by the growth of the empire. Perversely, the social and economic trends that were impoverishing small farmers and urban residents were the trends that made the upper classes fabulously wealthy. While it had been possible to enact social, economic, and political reforms in the early centuries of the Republic, by the 2nd century the nobles were unwilling to discuss issues of land reform, debt reduction, or hunger. This rejection of social change in the face of new challenges created by the empire generated growing political tensions in the Republic and eventually led to violent confrontations.

Chapter 9. Spain: Guerrilla War and Political Dissent

> I love the smell of napalm in the morning.
>
> —*Apocalypse Now*, a film released in 1979[1]

Scipio Africanus captured Spain from Carthage at the Battle of Ilipa in 206 BCE, and the treaty ending the Second Punic War gave Rome permanent possession of the entire peninsula. The Senate divided the newly acquired area into two provinces, Hispania Citerior (Nearer Spain) and Hispania Ulterior (Further Spain). Nearer Spain consisted of the Mediterranean coast from Saguntum to Emporiae, where the Pyrenees march into the ocean, and extended into the central Spanish highlands, including the valley of the Ebro River. Further Spain consisted of the southern coastal areas from *Carthago Nove* (New Carthage) to what we now know as the Straits of Gibraltar and the extremely fertile Baetis River valley. The region of the peninsula that is now Portugal was still relatively unknown to the Romans. To govern the new provinces, the number of praetors was increased from four to six, with one praetor for Nearer Spain and one for Further Spain.[2]

The new magistrates in Spain were soon engaged in warfare with local tribes. The Spanish tribes resented their new ruler's high taxes and objected to the ruthless exploitation of their resources by enterprising *equites*, for the Roman business elite immediately began taking the riches of the peninsula.

---

1 Directed by Francis Ford Coppolla, accessed at: www.Youtube.com, search for "Apocalypse Now," click on the "Napalm in the Morning" short video. In addition, click on "Helicopter Assault," to reproduce the movie atmosphere.
2 Cornell, *Atlas*, p. 48

In Further Spain, the fertile valley of the Baetis River produced a great abundance of wheat, olives, corn, and wine. There were also a large number of copper and gold mines; during the first decade of Roman rule, from 206 BCE to 197, about 4,000 pounds of gold flowed out of Spain and into Rome.[1]

The Iberian Peninsula proved an ideal place to wage guerrilla warfare.

The really stunning sources of wealth were some of the ancient world's largest silver mines. When the Greek historian Polybius visited the mines near New Carthage in the 140s BCE, he found a sprawling complex covering 100 square miles. He estimated that 40,000 Spanish slaves, working in horrendous conditions, produced a daily yield of 100,000 sesterces for the Roman businessmen who had been given control of the mines by the Senate.[2] The mining and smelting of silver was so extensive that archeologists have found lead levels from this period in the ice of Greenland's glaciers that were not matched again until after the industrial revolution in the 19th century.[3] During the ten years from 206 to 197, about 130,000 pounds of silver was shipped to Roman treasuries from Spain.

Sporadic warfare continued through the decade of the 180s until the arrival of the praetor Sempronius Gracchus in 181 BCE. With Rome in a lull between conflicts in Greece, the Senate was able to give Gracchus four legions.[4]

---

1 A. Schulten, "Roman Cruelty and Extortion" in Erich Gruen, ed., *Imperialism in the Roman Republic*, New York: Holt, Rinehart, Winston, 1970, p. 62

2 Boatwright, *The Romans*, p. 127

3 Holland, *Rubicon*, p. 41

4 Scullard, *Roman World*, p. 300

He inflicted stinging defeats on tribes in both Nearer and Further Spain, but had the intelligence to realize that only the resolution of grievances could bring real peace. He signed a peace treaty with the rebellious tribes that reduced the taxes they paid Rome. The historian Appian, using Polybius' account of the treaty negotiations, claims that Gracchus also, "gathered the poor together into a community and distributed land to them" offering a new livelihood to those warriors willing to put down their weapons.[1]

THE FIERY WAR

> The war between the Romans and the Celtiberians was called the "fiery war," so remarkable was the uninterrupted character of the engagements.... The engagements as a rule were only stopped by darkness, the combatants refusing either to let their courage flag or to yield to bodily fatigue, and ever rallying, recovering confidence and beginning afresh. Winter indeed alone put a certain check on the progress of the whole war and on the continuous character of the regular battles, so that on the whole if we can conceive a war to be fiery it would be this and no other one. *Polybius, The Histories (XXXV.1)*[2]

After more than 25 years of calm, the Spanish tribes began to feel, once again, that the corrupt and brutal rule of a succession of provincial governors had become an intolerable burden. The first tribe to break the peace was the Lusitanians, who lived in what is now modern Portugal. They were a more nomadic tribe than those living closer to Roman towns and possessed a fierce sense of independence. In 154 BCE, they raided Roman military camps and storehouses in Further Spain. Emboldened by their success, they attacked in greater force in 153, meeting an army led by the praetor L. Mummius. The Romans broke the Lusitanian ranks and started in hot pursuit, but the Lusitanians rallied and counter-attacked, killing or wounding 9,000 Roman soldiers and seizing a number of battle standards as the survivors ran for their lives.[3]

Encouraged by the Lusitanians' success, the Celtiberian tribe in Nearer Spain called the Belli defied a Roman edict and fortified the town of Segeda. In 152 the governor of the province, the consul Q. Fulvius Nobilior marched on the town, forcing the Belli to abandon it and take up residence in the territory of the Arevaci. Angry at the presence of Roman troops on their lands, the Arevaci set an ambush for Nobilior, killing or wounding 6,000 of his soldiers and overrunning his supply base. Nobilior and his remaining men were

---

1 Bernstein, *Tiberius Sempronius Gracchus*, p. 33
2 James Grout, *Encyclopaedia Romana*, "The Celtiberian War," available from http://penelope.uchicago.edu/-Grout/encyclopaedi_romana/hispania/celtiberianwar.html; accessed 22 July 2007.
3 Appian, *Wars in Hispania* #56

forced to spend the winter in a hastily built camp where they suffered from frostbite and hundreds died from the cold.[1]

A new Roman general, the consul M. Claudius Marcellus, arrived in Nearer Spain in the spring of 151 BCE, and, after a few months of campaigning, accepted a tribute of gold from the Celtiberians and signed a lenient peace treaty with his opponents.[2] Back in Rome, not knowing that peace had been declared, the consul L. Licinius Lucullus tried to draft new soldiers for the war. After two years of terrifying stories about the kind of battles being fought in Spain, the stunning response in militaristic Rome was a widespread avoidance of the draft.[3] At every social level, from the foot soldiers of the Second, Third, Fourth, and Fifth Classes, to the military tribunes from the *Equestrian* Order, serving in this dangerous war was rejected. Unlike the wars against Carthage, which were wars of national survival, or the wars in Greece and Asia Minor, which were wars for plunder, the on-going fight to maintain control of the remote province in Spain would never inspire enthusiasm in the general population. Defeating a Spanish tribe brought no plunder for ordinary soldiers and the many riches of the peninsula went directly into the pockets of wealthy *equites* and senators.

Responding to the outcry from their constituents, several tribunes vetoed parts of the levy that they claimed were unfair. The consuls then took the "virtually unprecedented step of attempting to carry on despite the veto."[4] Insulted, the tribunes escalated the conflict by imprisoning the consuls. After a tense day of debate, the Senate and the consuls stepped back from a constitutional crisis and agreed to use a lottery to determine which draftees had to go to Spain.[5] They also reduced the term of service from seven years to six.

Finally able to leave for Spain with fresh soldiers, Lucullus arrived to find that Marcellus has already signed a peace treaty with the Belli and Arevaci. A ruthless man, seeking his fame and fortune, Lucullus provoked a conflict with the Vaccaei, a tribe that had not participated in the rebellion. When they surrendered their town of Cauca, he had the adult males murdered and the town sacked.[6] This action, says Appian, writing a moral history of Rome from the perspective of the 2nd century CE, "brought infamy upon the Roman name."[7] It also made it much more difficult to negotiate future peace treaties with the Spaniards who, from then on, frequently chose death in battle to surrender.

---

1 Astin, *Scipio*, p. 37
2 Scullard, *Roman World*, p. 301
3 Astin, *Scipio*, p. 42
4 Astin, *Scipio*, p. 43
5 Taylor, "Forerunners of the Gracchi," p. 21
6 Bernstein, *Tiberius Sempronius Gracchus*, p. 50
7 Appian, *Wars in Hispania*, #52

Lucullus, still seeking booty, assaulted the city of Intercatia, but when he offered to make peace with them, "they reproached him for the slaughter of the Caucaei and asked him whether he invited them to the same kind of pledge that he had given to that people."[1] Furious, Lucullus placed the city under siege and both sides suffered greatly from hunger. Fortunately, Scipio Aemilianus, the son of the former consul L. Aemilius Paullus, victor over Perseus of Macedonia at Pydna, had volunteered to come to Spain during the turmoil over the levy. He had impressed the Spaniards with his bravery when he won a duel with a skilled Intercatian horseman.[2] When Scipio offered to guarantee a peace treaty, the people of the city trusted him and arranged a favorable peace treaty. To Rome's great shame, no charges for waging an illegal war were ever made against Lucullus when he returned to the city.

Later in 151 BCE the Lusitanians, once again in revolt, suffered an initial setback during a battle with the army of praetor Sulpicius Galba, but rallied and overran the Roman army, killing or wounding more than 7,000 soldiers. Galba was forced to evacuate large areas of Further Spain, taking thousands of refugees with him into winter camp.[3]

A Massacre in Spain and a New Imperial War

Concerned with the continuing uproar in a province that had belonged to Rome for 50 years, the Senate changed the beginning of the Roman year to January, rather than its traditional start in March, so that new commanders and their fresh troops could begin the long overland trip to Spain early enough to arrive in time for spring campaigning. In this way, the Celtiberian War led to changes in the calendar of the Republic and eventually the European world.[4]

Now, in 150 BCE, the Lusitanians were caught in a vice as the army of Licinius Lucullus moved into their territory from one direction and Sulpicius Galba attacked from another direction. When peace envoys came to Galba, he pretended to think they were making war because of the wretched farming conditions in the Spanish hills and promised to settle them in three farming areas.[5] The Lusitanians put down their arms, were separated into three groups, and then massacred "crying aloud and invoking the names and faith of the gods."[6] The survivors were shackled and sold into slavery. Only a handful of Lusitanians escaped, one of them Viriathus, the future guer-

1 Appian, *Wars in Hispania*, #53
2 Appian, *Wars in Hispania*, #54
3 Appian, *Wars in Hispania*, #58
4 Schulten, "Roman Cruelty," p. 65
5 Bernstein, *Tiberius Sempronius Gracchus*, p. 50
6 Appian, *Wars in Hispania*, #60

rilla chieftain. Appian says that in this way Galba "avenged treachery with treachery in a manner unworthy of a Roman, but imitating barbarians."[1]

With the Senate repeatedly showing its unwillingness to discipline members of the nobility who used their positions as governors to pillage and bully foreign peoples, the tribune L. Seribonius Libo introduced a bill proposing that the Lusitanian slaves be released and that a special court be created to try Galba for extortion. In the Plebeian Assembly, Cato the Elder, at 85 still Rome's guardian of traditional values, spoke against Galba.[2] The bill was only defeated after Galba made a weeping, hysterical defense of his actions, including bringing his teary-eyed children to the Forum. However, later in the year the Assembly created a permanent Extortion Court charged with examining the misdeeds of governors and other administrators of overseas provinces. With these acts, done without support of the Senate, the Plebeian Assembly began to take a more active role in foreign policy after years of passiveness.

While the moral character of the Roman people was sullied by these actions in Spain, the thirst for empire and pillage still raged in the Roman culture. In 148 BCE an old enemy, Carthage, suddenly looked vulnerable when King Massinissa of Numidia (a kingdom in the area now known as Algeria) provoked a conflict that ended in a stunning defeat of Carthage's army.[3] The loss of a 50,000-man army suddenly left Carthage vulnerable to attack. Eager to bring an end to their great rivalry, the Senate declared war on Carthage and sent a large army led by the two consuls for that year.

When the consuls approached the city they divided their forces. Manius Manilius attacked the city's outer walls while Lucius Marcius Censorinus brought his troops in ships to the walls guarding the harbor. Both consuls were lazy about planning their attack and the inexperienced citizens' army of Carthage easily repulsed them. Censorinus then built two enormous battering rams, one manned by his soldiers, the other by sailors from the Roman fleet. However, when the Romans battered down a portion of the city wall with their rams, the Carthaginians counter-attacked and drove them off. That night, the city sent two bands of volunteers with torches to attack the Roman camps and burn the rams, frustrating weeks of work.

Twice during this phase of the siege, Scipio Aemilianus saved the army from demoralizing defeat. Scipio, who was serving as a military tribune with the units led by Manilius, held his men back when the Cathaginians lured the consul into an ambush near a broken down section of the city wall. When Manilius and his men fled from the trap, Scipio and his soldiers acted as a rear guard to save them from disastrous losses. Later, when the Carthag-

---

1 Appian, *Wars in Hispania*, #60
2 Astin, *Scipio*, p. 58
3 Appian, *Wars in Hispania*, #72

inians staged a night attack on the consul's camp, Scipio led his men on a flanking march in the dark and fell upon the Carthaginians, forcing them to retreat back into the city. Thus, as the reputations of the consuls fell and all of Rome wondered at these multiple defeats, the name of Scipio Aemilianus was on everyone's lips.

THE RISE OF VIRIATHUS

By 147 BCE, the surviving Lusitanians in Further Spain had recovered from their defeats and, with a force of about 10,000 warriors, returned to harassing Roman settlements.[1] The Roman commander for that year, the praetor Caius Vetilius, who had more than 10,000 men in his army, chased them into a rugged hillside where they could not escape. However, as representatives from the Lusitanian army began bargaining with Vetilius over the terms of surrender, Viriathus addressed the rest of the army. He pointed out that some of them were survivors of the previous Roman massacre. He asked if they really trusted this Roman general to keep his oath and promised to save the army if they followed his orders. The Lusitanians rallied at these words and made Viriathus their leader. He led the swift Lusitanian cavalry in a diversionary attack while the foot soldiers scattered and fled.[2] Unable to keep up with the wily Lusitanian cavalry and unable to chase the Lusitanian soldiers for fear of cavalry attacks in the rear, Vetilius allowed the entire Lusitanian army to escape.

With Vetilius now in hot pursuit, Viriathus led his cavalry through a densely wooded hillside, where he had instructed the Lusitanian foot soldiers to gather. When Vetilius raced incautiously into the woods, the Lusitanians rose up and ambushed his columns of soldiers.[3] At least half of Vetilius' soldiers, including the old praetor, died during the confused fighting in the forest, while the other half fled to a fortified town on the seacoast. Viriathus had proven he was a master of guerrilla tactics and the mention of his name inspired Spanish tribes all over the peninsula. The first hero of the future Portuguese nation, Viriathus became known for his generosity when distributing captured booty with his troops and his willingness to share in their everyday hardships.

The news of yet another defeat hit Rome like a shock wave. The voters in the Centuriate Assembly, already angry and frustrated because the supposedly easy war against Carthage was going badly, turned against the candidates for consul offered by the discredited nobility.[4] Instead, they looked to the dashing young officer, Scipio Aemilianus. Scipio had excellent blood-

---

1 Appian, *Wars in Hispania*, #61
2 Appian, *Wars in Hispania*, #62
3 Scullard, *Roman World*, p. 302
4 Astin, *Scipio*, p. 64

lines; the son of L. Aemilius Paullus, he was also the grandson of Scipio Africanus, the man who defeated Hannibal at Zama. His heroics with Lucullus in Spain and his exploits during the siege of Carthage hinted that his military skills might equal those of his ancestors. However, he was not yet a praetor and was five years too young to be elected a consul.

In spite of his youth, many voters believed that Scipio should be a consul and riots disrupted the consular elections of 147. When the Senate, representing the established opinion of the nobility, refused to let the Centuriate Assembly violate the rules by electing Scipio consul, a tribune threatened to veto the elections.[1] Unwilling to face a constitutional crisis with angry crowds milling about in the Forum, the Senate gave in and Scipio was elected one of the two consuls for the following year. The Plebeian Assembly then encroached on another established privilege of the Senate and passed a law appointing Scipio as the consul who would take over command of the army that was besieging Carthage.

Social Conflict and Political Power

These extraordinary events displayed two serious fault lines in the solid foundation of unity that had marked Roman politics since the middle of the 4th century. The first crack was the division between the nobility and members of the First and Second Classes. Since the Lincinio-Sextian Plebiscite of 367 BCE, the prosperous landowners and merchants of the First Class, along with the established farmers that made up the Second Class, had accepted rule by the nobility. They had consistently voted for candidates from established families of the nobility in Centuriate Assembly elections and, in general, had acquiesced to the nobility's leadership during the First and Second wars with Carthage, the conquest of Greece and Spain, and the transformations of the Roman economy discussed in previous chapters.

Now, defeat in war and a serious loss of Roman honor as a result of the treacherous actions of her generals, led many to question the effectiveness of the old way of selecting leaders. Like the draft dodging and anti-war demonstrations of the Vietnam War era, draft dodging by the youth from the *Equestrian* Order and the First Class, which was to continue throughout the Spanish Wars, must have led to a change of heart on the part of a number of the members of these classes. The militarized political culture of Republican Rome made it impossible to generate an anti-war movement per se. Instead, some political leaders began thinking about how to use the general dissatisfaction with the nobility to advance their own careers.

The second crack in the foundation of unity was the breakdown of the Senate's hegemony in decision-making, along with telling demonstrations

---

1 Astin, *Scipio*, p. 65

of the power of the tribunes and the Plebeian Assembly to make essential decisions about war and peace.[1] During the previous century, with the office of tribune serving primarily as a stepping-stone to higher office and a place in the nobility, the Plebeian Assembly had lost its radical nature, but not its power to make laws. Similarly, the veto power of the tribunes had not lost its ability to disrupt the activities of leaders of the nobility. Beginning with the War in Spain, the growing divisions inside the nobility over the proper course to follow in managing the Republic and its unruly empire made it possible for dissenting political leaders, members of the nobility more attuned to the needs and attitudes of other classes in Roman society, to wield the tribunal power with new vigor.

THE SHADOW OF HONOR

Scipio Aemilianus took over the siege of Carthage with great skill and thoroughness. The dispirited Roman army, which had failed for two years in its attempts to capture the city, applied itself with new energy to the task. Every route for bringing supplies into the huge city, both land and sea, were blockaded and the soldiers and civilians inside the city were soon suffering from a lack of food and supplies. In desperation, the Carthaginians sent 50 triremes along with brigantines and other small craft to drive off the Roman fleet.[2] Foolishly losing the element of surprise by parading in front of their astonished besiegers, the Carthaginian rowers, sailors, and marines battled all day with the Roman fleet, their smaller boats smashing holes in their enemies' hulls, but were unable to break the Roman ranks. Retreating in some confusion for the evening, they were surprised when Scipio led an evening counter attack and many ships were sunk. After fierce fighting, Scipio was able to follow up this victory by building a fort at the entrance to the city's harbor, where the soldiers could shoot flaming spears into any boats that attempted to bring supplies into the city.

Scipio followed this up by capturing the city of Nepheris, breaking Carthage's last link to food supplies.[3] Then, after many foiled attempts, Roman troops were finally able to breach a wall. What followed was eight days of vicious street fighting, with Roman soldiers battling inhabitants block by block. "All places were filled with groans, shrieks, shouts, and every kind of agony. Some were stabbed; others were hurled alive from the roofs to the pavement . . ."[4] Finally, the city was captured and the 50,000 surviving residents of what once was the greatest city in the Western Mediterranean

---

1 Astin, *Scipio*, p. 67
2 Appian, *Wars in Hispania*, #121
3 Scullard, *Roman World*, p. 316
4 Appian, *Wars in Hispania*, #128

were sold into slavery or exiled, the city was burned, and the soil was declared *sacer*, or taboo, the gods preventing any further human use of the site.[1]

In Greece, there was a matching atrocity. The Achaean League, believing that Rome was distracted by the wars in Spain and Africa, declared war on Sparta. L. Mummius, the former governor of Spain, brought two legions to Greece and quickly defeated the small Achaean army. As the government of Corinth had twice insulted Roman envoys before the battle, the Senate decided to teach the rebellious Greeks a lesson. Mummius seized the great city, the inhabitants were massacred, the survivors sold into slavery, and the town was looted and burned.[2]. Four centuries of priceless art, statues, jewelry, and carvings were destroyed or carried off to Rome.

The savage destruction of two of the great cities of the Mediterranean world demonstrated Rome's military superiority and moral emptiness. After the events of 146 BCE, the Republic lost all pretense of moral superiority to other civilizations and was viewed by many people as a foreign oppressor. Even Polybius, the friend and advisor of Scipio Aemilianus, was disturbed by this new ferocity. Polybius, who began his great *Histories* with the idea of showing his Greek countrymen how it was that the Roman political system — with its elements of monarchy, aristocracy, and democracy — was superior to Greek political systems, found the new methods of Roman rule immoral. In his later works, written after these terrible events, he speaks of "ruthlessness, treachery, and the lust for power."[3] His most telling judgment was succinct, "Wrongdoing as an instrument of terrorization, to coerce unwilling subjects, belongs to the tyrant, who hates his people as much as they hate him..."[4]

It is difficult for the student of history to place a value on this loss of moral stature. We have seen, and will continue to see, concrete ways in which the acquisition of an empire placed unbearable demands upon the political system of the Republic. These effects can be traced and weighed. Moral authority is a slippery concept, without causal effect, yet present in every action by every person associated with the polity involved. It may be that a powerful state can ignore the opinion of the rest of humanity, but for how long? And when do foreign conquests and barbarity against less powerful people begin to pollute the political culture of the victorious power? Many ancient historians claimed that, as the citizens of the Roman Republic began depriving more and more people of their liberties, they set in motion some kind of ticking clock upon their own.

---

1 LeGlay, *History of Rome*, p. 100
2 LeGlay, *History of Rome*, p. 98
3 Green, *Alexander to Actium*, p. 279
4 Green, *Alexander to Actium*, p. 280

Defeat and a Widening War

The year 146 was not a time of universal triumph for Roman armies. In Further Spain, Viriathus and his Lusitanian army were unchecked by Roman legions during much of the summer. Then the praetor C. Plautius appeared with two legions and 1,300 cavalrymen.[1] Viriathus pretended to flee and Plautius sent an advanced guard to ensure the rout continued. Viriathus lured these soldiers into an ambush and killed or wounded 4,000 of them. When Plautius attacked with the main body of his army, Viriathus killed many Romans and forced them to go into winter quarters. The Lusitanians then dominated the Baetis River valley, collecting taxes from the owners of large estates.

Success eluded the Romans in Spain because it was a very different field of conflict from Carthage and Greece. The rough terrain and dispersed settlements of the Spanish tribes made it an ideal setting for guerrilla war. In fact, the word *guerrilla* is Spanish in origin, coming from the diminutive of *guerra*, war. Fittingly, the first known use of the term was coined to describe the tactics of Spanish soldiers who successfully resisted Napoleon's armies in the Peninsular War (1807–1814 CE).[2] From Spain, the use of the term spread to Latin America and then the United States. They were using small warfare tactics that had been used successfully for at least 2,000 years.

The Spanish guerrilla armies in the 2nd century BCE had a detailed knowledge of the terrain. In the rough hills, valleys, and forests of Spain's highlands, this made their small unit tactics superior to anything the Roman legions could do. In addition, the leader of a Roman army and his staff were officers with little knowledge of the geography of a battlefield because they rotated in and out of Spain so frequently. Those familiar with Sun Tzu's *The Art of War*, in which he claims that knowledge of terrain is one of the five main dimensions of the *tao* of war, will understand how this disparity in knowledge of terrain might make it devilishly difficult for the Romans to win battles against a competent commander like Viriathus. This yearly rotation had not been a problem when Romans were fighting in relatively well-known regions in Italy or Sicily. It had also not been a problem in Greece, where capturing a city or winning a formal battle on comparatively well-known terrain always ended a war.

As with the American effort in Vietnam, Roman forces were only able to securely control the coastal towns and the river valleys where settled farming occurred. Guerrilla armies were frequently successful raiding agricultural areas and, when pursued, fleeing into rougher terrain, where ambushes

---

1 Astin, *Scipio*, p. 99

2 *Columbia Encyclopedia* 6th *Edition*, "Guerrilla Warfare" available from www.bartleby.com, search 'guerrilla war' accessed 22 July 2007.

would lead to heavy Roman losses. In addition, the Spanish tribes were related but did not act together. This meant that defeating one tribe meant little to another.[1] As a result, pacifying the peninsula required an endless series of battles with the numerous tribes who were unhappy with Roman rule.

However, the Roman Senate was determined to press the fight. Scipio, the hero of Carthage, was now the dominant political personage in Rome. His adopted brother, Q. Fabius Maximus Aemilianus, was elected consul for 145 BCE and brought two additional legions to Spain. The Senate, however, was unwilling to risk compelling the veterans returning from Carthage and Corinth to go to Spain, so Fabius' two legions were newly drafted men with no military training.[2] After Viriathus inflicted a stinging defeat on his advanced guard, Fabius was forced to withdraw and spent the rest of the summer training his raw conscripts.

To widen the war, Viriathus persuaded the Numantines to rise up against Rome. Based in the central highlands of Spain, they were Nearer Spain's most disciplined warriors. The town of Numantia was located on a hill at the junction of two major rivers. It was nearly impossible to storm because of a double row of fortified walls on the crest of the steep hill. While they were not an advanced civilization, they made magnificent iron weapons, which made them formidable opponents in battle.[3] In 143, the consul Caecilius Metellus Macedonius took over the army in Nearer Spain, but was unable to interrupt the Namantine's sources of food and water and compel them to surrender.

In 141, another of Scipio's allies, consul Fabius Servilianus, assumed command of the army in Further Spain.[4] In addition to two more new legions from Italy, Servilianus brought 10 elephants and 300 cavalry from the new Roman province of Africa, the new name for the area formerly ruled by Carthage.[5] Servilianus advanced upon Viriathus and won an initial triumph over his soldiers; however, Viriathus rallied his men when the Roman pursuit became disorderly and led a counter-charge, killing or wounding 3,000 Romans. The Romans fled into their camp and were barely able to defend it from the Lusitanian advance.

When Viriathus retreated back into Lusitania in 140 to rest his weary army, the Romans began attacking and plundering towns that had provided Viriathus with support. Viriathus brought his army up and counter-attacked at Erisana, defeating Servilianus and surrounding his army.[6] To save his men

1 Boatwright, *The Romans*, p. 124

2 Astin, *Scipio*, p. 103

3 Scullard, *Roman World*, p. 303

4 Astin, *Scipio*, p. 123

5 Appian, Wars in Hispania, #67

6 Scullard, *Roman World*, p. 302

from death, Servilianus negotiated a peace treaty with the Lusitanians. In it, Viriathus was recognized as a "Friend of the Roman People" and the Lusitanians were allowed to keep the land they occupied.[1] The Senate then ratified the treaty and the war in Further Spain seemed to be over, with Roman influence greatly reduced in that part of Spain.

The dismal failures of the Roman army in Spain, where much blood was shed, generals were frequently incompetent, and little plunder was available even when a victory was obtained, soured the political climate in Rome during 140 BCE. While our sources for this period are scanty, there must have been continuing difficulty finding eligible farmers to be drafted, because the consul C. Laelius proposed some type of agrarian reform law.[2] Given the widespread draft evasion going on in the *equites* and in the First Class, the burden of fighting and dying in the Spanish war must have fallen on the less politically connected Second through Fifth Classes. Laelius' law was probably designed to give small plots of land to poor urban citizens in order to replenish the depleted ranks of able-bodied males from these classes who did much of the fighting and dying in Spain.

The growing shortage of service-eligible, property-owning citizens in the 2nd century was highlighted by the fall in the minimum property standard. For a Roman citizen to serve in a legion, he had to have *adsiduus* status, enough wealth to be eligible for the Fifth Class in the Centuriate Assembly. As small farmers were killed or displaced during the 2nd century, the minimum qualification, in an age of steady inflation, was reduced from 11,000 HS in 200 BCE to 4,000, and then to 1,500 by 130.[3] With this falling wealth standard, even small allotments of land for the urban poor would have greatly increased the pool of citizens eligible for the draft. However, strident opposition from members of the nobility, who were busy buying up small farms to build up their *latifundias*, caused Laelius to withdraw his proposal without a vote occurring.[4]

DEEPENING CONFLICT IN ROME AND SPAIN

Q. Servilius Caepio, brother of Q. Fabius Maximus Servilianus, completed the family's trilogy of consulships, by attaining the office in 140 BCE. Quite possibly with Scipio's encouragement, (Scipio was a hard liner about maintaining the empire with force) in 139, Caepio broke the treaty with the Lusitanians and resumed the war. A tribune named Ti. Claudius Asellus, tried to veto his leaving Rome to join the army in Further Spain, but he was physically intimidated by Caepio's lictors. When they crowded around

---

1 Appian, *Wars in Hispania*, #69
2 Astin, *Scipio*, p. 126
3 Bernstein, *Tiberius Sempronius Gracchus*, p. 75
4 Astin, *Scipio*, p. 126

the unarmed tribune and threatened him with their sharp axes he withdrew his veto.[1] After he left for Spain, the Senate responded to public discontent by passing a decree against drafting new soldiers to reinforce his army. The decree was proposed by Appius Claudius Pulcher, a descendent of the Claudius Pulcher who tried to redistribute the freedmen into the rural tribes in 312 BCE. Reflecting the growing political divisions in the nobility, Claudius had emerged as both an opponent of Scipio and of his war policies in Spain.

The tribune Claudius Asellus then prosecuted Scipio on an unknown charge. While it was common in Rome for a political rival to try to discredit a foe by filing legal charges and hoping a jury might be swayed into sending him into exile, it was unusual for a tribune to file charges against a former consul and censor. No one could imagine that a jury might convict a man of such stature unless there were sharp divisions in the nobility over the aggressive policies Scipio supported in Spain and his frequent attempts to influence elections. Scipio was acquitted, but it must have been a serious case, because he was forced to make more than one speech defending his activities as censor in 142 and 141.[2]

Servilius Caepio proved to be an able general and his army forced Viriathus to retreat in Lusitania. Frustrated at Viriathus' ability to avoid a decisive battle, Caepio bribed three of Viriathus' most trusted officers and had them assassinate him while he slept in his tent. Thus ended an amazing career, where a man who had grown up as a simple shepherd repeatedly defeated the most powerful army in the world. This cowardly action, which violated every tenet of how Romans were expected to wage an honorable war, paid immediate dividends as Caepio quickly defeated Viriathus' successor and accepted the surrender of his army, ending the war with the Lusitanians. The reader might contrast Caepio's tactics with those of the consul Marcus Furius Camillus when he was given the opportunity to use the children of Falerri as hostages (see chapter 2).

In the wake of the controversy created by the consul Caepio breaking a treaty against the will of a tribune and then gaining a dishonorable victory through assassination, the tribune Gabinius proposed a law that was bitterly opposed by most of the Senate and the nobility. The *Lex Tabellaria*, passed by the Plebeian Assembly in spite of the Senate's opposition, established secret balloting in all elections.[3] The measure is another sign of the nobility's weakened hold over the Assembly because the law greatly limited the nobility's ability to oversee the votes of their clients. No longer was it possible for poll watchers to report to wealthy landowners how their clients voted in elections.

---

1 Astin, *Scipio*, p. 127
2 Astin, *Scipio*, p. 127
3 Astin, *Scipio*, p. 128

The long term effect of the new law is clear: public popularity, as opposed to manipulated votes through the client system, was, from now on, the decisive element in elections. This did not mean that people outside of the nobility would be elected to political office. The deference given to noble families and to the custom of centuries of aristocratic rule prevented this departure from the established ways. However, it meant that dissident members of the nobility could act against the interests of the leading families and still be elected to high political office. The key would be to propose policies that would gain favor in the First and Second Classes of the Centuriate Assembly.

Meanwhile, in spite of the assassination of Viriathus, the war raged on in Nearer Spain. The consul Q. Pompeius Aulus attempted to lay siege to Numantia, but his soldiers were repeatedly ambushed as they foraged in the forest, dug trenches, or searched for fresh water. Several frontal assaults upon the city's well-built fortifications were also repulsed with heavy losses.[1] The army then went into winter camp near Numantia, a decision that cost many Roman lives as the snow and cold led to widespread hunger and disease.

With the Senate's determined to continue the war in Nearer Spain, the war-weary citizenry was confronted with yet another draft of soldiers. By 138 BCE, dissent over the war must have been affecting morale in the legions because, in addition to avoidance of the draft, desertion from Rome's legions had become a problem. As part of the public preparation for conducting the new levy, the consuls had deserters from the army in Spain whipped in the Forum.[2] Once again, shock waves must have rippled through Rome at this unprecedented event. The Forum, for 370 years, had been the place where political leaders and the public would meet to debate and vote on the vital issues facing the Republic. If there was any place in Rome where *res publica* had meaning as government through consent of the governed, then the Forum was that location. To defile the Forum with this brutal assertion of state power over individual citizens, while not illegal, certainly made the statement that behind the political spectacle of speeches and voting, the Senate was willing to impose its will upon the rest of the citizenry.

By this time, however, the Senate was no longer the only political body in the Republic that counted. In response, the tribunes C. Curiatius and S. Licinius demanded that each tribune be allowed to exempt 10 persons (probably politically connected sons of *equites* and the First Class) from the draft. When the consuls refused, they were fined and imprisoned by the tribunes.[3] Unfortunately, we have no historical record of how this dramatic confrontation was settled. Given the Senate's earlier inclination to avoid constitu-

---

1 Scullard, *Roman World*, p. 304

2 Astin, *Scipio*, p. 130

3 Astin, *Scipio*, p. 130

tional confrontations with tribunes, and the suspicion that a serious conflict would have led to a more extensive discussion of the incident in historical records, it is certainly possible that some sort of tribunal exemption or appeals process was created to diffuse the dispute.

Bad blood probably lingered because, later in the year, the tribune C. Curiatius held some type of *contio* in the forum and asked the consuls to use government funds to buy corn for hungry plebeians.[1] Keep in mind that political leaders staged *contios*, pre-announced public meetings in the Forum, with the purpose of stating a position on an issue and, if possible, forcing an opposing politician to defend their viewpoint in front of an unsympathetic crowd. In this situation, the crowd may have been quite ugly because there was a shortage of corn in the city (Spain had been a big exporter of corn to Rome) and the plebeians were hungry. C. Curiatius was successful in creating more controversy because the consuls, as expected, refused his request and were roundly booed by the assembled throng.

Here we begin to see the political power that could be wielded by an active, assertive tribune. It is unlikely that Curiatius expected a positive response from the consuls. His only reason for pressing the issue would have been to discredit the consuls and, perhaps, to highlight another way in which the Senate was becoming separated from the rest of the public. Given the growing importance of public opinion in the settling of close elections, political leaders allied to these particular consuls may have found it harder to rally voters to their cause in the next round of elections. In these subtle ways, the unity of the nobility and the strength of its rule over the Republic were being undermined. When a tribune, possibly Curiatius, died later in the year, large crowds attended the funeral in tribute — showing that tribunes, for the first time since the Compromise of 367 BCE, had become important political people in their own right.[2]

As the level of political conflict grew, it is interesting to note what did not happen in Roman politics. There was no peace movement to pose alternatives to militarism and the creation of empire, and no peace movement ever emerged during the following years of escalating domestic conflict. Even when the plebeians began to break through the deferential dimension of Rome's political culture and act independently through the Plebeian Assembly, they still valued possession of an empire. Defeat in the Spanish War discredited the leaders who prosecuted that war, but did not discredit the idea of going to war to maintain the empire. For example, the Plebeian Assembly never objected when the Senate rejected peace treaties negotiated by consuls in the field.[3]

---

1 Astin, *Scipio*, p. 130

2 Astin, *Scipio*, p. 130

3 Shulten, "Roman Cruelty," p. 65

DEFEAT AND DIVISION

In 137 the consul C. Hostilius Mancinus came to Spain and proved himself an incompetent general. His army of 20,000 men suffered several defeats at the hands of the Numantians. Then, alarmed that another tribe was coming to reinforce his victorious foe, he abandoned his fortified camp and retreated to an old campground with few fortifications.[1] Surrounded by Numantian soldiers who were preparing to massacre his entire army, Mancinus sent his quaestor, Tiberius Sempronius Gracchus, to negotiate a peace treaty. Tiberius, whose father had negotiated the celebrated treaty of 179, was trusted by the Numantians and managed to negotiate a peace treaty that proclaimed the Celtiberian tribe's independence and saved the army from a terrible massacre. Mancinus then bound himself to the treaty with a solemn oath.[2]

The Senate, led by Scipio, remained determined to accept only unconditional surrender in Spain and rejected the treaty when Mancinus brought it back to Rome. After a fierce debate, Mancinus, a Roman consul and nobleman, was repudiated by the Senate and "with shameful hypocrisy" sent naked and in chains back to the Numantians as per the terms of his oath.[3] Scipio, Tiberius' uncle, saved him and the other officers in the army from a similar fate by claiming that the officers were only following the orders of the general with *imperium*.

Far from feeling grateful, Tiberius considered the Senate's actions dishonorable and split from Scipio's political faction. He had established political ties with another faction during the 140s when he married the daughter of Appius Claudius Pulcher. After the Mancinus affair, Tiberius, the proud son of a famous Roman family, became an ally of Claudius and a faction of distinguished men who believed that the Senate has lost its bearings.

In the middle of this bitter debate, the tribune L. Cassius Longinus Ravilla sponsored a bill that was passed by the Plebeian Assembly over the objections of the Senate and the consuls. The *lex Cassia* mandated secret ballots for all jury trials, making it harder to bribe juries and more difficult to target reprisals on jurors who voted against the interests of powerful members of the nobility.[4]

While these conflicts were occurring in Rome, the other consul of 137,, A. Aemilius Lepidus, had taken command of Mancinus' demoralized army. Looking for an easy victory, he falsely accused the Vaccaei of aiding the Numantians and ravaged their farmlands. With the aid of Decimus Brutus, commander in Further Spain and his brother-in-law, he laid siege to Pallantia

---

1 Appian, Wars in Hispania, #80
2 Astin, *Scipio*, p. 131
3 Scullard, *Roman World*, p. 304
4 Astin, *Scipio*, p. 131

their principal city.[1] Unfortunately for Aemilius, the Vaccaei showed surprising resilience and the siege was not finished when winter began to descend upon Spain. The Roman food supply gave out and soldiers began dying of hunger and disease. When they could take no more, Aemilius had them withdraw in the middle of the night, leaving behind their sick and wounded. The retreat became a disorderly race and the Vaccaei spent the following day attacking their flanks and ambushing stragglers. Finally, at nightfall, the victorious Spaniards withdrew and the army slept, exhausted, in full battle dress.[2] When the Senate heard about this disaster, Aemilius was recalled in disgrace and stripped of his consulship.[3] It was the first time in the Republic's history that a consul was relieved of office in the middle of his term.[4]

TURNING POINT: 134 BCE

Frustrated and frightened by the continuing war in Spain, the Centuriate Assembly turned, as it had in 146, to Scipio Aemilianus. He was elected consul again, in spite of the recent law forbidding one person from holding a second consulship. In response to this new violation of the Republic's constitutional order, the Senate refused to levy troops or give Scipio money for the upcoming campaign.[5] Reinforcing the notion that Spain had become his own private war, Scipio raised a personal guard of 500 officers and men, recruited from allies and friends from every province of the empire. After raising this private army, a foreshadowing of the private armies that participated in the civil wars of the 1st century, Scipio took over the demoralized legions in Spain and spent many months training and drilling them to restore order and their fighting spirit.

With his army restored, Scipio systematically laid siege to Numantia in 133 BCE with 20,000 Roman legionaries and another 20,000 soldiers donated by Rome's Spanish allies. He went into the countryside near the city and burned any crops that he could not gather for his own army. Aware of the Spanish ability to ambush and out maneuver Roman soldiers, he only marched along secure roads and did not pursue bands of warriors who harassed his troops when they went to get water. Rather than trying to storm the impregnable fortress, Scipio built a ditch and large wall around the entire city.

---

1 Appian, *Wars in Hispania*, #80

2 Appian, *Wars in Hispania*, #82

3 Astin, *Scipio*, p. 133

4 James Grout, *Encyclopaedia Romana*, "The Celtiberian War," available from http://penelope. uchicago.edu/-Grout/encyclopaedi_romana/hispania/celtiberianwar.html; accessed 22 July 2007

5 Astin, *Scipio*, p. 134

Once the siege was established, Scipio then built small forts around the first perimeter and connected them with walls.[1] The most difficult part of the siege was the river Durius, which flowed through the city and could not be blockaded. To prevent food and reinforcements from coming along the river, Scipio built towers on either side of the river and placed large timbers, bristling with spears and knives, floating on a rope between them. This made it nearly impossible to move boats up stream and thwarted any attempt to swim.

After a grueling six-month siege, the 4,000 Numantian defenders were forced to surrender. So great was their love of liberty and so powerful their anger at losing their homeland, most of the defenders killed themselves rather than be sold into slavery by the conquering army. As he did with Carthage, Scipio burned down the city, ending the war with a people who had defied the world's most powerful army for twelve years.

With Scipio's victory, the Senate got what it wanted, unconditional victory over the Spanish tribes, with an unrestricted ability to dictate how the provinces would be governed. Given the enormous cost in blood, money, and political disorder that the conflict had generated, it would be well for us to ponder why the Senate resisted relatively fair treaties with both the Lusitanians and the Numantians. There seems to be two interwoven reasons, each of which is important, neither of which is sufficient on its own to justify the Senate's actions.

First, influential members of the nobility and members of the *publicani* wanted to be able to exploit Spain's gold and silver mines.[2] Dozens of corporations had been set up by the leading *equites* to build and operate these mines, and they had become an inexhaustible source of enormous wealth. The *publicani* who profited from the mines must have been generous financial supporters of candidates for office who pledged to continue the war. Neither group of men would let go of a land with such valuable natural resources merely because of casualties suffered by the lowly citizens of the Second through Fifth Classes.

A second reason for prosecuting the war until victory was the need to "maintain Roman military prestige." The string of humiliating defeats led to an insistence on victory.[3] Military prestige is a vital resource for an empire. Victory over the rebellion had to be obtained regardless of the cost. If not, then the Spanish fight for freedom would have served as a bad example for the other conquered peoples of the empire. The Senate probably feared that a Spanish victory might have served as inspiration for further revolts in Macedonia and Greece. There was a slave uprising on Sicily in 134 that, while

---

1 Appian, *Wars in Hispania*, #90
2 Astin, *Scipio*, p. 156
3 Astin, *Scipio*, p. 156

based on local factors, surely must have drawn hope from the stubborn resistance of the Numantians.

We can postulate one of the dynamics of any large empire: resistance in one part of the empire becomes a threat to stability in the rest of the empire. The larger, the more hated the empire, the more frequently will resistance take shape and armed force be needed to crush the bad example set by this resistance. Empires then, by their very nature, are likely to be in a continual state of military alarm.

The Roman nobility paid a severe short- and long-term price for maintaining their wealth and their empire in Spain. The moral authority of the Senate, unchallenged after the defeat of Hannibal, was badly damaged by the string of costly defeats and the widespread resistance to the draft. The decline of the Senate as an institution was matched by the rise in influence of the tribunes and the Plebeian Assembly. Subservient for years, they now became rival power centers that would, off and on, match wits and words with the Senate until the end of the Republic. The wars in Spain also led to serious splits within the nobility and within the Senate, creating a situation where dissident members of the nobility were willing to openly challenge the policies of the major families.

In addition, the secret ballot law made the Centuriate Assembly and Tribal Assembly far less susceptible to control though the clientele system. During the remaining years of the Republic, voters in the First and Second Classes, who frequently viewed the nobility as a group opposed to their own interests, dominated these Assemblies. They were to prove themselves willing, on a regular basis, to elect dissenting members of the nobility to important political offices. Suddenly, landless farmers, unemployed plebeians, and destitute families found members of the nobility who would give voice to their grievances. The Republic would never be the same.

The same year that Numantia was destroyed, 133 BCE, the Plebeian Assembly elected a prominent member of the nobility to be one of the ten tribunes. Tiberius Gracchus, returning to public life after several years in seclusion, was elected tribune for the year 132. Immediately after taking his oath of office, Tiberius introduced a sweeping agrarian reform law, setting off a process that would compress all of these swirling political trends into an explosive mixture, needing only a single misstep to produce an historic tragedy.

Chapter 10. The Brothers Gracchi and the Limits of Reform

> When considering any period, historians have to ask to what extent those living at the time were in a position to influence the processes of change taking place in their midst. At some times this is not very important... In other periods change takes place very slowly. But when it becomes rapid and moves in an undesirable direction, undermining the foundations of an existing order, the urgent question arises as to how it is possible, in a given situation, to gain control of the processual changes.[1]

> — Christian Meier, *Caesar: A Biography*

Like Franklin D. Roosevelt, many people considered Tiberius Gracchus, Tribune of the Roman Plebeians, a traitor to his class. He certainly could not be classified as a rebellious outsider. The eldest son of a man who had twice been elected consul, Tiberius became the head of one of the ambitious plebian families who rose to become part of the Roman nobility. By the time Tiberius was elected tribune, the nobility had been Rome's ruling elite for more than two hundred years.

Tiberius Gracchus' family played a leading role in the nobility's triumphs. His great grandfather, Tiberius Sempronius Gracchus, was elected consul in 238 BC, officially placing the family in the ranks of noble families.[2] During his one-year term of office Gracchus led a successful expedition against the Carthaginian island of Sardinia.

---

1 Meier, *Caesar*, p. 493
2 Bernstein, *Tiberius Sempronius Gracchus*, p. 23

His son, another Tiberius, was a fierce warrior, gaining fame in the war against Hannibal by training an army of slaves, boys, and recently-released criminals hastily assembled to protect Rome after the terrible defeat at Cannae. They routed a segment of Hannibal's army after an electrifying speech by Tiberius promising freedom to any slave who brought back the head of a Carthaginian soldier.[1] Elected consul for a second time in 213 BC, he was killed in an ambush near the town of Capua, one of the many nobles who died leading their legions.

After defeating Hannibal, Rome conquered the wealthy Greek kingdoms established after Alexander the Great's death and established colonies in Spain. The Gracchi were prominent during this period as well. Tiberius' father, Tiberius Sempronius Gracchus, nephew of the great general, was elected Tribune of the Plebeians in 184 BCE and became an ally of Scipio Africanus, the legendary general who defeated Hannibal at Zama. He married the great man's daughter, Cornelia, to seal an alliance between the two families. Sempronius went on to be elected consul in 177, censor in 169, and was re-elected consul in 163. As we saw in the last chapter, he had governed one of Rome's provinces in Spain, defeated the rebellious Celtiberians, and negotiated a just peace that lasted until 153. Sempronius Gracchus also led a number of diplomatic missions on behalf of the Senate to the important Greek city-states of Pergamon, Athens, and Rhodes.

When Tiberius Sempronius Gracchus was born in 163 BC, his future as a leading statesman of Rome was practically assured. In conservative, traditional Rome, sons of former consuls were assured of support from many voters who preferred their leaders to have successful military backgrounds. Cornelia, his mother, became legendary for the virtuous upbringing she provided her sons, Tiberius and his brother Gaius, born in 154. With Rome rapidly absorbing the Hellenistic culture of her latest conquests, every noble family sought suitable tutors who could teach their sons about the great thoughts of Plato, Socrates, and Demosthenes. Diophanes of Mytilene, a well-known orator and philosopher, was hired as the boys' tutor. The memory of their father's brilliant career must have fired the boys' imaginations, especially since he died when Tiberius was only ten and Gaius just an infant.

All of that was before the guerrilla wars in Spain. Like the United States in Vietnam, the greatest military power in the Mediterranean world could not defeat the guerilla tactics of the Spanish tribes. As defeat followed defeat, the Romans grew more frustrated and the list of atrocities, broken treaties, and dishonored reputations grew longer.

Even Tiberius Gracchus was stained by the Spanish war. At the age of 18, he had been one of the first Roman officers to scale the walls of Carthage and

---

1 Bernstein, *Tiberius Sempronius Gracchus*, p. 24

in 138 BCE, he was elected quaestor, the first step in the *cursus honorum*. In 137, he served in the army taken to Spain by the consul C. Hostilius Mancinus. In the previous chapter, we saw how his army was defeated and surrounded by the Numantines. Rather than massacre the 10,000 men in the helpless army, the Numantines let them go in return for Tiberius Gracchus' pledge to convince the Roman Senate to approve a peace treaty addressing Numantine grievances.[1]

To his horror, the Senate refused to ratify the treaty. Foreshadowing debates in the US during the Vietnam War, conservative senators argued that for a great military power to settle for anything less than victory would send a message of weakness to other nations eager to escape rule by a foreign power. Scipio Aemilianus and his allies in the Senate said that Mancinus and Gracchus had dishonored Rome by accepting peace; honorable commanders would have died before they submitted to such humiliation. His command-ing general was condemned and exiled, but Gracchus was spared from that fate because he was not the officer-in-charge.

Alienated from the Senate, but treated as a hero by the families and friends of the soldiers he had saved from certain death in an unpopular war, Tiberius retreated to his family home. He was not alone in his discontent with Scipio and the Senate's insistence on continuing the war. Appius Claudius Pulcher and a group of prominent senators were pondering how to address some of the Republic's most pressing problems in a way that would make their reform-oriented faction more popular than Scipio's group. It is not hard to imagine Tiberius actively participating in the discussions led by his father-in-law.[2]

A former consul and *Princeps Senatus*, Claudius had often clashed with Scipio. In 142 BCE, he had run for the office of censor but had lost to Scipio, who was too young for the position and had never served as a praetor. Scipio, however, was "popular" with the crowd in the Forum and a military hero, political assets that were more important now that Rome was crowded with people who were displaced from the countryside.[3] This must have been a bitter disappointment for the man whose ancestor of the same name had been wildly popular in the 4th century when he had aided the freedmen and built Rome's first great road and aqueduct. It is possible that from this time on, Claudius was determined to compete against Scipio and his allies for popularity with the voters of the city. For example, in 139, with Scipio's en-couragement, the consul Gnaeus Servilius Caepio went to Spain to provoke an unpopular new war with Viriathus and the Lusitanians. Trying to trip

1 Astin, *Scipio*, p. 131
2 Bernstein, *Tiberius Sempronius Gracchus*, p. 119
3 Boatwright, *The Romans*, p. 153

him up, Claudius persuaded the Senate to pass a decree blocking the use of a levy to raise more troops for the treacherous campaign.[1]

Then, in the elections of 135 BCE, Scipio once again flouted the electoral laws, getting elected consul for a second time.[2] Given his actions in 139 against Caepio, Claudius was likely to have been one of the men who initiated a Senate decree refusing to levy new troops or to provide Scipio with money to finance his campaign in Spain. Scipio by-passed the Senate and recruited a new legion from cities in Italy and from detachments sent by eastern kings who saw him as the leading man in Rome and wanted to gain his favor.[3] During 134, while Scipio was in Spain laying siege to Numantia, Claudius and his allies decided on a bold countermeasure.

Land Reform and Political Power

Claudius' group included P. Mucius Scaevola, who would soon be elected consul for the year 133 and P. Licinius Crassus Mucianus (a man could end up with four names if he was adopted into another noble family), who had recently served as praetor. Both of these men were leading advocates in Rome's courts of law. In addition, one of Licinius' ancestors was the consul in the 4th century who passed a law decreeing that no Roman could own more than 500 *iugera* (300 acres) of public land, the *ager publicus*.[4] This law was widely ignored by the 2nd century, as hundreds of *iugera* of public land were added to the *latifundia* of wealthy nobles and *equites*.[5] The wealthy aristocrats were given temporary use of the land, *possessio*, while the land continued to be owned by the state. However, by the end of the 2nd century the *possessores* came to see themselves as the real owners.[6]

This abuse of a public land law was the key to a land reform program that had a chance of working. As in the United States, the rights of private property were sacred in Rome and no law that proposed to take agricultural land from aristocrats and re-distribute it among the poor had a chance of passing.[7] So the heart of the Claudian group's land reform bill was a call for enforcement of the ancient limits of 500 *iugera* on the rental and use of public land. A land commission would be created to survey public lands and reclaim land when a family had taken too much. The reclaimed land would be distributed to landless people in blocks of 30 *iugera*, enough to operate a prosperous farm.[8]

1 Astin, *Scipio*, p. 126
2 Astin, *Scipio*, p. 134
3 Boatwright, *The Romans*, p. 155
4 Matyszak, *Chronicle*, p. 128
5 Bernstein, *Tiberius Sempronius Gracchus*, p. 124
6 LeGlay, *History of Rome*, p. 110
7 Bernstein, *Tiberius Sempronius Gracchus*, p. 123
8 Matyszak, *Chronicle*, p. 129

This simple reform would address several pressing problems. It would help thousands of people either leave the slums of Rome or stop being day laborers in the countryside and become citizen farmers. This return to the land would lift them out of poverty and increase the number of property owning Romans who could serve in the depleted legions of the military. These changes would also lower social tensions in the city and in the countryside by giving the recipients new hope and new attachments to the Republic. It had happened before. The creation of colonies and the distribution of new lands to plebeians in the 4th century created a large class of loyal small farmers. Several talented young members of the nobility, M. Fulvius Flaccus, C. Papirius Carbo, and C. Porcius Cato, grandson of Cato the Censor, were recruited to support the proposed land law.[1]

The reform group knew that the Senate would be inhospitable to even this mild proposal. When the consul C. Laelius had brought the idea of a land reform law before the Senate in 140 BCE, the resulting outcry from senators led him to abandon the idea before placing the matter before the Plebeian Assembly.[2] It would violate a great many customs for the in-coming consul P. Mucius Scaevola to introduce the bill directly to the Assembly without consulting the Senate. What was needed was a strong Tribune of the People who could introduce their reform law directly to the Assembly. It was a time-honored political strategy — this would not be the first time that a tribune would propose legislation on behalf of more senior and powerful politicians.[3] Tiberius Gracchus was eager for the task.

When his term began in 133, Tiberius offered his land reform bill to a crowded session of the Plebeian Assembly. With a throng of senators listening intently and the Forum filled with people eager to hear what the famous tribune would say. This is how Tiberius began:

> The beasts of Italy have a house and home; they know where they can find shelter. But the men who risked their lives in fighting for Italy are granted only air and light; house and home are denied them and they are left to wander with their wives and children in the open air...They have neither ancestral altar or tombstone. They die for foreign luxury and riches, in name the masters of the world, in fact not even masters of their own plots of land.[4]

The effect on Rome was electric. Tiberius became a hero to the average Roman. Each morning when he arose, a crowd of men waited for him, eager to be part of his *ambitions* (formal political walks) through the Forum. Enthusiastic laborers and tenant farmers from the countryside poured into the city to vote for Tiberius' bill during the 20- day waiting period between when a

1 Astin, *Scipio*, p. 191

2 Alfoldy, *Social History*, p. 63

3 Bernstein, *Tiberius Sempronius Gracchus*, p. 119

4 Alfody, *Social History*, p. 53

bill was proposed and when it was voted upon. The ancient scholar Diodo-rus wrote that the voters came into Rome "like so many rivers into the all receiving sea.[1]

The nobles and *equites* who had grown rich using the public lands were furious at this proposal to seize what they regarded as their property. When Tiberius' bill was read to the Plebeian Assembly, a tribune aligned with the Senate named Marcus Octavius vetoed the legislation. This act was unprece-dented. No tribune had ever vetoed a piece of legislation so obviously favored by a majority of plebeian voters; it was literally "a betrayal of his trust as a Tribune of the People."[2] In the past, tribunes had primarily vetoed the ac-tions of praetors and consuls. Vetoes of legislation proposed by another tri-bune were usually withdrawn if there was clear support for the legislation.[3]

Tiberius tenaciously fought for his bill; in actions reminiscent of the Tri-bunes of 377–367, he vetoed every piece of official business in Rome, halt-ing public finances, trials, and even meetings of the Senate.[4] He also staged a series of debates with Octavius in the Forum, at one *contio* he offered to compensate his rival from his own pocket, a ploy that highlighted Octavius' extensive holdings of public lands.[5] But Octavius would not withdraw his veto.

Octavius' veto was not simply the act of a stubborn man protecting his vast estates from confiscation — he was supported by most of the Senate.[6] These actions showed an astonishing resistance to any action designed to improve the lot of a population that was becoming poorer and more desper-ate every year. During the conflict with Tiberius, the Senate refused to play its traditional role of guardian of the interests of the entire community. Since the Great Compromise of 367, the Senate had taken upon itself the task of being the steward for the entire society. Through its representatives in the Senate, the nobility had compromised with other social groups when they had called for reforms.[7] In this new crisis, the heady wealth and power of em-pire turned the vision of the nobility inward, toward their narrow interests, and away from the *res publica* that had been so important to their ancestors.

At the next session of the Plebeian Assembly, Tiberius increased the pres-sure on Octavius by moving that the Assembly remove him from his position, a kind of impeachment that had never occurred in Rome before. Tiberius justified this unprecedented step by saying that Octavius was not acting in the interest of the plebeians and pointed to Scipio's argument just a year

1 Stockton, *The Gracchi*, p. 20

2 Bernstein, *Tiberius Sempronius Gracchus*, p. 174

3 Boatwright, *The Romans*, p. 159

4 Matyszak, *Chronicle*, p. 129

5 Matyszak, *Chronicle*, p. 129

6 Bernstein, *Tiberius Sempronius Gracchus*, p. 174

7 Meier, *Caesar*, p. 35

before that the people had a right to choose who they wanted as their leaders.[1] When Octavius again refused to withdraw his veto, the 35 tribes voted unanimously to remove him. The Assembly then overwhelmingly passed the land reform bill.

Then, in his moment of triumph, Tiberius made a grave mistake. He appointed himself, his father-in-law Claudius, and his brother Gaius to the Agricultural Commission that was empowered to distribute land. Distributing land to poor citizens was a well-known and controversial way to win the allegiance of rural votes. The most recent incidence had occurred in 198 BCE, when T. Quinctius Flamininus was head of the commission that distributed farmland to Scipio Africanus' soldiers at the end of the Punic War.[2] The popularity gained from his outspoken role as the soldier's advocate led to his being elected consul at the age of 30, years ahead of when most people ran for consul and before he was elected praetor. He later was elected censor in 189.

By appointing himself and members of his family to the Land Commission, Tiberius made it easy for his enemies in the nobility to claim that he was carrying out this reform in order to increase his family's political power. In *contios* designed to arouse suspicions in the public's mind, his opponents linked Tiberius to revolutionary traditions in the Greek world, where the redistribution of land and the abolition of debts were the basic appeal of radicals who were leading rebellions against oligarchies.[3] For example, Cleomenes III had cemented his position as King of Sparta at the end of the 3rd century by rallying the common people around just such a revolutionary program. Aristocracies around the Mediterranean were frightened by his decade of success as a reformer and remained on the alert for similar uprisings.[4]

While Roman citizens celebrated the possibility of farmland for the poor, the Senate moved to phase two of its resistance, refusing to allocate money for the Land Commission's activities. At this critical moment, Attulus III, King of the rich city-state of Pergamum, who had no sons, died and willed his kingdom to Rome. This seemingly bizarre event was triggered by Attulus' understanding of Rome's growing power in the east and by his desire to prevent his crown from going to his illegitimate half-brother Aristonicus.[5] Roman legions were able to crush the revolt Aristonicus led against his brother's will and the wealthy, new province of Asia was created.[6]

The immediate impact in Rome was the transfer of Attulus' personal fortune to the Roman treasury. Tiberius boldly placed a bill before the Plebeian

1 Astin, *Scipio*, p. 207
2 Vishnia, *State, Society, Leaders*, p. 117
3 Bernstein, *Tiberius Sempronius Gracchus*, p. 179
4 Green, *Alexander to Actium*, pp. 258-260
5 Green, *Alexander to Actium*, p. 217
6 Green, *Alexander to Actium*, p. 521

Assembly, assigning the money to the operations of the Land Commission. The people, hungry for land, voted overwhelmingly for this law, usurping the Senate's privileged role in foreign policy and financial decision-making. Tiberius became the dominant figure in the city; three or four thousand people always accompanied him when he left his house to venture into the Forum.[1] However, he was now the target of charges that he wanted to be king. These attacks were reminiscent of the conservative assault on M. Manlius Capitolinus, the aristocrat who rallied the plebeians against debt laws in the 4th century. After a time, the unrelenting, distorted criticism from conservative leaders created doubt and hesitation among people who had initially supported Tiberius. Perhaps more alarming, his opponents in the Senate were preparing the way for the charges of treason that would surely be laid against him when his term of office ended.[2]

The threat of a trial was a serious problem for Tiberius. As a tribune, he could not be charged with crimes. However, after his term ended, he no longer had the shield of legal immunity. The penalty for treason was exile and seizure of his property. The likelihood of conviction was now very high because the juries for treason trials consisted entirely of members of the nobility. To avoid this fate, Tiberius decided to run for re-election. This was against tradition, as there had been no consecutive terms for a tribune in over two hundred years.[3] However, the laws only forbid the re-election of a magistrate and it was not clear that this term described a tribune. Of course, at the time of the Great Compromise of 367, two men were re-elected tribune ten times. That precedent seems to have had no impact in 133.

On Election Day, in the late summer of 133, the city was very tense, but not as crowded as in past showdowns because many of Tiberius' supporters were involved in the harvest and unable to come to the city.[4] Still, the first two tribes supported his bid for a second term and sentiment seemed to be on his side. At this point, several hostile tribunes who had previously been unwilling to block him vetoed his candidacy. The Plebeian Assembly broke up in confusion because it was unclear whether tribunes could veto an election.

The next day, when the Assembly resumed voting, the tribunes again vetoed Tiberius' candidacy. When Tiberius and his supporters ignored them and continued the voting, a fight broke out.[5] Meanwhile, at an angry meeting of the Senate, the *pontifex maximus*, a hard-line conservative named Scipio Nasica, demanded that Tiberius' ally, the consul Mucius Scaevola, authorize

1 Bernstein, *Tiberius Sempronius Gracchus*, p. 210

2 Astin, *Scipio*, p. 213

3 Astin, *Scipio*, p. 215

4 Matyszak, *Chronicle*, p. 130

5 Astin, *Scipio*, p. 222

the use of force to break up the fight and prevent the "illegal" re-election of the renegade tribune.[1] When Scaevola refused, Nasica led a group of Senators and their clients to the Rostra and attacked Tiberius and his followers. In the riot that followed, Tiberius and at least a hundred of his supporters were beaten to death. Their bodies were thrown in the Tiber River like common criminals.[2] A shock wave ran through the city — for the first time since Rome's independence, a political dispute was settled by killing other Roman citizens.

Scipio Nasica became the living symbol of the murder of a tribune and was pelted with stones and abuse whenever he went about the city. At the advice of the Senate, he went into self-imposed exile and died a year later in Asia province. To calm the public, the Senate quickly passed a decree affirming the existence of Tiberius' land reform law and Mucius Scaevola took his place on the Land Commission. A little later, when he and Claudius died, younger supporters of Tiberius, M. Fulvius Flaccus and C. Papirius Carbo were named to the Commission, which continued its work until 129 BCE.[3] Boundary markers set up by the Commission have been discovered in Campania, Picenum, and Samnium, showing that thousands of families benefited from Tiberius' sacrifice.

With order restored, the nobility moved to punish Tiberius' followers. The consuls of 132 set up a special senatorial court to prosecute people who had supported Tiberius.[4] The court condemned a number of Tiberius' supporters who were not members of the nobility and they were executed or sent into exile. It is unclear who they were or what crimes they were said to have committed, but the message from the Senate to the general population was clear — a member of the nobility might defy the Senate and pass a few laws, but he can not protect you from our revenge.

In the 4th century, territorial conquest and social reforms had soothed political conflicts in the city by satisfying the needs of large sections of the population.[5] In the 2nd century, territorial conquest was creating acute social problems. A modest reform attempt had provoked a violent reaction, splitting the ruling nobility, and pitting the Senate against the mass of the population.[6] The empire, which had initially enhanced the Republic, was now pulling it apart. Cracks in the political system that had opened during the war in Spain — between the Plebeian Assembly and the Senate and between reform and conservative factions in the nobility were now hardened into

---

1 Boatwright, *The Romans*, p. 160
2 Matyszak, *Chronicle*, p. 132
3 Boatwright, *The Romans*, p. 160
4 Henry Boren, *The Gracchi*, Woodbridge, CT: Twayne, 1968, p. 70
5 Meier, *Caesar*, p. 36
6 Alfoldy, *Social History*, p. 62

the structure of the Republic by the Senate's violent response to the reform movement. Looming over future conflicts would be the figure of Tiberius Gracchus, a model of enlightened reform for the great mass of the population and some members of the nobility, a symbol of mob disorder and a threat to private property for those with wealth and privilege.[1]

* * *

THE REFORM COALITION OF GAIUS GRACCHUS

The plan hatched by Appius Claudius and his Senate partners was a political success in spite of the turmoil and tragedy surrounding Tiberius' death. All of Tiberius' supporters became very popular; M. Fulvius Flaccus was elected consul in 125, C. Papirius Carbo was elected consul in 120, and C. Porcius Cato was elected consul in 114. Most remarkably P. Licinius Crassus Mucianus was elected consul just a year later, in the summer of 132. Clearly, the voters in the First and Second Classes of the Centuriate Assembly felt that the land reform law was a good idea. Another way of gauging public opinion was the fate of Scipio Aemelianus, the most popular man in Rome for 15 years. He was still in Spain in 133 and, when he heard of Tiberius' death, said, "So may perish others who venture on such wickedness."[2] Upon returning to Rome, the conqueror of Numantia was heckled because of his opposition to the land reform bill. The popularity he had worked so hard to gain vanished in the new world created by the events of 133.

The city remained tense for the next decade, displaced farmers continued to move into the city and there were years when hunger and unemployment filled the streets with angry crowds.[3] Political dissent was muted because people were understandably cautious after the violent nature of Tiberius' murder in the Forum. Most of all, everyone was waiting for Gaius Gracchus to take up the mantle of reform. In the family-oriented culture of Rome, it seemed only natural that the younger brother would assume leadership of the reform movement sparked by the bravery of the older brother. Only 20 when his brother was killed, Gaius worked on the Land Commission for several years and was then elected quaestor by the Tribal Assembly in 126. When he returned from Sicily in 124 to run for tribune, he received a hero's welcome.[4] "An immense crowd that the Campus Marti could not contain" elected him to one of the ten tribune positions.[5]

Gaius Gracchus inherited his brother's role as leader of the reform movement and he proved to be an extraordinary politician and administrator. The

1 Alfoldy, *Social History*, p. 75
2 Boatwright, *The Romans*, p. 160
3 Boren, *The Gracchi*, p. 90
4 Boatwright, *The Romans*, p. 161
5 LeGlay, *History of Rome*, p. 112

new tribune was not like his brother. Tiberius was cool and reasoned, while Gaius was fiery and animated. Cicero claimed he was the best public speaker of the age, able to incite the emotions of thousands of people packed into the Forum.[1] He even had a flute player nearby to sound a warning note if his voice became too shrill with passion when he spoke to an audience.

Most notably, Gaius had an incredible political mind. Unlike Tiberius, who focused on a single dramatic law, and more like the tribunes who forced the Great Compromise of 367, Gaius introduced an entire legislative program. His first priority was to restore civil liberties that had been trampled on by the Senate during its prosecution of Tiberius' supporters. The Senate's trials in 132 violated the hard won right of a citizen to *provocatio*, trial by a citizen's assembly in a capital case. To restore this fundamental right and block the Senate from launching legal prosecutions of its opponents, Gaius successfully proposed a law barring praetors and consuls from imposing a capital sentence as part of a special investigation unless this power was authorized by a vote of a citizens' assembly. The law was retroactive (a feature of Roman law that was dropped by the English) and P. Popillius Laenas, who (as consul in 132) presided over the execution of Tiberius' supporters, went into exile to avoid prosecution.[2]

Gaius then persuaded the Plebeian Assembly to pass a series of laws designed to win the favor of significant groups in Roman society in order to draw them into his reform coalition. For rural laborers and tenant farmers, he introduced a modified land reform law that would take back more public land and give it to poor citizens. Another law prohibited the drafting of boys under the age of 17 and required the army to provide clothing for its soldiers.[3]

For the *equites*, Gaius introduced a jury law that excluded senators from the juries that passed down verdicts for cases involving corruption in provincial government. Juries full of *equites* would now sit in judgment of ambitious nobles who served as magistrates in the provinces.[4] In addition, the *publicani* were given the right to collect taxes in the wealthy new province of Asia, the former Kingdom of Pergamum. This was called "tax farming" and was a source of great riches for those international businessmen who were chosen to collect taxes.

For the urban proletariat, Gaius had his most spectacular innovations. The *lex Sempronia frumentaria* gave every resident of the city a bushel of corn (40 lbs.) every month, at a price reduced by a state subsidy paid for with rev-

---

1 Matyszak, *Chronicle*, p. 134
2 Boatwright, *The Romans*, p. 162
3 Boren, *The Gracchi*, p. 94
4 Matyszak, *Chronicles*, p. 135

enues from the tax farming of Asia province.[1] It was the first social welfare legislation enacted in Rome and enraged most senators. The story is told that Gaius Gracchus saw Piso Frugi, one of the most outspoken opponents of the law and a very wealthy man, standing in line for a bushel of corn. When Gaius asked what he was doing in line, Piso explained, "If you stole my property and distributed it among the Roman people, you would also find me here, queuing to get some of my own back again."[2] If he had lived in the 19th century Senator Frugi would have been a good friend of Ebenezer Scrooge.

Gaius also had the Plebeian Assembly authorize a number of public works projects and then managed their construction himself.[3] He supervised repairs to a number of major roads near and through the city, providing steady wages to hundreds of unskilled workers.[4] As part of his attempt to manage hunger in the city, Gaius built large grain storage facilities near the docks along the Tiber River. With these enormous storage bins, the state could influence the price of grain in the city, bringing a measure of stability to the very erratic market for corn and grain.

Gaius needed more than one year to implement all of these changes, so he made himself available for a second term but did not announce himself as a candidate. The Plebeian Assembly then elected only nine tribunes for the year 122 and, with a special vote, invited the non-candidate to become the 10th tribune.[5] The Senate, presented with a *fait accompli*, had to let the election stand. Gaius was the most powerful man in Rome.

THE NOBILITY STRIKES BACK

Gaius then stunned the Senate by introducing a law granting citizenship rights to all Italians who currently had Latin rights and the privileges of Latin rights to all of the other residents of Italy. It was a bold move designed to address the changing nature of Rome's relationship with its Latin and Italian rights allies. Since the Second Punic War the exchange of goods, people, and culture between communities on the Italian peninsula had lessened differences between the Romans and other tribal peoples. Latin colonies had always been bastions of Roman culture and institutions and these practices now spread into many other allied communities.[6] The Latin language and Roman law were practiced widely, towns began calling their ruling council a Senate, and officials had Latin titles such as quaestor. In addition, ties of mutual political interest linked the leading families of Italian towns with

1 LeGlay, *History of Rome*, p. 112
2 Matyszak, *Chronicle*, p. 135
3 Matyszak, *Chronicles*, p. 136
4 Boren, *The Gracchi*, p. 101
5 Boren, *The Gracchi*, p. 173
6 Boatwright, *The Romans*, p. 144

the nobility and ties of commerce and trade linked the *Equestrian* Order with businessmen from other regions of Italy.

On the other hand, there were many suspicions left over from the Punic War. Many communities in southern Italy had sided with Hannibal when it looked like he might win. After the war, Roman officials made random efforts to search for disloyalty in Italian communities and became more intrusive in the management of local affairs. This legal harassment reached new heights during the Bacchus affair in 186 BCE.

During the difficult period of the Punic Wars, many new cults from the Hellenistic east came to Rome as people sought relief from their hardships and sacrifices. The cult of Bacchus was based on worship of the Greek god Dionysus, who represented the force of life in all growing things. He was best known as the god of wine and the cult was based on wild frenzied worship.[1] The dangers of excess typified by Dionysus were, in the Greek world, balanced by an understanding that denial of our basic instincts is also unhealthy. The 5th century playwright Euripides explores these themes in one of his most famous tragedies, *The Bacchae*.[2] In Italy, participants in the cult met secretly at night and engaged in wild dancing, drinking, drumming, and sexual activity.[3]

This quasi-religious activity, done in secret and outside of the traditional religious framework was alarming to the solid citizens of the Senate. The level of organization the Bacchus cult had achieved by this time is demonstrated by the Senate's decree suppressing its activities. It ordered the arrest of priests, forbid gathering for rituals and nocturnal meetings, called for the dismantling of shrines, prohibited the mixing of men and women for rituals, and forbid the swearing of oaths.[4] The consul Spurius Postumius Albinus spent his entire year in office enforcing the decree throughout the Italian peninsula. The historian Livy believed that this ancient witch-hunt resulted in many executions. It is possible that, in an atmosphere of accusation and suspicion, the heaviest weight of the investigation fell on Italian communities suspected of lacking adequate loyalty to Rome.

It is within this context of growing ties mixed with increasing tensions that Gaius Gracchus introduced the citizenship law. While in the long run it was an act of great statesmanship that would have increased the prosperity and political unity of Italy, in the short run it destroyed the foundations of Gaius' popularity. When Gaius was re-elected, the Plebeian Assembly had also selected a young noble named Livius Drusus to be one of the tribunes.

---

1 Michael Stapleton, *The Illustrated Dictionary of Greek and Roman Mythology*, New York: Peter Bedrick Books, 1978, p. 69

2 Stapleton, Dictionary of Mythology, p. 69

3 Boatwright, *The Romans*, p. 142

4 Boatwright, *The Romans*, p. 142

Drusus had close ties with a group of people who had been allied with Scipio Aemilianus. These individuals wanted to enact limited reforms to improve the aristocratic system and were willing to accept more power for the *equites* and cheaper grain for the plebeians in order to forestall more radical changes.[1]

Livius Drusus' role was to seek ways to undermine Gaius' popularity with groups in his coalition and the citizenship law offered the perfect opportunity to separate him from the urban proletariat. "He attacked the enfranchisement of the Italians, pointing out that more for everyone meant less for those who already had it. So, posing as a popular champion, Drusus vetoed Gaius' proposal."[2] He then persuaded the Plebeian Assembly to pass a law eliminating the rents paid by people who had just been given public lands. While this was very popular in the countryside, the law also made the land private property and gave the new owners the right to sell their land. This made the new farmers vulnerable to the same forces that had pushed so many small farmers off their land in the first place.[3] At the same time, the Senate reassured the *equites* that it would retain the laws giving them control of the juries and the right to collect taxes in the province of Asia. By this time, the wealthy *equites* were uncomfortable with Gaius' populist activities and they quickly dropped their support for him.[4]

Meanwhile, Gaius, filled with the excitement of starting a new venture, had made the mistake of going to Carthage to oversee the creation of a new colony. When he returned, Gaius was dismayed by the success of Drusus' measures and disillusioned by the fickleness of the *equites* whom he thought were his allies. The counter-attack by the nobility radicalized Gaius; he moved from his beautiful home on the Palatine hill to a slum area near the Forum and went about the city followed by bands of loud, roughneck supporters. With so many allies now turned against him, Gaius was unable to win a third term as tribune.

The next year, one of the new consuls, Lucius Opimius, induced a tribune to propose that the legislation setting up the colony at Carthage be repealed. Gaius and his ally, Fulvius Flaccus, came to a meeting of the Plebeian Assembly determined to block this proposal. A fight broke out in the very tense atmosphere and one of Opimius' clients was killed.

This was the excuse the Senate was waiting for. Opimius called an emergency session and the body passed a new decree that came to be known as the *senatus consultum ultimum*. This Senate resolution stated that the consuls were to make sure that no harm came to the Republic. "This meant the use

---

1 Boren, *The Gracchi*, p. 111
2 Matyszak, *Chronicles*, p. 136
3 Boren, *The Gracchi*, p. 113
4 Stockton, *The Gracchi*, p. 191

of unrestrained police power, if necessary without regard for civil liberties."[1] The consul had arranged for a detachment of Cretan archers, non-Roman soldiers, to be stationed near the city and he sent them and a mob of armed nobles and equites to attack Gaius and his followers. Gaius had hoped that in a direct confrontation the people of Rome would rise up against the nobility, but this did not happen. Gaius, Flaccus, and several thousand loyal supporters were massacred. Gaius' and Flaccus' heads were cut off and brought to the consul for rewards.[2]

In spite of the new law against Senate inquisitions, Opimius set up a special court that condemned dozens of Gaius' political supporters to exile or death. When the consul was later prosecuted for killing Roman citizens in violation of recent and ancient *provocatio* laws, the jury, consisting of members of the nobility, ruled that the *senatus consultum ultimum* placed him beyond the restrictions of any laws.[3] This new weapon, which came to be known as the "Ultimate Decree," placed the Senate above the *res publica* and the Centuriate and Plebeian Assemblies. From now on, every citizen knew that when the Senate felt its interests were being threatened, it would use force to ensure its supremacy.

While the Senate had won the battle against reform, the second naked display of power in a decade tarnished the aura of legitimacy that the nobility had so carefully developed for more than two hundred years. In the long run, for Rome to survive as a Republic, the ruling elite's right to rule needed to be based on some level of consent from those being governed. However, from now on, the Roman people deferred not to the superior *dignitas* of the nobility, but to its superior power.

THE POPULARES MOVEMENT

For the rest of the existence of the Roman Republic, the conservative majority in the Senate was challenged by members of the nobility who believed that the reforms championed by the Gracchi brothers needed to come to fruition. Frequently, these challengers sought the position of tribune in order to enact a legislative agenda that included one or more of the types of reform proposed by the Gracchi. As in previous centuries, these reform tribunes were members of the nobility.[4] Only members of the nobility had the financial, family, and political resources to build a following among the urban population and also have enough connections in the rural tribes to win election in the Plebeian Assembly.

---

1 Meier, *Caesar*, p. 39
2 Boren, *The Gracchi*, p. 124
3 Meier, *Caesar*, p. 39
4 Alfoldy, *Social History*, p. 54

Sometimes a charismatic noble would have an already formed agenda and impose his will on the Assembly. At other times, tribunes would respond to problems or crises by suddenly seizing the mantle of reform. As the troubles of the Roman Republic deepened, tribunes were often allies or followers of successful generals, and the legislative program was a mixture of the two men's political agendas. Those tribunes and generals who sought reforms through popularity in the Plebeian Assembly were known as *populares*. While they often cooperated with one another, they never formed a cohesive political party.

Populares were in no way a peace group or critics of the empire. *Populares'* measures were primarily designed to distribute the riches of empire more equitably and to manage the empire more efficiently. Many of the Republic's most successful generals found themselves opposed by the Senate during this period and supported tribunes who would press land reform or other issues that discredited the Senate. The prohibitions against re-election of tribunes made it impossible for any one leader to press for reforms over a period of years. As a result, *populares'* reform issues arose occasionally, in particular situations, rather than on a yearly basis.

The Empire under Attack and the Rise of Marius

Just eight years after the death of Gaius Gracchus a series of military defeats on the northern borders of Italy and in Africa would shake the foundations of the Senate's control of the city's politics. For unknown reasons, two large Germanic tribes, the Cimbri and the Teutones, who had lived for centuries in northern Germany, began migrating south. They inflicted costly defeats on Roman armies in 113 and 112 and then invaded Gaul. Meanwhile, in 111 BCE, the barbarian army of the Numidian king Jugurtha crushed a Roman army in northern Africa.[1] Public indignation over these of defeats prompted a tribune to successfully propose a law creating a special court, with *equite* jurors, to investigate the Senate's conduct of foreign policy. This investigation in 109, which would never have happened before the war in Spain and the conflicts with the Gracchi, led to the exile of a number of nobles accused of accepting bribes from Jugurtha, including L. Opimius, the consul who had led the massacre of Gaius Gracchus and his followers.[2]

Turning from the nobility, the Centuriate Assembly elected Gaius Marius, a "new man" whose family had never held a praetor or consul position, to be consul and approved a law making him head of the army in Africa. Then, in his quest for greater *dignitas*, he struck up an alliance with Gaius Julius Caesar, arranging for Marius to marry Caesar's oldest daughter, Julia. When

---

1 Cornell, *Atlas*, p. 60
2 Matyszak, *Chronicle*, p. 141

Gaius Julius Caesar's son, also named Gaius, had a son in 100 BCE, Marius became the uncle and role model for Julius Caesar.

Marius and his *legat* Cornelius Sulla captured Jugurtha in the year 105. With this victory Marius and Sulla became heroes to the Roman people, in contrast to the consuls who suffered a devastating defeat in 105, with more than 50,000 killed or wounded in a fierce battle with the German tribes. The Plebeian Assembly reacted to this disaster by stripping the consul Caepio of his *imperium* and sending him into exile.[1] In an unprecedented event, Marius, was elected consul again for the year 104 even though he had not yet returned from Africa. Desperate for new men to stop the advancing Germans, Marius abandoned the requirement that recruits be men with status in the Centuriate Assembly and accepted anyone from the proletariat who volunteered for service. "Soldiering became a form of employment for men who owned no land."[2] After 400 years of a part-time citizens' army, the social changes created by the conquest of an empire forced the Republic to switch to a professional army. This army proved to be more efficient than the previous citizen legions but also far less loyal to the Republic and its political institutions.

Marius had a marvelous flair for motivating soldiers and his new army was soon a well-developed fighting machine. His army crushed the Teutones in Gaul and then destroyed the Cimbri in northern Italy. Julius Caesar's uncle was the nation's savior, winning re-election as consul for the years 103, 102, 101, and 100.

The recruitment of proletarian armies added a new, explosive twist to the already heated issue of land reform and redistribution. These soldiers, once their term of enlistment was finished, had no farmland to return to.

> The consequence however was that the proletarian armies began to demand some permanent reward for their services, and since the state was not prepared to institute a regular system of granting land allotments to discharged veterans, the men looked instead to their commanders to make provision for them.[3]

The key phrase in this statement is "the state was not prepared," another way of saying that the Senate was unwilling to give good farmland to mere proletarians. As it had at the time of the Gracchi, the nobility refused to accommodate the welfare of other elements of Roman society.

In 103, a weakened Senate could not prevent an ambitious tribune, L. Appuleius Saturninus, from allying with Marius and persuading the Plebeian Assembly to give generous allotments of land in Africa to Marius' veterans from the war against Jugurtha.[4] Elected tribune again for the year 100, he and

---

1 Cornell, *Atlas*, p. 61
2 Cornell, *Atlas*, p. 61
3 Cornell, *Atlas*, p. 61
4 Matyszak, *Chronicles*, p. 147

Marius pushed through a land distribution bill that would give farmland in Gaul and in the Po River Valley to Marius' veterans and other poor Roman citizens.[1] However, Saturninus, like Tiberius before him, was concerned about being prosecuted after his term was over and ran for re-election. He won but a candidate for consul was murdered during a chaotic fight at the election stalls and the Senate passed the *senatus consultum ultimum*. Marius was forced to arrest Saturninus and his ally Glaucia. A band of young nobles then stoned Saturninus and his supporters to death and the Senate repealed the land distribution law.

Marius was discredited by the conflicts over Saturninus and retired to private life. His veterans, along with proletarians in the city, had received no benefits and Rome was again full of unhappy citizens. During the decade of the 90s there were also rising tensions in the empire. The Italian and Latins deeply resented being second-class members of the alliance and the provinces seethed under the rapacious rule of *publicani* tax farmers and greedy provincial governors. By the year 91, almost in desperation, one of the leading young members of the nobility, Livius Drusus, became a tribune and tried to enact a reform program to hold the Republic and its empire together. Unfortunately, the polarized politics of the time meant that, rather than creating a coalition as Gaius Gracchus had done, Drusus gave nearly everyone something to dislike. After the collapse of his legislative program he was stabbed by an anonymous assassin and died the next morning.[2]

The death of their last hope for relief sparked a general uprising of the Italians, a bloody conflict that became known as the Social War. From this point in 91 BCE, Rome's citizens were engaged in either civil wars or desperate repression of revolts within the empire for the next twenty years. The empire, which had brought Rome so much wealth, now brought rivers of misery. Subjugated peoples in Spain, in Italy, in Greece, and Asia Minor all took turns revolting against the harshness of Roman rule. The impact of these blows staggered the Republic and weakened the representative institutions and political practices that were at the heart of this unique society. As a result, when they were not fighting to defend their empire, the Romans were fighting each other in a series of civil wars that left thousands dead and eventually extinguished the spark of *libertas*.

---

1 Boatwright, *The Romans*, p. 174
2 Boatwright, *The Romans*, p. 180

CHAPTER 11. CLASH OF THE TITANS

> When our state had grown powerful through toil and the practice of justice, when great kings had been subdued in war, when barbarian nations and mighty peoples had been subjugated by force, when all the seas and lands lay open, fortune began to grow cruel and cast confusion on all our affairs. The lust for money and then for empire grew apace. At first the vices spread slowly and sometimes were punished; but later when the disease spread like a plague, the state was changed, and what had been a dominion of highest virtue and equity was transformed into one of cruelty and intolerance.
>
> —Sallust, *Bellum Catilinae* 20 BCE.[1]

The Social War was a terrible test of will and military cunning because the rebel Italian alliance had 100,000 trained soldiers. It quickly overran many strategic towns in central Italy and inflicted humiliating defeats on Roman legions. Not until the next year, when Gaius Marius and L. Cornelius Sulla, heroes of the wars against Jugurtha and the Germans, were in charge of the northern and southern sectors of the war did the tide began to turn against the Italians. The Romans also took some of the steam out of the rebellion by addressing its root cause. Julius Caesar's father's cousin, L. Julius Caesar, consul in 90, was able to get a law passed granting voting citizenship to all Italians who were not in rebellion and those willing to lay down their

---

1 As quoted in, Erich Gruen, "Introduction," in Erich Gruen, ed. *Imperialism in the Roman Republic*, New York: Holt, Rinehart, Winston, 1970, p. 2

arms. These concessions persuaded Italians in Etruria, Lucania, and Campania to stay out of the conflict, greatly simplifying Rome's task.

Roman armies gradually subdued the last rebel cities in 88, but the two consuls for that year, L. Cornelius Sulla and Q. Pompeius Rufus were immediately confronted with a new disaster. With Rome distracted, King Mithridates Eupator IV of Pontus (an old kingdom in Asia Minor located on the south shore of the Black Sea) invaded Asia province. There, the Greek residents greeted him as a liberator. To show their loyalty to the new leader and take some measure of revenge for 40 years of misrule, the Greeks massacred the Roman politicians, bureaucrats, tax collectors, and businessmen who had exploited them. Between 40,000 and 80,000 Romans and Italians were killed.[1] The city of Athens, once a Roman ally, then invited Mithridates to come and liberate Greece as well.

As it had in the past, the complexities of managing an empire in crisis led to political deadlock and new bloodshed in Republican Rome. P. Sulpicius Rufus, a reformer and friend of the murdered tribune Livius Drusus, was elected tribune for 88. His goal was to enroll the newly enfranchised Italian voters in all of the 35 tribes, a reform that would radically alter the electoral system, especially the Tribal Assembly which elected tribunes and quaestors — entry points to the *cursus honorum*. Many *equites* supported Sulpicius because they wanted an influx of new citizens to dilute the power of the nobility and bring more influence to prominent members of the First Class.[2] Determined to avoid the fate of previous reform tribunes, Sulpicius created a bodyguard of young equestrians that was nicknamed the "anti-Senate" by members of the nobility.[3]

Led by Sulla and Pompeius Rufus, the Senate blocked Sulpicius' bill, instead passing a resolution calling for all of the new citizens to be enrolled in eight new tribes that would vote after the original 35 tribes.[4] The Senate also appointed Sulla to command the army that would restore Asia province to the empire. Furious at being spurned by the Senate and the consuls, Sulpicius formed an alliance with old Gaius Marius. In return for Marius' help getting the Plebeian Assembly to distribute the Italians into all of the tribes, Sulpicius agreed to have the Assembly reassign Sulla's command to Marius. With the help of a mob of Marius' old soldiers, Sulpicius was able to get both laws passed.

Robbed of his chance for gold and glory, Sulla retreated to Campania and mobilized the five legions that he led during the Social War. Shrewdly, he spoke to his soldiers, telling them about his reversal of fortune and warning

---

1 Boatwright, *The Romans*, p. 215

2 Meier, *Caesar*, p. 76

3 Kahn, *Education of Caesar*, p. 40

4 Boatwright, *The Romans*, p. 184

them that, as Sulla's men, they would probably not get their fair share of the booty that would go to the victorious Roman army that re-conquered the east. The reaction was alarming for anyone who believed in the political institutions of the Republic. The men showed their loyalty to their commanding general rather than the Republic by stoning to death the legates sent from Rome to take over from Sulla. They marched on Rome, followed him across the *pomerium*, and killed any citizens who tried to defend the city. Sulla hunted down the *populares* tribune Sulpicius and placed his head on a pike in the Rostra. The Senate declared Marius an outlaw and he was forced to flee to Africa. With his main rivals dead or in exile, and their citizenship law nullified, Sulla march off to attack Athens and Mithridates.

For the first time in Rome's history, a Republican army had attacked the city to settle a political dispute. If the killing of the Gracchi had violated rules of conduct that allowed the Republic to foster civilized disagreement, then Sulla's action threatened the social compact that connected Romans as citizens. When his soldiers occupied the city and crossed the *pomerium*, they initiated a new era. "Competition for honors had always been the lifeblood of the Republic, but now something deadly had been introduced into it, and its presence there, a lurking toxin, could not easily be forgotten."[1]

As soon as Sulla left, the two newly elected consuls for 87, L. Cornelius Cinna and Gnaeus Octavius, quarreled over the same vexing issue of where to place the newly enfranchised Italian voters. Again, the nobility would not accept any changes in the status quo, there was rioting in the streets, and the *populares* consul Cinna was forced to flee the city. He managed to rally support in a number of Italian towns and, when Marius triumphantly returned from Africa with some of his former soldiers, Cinna marched on the city. They routed the dispirited force protecting the city after Pompey Strabo, leader of the only other effective fighting force, died of plague. Cinna and Marius proclaimed themselves consuls for the year 86 and, after a brief period revenge killings, old Marius died, leaving Cinna to face Sulla's rage.

Sulla's Revenge

Pompey Strabo's son, Gneaus Pompey, inherited his father's power base in Picenum and Cisalpine Gaul. At 19, Cn. Pompey was already a charismatic leader. He had a noble face with shaggy blond locks that reminded on-lookers of how Alexander the Great was portrayed in statues.[2] He always played the part of the boyish hero, blushing when complimented, always modest in public. Matched with his record of military triumphs, this personality made him a celebrity. His standing among the common people would always be

---

1 Holland, *Rubicon*, p. 70
2 Kahn, *Education of Caesar*, p. 67

greater than that of his rivals.[1] Pompey's political ambitions mirrored his public image; he sought honor and fame and was happiest when the Senate praised him. He repeatedly demonstrated that he was not grasping for political power by demobilizing his army once he received what he believed was proper recognition.[2]

Shortly after Cinna took over the city, Pompey was prosecuted for not returning to the state money seized during the Social War. His team of defense advocates demonstrated the respect other powerful people already had for him. It included the former consul L. Marcius Philippus, Q. Hortensius the leading advocate in the city, and Cn. Papirius Carbo, who would become Cinna's colleague in the consulship the next year.[3] In a final, typically Roman twist, Pompey became engaged to the daughter of the president of the court during his trial. When he was acquitted, the crowd in the Forum sang a popular wedding march.[4]

Rome was calm for three years while Sulla inflicted defeats on Mithridates, but was unable to capture the wily king. Sulla now itched to return to Rome and, in 85 BCE, he hastily signed a peace treaty that returned Asia province to Rome but left the unrepentant king on his throne. Cinna, reelected consul for three straight years, decided to fight Sulla in Greece and tried to force his soldiers to cross a storm-tossed Adriatic Sea. After one ship was lost, the men mutinied and murdered the consul. After Cinna's death, the nobility abandoned the *populares* regime and three wealthy young aristocrats, Pompey, M. Licinius Crassus, whose father was murdered by Marius, and Metellus Pius, head of the powerful Metelli family, each recruited private armies and joined Sulla.

It took Sulla and his allies almost a year to capture the city because, while they were poorly led, many Italians and Romans knew that Sulla was determined to return the nobility to its position of dominance in Roman society and they fought his experienced armies with grim desperation.[5] When, after thousands of deaths, the city was finally captured, the restored Senate voted Pompey his first actual title. With the *imperium* of a praetor (if not the actual legitimacy of being elected to an office) he led his army to Sicily and then Africa and crushed rebel holdouts. His troops now hailed him as *Magnus* (the Great), in echo of his association with Alexander. When Pompey Magnus returned to the city, he brought his soldiers with him and demanded the honor of a triumph. No man who had not been elected to the office of praetor had ever been granted the right to have a triumph. However, when Pompey

1 Holland, *Rubicon*, p. 137
2 Meier, *Caesar*, p. 127
3 Seager, *Pompey*, p. 25
4 Southern, *Pompey the Great*, p. 20
5 Southern, *Pompey the Great*, p. 23

boldly told Sulla, "More men worship the rising sun than the setting one," Sulla relented.[1] Pompey, of course, had a surprise for his parade; his golden chariot would be pulled through the streets of the city by two African elephants. Alas, to the amusement of the crowd the great beasts were too large to fit through the city gate and Pompey the Great was forced to ingloriously dismount and ride behind a chariot pulled by white horses, like all of Rome's previous heroes.[2]

Pompey's triumphant day was followed by a descent into public hell. Sulla ruled the city as unquestioned dictator. His first order of business was to kill the *populares* whose push for reforms had ignited the troubles. He posted a series of lists in the Forum of prominent *equites* and nobles who had supported Marius or Cinna, perhaps 500 to 800 men. They were all condemned to death. Anyone could kill a person whose name appeared on one of these lists and bring the head in to receive a reward. The sons of a man who was *proscribed* in this way were barred from holding public office in the future and his property was put up for auction and sold to one of Sulla's supporters.

In a society that had prided itself on following the rule of law, this chaotic hunting down and killing of great numbers of leading citizens — with no trials and no rights — was an enormous shock.[3] Armed men, seeking rewards, roamed the streets and killed doomed individuals as soon as new lists were posted. After the initial political killings, further lists degenerated into a settling of blood feuds and family rivalries. In addition, Sulla's unscrupulous allies placed rich men on the lists in order to acquire their properties. One wealthy man, upon seeing his name on a list, is said to have remarked, "Ah, I see that my Alban farm has informed on me."[4] Another 1,000 to 2,000 *equites* and nobles were murdered and their property re-distributed to Sulla's allies. The ill feelings from this horrible time divided the Republic for years.

In the midst of this terror, not everyone obeyed the dictator. Gaius Julius Caesar, a nephew of Gaius Marius, had married Cinna's daughter Cornelia. To force a show of loyalty and to soil Caesar's *dignitas* with the betrayal of his wife and her family, Sulla called the 18-year-old Caesar in for a meeting and demanded that he divorce Cornelia.[5] The youth was tall and slender, with blond hair and large dark eyes. A stylish dresser and an articulate speaker, he seldom drank and could ride horses and use swords with the best-trained soldiers.[6] Still a teenager, with his family on the losing side in a civil war, and facing a murderous dictator, Caesar refused. Purple with rage, the dictator

---

1 Seager, *Pompey*, p. 28
2 Matyszak, *Chronicles*, p. 182
3 Boatwright, *The Romans*, p. 194
4 Matyszak, *Chronicles*, p. 169
5 Meier, *Caesar*, p. 92
6 Matyszak, *Chronicles*, p. 201

took away Cornelia's dowry and Caesar's inheritance, but the young man would not give in.

When he left Sulla's palace, his mother gave him a disguise and sent him away to live in the hills. Then she rallied all of the relatives she knew who were on good terms with Sulla and together they convinced the dictator not to proscribe the boy. Legend is that he told them, "Bear in mind that the man you are so eager to save will one day deal the death blow to the aristocracy . . . for in this Caesar there is more than one Marius!"[1] Caesar's bravery and Sulla's warning reinforce other comments in the ancient literature that, even as a youth, he had an unusually charismatic and commanding presence, a personality that won him respect and loyalty from many types of people.

The second phase of Sulla's plan to save the Republic was to muzzle the office of tribune. He decreed that no person who was elected tribune could run for higher office, making it a dead end for ambitious members of the nobility. He also declared that tribunes could only bring proposed laws before the Plebeian Assembly when the Senate had already approved them. Finally, he said that individuals must wait for ten years before seeking re-election as tribune, making it impossible to use the position as a base for mobilizing opposition to the Senate.[2] To show the plebeians that the nobility now controlled the city, Sulla eliminated the grain subsidy, which had been around in one form or another for 43 years, since the time of Gaius Gracchus.

A DECADE OF CONFLICT

Believing that he had restored the power of the nobility, Sulla resigned as dictator in 79 BCE and presided over the first peacetime elections in Rome since 91. One of the new consuls, Q. Lutatius Catulus, would be a leader of the patrician branch of the nobility for the next 15 years. His colleague was M. Aemilius Lepidus, a man who had changed sides frequently during the 80s. Sulla opposed his candidacy, but Pompey the Great supported him because he had been an officer in his father's army during the Social War.[3] Lepidus soon began making speeches in the Forum against Sulla's new laws, advocating for the return of children of the proscribed from exile, restoring the power of the tribunes, and bringing back the grain subsidy. The fact that these speeches brought him instant popularity and support in many parts of Italy speaks to the discontent that Sulla could not erase.[4] When unhappy farmers and sons of proscripted men formed a rebel army, Lepidus declared

---

1 Kahn, *Education of Caesar*, p. 60

2 Southern, *Pompey*, p. 30

3 Kahn, *Education of Caesar*, p. 71

4 Boatwright, *The Romans*, p. 204

that he should be re-elected consul and marched on Rome at their head.[1] Catulus was able to defeat him in a small battle near Rome.

The end of open rebellion did not mean an end to agitation. In 76, the tribune Gnaeus Sicinius made speeches in the Forum calling for a restoration of the ancient privilege of the people to be led and protected by tribunes.[2] The following year, the tribune Quintus Opimius used his veto power to hinder the consuls' actions. As punishment several leading members of the nobility took Opimius to court in 74, after his period of immunity as tribune had expired. The jury of Senators imposed an enormous fine on him, which led to his property being confiscated and his finances ruined.[3] This blatant use of the courts to stifle dissent confirmed the fears the Gracchi brothers had of persecution after their term of office expired.

Opimius was not the only problem in 75. There were severe grain shortages that year, with the price of corn jumping out of the reach of thousands of residents. Our sources refer to more than one public disturbance, and on one occasion Cotta and his consular colleague were surrounding by angry, hungry citizens in the Forum.[4] They retreated to the home of a nearby supporter and the next day Cotta went to the Forum to confess that he was not to blame for the shortages. Instead, he claimed that the stress of multiple rebellions in the empire meant there were no state funds to subsidize the price of corn.[5] He had the audacity to add that their hunger should to be viewed as a necessary sacrifice in order to maintain the empire. The historian Sallust has Cotta saying, "The price of supreme power is great anxiety, many heavy burdens. It is vain for you to attempt to avoid them and to look for peace and prosperity."[6]

The leaders of the nobility were too practical to believe that mere rhetoric would calm the hungry plebeians. Demonstrating where the wealth acquired in Rome's wars had accumulated, Q. Hortensius, a leader in the Senate, distributed grain to the city's residents at subsidized rates for several weeks.[7] Cicero, serving as quaestor in Sicily was able to send emergency shipments to the city from the island's storage bins. No changes occurred in 74, perhaps because another wealthy member of the nobility, Marcus Seius, used his own funds to distribute grain at below market prices.[8]

In 73, when the noted historian C. Licinius Macer was elected tribune and delivered eloquent speeches against the nobility, the consuls again used

---

1 Gruen, *Last Generation*, p. 14
2 Seager, *Pompey*, p. 33
3 Gruen, *Last Generation*, p. 25
4 Kahn, *Education of Caesar*, p. 82
5 Gruen, *Last Generation*, p. 36
6 Kahn, *Education of Caesar*, p. 83
7 Gruen, *Last Generation*, p. 36
8 Gruen, *Last Generation*, p. 36

coercion as Macer "was shouted down."[1] However, they also persuaded the Senate to allocate money for the purchase of corn in Sicily to be distributed at below market prices. In his speeches, Macer cautioned the plebeians not to express gratitude for the grain laws, "by which they have valued all your liberties at five pecks [monthly] per man, an allowance not much greater than the rations of a prison."[2] He also warned them that by falsely promoting "hysteria" about threats to national security, "a few men [had] taken possession of the treasury, the armies, the kingdoms, and the provinces."[3]

By this time, the Senate could ill afford bread riots among the plebeians, for in the summer of 73 a group of gladiators broke out of their training camp in Campania. During the 1st century, as the ideology of empire took a deeper hold on the self-image of Roman citizens, the sport of watching foreigners fight to the death in organized combat became very popular. To reinforce the idea that the desperate men struggling for their lives in the arena were representative of the barbarian peoples who made up the empire, the gladiators were dressed and armed like Roman opponents, brimmed helmets and feather crests for the Samnites, loincloths and spears for the Gauls, mailed armor for Thracians.[4] Men from all over the Mediterranean region, Spaniards, Gauls, Macedonians, Greeks, and North Africans lived and trained together, and then killed one another in savage combat. Such men, when working together as escaped slaves, were formidable adversaries. A praetor with three thousand men chased them to the slopes of Mt. Vesuvius, where the gladiators attacked from the rear and routed the legion.[5]

This was just the first defeat. The gladiators had a leader, Spartacus, who inspired them to work together and could enforce military discipline in combat. Everywhere the growing band went there were dozens of slaves to be freed and then armed. The little army looted towns in central Italy and then crushed another praetor in battle. The slave army plus its camp following of women and children may have grown to total 100,000 individuals in all as it marched north up the peninsula burning, looting, and freeing slaves. One element of the cohesion of this disparate band of individuals was Spartacus' attempt, "unique among the leaders of slave revolts in the ancient world," to keep a sense of egalitarianism within his army.[6] Gold and silver loot, for example, was shared equally among all the former slaves. On a peninsula where perhaps one third of the population was enslaved this was every Roman's

1 Gruen, Last Generation, pp. 25 & 36
2 Kahn, *Education of Caesar*, p. 94
3 Kahn, *Education of Caesar*, p. 93
4 Holland, *Rubicon*, p. 140
5 Holland, *Rubicon*, p. 141
6 Holland, *Rubicon*, p. 144

nightmare, that those in bondage would rise up, murder their masters, and take over society.

Once again, the empire was spinning out of control. The Senate took command of the legions on the Italian peninsula from the two elected consuls and gave a special grant of *imperium* to an ambitious political leader, the praetor, Marcus Licinius Crassus. In this emergency, Crassus needed experienced officers and there was a young, accomplished, nobleman in Rome who was available for service — Julius Caesar. To avoid Sulla's wrath, Caesar had gone to Asia province in 79 and participated in the siege of Mitylene as a junior officer. During the assault on the city's walls, his legion had wavered under a counter-attack but Caesar rallied the soldiers and saved several men's lives with his decisive leadership. After the victory, the provincial governor awarded him a wreath of oak leaves, the *corona civica*, an award whose origins stretched back to the time of Romulus.[1]

In 75, while he was traveling to another posting in Asia Minor, pirates captured him. Caesar spent more than a month with the pirates and charmed his captors. He wrote poetry and read it to them, demanded quiet when he wanted to sleep, and assured them, to much laughter, that he would have them all hanged when he was freed.[2] After his ransom was paid, he immediately hired a few ships, chased down the pirates and captured them. To fulfill his vow, he had them all crucified, but because he bore them no ill will, he had them killed before their crosses were set upright.

He returned to Rome, where he had been selected to become a member of the college of *pontifices* in his absence. This was an important honor and showed that his reputation had overcome its initial shadow from being a member of Marius' family.[3] Young noblemen were often brought into the college at an early age. There were many ceremonies and rituals to learn and it was important that some members served a long time to ensure stability and competence in the group. There may also have been some hope of bringing the impetuous but talented youth closer into the established circle of the nobility.[4]

With the prestige of this religious office behind him, he was easily elected to the post of military tribune in 73.[5] He then proceeded to show his *populares* leanings by speaking out in support of the tribune C. Licinius Macer and his campaign for a restoration of the powers of the tribunes.[6] This act might have been his first point of contact with Crassus. Crassus was an admirer

---

1 Kahn, *Education of Caesar*, p. 64
2 Meier, *Caesar*, p. 108
3 Meier, *Caesar*, p. 111
4 Meier, *Caesar*, p. 111
5 Kahn, *Education of Caesar*, p. 92
6 Gruen, *Last Generation*, p. 78

of Macer's historical work, was Macer's advocate when he was prosecuted in 66, and supported restoration of tribunal powers when he was elected consul in 70.[1] While we have no specific record confirming that Caesar participated in Crassus' campaign against Spartacus, Caesar refers to his role in putting down the slave rebellion in his *Commentaries*, which were written about his conquest of Gaul.[2]

The command against Spartacus was Crassus' big chance to impress the public with his military skills. He quickly bottled Spartacus up at the toe of Italy. Unable to cross to Sicily, the heartland of previous slave rebellions, Spartacus broke out of the trap and then turned to initiate one final battle. Crassus' men held firm and Spartacus, along with most of his slave army, was killed. In a grim reminder to slaves of the punishment for rebellion, the 6,000 soldier/slaves who were foolish enough to surrender were crucified along the Appian Way, from Capua to Rome.[3]

Pompey the Great, returning from Spain, got into the final act, intercepting a group of slaves who were fleeing to the north and executing them on the spot. Now both men approached Rome with their armies. The Senate feared Pompey's ambitions, but once again he was seeking praise and recognition, not ultimate power. When the Senate agreed to let him run for consul, even though he had never been a quaestor or praetor and by Sulla's laws was too young (age 35) to run for the consulship, Pompey celebrated another triumph and sent his army home.[4]

Crassus, too, wanted the consulship; however, recognizing Pompey's overwhelming popularity, he was careful to seek his support in the coming election. One can easily imagine that his emissary to Pompey was a loyal junior officer in whom he had great confidence, a shrewd negotiator who could stroke Pompey's ego without giving away too many bargaining chips. We have no hard evidence that Caesar handled the negotiations between the two leaders, but we do know that he became an outspoken backer of Pompey during the following decade, often standing alone in the Senate in support of the general's ambitions.[5]

POMPEY AND CICERO TRIUMPHANT

Pompey the Great and Marcus Crassus were easily elected to the consulship in 70, a turning point because one of their first acts was to restore the powers of the tribunes and the Plebeian Assembly. The Senate, aware of the

---

1 Gruen, *Last Generation*, p. 74
2 Kahn, *Education of Caesar*, p. 96
3 Meier, *Caesar*, p. 120
4 Boatwright, *The Romans*, p. 208
5 Gruen, *Last Generation*, pp. 79-81, examines the question of Caesar's relationship with Pompey

popularity of the consuls and of the legislation, endorsed the change, though grudgingly.

The year 70 was also a time when M. Cicero came to full public prominence. Like Marius, he was regarded as a "new man," because no one in his family had been elected to an office on the *cursus honorum*. As noted in chapter 2, he studied with the prominent advocate Marcus Antonius and slowly earned a reputation as one of the better defense lawyers in Rome. Unlike Rome's successful generals or its long-standing noble families, Cicero was never able to develop a large *clientela* or have a group of senators who supported his schemes. He was unique in being prominent and influential without possessing a great deal of power.[1]

He is second only to Caesar in modern memories of Rome because he wrote a series of books on political and moral philosophy that miraculously have been preserved. His theories about harmony between the social orders and between the past and the present were beautifully written and influenced the thinking of intellectuals during the Enlightenment in Europe. A large number of Cicero's court speeches have been preserved as well. They are invaluable to historians because in them he frequently refers to events in Rome's past, providing useful confirmation about which stories are myths and which are factual. He also wrote a great number of letters to his friend Atticus that were filled with detailed political gossip and references to events during his lifetime.

Cicero was not overly popular during his lifetime. He was not a brave man and frequently shuttled about between political factions, supporting this person and then that one, a tendency that left everyone angry and suspicious of his motives. In the early part of his career he occasionally supported *populares* issues, but he became more conservative, frequently speaking out to maintain the privileges of the nobility. In a society where the pursuit of *dignitas* and glory was standard behavior, Cicero stood out for his vain and boastful nature. Finally, Cicero closely identified with the nobility and thought that the common people were, well, the scum of the earth. While many nobles had similar thoughts, he sometimes stated his beliefs openly. Once he had been elected consul and no longer had to campaign for political office, Cicero openly insulted the citizenry in his public speeches, earning himself the hatred of the average Roman.

As related in chapter 2, in 70 Cicero prosecuted Gaius Verres, the corrupt governor of Sicily. He was so eloquent in his denunciation of corrupt juries that Q. Hortensius, the leading advocate of the era, resigned from the defense team and Verres went into exile. In addition to gaining him tremendous fame, the rules of legal procedure said that an advocate could claim the

---

1 Holland, *Rubicon*, p. 126

rank of the criminal he successfully prosecuted.[1] Verres was a praetor, so Cicero gained the right to speak in Senate debates ahead of all quaestor-rank Senators. His influence in the Senate jumped accordingly and he easily won election as praetor in 66 BCE.

As this new generation came to power, the empire remained in turmoil. The break-up of social order that accompanied Roman conquests in Greece and Asia Minor had left many men with military skills rootless and without a suitable livelihood. The many small inlets and anchorages along Asia Minor's southern coastline provided them with safe bases for hiding and refitting pirate ships. By the decade of the 60s, the pirates had gone beyond attacking ships in the Aegean Sea and operated hundreds of vessels around the Mediterranean. In their most outrageous operation, the pirates attacked Rome's port of Ostia, burning grain ships in the harbor and warehouses stuffed with food for the growing metropolis.[2] The threat could no longer be ignored — these raids caused grain prices to soar and thousands in the capital were hungry and restless.

Once again, attempts to manage disorder in the empire touched off fierce conflict in the city. A supporter of Pompey, the tribune Gabinius, proposed a law in the Plebeian Assembly that one man be given *imperium* over all of the Mediterranean Sea with a three-year command and 200 ships.[3] This proposal, presented without the backing or consultation of the Senate, showed the significance of the restoration of the tribune's powers in 70. Opposition in the Senate was immediate and violently hostile. The consul C. Piso, for example, warned that Pompey would meet the fate of Romulus (remember the myth about his disappearance during a thunderstorm) if he took this command.[4]

As in the days of Tiberius Gracchus, a group of senators moved to physically attack Gabinius, but Caesar intervened and brought the embattled tribune out to the Forum where a crowd of plebeians protected them.[5] The Senate convinced a tribune to place a veto upon the legislation, but Gabinius immediately had the Plebeian Assembly divide into tribes and begin voting to impeach the Senate's tribune. For this act, Tiberius had been murdered, but the balance of forces was more even now: after the 17th tribe voted for impeachment the intimidated tribune withdrew his veto.[6] The Plebeian Assembly passed one law creating the office and another appointing Pompey to the position.

1 Holland, *Rubicon*, p. 132
2 Meier, *Caesar*, p. 142
3 Seager, *Pompey*, p. 44
4 Seager, *Pompey*, p. 44
5 Kahn, *Education of Caesar*, p. 116
6 Boatwright, *The Romans*, p. 213

Pompey the Great then showed he had the kind of organizational skills displayed by Dwight Eisenhower when he coordinated the air, naval, and land aspects of the invasion of Europe. He divided the Mediterranean into sections, gave each section to a commander with detailed instructions, and "swept from west to east in 40 days."[1] When the pirates were forced into their last strongholds along the coast of Asia Minor, Pompey assaulted them with his superior forces, capturing more than 20,000 pirates and 100 ships. He then showed great wisdom by re-settling the pirates in agricultural areas of Asia Minor and Greece that had been depopulated by wars.[2] The southern coast would always be a hiding place for pirates, but they would never again threaten the stability of the Mediterranean economy. The Plebeian Assembly then defied the Senate again and appointed Pompey as provincial governor of Asia Minor and told him to finish the war against Mithridates.[3] Over the next three years Pompey defeated Mithridates, made Syria a Roman province, and set up a series of client-kings in Palestine who regularly paid tribute to Rome.

Stung by these events, the conservative leaders of the Senate came to see Pompey as a threat to impose one-man rule and resolved to do everything in their power to thwart his ambitions. They also saw themselves as noble defenders of the ancient tradition of Senatorial leadership of the Republic. Cicero put it this way, "Those who have wished their deeds and words to be pleasing to the multitude have been held to be *populares*, and those who have conducted themselves in such a manner that their counsels have met the approval of all the best men have been held to be *optimates*."[4]

Men like Q. Catalus and then M. Cato, who were outspoken in their defense of every privilege of the nobility, led the *optimates*. The *optimates* operated as a disciplined group and were supported by some of the leading families of the nobility. Catalus summed up their program with the slogan, "Let no innovation be made contrary to usage and the principles of our forefathers."[5] Ironically, by blocking both Pompey's ambitions and the reforms offered by the *populares*, the *optimates* would eventually force these individuals with very different agendas to work together.

In the summer of 64, a bitter election campaign for the consulships of 63 took place between Cicero and two men of questionable reputation, Gaius Antonius Hybrida and Lucius Sergius Catiline, who ran together for the two open positions. Crassus, looking for consuls who would support his interests, probably provided them with crucial financial support and Caesar, who

---

1 Matyszak, *Chronicles*, p. 185

2 Seager, *Pompey*, p. 48

3 Seager, *Pompey*, p. 49

4 Taylor, *Party Politics*, p. 11

5 Kahn, *Education of Caesar*, p. 139

had served with Catiline in the army, probably helped them seek votes because of their *populares* leanings.[1] In normal times, Cicero, a new man and not a military hero, would have had trouble getting enough votes in the Centuriate Assembly to become a consul. However, these were not normal times and the *optimates* decided to give him financial support (for bribes) that helped him defeat Catiline.

Caesar and other *populares* immediately challenged Cicero to either defend the privileges of his new supporters in the nobility or to support the interests of the rest of the population. In the spring of 63, they put together a land reform bill that proposed the creation of a commission of ten senators, elected by the Plebeian Assembly, that would sell public lands held in the empire and use the money to buy farmland in Italy.[2] Proposed by the tribune P. Servilius Rullus, the bill was clearly designed to be a mechanism for distributing land to Pompey's soldiers when he returned from the east and, like Tiberius Gracchus' proposal, provide the urban poor with an opportunity to leave the city and gain some measure of rural prosperity.[3]

Cicero immediately attacked the bill. To the general population in the Forum he claimed that it harmed Pompey by not allowing him to be a member of the commission (of course, he was not present in Rome) and he attacked Rullus as a rebel who was trying to create a commission of people who would have the power of kings.[4] (Remember in 380 BCE how Manlius Capitolinus, a leader who wanted to reform the debt laws, was accused of wanting to be a king, see chapter 3.) In the Senate, he warned the fabulously wealthy leaders of the nobility that giving land to the poor could not be carried out "without draining the treasury."[5] After much controversy, a tribune who supported the *optimates* threatened to veto the legislation and Rullus dropped his proposal.[6]

The next challenge came over the right of the Senate to issue the *senatus consultum ultimum*, the ultimate decree, which allowed consuls to kill citizens without a trial. A tribune, who was an ally of Caesar and Pompey, T. Labienus, brought a prosecution against an elderly Senator, C. Rabirius, for participating in the murder of the *populares* tribune Saturninus in 100 after the *ultimum* had been declared by the Senate.[7] Their goal was to demonstrate to the Senate how unpopular this violation of the right to a trial had become.[8] To escape being condemned by Caesar and a relative who had been

---

1 Kahn, *Education of Caesar*, p. 130
2 Boatwright, *The Romans*, p. 220
3 Seager, *Pompey*, p. 68
4 Boatwright, *The Romans*, p. 221
5 Kahn, *Education of Caesar*, p. 140
6 Kahn, *Education of Caesar*, p. 143
7 Millar, *The Crowd in Rome*, p. 106
8 Kahn, *Education of Caesar*, p. 144

appointed special judges in the case, Rabirius was forced to appeal to the Centuriate Assembly.

With thousands of Romans assembled on the Campus Marti, buzzing with excitement, Cicero again took the side of the Senate. He argued in favor of the ultimate decree, while Labienus, assisted by Caesar, claimed that use of the decree was an abuse of power that threatened the liberty of the people.[1] Cicero, voicing the *optimates'* view of politics in Rome, encouraged "good and courageous citizens . . . to block all approaches of revolution."[2] Then, carried away by his rhetoric, he made the mistake of approving of Saturninus' murder: "Would that my case gave me the chance to proclaim that my client's was the hand that struck down that public enemy, Saturninus."[3] The crowd booed the man they once thought was their champion. The assembled voters were about to condemn the old man to death when Caesar, his point made, had the praetor Metellus Celer lower a ceremonial flag, signaling that the Assembly had to immediately adjourn.[4]

Soon after, Caesar, with heightened status and the votes of Pompey's supporters, was elected *pontifex maximus* and then praetor for the year 62.[5] Those elections saw yet another electoral defeat for Catiline. He declared his candidacy for the consulship early on and waged a stirring campaign, drawing huge crowds to the Forum. He attacked the *optimates* and moneylenders and promised cancellation of debts and passage of Rullus' land reform law. While Crassus and Caesar would not go so far as to support a person who advocated for the cancellation of debts, he attracted to his cause the urban poor, rural farmers who were dispossessed, and men of all classes who were in debt and could not break free — in other words citizens from every social group in the Republic.[6]

His supporters also included participants in some sort of counter-culture that flourished among the sons and daughters of both nobles and *equites* in this period. They were uninterested in "the ways of the ancestors" and were drawn to the more egalitarian world that Catiline talked about in his speeches. Cicero saw them as unmanly, "with their hair combed, sleek fellows, either beardless or abundantly bearded, with tunics that reach to the ankles and the wrists, clad in veils, not in togas." They spent their time "not only to love and be loved, not only to dance and sing, but also wave daggers and sprinkle poisons."[7] Cicero would gladly have made common cause with Spiro Agnew.

1 Hutchinson, *Catiline*, p. 68
2 Kahn, *Education of Caesar*, p. 145
3 Kahn, *Education of Caesar*, p. 145
4 Seager, *Pompey*, p. 70
5 Gruen, *Last Generation*, p. 81
6 Hutchinson, *Catiline*, pp. 78 & 79
7 Kahn, *Education of Caesar*, p. 152

Cicero campaigned vigorously against Catiline and, just days before the election, confronted him in the Senate. In response to Cicero's questioning, Catiline said, "I can see two bodies in the Republic, one thin but with a large head, one huge, but headless. Is it really so terrible if I offer myself to the body which is lacking a head?"[1] Catiline would have easily been elected tribune, but the members of his coalition were not numerous in the First Class of the Centuriate Assembly and he lost the race for consul for the second time.[2] However, Catiline, like Lepidus in 78, had ignited a firestorm of discontent in the countryside. His supporters in Etruria had formed a para-military organization under the guidance of one of Catiline's associates, C. Manlius. Cicero repeatedly attacked Catiline in the Senate and, with few allies in the nobility, Catiline finally left the city and joined Manlius' army.

Since most of our information about the downfall of Catiline come from Cicero's almost hysterical writings, there is no consensus on whether there actually was a conspiracy to launch an uprising.[3] What did happen is that, after Catiline left Rome, Cicero brought five members of Catiline's circle to the Senate, presented vague proof that they were conspiring against the Republic, and urged the Senate to sanction his use of the ultimate decree to execute them without a trial. This touched off the debate that climaxed with the dramatic exchange between Caesar and Cato described near the end of chapter 3. After the trial of Rabirius, we can see how Caesar's warning about the unpopularity of the ultimate decree would have carried weight with the Senators (with good reason as we shall see). However, Cato's eloquent denunciation won the day, and Cicero promptly executed the five men without a trial. A few months later, Catiline's ragged little army was eliminated, almost to the man, by a Roman army.

Pompey the Great returned from the East in 62 BCE, shortly after these turbulent events. He staged an enormous triumph, highlighted by his claim to have brought fourteen "nations" into the Republic's growing empire. As befit his vanity, during the parade he wore a cloak he had been given in the East that reportedly had been worn by Alexander the Great.[4] From his conquests, Pompey presented 20,000 *talents* in gold and silver (approximately 1,100,000 pounds) to the Roman treasury, his soldiers and officers received lavish gifts, and he took his place as the wealthiest man in the city.[5] Unlike Sulla, he did not use his army to intimidate the Senate; instead he released them from service after the triumph.

---

1 Holland, *Rubicon*, p. 198

2 Boatwright, *The Romans*, p. 222

3 Seager, *Pompey*, p. 71

4 Seager, *Pompey*, p. 80

5 Boatwright, *The Romans*, p. 227

Unwilling to acknowledge Pompey's achievements, the *optimates* thwart-ed his interests at every turn. As a sign of his willingness to become a mem-ber of the establishment, and a clear indication that he did not think of him-self as a *populares*, Pompey divorced his wife Mucia and proposed marriage to one of Cato's nieces. Instead of welcoming this marriage alliance that could have cemented Pompey in the *optimates'* camp, Cato denounced Pompey and refused the offer.[1] When Pompey asked that the Senate ratify his treaties with kings in the East, Cato led the opposition and combined with Crassus to defeat the measure. When Pompey asked that his long-serving soldiers be given land so they could become farmers, Cato and Crassus led the success-ful opposition. Secure in his control of the Senate, Cato then turned on his quiet ally, Crassus, and had that body refuse to change the amount of money a group of *publicani* administering Asia province owed the treasury.[2] This led to tremendous losses for these very influential businessmen and came as a nasty shock for Crassus, who was one of their leaders and had been enjoying Cato's harassment of Pompey.

THE CONSULSHIP OF JULIUS CAESAR

When Caesar returned from his term as governor of Spain to run for the consulship in the summer of 60 BCE, his two old allies Crassus and Pompey, though not *populares*, were very angry with Cato and the *optimates*. After Caesar became the senior consul, winning the most votes in the Centuri-ate Assembly, he negotiated a reconciliation between Pompey and Crassus. In what became known informally as the First Triumvirate, they agreed to work together to pass legislation favorable to each other. At the beginning of his first month as presiding officer of the Senate, in 59, Caesar advanced a land reform bill for Pompey's long waiting veterans and for the urban plebe-ians. Cato, faced with a bill that met all his previous objections, said merely that land reform was not in the interest of the state and proceeded to filibus-ter against the legislation.[3]

Disgusted with Cato and the *optimates*, Caesar introduced his laws in the Plebeian Assembly. After a bitter debate marked by physical conflict, the Assembly passed the land reform bill, a law ratifying Pompey's treaties in the East, a law reducing the *publicani's* debts to the treasury, and finally, legisla-tion giving Caesar command of the provinces of Cisalpine and Transalpine Gaul along with four legions after his term as consul was over.[4] To cement their partnership, Pompey married Julia, Caesar's daughter by his first wife Cornelia. Later in the year, Caesar convinced the Plebeian Assembly to pass

---

1 Seager, *Pompey*, p. 76
2 Seager, *Pompey*, p. 82
3 Seager, *Pompey*, p. 86
4 Boatwright, *The Romans*, p. 236

another land reform law giving fertile acreage in Campania to any father in Rome who had three or more children.[1]

The *optimates* were angry at this unprecedented outburst of legislation, but they expected Crassus to have shifting political alliances and did not attack him directly. Caesar was vilified, but he soon left for his command in Gaul. Cato and the *optimates* focused their fury on Pompey, whose standing amongst the nobility declined, causing him great discomfort and reducing his ability to influence elections.[2]

However, politics in the city was dominated not by the *optimates*, but by one of the tribunes of 58, Publius Clodius Pulcher. He was following a long line of reformers in the *Claudii* family that included Appius Claudius Caecus, who built the Appian Way in the 4th century and Appius Claudius, the father-in-law of Tiberius Gracchus and sponsor of his land reform legislation.[3] An active member of the counter-culture in the 60s, Clodius developed close relationships with leaders from Rome's poor neighborhoods and stunned the *optimates* by proposing to legalize the activities of the *collegia*, religious and social organizations in Rome's poor neighborhoods, which had been banned in 64 by the Senate. Clodius' second piece of legislation made the grain distribution free to all residents of the city over the age of ten. The best estimates are that roughly 300,000 residents took advantage of this free grain distribution.[4]

Clodius' final piece of legislation reaffirmed the ancient principle that no Roman citizen should be executed without trial. The new law stated that anyone guilty of such an offense would be condemned to exile. Aimed at Cicero, the law suddenly revealed that Cicero's service to the *optimates* had won him no loyalty in a fight. So, to the delight of the urban plebeians and other *populares*, Cicero went into exile in Greece. Clodius had Cicero's mansion on the Palatine hill razed as part of his punishment. He then purchased the property and built a shrine on it dedicated to the liberty of the people of the Republic, the *aedes Libertatis* (an *aedes* was a one-room temple).[5]

Clodius' triumph was short-lived. By the spring of 57, the tribune Titus Milo, an ally of Pompey and supporter of the *optimates*, had organized gangs of gladiators and former soldiers. They were more than a match for the unarmed men from the *collegia* who rallied when Clodius needed them. No longer intimidated by Clodius, Pompey led a campaign that resulted in a special meeting of the Centuriate Assembly in August of that year. Men of property and influence from all over Italy came to the city to bring Cicero back from

---

1 Taylor, *Party Politics*, p. 134
2 Gruen, *Last Generation*, pp. 92 & 93
3 Gruen, *Last Generation*, p. 97
4 Tatum, *Patrician Tribune*, p. 122
5 Tatum, *Patrician Tribune*, p. 162

exile.[1] No longer intimidated by Clodius the *optimates* stepped up their attacks on Pompey and announced that one of their members was going to run for the consulship for the year 55 on the platform of taking away Caesar's command in Gaul.

These new threats to Caesar's position and to Pompey's influence led them to engineer a surprising realignment of political alliances in the city. Caesar met with Crassus in Ravenna[2] and then with Pompey in the small town of Luca. Another significant participant in the meeting at Luca was Appius Claudius Pulcher, Clodius' older brother who was then praetor and needed support for his bid for the consulship of 54.[3] Fences were mended all around — Clodius would stop his attacks on Pompey, Cicero would support Caesar getting his command in Gaul renewed, and Appius would gain support in his quest for the consulship. Most crucially, Pompey and Crassus agreed to stop backstabbing each other and to jointly seek the consulship for 55.[4]

This complex alliance was initially successful. Pompey and Crassus were elected after a bitterly contested election and Cato lost his bid to become praetor. Caesar's command was extended, and Pompey was given command of Spain for five years. Most significantly, Crassus was given a five-year command in Syria and control of enough legions to launch a new attack against the Parthian empire (formerly Persia).[5] Crassus was now determined to win the kind of military glory that would make him equal in public esteem with Caesar and Pompey.

In the long run, the alliance failed dramatically. These moves by the triumvirate, unlike Caesar's legislative program in 59 or Clodius' new laws in 58, held no benefits for the *populares* constituency in Rome, nor did they promote any aspect of the public good. Instead, they were directed primarily at giving Caesar, Pompey, and Crassus control of most of the Republic's legions and a wide mandate to launch new wars.[6] In particular, Crassus' unprovoked war against Parthia, an unknown and feared opponent, aroused popular opposition and resistance. As he left the city with his army in 54 BCE, a tribune, chanting beside a ceremonial fire, put an ancient curse on his venture.[7] The next year, when his army marched across the desert toward Babylon, a host of swift Parthian archers on horseback surrounded Crassus and showered

1 Millar, *Crowd in Rome*, p. 37
2 Seager, *Pompey*, p. 118
3 Tatum, *Patrician Tribune*, p. 215
4 Boatwright, *The Romans*, p. 239
5 Boatwright, *The Romans*, p. 239
6 Taylor, *Party Politics*, p. 143
7 Holland, *Rubicon*, p. 257

his men with arrows. Crassus, his son Publius, and 30,000 legionnaires died in Rome's worst defeat since the wars with the German tribes.[1]

The *populares* cause had lost its way in the temptations of empire. Their battles had always been a combination of calls for more social justice at home and more efficient management of the empire abroad. Recall that one of Tiberius Gracchus' motives for implementing land reform was to restore the class of small farmers who had been the backbone of the legions for many years. Between 58 BCE and the agreement at Luca, the balance shifted from reforms to primarily military and personal considerations. Caesar was caught up in a bloody nine-year conflict to subdue the fiercely independent tribes of Gaul. By the time he emerged victorious in 50 BCE, one million Gauls had died and another million had been sold into slavery.[2] This savagery expanded the empire, but did not improve life in either Rome or Gaul. Crassus' invasion of Parthia, had it not been cut short by the Parthian victory, would likely have been equally bloody. The triumvirate and their supporters were seduced by the glory of empire and the gleaming wealth available from personal conquest. The *populares* quest for social justice was now secondary to the struggle for political power and glory.[3]

With Crassus dead, there were now only two triumvirs left. Their strongest personal connection had already been broken in 54 when Julia, Caesar's only daughter and Pompey's beloved wife, died in childbirth. In the meantime, electoral corruption reached a crisis point in the city. In September of 54, just before the elections for the consulships of 53, it was revealed that the two sitting consuls, Appius Claudius and Domitius Ahenobarbus had made a written election agreement with two candidates, Domitius Calvinus and Gaius Memmius. It said that in return for money and support the candidates would ensure that the consuls were given lucrative provincial governorships after they left office.[4] All four candidates for consul were brought to trial for bribery, the election had to be delayed until the following spring, the sitting consuls were disgraced, and the Republic had no public officials during the first half of the year 53 BCE.[5]

The summer and fall of 53 were chaotic. Clodius was striving to be elected praetor for the year 52 and his street-fighting opponent Milo was campaigning to be elected consul. Both men put as much energy into disrupting his rival as waging his own campaign and that meant a series of gang fights that disturbed the city for months and forced elections to be postponed again. Then, in January of 52, Milo and Clodius accidentally met on a road outside

---

1 Boatwright, *The Romans*, p. 239
2 Boatwright, *The Romans*, p. 242
3 Alfoldy, *Social History*, p. 84
4 Tatum, *Patrician Tribune*, p. 232
5 Seager, *Pompey*, p. 131

of Rome and, in the ensuing fight between their followers, Clodius was murdered. When Clodius' body was returned to Rome, the distraught population blamed the Senate and used the *curia*, the ancient home of the Senate, as his funeral pyre.[1] This act of public violence, in stark contrast to the passive reaction to the murder of the brothers Gracchi, showed that the legitimacy of the nobility had ceased to act as a control on political conflict in the city.[2] Faced with widespread public defiance, the Senate proclaimed the *senatus consultum ultimum* and, because there were no consuls, passed a special law making Pompey sole consul.[3] With the Republic collapsing into chaos, even Cato supported this new extraordinary command for Pompey.

The Descent into Monarchy

The new command broke the spell of Pompey the Great being rejected and hounded by Cato and the *optimates*.[4] As kings and emperors did, he restored order in the city by bringing in several legions to police the Forum and the neighborhoods. Pompey then had the Senate pass the *lex Pompeia de vi*, which streamlined the judicial process in cases of civil disorder.[5] Milo was tried and sent into exile, as were Sexus Cloelius, Clodius' long time assistant, and the tribunes Munatius Plancus and Pomeius Rufus, who had encouraged the burning of the *curia*.[6]

With Pompey, the greatest soldier of the age, on their side and Clodius, the leader of the urban plebeians, dead, the *optimates* now turned to the elimination of Caesar. Cato vowed to pursue Caesar in court when he returned from Gaul, and with the new surge of conservative strength it seemed possible that Caesar would be convicted and exiled. To prevent this, Caesar convinced the tribunes of 52 to enact a law allowing him to run for consul while he was still in command of his army in Gaul and thus immune to prosecution.[7] However, by the spring of 50 BCE the *optimates* claimed that his appointment as leader of the army in Gaul had expired and the law no longer provided him with immunity. The senior consul for that year, C. Marcellus, called repeatedly for Caesar to lose his command and be brought to trial.[8]

Then, in the summer of 50, Pompey fell ill with a fever and appeared to be on the verge of death. All over Italy offerings were made for his health and when he recovered there was widespread rejoicing. Unfortunately, Pompey interpreted this support as meaning that citizens would rally to his side if he

---

1 Boatwright, *The Romans*, p. 243
2 Nippel, "Policing Rome," p. 28
3 Tatum, *Patrician Tribune*, p. 241
4 Holland, *Rubicon*, p. 282
5 Gruen, *Last Generation*, p. 235
6 Tatum, *Patrician Tribune*, p. 241
7 Seager, *Pompey*, p. 138
8 Gruen, *Last Generation*, p. 479

fought against Caesar. He began to boast that, "wherever he stamped his foot in Italy, companies of foot and horse would spring up from the earth."[1]

With a civil war looming in December of 50, the tribune C. Scribonius Curio, proposed that both Caesar and Pompey give up their commands. The Senate voted 370 to 22 in favor, a vote that showed only Pompey, Cato, Caesar, and a small number of *optimates* were interested in a war.[2] However, Cato and the war faction asked Pompey to take command of all the legions in Italy and then convinced the Senate to pass the *senatus consultum ultimum* condemning Caesar as an enemy of the state. The tribunes supporting Caesar, including Mark Antony who was a successful leader in Caesar's army, were forced to flee for their lives.[3] Caesar now faced the same "ultimate decree" that had led to the deaths of Gaius Gracchus, Saturninus, Lepidus, and Catiline. Unlike them, he commanded an army — so he chose to lead it cross the Rubicon River in northern Italy rather than resign and submit to the Senate's will.

When Caesar took a single legion and marched on Rome in the middle of winter, there was no resistance. A sense of horror gripped the nobility as rumors swept the city that Caesar was preparing lists of the proscribed. When the population, unwilling to fight for the *optimates*, refused to enlist in Pompey's army no matter how often he stomped his foot, he panicked and ordered the Senate to evacuate Rome and soon after retreated to Greece.[4]

> Cato, contemplating the results of his greatest and most ruinous gamble, did nothing for his followers' morale by putting on mourning clothes and bewailing the news of every military engagement, victory as well as defeat.[5]

When Caesar easily defeated his bitter enemy, Domitius Ahenobarbus, at Corfinium on the road to Rome, he pardoned his foe and allowed him to go free. News that Caesar would not be Sulla swept Italy, and the possibility of the Senate benefiting from a general uprising against Caesar disappeared.[6]

In 48 BCE, Caesar brought his army to Greece where the two armies of the Republic met near the city of Pharsalus. After all of those meetings and letters, the marriage ceremony with Julia, the plotting of legislative strategies, and support for one another's political ambitions — it had come down to Pompey the Great versus Julius Caesar. The titans clashed with Rome and its empire as the prize. After a bitter morning of fighting Caesar's experienced veterans crushed the larger, but poorly trained *optimate* army. Pompey fled to Egypt, hoping to gain ships and soldiers from the young king of Egypt who owed his throne to a law Pompey's passed in 55. However, King Ptole-

1 Seager, *Pompey*, p. 146

2 Boatwright, *The Romans*, p. 245

3 Boatwright, *The Romans*, p. 247

4 Seager, *Pompey*, p. 154

5 Holland, *Rubicon*, p. 300

6 Holland, *Rubicon*, p. 302

my XIII and his advisors feared Caesar's wrath if they helped Pompey, so they had him assassinated.

With customary audacity, Caesar came and took up residence in Egypt's imperial palace, announcing that he was willing to mediate the simmering conflict between the young king and his exiled sister, Cleopatra VII. She and her brother were direct descendents of Ptolemy Soter, one of Alexander the Great's generals. After Alexander's death he took one slice of the empire, Egypt, for himself and established a monarchy that lasted until the reign of Cleopatra and her brother. Thus, Cleopatra was not Egyptian but of Greek/Macedonian blood. She and her brother were struggling to rule an ancient nation from the city that still held Alexander's mausoleum, as well as the Great Library, stuffed with the great works of literature, science, architecture, math, and history written during Greece's classical age and the Hellenistic era that followed.

Smuggled one evening into Caesar's headquarters wrapped in a rug, she was not a great beauty, but her vivid personality was almost tangible. Plutarch wrote, "Her sex appeal, together with the charm of her conversation, and the charisma evident in everything she said or did, made her quite simply irresistible."[1] They were instantly a couple and Caesar spent the next six months fighting her brother's army. Reinforcements finally arrived from Asia Minor and Caesar made his lover the sole ruler of Egypt. Before Caesar left she was pregnant with a son, Ptolemy Caesar, nicknamed "Caesarion."[2] To solidify his hold on the Republic and its empire, Caesar raced around the Mediterranean, defeating *optimate* armies in Asia Minor, Spain, and North Africa.

During the three years of civil war with the *optimates* Caesar governed Rome through the normally short-term office of "dictator." During his stays in Rome he found land for his veterans in North Africa, Spain, and Greece, began planning for a great library, reformed the calendar to the one still used today, and passed debt relief measures. However, with absolute power, Caesar showed a growing lack of respect for the cumbersome electoral offices and procedures that had been so important in the old Republic.[3] Many nobles remained sullen, angry at the loss of their political privileges. Caesar was voted many honors by the Senate, which was dominated by men he appointed from the *Equestrian* Order and from ruling groups in Italian cities. He rejected being called a king, but did everything possible to enhance his personal authority. Most significantly, he took the title of perpetual dictator in February of 44. This final title, confirming the end of Republican institu-

---

1 Quoted in Holland, *Rubicon*, p. 318
2 Boatwright, *The Romans*, p. 253
3 Meier, *Caesar*, pp. 463 & 464

tions and practices, was the spark for the conspiracy that resulted in his assassination on the Ides of March, 44 BCE.

Brutus and Cassius, the leaders of the assassination plot, fled to Greece, while Mark Antony, who was serving as consul with Caesar, Aemilius Lepidus, who commanded the legions in Italy, and Caesar's 19 year old nephew, Octavian, maneuvered against the Senate. Eventually, they signed a formal agreement to share absolute power over the empire, a contract known as the Second Triumvirate. To raise cash to pay their enormous armies, the triumvirs initiated several rounds of proscriptions. Two thousand *equites* and 300 senators, including Cicero, were murdered and their property was confiscated.[1] Antony and Octavian then took their imperial army to Greece where they decisively defeated Brutus and Cassius near the town of Philippi in 42 BCE.

They divided the empire, with Antony ruling the eastern Mediterranean, Octavian ruling Italy and Spain, and Lepidus controlling North Africa. As leader of the Roman east, Antony sailed to Alexandria to negotiate with Cleopatra, the leader of the largest kingdom in the empire. Within a year their negotiations produced twin sons. After several years of tense coexistence, Octavian disposed of Lepidus, invaded Antony's territory in Greece, and defeated Antony and Cleopatra at Actium, in western Greece, in 31 BCE. A year later Octavian stormed into Alexandria and the two rulers of the eastern empire committed suicide.

The sole ruler of Rome, in 28 Octavian reached an agreement to restore a small amount of power to the Senate in return for the senators granting him the role of governor of several rich provinces and the two-dozen legions stationed in them. The Senate also gave the victor at Actium a new name, Augustus (sacred or venerable,) and renamed the month of his birth after him. (A few years earlier, the Senate had declared his uncle, Julius Caesar, a god and named the seventh month of the year after him.) From Augustus sprang the first imperial family of the Roman Empire, the Julio-Claudians. It would be more than 1,300 years before *libertas* was given another chance to flourish in the political form known as a republic.

---

1 Boatwright, *The Romans*, p. 272

CHAPTER 12. THE AMERICAN EMPIRE AT WAR

> I am saddened that it is politically inconvenient to acknowledge what everyone knows: the Iraq War is largely about oil.[1]
>
> —Alan Greenspan, former Chairman of the Federal Reserve System

The Cold War provided United States decision makers with an on-going context in which to place their long-term strategy of promoting open markets for American goods and services. In the same way that the Roman Republic's 3rd century policy of "defensive imperialism" led to a logical progression of conflicts that expanded Rome's sphere of influence, so too, the "containment strategy" against Soviet and Chinese communism led to a series of actions that projected American influence into many areas of the globe. While the Roman Republic expanded by seizing colonies, the United States expanded by creating military, political, and economic ties with any country whose rulers were willing to join with the United States in the fight against communism — an empire of military bases, oil leases, and trade agreements without the politically unpopular role of direct ownership of colonies.

The end of the Cold War, like the Roman destruction of Carthage and annexation of Greece in 146 BCE, marked the end of the period where an aggressive foreign policy might be described as a legitimate response to

---

1 Robert Weissman, "Greenspan, Kissinger: Oil Drives U.S. in Iraq, Iran," *The Huffington Post*, 9.17.07; available from: http://www.huffingtonpost.com/robert-weissman/greenspan-kissinger-oil_b_64659.html; accessed on 16 December 16, 2007

military threats to the homeland. Just as the Roman legions dominated the Mediterranean area after 146, so too, the United States entered a period of unchallenged military superiority. The Roman response to this new security environment was to increase their efforts to control the Spanish peninsula and begin the process of dominating the area known as Asia Minor. During the Clinton administration the United States promoted "globalization," an economic and political strategy for opening up the economies of former communist bloc nations and any remaining economies that were still tightly regulated by the national government. For the Clinton administration, military power was secondary to a series of aggressive "free trade" agreements and actions by the International Monetary Fund.

RISE OF THE NEO-CONSERVATIVES

However, during the 1990s a number of conservative intellectuals and policy analysts developed a longer-term theory about how to preserve and expand the American empire that had emerged from the Cold War period. Based in think tanks like the American Enterprise Institute, and supported by grants from conservative foundations like the Bradley and Olin Foundations, these neo-conservative theorists wanted to ensure that no country became powerful enough to threaten the United States in the future. They also wanted to enhance American influence by extending the globalization process into every country in the world.

While most Republicans and Democrats would agree with the thrust of this argument, the neo-conservatives went a step further and said that the United States should try to replace authoritarian governments that refused to adopt free market reforms. This is the famous "regime change" idea that became prominent in the period before the invasion of Iraq.[1] Instead of working through the United Nations, neo-conservatives wanted the US to act on its own, to exercise "benevolent hegemony" in situations where the globalizing world order was impeded by an authoritarian regime.[2] This "go it alone" idea was based on the belief that the United States has a uniquely positive historical role. America, said the neo-conservatives, is an exception to all empires that came before — she is able to consistently act in ways that bring benefits to the whole world. Francis Fukuyama says this is an example of what he terms "American exceptionalism." American exceptionalism is the "implicit judgment that the United States is different from other countries and can be trusted to use its military power justly and wisely in ways that other powers could not."[3]

1 Francis Fukuyama, America at the Crossroads: Democracy, Power, and the Neo-Conservative Legacy, New Haven: Yale University Press, 2006, p. 49
2 Fukuyama, *Crossroads*, p. 95
3 Fukuyama, *Crossroads*, p. 101

During the late 1990s, many neo-conservatives participated in the Project for the New American Century (PNAC), a working group guided by neo-conservative William Kristol, editor of the prominent conservative magazine *The Weekly Standard*. In a widely read essay published in 1996, Kristol, the former chief of staff for Vice President Dan Quayle, called for the United States to exercise "benevolent hegemony." American policy should be one of "resisting, and where possible undermining, rising dictators and hostile ideologies."[1] In the late 1990s, the PNAC issued a series of public letters calling for the US to invade and occupy Iraq, to support Israel against the Palestinians, and to threaten Iran with invasion if it did not stop supporting terrorist organizations.

The PNAC also issued a report on defense issues that emphasized the need for American troops to be trained and equipped to rapidly move to scenes of conflict any place on the globe. This ability, the report claimed, is essential for the successful carrying out of one of the "four core missions" of America's military forces, to "perform the constabulary duties associated with shaping the security environment in critical regions."[2] In order to more effectively carry out these "constabulary duties," the report calls for a major repositioning of US land, naval, and air forces out of older European bases and into the Middle East and Southeastern Asia.

When the Bush administration was formed in 2001, a number of influential neo- conservatives moved into important policy positions. To name just a few, Paul D. Wolfowitz became Deputy Secretary of Defense; Douglas Feith, became Deputy Undersecretary of Defense for Policy (the number three position in the agency), Richard L. Armitage became Deputy Secretary of State (the number two position in the agency), and Lewis "Scooter" Libby became Vice-President Richard Cheney's chief of staff.

In addition to this general support of a more active military presence, Vice-President Cheney and Secretary of Defense Rumsfeld had been involved for years in activities designed to secure Middle East oil resources. For example, during the late 1990s Dick Cheney, while CEO of Halliburton, served as a member of Kazakhstan's Oil Advisory Board and helped negotiate a deal between Chevron and Kazakhstan to build an oil pipeline under the Caspian Sea and through Armenia to a Turkish port in the Mediterranean Sea. Chevron's chief political advisor during the negotiations was Condoleezza Rice, then a Stanford University professor. She became President Bush's first National Security Advisor and later Secretary of State.[3]

Early in the Bush administration the National Energy Policy Development Group, led by Vice-President Cheney, explicitly made the linkage

1 Fukuyama, *Crossroads*, p. 41
2 Project for the New American Century, "Rebuilding," Sept. 2000, p. iv
3 Johnson, *Sorrows*, p. 173

between the aggressive use of military power and the on-going American effort to secure control of oil resources. The Group predicted domestic oil production would fall gradually from 8.5 to 7.0 million of barrels a day while consumption would rise from 19.5 to 25.5 million barrels a day. To fill the gap, oil imports would have to rise steadily from 11 million barrels a day in 2001 to 18.5 million barrels per day in 2020, almost three-quarters of the oil used by the American economy. As a consequence, the report calls upon the federal government to redouble its efforts to secure safe and dependable access to foreign oil sources.[1]

After the Group issued its report, the Defense Department followed up by developing a document called the Quadrennial Defense Review (QDR) which analyzed America's strategic situation in 2001. In this document, written primarily before 9/11, Donald Rumsfeld's military staff echoed the PNAC's call for the ability to send US military units to hot spots anywhere on the globe, claiming that "the United States must retain the capability to send well-armed and logistically supported forces to critical points around the globe, even in the face of enemy opposition."[2] The document also:

> Explicitly identifies overseas oil-producing regions as "critical points" that American military forces may conceivably have to invade, going on to assert that because the Middle East, in particular, includes several states with formidable conventional capacities as well as the capacity to manufacture weapons of mass destruction (WMD), American forces must be strong enough to overpower them and eliminate their WMD stockpiles.[3]

September 11 and The Bush Doctrine

The horror of 9/11 created a new situation; the United States was now involved in a protracted struggle against a determined foe. Ironically, the war on terrorism was now unavoidably attached to the process of globalization.

> Before September 11, the conventional wisdom had been that globalization was fast making war obsolete; after September 11, the conventional wisdom was that globalization was making war an all but permanent and inescapable part of life in the twenty-first century.[4]

On September 20, 2001 President Bush appeared before a joint session of Congress and declared that the civilized world was now in an endless conflict with a terrorist organization that would not hesitate to use violence

---

1 Klare, *Blood*, p. 62

2 *Department of Defense*, "Quadrennial Defense Review 2001," 9.30.2001, p. 43; available from www. comw.org/qdr/qdr2001.pdf; accessed 10 September 2006

3 Klare, *Blood*, p. 71

4 Bacevich, *American Empire*, p. 225

while in the process of "imposing its radical beliefs on people everywhere."[1] Taking up the language of the neo-conservatives, Bush emphasized, "Freedom itself is under attack." Because of the high stakes in this conflict the President insisted that every nation take sides, famously declaring, "Either you are with us or you are with the terrorists."[2] Congress responded by voting for the President to use "all necessary and appropriate force" against those who had participated in planning the September 11 attack and anyone who assisted them.

The President now had authorization from Congress, the support of the whole American people, and friends in every corner of the globe. Attention immediately focused on the Taliban government in Afghanistan, which offered safe harbor to Osama bin Laden and al-Qaeda's leadership group. The United States provided air support and technical assistance to the Afghan tribal warlords that opposed the Taliban and the Alliance quickly routed their foes. Most of al-Qaeda's leaders and cadre escaped into the wild mountains along the border with Pakistan, and a new government that was an uneasy balance between a national, western-oriented executive and local, traditional tribal leaders and warlords came into being.

While al-Qaeda was a loosely organized terrorist organization, the neo-conservatives in the White House and the Pentagon were also interested in seizing this opportunity to bring rogue states into line and to secure new oil resources. For example, at an emergency meeting at Camp David on September 15, 2001, Deputy Secretary Wolfowitz advocated attacking Iraq as well as Afghanistan and followed this up with a series of memos to Defense Secretary Rumsfeld outlining the case for taking out Saddam Hussein.[3] In early 2002, the President launched a campaign to link the horrors of terrorism to the activities of rogue states. In his 2002 State of the Union Address, the President painted a frightening picture of worldwide terrorist activity:

> What we have found in Afghanistan confirms that, far from ending there, our war against terror is only beginning. Most of the 19 men who hijacked planes on September the 11th were trained in Afghanistan's camps, and so were tens of thousands of others. Thousands of dangerous killers, schooled in the methods of murder, often supported by outlaw regimes, are now spread throughout the world like ticking time bombs, set to go off without warning.[4]

---

1 *George W. Bush*, "Address to a Joint Session of Congress and the American People," available from www.White House.gov/news/ releases/2001/09/20010920-8.html; accessed July 26 2007

2 *George W. Bush*, "Address," www.White.House.gov/news/releases/2001

3 *9/11 Commission Report*, "Ch. 10 Wartime," p. 335; July 22, 2004; available from http://www.9-11commission.gov/report/index.htm; accessed 26 July 2007

4 George W. Bush, "Address to the Congress and the American People," available from www. White House/press/release/2002/01/20020129-11.html; accessed 26 July 2007

The President then tied three countries, North Korea, Iran, and Iraq, to this terrorist threat:

> States like these, and their terrorist allies, constitute an axis of evil, arming to threaten the peace of the world. By seeking weapons of mass destruction, these regimes pose a grave and growing danger. They could provide these arms to terrorists, giving them the means to match their hatred.

He then laid out a line of reasoning that became known as the "Bush Doctrine":

> I will not wait on events, while dangers gather. I will not stand by, as peril draws closer and closer. The United States of America will not permit the world's most dangerous regimes to threaten us with the world's most destructive weapons.

The Bush Doctrine, as this line of reasoning came to be known, merges the threat from terrorist groups with the possession of weapons of mass destruction by so-called rogue states. The formal statement of the Bush Doctrine, in *The National Security Strategy of the United States of America 2002*, claims, "Secure in their alliances, neither rogue states nor their terrorist partners can be deterred by the threat of massive retaliation from superior military forces."[1] Leaders of rogue states are likely to take risks and gamble with the lives of their people because terrorist soldiers are willing to seek "martyrdom in death" and have no homeland that will absorb retaliation because of their reckless actions.[2]

The NSS.USA.2002 goes on to say that, as a result of this reckless martyrdom, the United States must assume rogue states that seek to possess weapons of mass destruction and their terrorist partners are *imminent threats* to American security. Weapons of mass destruction, because of their potential to inflict widespread suffering, greatly increase the urgency of our response to these imminent threats:

> We must adapt the concept of imminent threat to the capabilities and objectives of today's adversaries....The United States has long maintained the option of preemptive actions to counter a sufficient threat to our national security. The greater the threat, the greater is the risk of inaction — and the more compelling the case for taking anticipatory action to defend ourselves, even if uncertainty remains as to the time and place of the enemy's attack.[3]

Perhaps the most important words in this paragraph come at the very end — *even if uncertainty remains...* This phrase contains within it the rejection of hundreds of years of attempts to contain warfare between nation states. While international law recognizes that nations have the right of self-defense against imminent threats to their security, the Bush Doctrine, as it was ap-

---

1 *The National Security Strategy of the United States of America 2002, p.15*; available from http://www.whitehouse.gov/nsc/nss.html; accessed 25 July 2007

2 NSSUSA 2002, p. 15

3 NSSUSA 2002, p. 15

plied to Iraq in 2003 and to Iran in 2007 stretches the meaning of "imminent" in ways that obscure the very sense of the word. As Michael Kinsley put it:

> Striking first in order to pre-empt an enemy that has troops massing along your border is one thing. Striking first against a nation that has never even explicitly threatened your sovereign territory, except in response to your own threats, because you believe that this nation may have weapons that could threaten you in five years, is something very different.[1]

In practice, the Bush Doctrine, as applied during the build up to the invasion of Iraq and the threatened attack on Iran, means that a decision by the United States to go to war against a rogue state will take place in a fog of intelligence reports about weapons developments. In the process, American leaders will make negative assertions about the intentions, rationality, and humanity of the other state's leaders and there will be a variety of allegations about ties or potential ties the rogue state has to a number of shadowy terrorist organizations.[2] This fog of accusation is built into the doctrine because preemptive military action must be justified by showing hot links between a rogue nation, the acquisition of weapons of mass destruction, and a menacing terrorist organization.

To bypass international law and justify preemptive attacks, the Bush Administration claimed in 2002 and 2003 that the Iraq was collaborating with al-Qaeda and, in 2006 and 2007 claimed that Iran was developing nuclear weapons that would be used by Hezbollah and other terrorist groups. Once a link like that was made (or at least stated repeatedly), then US decision-makers were able to argue that the offending terrorist organization would use a weapon of mass destruction without hesitation and without a hint of warning, thus triggering the US's right to defend itself and its allies from imminent attack.

For example, at a campaign event in Cincinnati in October of 2002, President Bush said that Iraq "possesses and produces chemical and biological weapons" and "could have a nuclear weapon in less than a year."[3] He went on to claim, "Iraq has trained al-Qaeda members in bomb making and poisons and deadly gases" and, "Saddam Hussein is harboring terrorists and the instruments of terror, the instruments of mass death and destruction." In words that echoed the theme of approaching danger in his 2002 State of the Union address, President Bush warned, "We cannot wait for the final proof — the smoking gun — that could come in the form of a mushroom cloud."

---

1 Michael Kinsley, "Unauthorized Entry: The Bush Doctrine: War Without Anyone's Permission,"
Slate.msn, 3.20.03, available from www.Slate.msn.com/id/2080455; accessed 11 September 2006
2 Richard Falk, "The New Bush Doctrine," *The Nation,* July 15, 2002, available from www.thenation.com/doc/2002715/Falk; accessed 12 September 2006
3 Glen Greenwald, "The President has 'made his choice' — more wars." *Unclaimed Territory,* 8.31.2006, available from glenngreenwald.blogspot.com; accessed 12 September 2006

The deception buried in this repeatedly stated justification for pre-emptive war against Iraq was that there were no ties between Saddam Hussein and al-Qaeda — and Iraq did not possess weapons of mass destruction. To make their case, administration officials had to search for shaky intelligence produced by unreliable sources. For example, Vice-President Cheney repeatedly said that a Czech intelligence official saw lead hijacker Mohamed Atta meet with an Iraqi agent in Prague just five months before 9/11.[1] This assertion was decisively refuted by the 9/11 Commission, which said the facts indicate that Atta was already in the US at that time and never left. In April of 2007, the Defense Department's acting Inspector General, Thomas F. Gimble, released a declassified report stating that there is no evidence of cooperation between al-Qaeda and Saddam. The report found that the Defense Intelligence Agency had decided in 2002 that "available reporting is not firm enough to demonstrate an ongoing relationship" between the Iraqi government and al-Qaeda.[2]

Where did the President and Vice-President get information asserting there was a link? Undersecretary of Defense Douglas Feith, one of the signers of the 1998 letter calling for the removal of Saddam, set up a special "intelligence unit" in his office after 9/11. This unit developed a briefing claiming that the relationship between Iraq and al-Qaeda was "mature" and "symbiotic," and there were 10 ways in which the two cooperated, including training, financing, and logistics.[3] Feith's briefing also said that the CIA's report of no connection between Iraq and al-Qaeda "ought to be ignored." Feith and his team presented this "intelligence" report to Vice-President Cheney's chief of staff "Scooter" Libby, Defense Secretary Donald Rumsfeld, CIA Director George Tenet, and deputy national security adviser Stephen Hadley.[4] The Inspector General's report asserts that in bypassing established intelligence agencies Feith had acted "inappropriately but not illegally."[5] The steady stream of false claims based on this mis-information had its desired effect — by March of 2003, two-thirds of Americans believed that Iraq was directly involved in the 9/11 attacks.[6]

Similar levels of misinformation were used to assert that Iraq was bristling with weapons of mass destruction. For example, in September of 2002, CIA Director George Tenet and Vice President Dick Cheney went to Capitol Hill to brief four top Senate and House leaders on what one participant

---

1 Thomas Oliphant, "Facts vs. Fiction," *Boston Globe*, 8.29. 2004.
2 R. Jeffrey Smith, "Saddam's Ties to al-Qaida Discounted," *Washington Post*, 4.6.07; available from http://www.washingtonpost.com/wp-dyn/content/article/2007/04/05/AR2007040502263_pf.html; accessed 7 April 2007
3 Smith, "Saddam's Ties," 4.6.07
4 Smith, "Saddam's Ties," 4.6.07
5 *The Associated Press*, "Cheney Reasserts al-Qaida-Saddam Link," 4.5.07
6 Thomas Oliphant, "Facts vs. Fiction," *Boston Globe*, 8.29. 2004

described as a "smoking gun."[1] They claimed that new intelligence evidence "proved" that Iraq had developed unmanned airborne vehicles (UAVs) that could deliver chemical or biological agents. In his speech before the United Nations Security Council in January of 2003, Secretary of State Colin Powell repeated that warning saying, "Iraq could use these small UAVs, which have a wingspan of only a few meters, to deliver biological agents to its neighbors or, if transported, to other countries, including the United States."[2]

The truth is that this claim about the supposed capabilities of the UAVs, originally put forward by the CIA, was disputed in October of 2002 by Air Force intelligence, which thought the vehicles were primarily for reconnaissance. Powell knew about this dissent and chose to ignore the Air Force because the administration was desperately searching for scary intelligence to justify the war. After Iraq was occupied, US weapons inspectors carefully inspected several UAVs and confirmed the Air Force's opinion about the tiny aircraft.

The virtue of this approach was that this inflammatory language allowed the President to set the terms of debate during the mid-term elections of 2002, during his re-election campaign in 2004, and in the early stages of the 2006 Congressional elections. This strategy was aided by the timidity of the Democratic Party, most of whose members are unwilling to appear weak on national defense even in the face of reckless threats of war by the President and his supporters. However, the page scandal that rocked the capital in October of 2006 dominated the headlines for several weeks and distracted public attention from foreign affairs. Then, in late October, the rising tide of violence in Iraq overshadowed the President's terrorism message, suddenly turning the election into a referendum on the failures of the Iraq War.

IRAQ AND THE AMERICAN EMPIRE

The Bush Doctrine is rooted in the neo-conservative impatience with diplomatic, cultural, and economic means of expanding the American empire in the post-Cold War world. While the tactics they advocate are more aggressive and go-it-alone than those used by previous American Presidents, their goals remain remarkably similar. Since the Rough Riders rushed up San Juan Hill, American diplomats, politicians, and military leaders have pursued the related goals of: (a) creating open markets for American goods, cultural products, and investments (b) securing steady supplies of inexpensive oil and, (c) enhancing American influence through a network of military bases and alliances. An examination of the Bush administration activities

---

1 Glenn Kessler & Walter Pincus, "Misfires of a 'smoking gun' in Iraq Debate," *Washington Post*, available from http://seattletimes.nwsource.com/html/nationworld/2001848577_powell01. html; accessed 25 July 2007
2 Glenn Kessler & Walter Pincus, "Misfires of a 'smoking gun'"

during the occupation of Iraq reveals continued adherence to this long-term strategy of empire.

OPEN MARKETS

The National Security Strategy of the United States of America 2002 has an entire section devoted to the open markets strategy. It is titled, "Ignite a New Era of Global Economic Growth through Free Markets and Free Trade."[1] As in policy statements issued by previous presidents, the NSS.USA2002 calls for a bundle of economic policies that, if followed, would open up a nation's economy to the world market and give transnational corporations freedom to invest in previously protected markets. The document states that "economic growth and economic freedom" can be achieved through policies such as: pro-growth legal and regulatory policies to encourage business investment; tax policies — particularly lower marginal tax rates — that improve incentives for work and investment; free trade that provides new avenues for growth and fosters the diffusion of technologies and ideas that increase productivity and opportunity.[2] Secretary of State Madeline Albright or Secretary of State John Hay could easily have written this section of the NSS.

Occupied Iraq was to be a NSSUSA showcase. The criticism that the Bush administration did not have a post-war "plan" for running Iraq completely misses the point. There was a plan and it was taken from the standard International Monetary Fund (IMF) package of demands that are forced upon nations that come to it hat-in-hand because of a currency crisis. To get a loan from the IMF, a country must adopt pro-business legal policies, privatize public businesses and utilities, fire government workers, allow transnational banks to operate in the country, and open the economy to foreign investment and ownership. In most countries these changes come half-heartedly as the nation in trouble surrenders portions of its economic sovereignty to the IMF, but manages to retain some portion of its original economic rules. However, in Iraq, a conquered country with no armed forces and few political groups, US administrators could adopt these IMF policies without any restrictions or moderation.[3]

L. Paul Bremer, who was appointed the Administrator of the Coalition Provisional Authority (CPA) on May 6, 2003, was in charge of implementing the radical program of economic openness. Bremer's first official act was to fire 500,000 people who worked for the Iraqi government.[4] The purge included more than 400,000 soldiers and officers of the Iraqi armed forces and

1 NSS.USA2002 p. 17

2 NSS.USA.2002 p. 17

3 Naomi Klein, "Baghdad Year Zero: Pillaging Iraq in Pursuit of a Neocon Utopia," *Harpers.org*, Sept. 2004; available from http://www.harpers.org/archive/2004/09/0080197; accessed 22 July 2007

4 Klein, "Year Zero," Sept. 2004

a great many doctors, nurses, printers, bureaucrats, oil industry professionals, etc. In an economy with approximately 6.5 million workers, this meant more than 8% of the workforce was suddenly unemployed. The official line was that this was the first stage of de-Ba'athification, a process where an individual could re-apply for his or her job once it had been determined that it was an essential position. As part of the application process the individual would have to prove that he or she had no political ties to Saddam Hussein's Ba'ath Party, which had ruled the country for so many years. Of course, in neo-conservative Iraq most government jobs were not considered essential and would never be restored by the provisional authority.

Bremer's next economic decision was to open up the country's borders to foreign trade; there were to be no tariffs on imported goods, no duties on exported products, no inspections of shipments, and no taxes. Bremer stated that Iraq was "open for business."[1] The CPA also had a plan for privatization of the country's main businesses:

> In June, Bremer announced that the 200-state owned companies that dominated the Iraqi economy would be sold to private owners as soon as possible. To ensure that multi-national corporations would step up and purchase these companies, Bremer made it possible in September of 2003 for foreign companies to own 100% of Iraqi businesses outside of the oil sector. In addition, investors could take all of the profits they made in Iraq out of the country; they would not be required to reinvest their earnings in the country or to pay taxes on those profits.[2]

Foreign banks were allowed to come into Iraq under similar rules. "All that remained of Saddam Hussein's economic policies was a law restricting trade unions and collective bargaining."[3] These labor laws were reinforced when Bremer issued Order #19, which limited assemblies and marches, and outlawed public gatherings without permission from the CPA. "Thus, in effect, outlawing protests for workers' rights, since, naturally, the CPA won't authorize such protests..."[4]

These revisions were greeted with enthusiasm by the neo-conservatives in Bush's administration. Secretary of Defense Rumsfeld said that the new policies were "some of most enlightened and inviting tax and investment laws in the free world."[5] *The Economist*, a transnational business-oriented magazine, said that Iraq was now "a capitalist dream" and the new laws

1 *Chicago Tribune*, May 26, 2003, quoted in Rania Masri, "Freeing Iraq's Economy — For its Occupiers," *Swans*; available from www.swans.com/library/at10/iraq/masri.html; accessed 14 September 2006

2 Kamil Mahdi, "Privatization won't Make you Popular," *The Guardian*, November 26, 2003; available from http://www.commondreams.org/scriptfiles/views03/1126-12.htm; accessed 17 September 2006

3 Klein, "Year Zero," Sept. 2004

4 Rania Masri "Freeing Iraq's Economy — for its Occupiers" *Swans*; *available from* www.swans.com/library/art10/iraq/masri.html; accessed 14 September 2006

5 Klein, "Year Zero," Sept. 2004

were "the wish list of foreign investors." However, with no protection from foreign imports, domestic Iraqi companies faced crippling foreign competition. In just a month after the removal of tariffs:

> "Textile plants and clothing factories [in Iraq were] devastated by the influx of cheap clothing, much of it made in China... the nation's farmers are also being jolted by the elimination of most agricultural subsidies.... [Iraq's poultry industry] can't compete against containers full of American Tyson chicken legs, which are shipped to the Middle East at bargain-basement prices."[1]

Local businesses rapidly went bankrupt and state-owned firms had to lay-off workers because they were barred from participating in the reconstruction process. This economic collapse, combined with the soldiers and government workers who Bremer dismissed in the first month of the occupation led to an enormous increase in the country's unemployment rate by the fall of 2003. Protests in Baghdad and in the Sunni triangle multiplied. In the worst confrontation, American troops fired on a peaceful protest in Fallujah, killing 13 civilians.[2] This was actually a typical response to Iraqi protests:

> Top officials of the CPA and the US military command considered these demonstrations, peaceful or not, the most tangible signs of ongoing Ba'athist attempts to facilitate a future return to power. They therefore applied the occupation's iron heel on the theory that forceful suppression would soon defeat or demoralize any "dead-enders" intent on restoring the old regime...Home invasions of people suspected of anti-occupation attitudes or activities became commonplace, resulting in thousands of arrests and numerous firefights. Detention and torture in Abu Ghraib and other American-controlled prisons were just one facet of this larger strategy, fueled by official pressure — once a low-level rebellion boiled up — to get quick information for further harsh, repressive strikes.[3]

The twin policies of economic depression and military repression generated dozens of new recruits every week for the growing Iraqi resistance movement that winter. Still focused on Saddam's Ba'athist Party, American officials felt that the capture of Saddam in December of 2003 would lead to a rapid collapse of resistance. Instead, the forces of nationalism and economic desperation fed an opposition movement that grew in sophistication and effectiveness each month.

By the end of November, faced with opposition from the Iraqi ministers appointed by the US after the invasion, the plan to sell all of the state's companies immediately had to be slowed:

---

1 *The San Francisco Chronicle*, July 10, 2003 quoted in Rania Masri, "Freeing Iraq's Economy — For its Occupiers," *Swans*; www.swans.com/library/at10/iraq/masri.html

2 Michael Schwartz, The Economics of Occupation," *TomDispatch*, 3.28.06, available from www.tomdispatch/index.mhtml; accessed 14 September 2006

3 Michael Schwartz, The Economics of Occupation," *TomDispatch*, 3.28.06, available from www.tomdispatch/index.mhtml; accessed 14 September 2006

> With goodwill toward Americans ebbing fast, Bremer and his lieutenants have also concluded that it does not make sense to cause new social disruptions or antagonize Iraqis allied with the United States. Selling off state-owned factories would lead to thousands of layoffs, which could prompt labor unrest in a country where 60 percent of the population is already unemployed.[1]

Then, at the end of March 2004, the CPA closed down the newspaper *al Hawza*, which was published by the radical cleric Moqtada al Sadr. Bremer accused *al Hawza* of publishing "false articles" that "could pose the real threat of violence."[2] As an example, Bremer pointed to a newspaper article saying that the CPA "is pursuing a policy of starving the Iraqi people to make them preoccupied with procuring their daily bread so they do not have the chance to demand their political and individual freedoms." Al Sadr's organization, the Mahdi Army engaged in high profile street demonstrations and, when American troops tried to occupy their offices, began fighting in the streets of Baghdad.

Worse was soon to come. Just days later, four American mercenaries were killed in Fallujah and their bodies were burned and put on public display. US marines immediately put Fallujah under siege and the whole country seemed to explode into violence. Unfortunately for foreign investors, guerilla groups all over the country adopted the Fallujah example. A wave of kidnappings and murders of foreign businessmen culminated in the kidnapping and beheading of Nicholas Berg, a grim warning to anyone thinking that Iraq was truly open for business.[3] Since the violence in Iraq has never receded since the spring of 2004, almost no foreign investment has come into the country.

THE PROMISE OF IRAQI OIL

Iraq has the world's second largest proven oil reserves, estimated at 112.5 billion barrels. This is 11% of the world's total proven reserves and there are estimates that the country may actually have 250 billion barrels, a total similar to Saudi Arabia's estimated reserves.[4] These oil riches have attracted western attention since the early 20th century. After World War I, Great Britain claimed the area during the break-up of the Ottoman Empire, but was forced by a nationalist opposition movement to grant Iraq full independence in 1932. After independence, British, American, Dutch, and French oil firms pumped Iraqi oil under the auspices of a joint venture company called

---

1 Rajiv Chandrasekaran, "Threats Force Retreat from Wide-Ranging Plans for Iraq," *Washington Post*, December 28, 2003; available from http://goldismoney.info/forums/showthread. php?t=6353; accessed 19 July 2007

2 Klein, "Year Zero," Sept. 2004

3 Klein, "Year Zero," Sept. 2004

4 James A. Paul, "Iraq the Struggle for Oil," *Global Policy Forum*, December, 2002; available from http://www.globalpolicy.org/security/oil/2002/08jim.htm; accessed 20 September 2006

the Iraq Petroleum Company (IPC). In 1958 the constitutional monarchy set up at the time of independence was overthrown in a military coup and King Faisal II and a number of leading politicians were murdered.

In 1961, General Abdul-Karim Qassem, leader of the coup, nationalized any oil fields not yet explored by IPC. In response, with CIA assistance, members of the Ba'ath Party, a nationalist, anti-communist group made up of young officers and professionals, assassinated General Qassem in 1963.[1] After a chaotic period of military rule, the Ba'ath's became the dominant political organization in the country. In 1979, Saddam Hussein succeeded General Ahmed Hasan al-Bakr, as head of the Ba'ath Party and as Prime Minister.

Following Iraq's crushing defeat in the month-long Gulf War of 1991, the United Nations imposed harsh economic sanctions on Saddam's regime and the United States created no-fly zones over the Kurdish areas of northern Iraq and the Shiia areas of southern Iraq. By 1997, support for sanctions was fading and more and more supplies were being smuggled into the country.[2] Saddam took advantage of the change in world opinion and began negotiating oil contracts with French, Russian, and Chinese oil companies. Russia's Lukoil received a contract to develop the West Qurna oil field, China National signed an agreement to develop the huge North Rumailah oil field along the Saudi Arabian border, and the French oil company Total was given the rights to develop "the fabulous Majnun field."[3] Only the continuing barrier of the U.N. sanctions prevented these countries from investing huge sums in Iraq and gaining secure access to the second largest source of petroleum in the world.

These new oil contracts increased American hostility to the Saddam regime. The possibility that American and British companies would be shut out of this key source of oil by geo-political rivals Russia and China, and by the always-annoying French, was a stark threat to one of the American empire's principal goals — controlling access to oil. As a result of these geo-political rivalries, the Security Council debate over US plans to invade Iraq took place under the shadow of Iraqi oil derricks. Each of the five permanent members of the Council — the United States, Britain, France, Russia, and China — had a vested interest in the fate of Iraq's oil fields.

Once again, the Bush administration did have a plan for oil in post-war Iraq. While the military carelessly allowed looters to steal priceless artifacts from the Iraqi National Museum, military planners had carefully planned the occupation and preservation of the Iraqi Oil Ministry. "World opinion had little difficulty in mistaking US priorities."[4] The neo-conservatives wanted

---

1 Johnson, *Sorrows*, p. 223
2 Klare, *Blood*, p. 95
3 Paul, "Struggle for Oil," August 2002
4 Phillips, *American Theocracy*, p. 75

to sell-off all of the country's oil fields to transnational oil companies. Their hope was that massive increases in the production of Iraqi oil would destroy the OPEC cartel's ability to set prices, triggering a sharp drop in oil prices. Iraqi leader in exile, Ahmed Chalabi, agreed to this giant asset sale shortly after US forces captured Baghdad.[1]

However, the major oil companies had no interest in reducing the price of oil and their profit margins. They also feared the reaction of Iraqi citizens to the loss of their country's oil assets. To prevent this outcome, the oil industry giants arranged for Philip Carroll, the former CEO of Shell Oil, USA, to be appointed head of Iraqi oil production a month after the invasion. He later told BBC News that he informed Paul Bremer in May of 2003, "There was to be no privatization of Iraqi oil resources or facilities while I was involved."[2]

As an alternative, analysts at the James Baker Institute in Texas drew up a plan in January of 2004 that called for the creation of a state-owned oil company that would enter into joint ventures with transnational oil companies.[3] (President Reagan's former Secretary of State, James Baker was the co-chair of the Iraq Study Group. His legal clients include Exxon-Mobil and the Saudi Arabian government.) This plan too, had to be abandoned when the Iraqi opposition movement made it dangerous for foreign personnel to live and work in the country during 2004.

By the summer of 2007, no final plans had been made for involving transnational oil companies in the development of Iraq's oil fields. Rising levels of violence made it very difficult to keep oil flowing to market. In July of 2006, US Comptroller General David M. Walker told Congress that oil production was still below prewar production levels. Attacks by the opposition movement damaged both pipelines and pumping stations and made it dangerous to carry out maintenance work on the country's aging oil infrastructure.[4] Millions of dollars of US reconstruction funds that were originally intended to upgrade the country's oil pumping and distribution system had to be diverted to pay for security activities and repairing damaged facilities.

Who will benefit from Iraq's fabulous oil wealth is still an open question. The coalition government headed by Prime Minister Nuri al-Maliki has consented to signing Production Sharing Agreements (PSAs) with US oil companies, but the PSA is a controversial method, so biased in favor of the oil

---

1 Greg Palast, "Secret U.S. Plans for Iraq's Oil," broadcast on *BBC Newsnight*, 3.21.05; available from www.gregpalast.com/secret-us-plans-for-iraqs-oil/; accessed 23 September 2006

2 Palast, "Secret U.S. Plans," 3.21.05

3 Palast, "Secret U.S. Plans," 3.21.05

4 Walter Pincus, "Corruption Cited in Iraq's Oil Industry," *Washington Post*, 7.17.2006; available from http://www.washingtonpost.com/wp-dyn/content/article/2006/07/16/AR2006071600774.html; accessed 21 August 2006

companies that they are not used by most oil producing countries.[1] While a PSA states that the government is the "owner" of the resource, in practice the terms of the contracts are written so that the company has complete management control and the lion's share of the profits. In hard-ball negotiations the Paris Club of Creditors, which includes US, Britain, France, Germany, Russia, Japan, Canada, and Italy, agreed to forgive 80% of Iraq's $39 billion foreign debt to members of the Club in return for the government persuading Parliament to approve a law authorizing the signing of PSAs with oil firms.[2]

A study by the Global Policy Forum shows that the impact on Iraq's future could be staggering. The key finding of their econometric study was:

> At an oil price of $40 per barrel, Iraq stands to lose between $74 billion and $194 billion over the lifetime of the proposed contracts, from only the first 12 oilfields to be developed. These estimates, based on conservative assumptions, represent between two and seven times the current Iraqi government budget.[3]

The decision on whether or not to use PSAs is crucial because they usually run for 30 to 40 years and have "stabilization clauses" that make it impossible for future governments to alter the terms of the contract.[4] The negative aspects of PSAs are one of the major reasons that no "oil sharing" agreement was passed by the Iraqi Parliament in 2007, in spite of vociferous demands by the Bush administration and the US Congress.

This tug-of-war in Iraq is taking place in the context of a much larger struggle between the world's oil-rich countries and the United States for control of oil resources in the decade starting in 2010. Booming demand from China and India and other Asian economies has sparked an international scramble for long-term oil contracts with producer countries. As the price of oil approaches $100 per barrel, many producer nations, especially Russia, Venezuela, and Iran have used their new wealth to create alliances with countries that are unhappy with the aggressive foreign policy of the Bush administration. With big, hungry oil consumers in China and the European Union, they do not have to bend to US demands and, as peak oil approaches, they are accumulating large reserves of cash to cushion their economies.

The Bush administration's response to the looming crisis of peak oil has been to resist all attempts to remove our troops from Iraq. Deeply opposed

---

1 Greg Muttitt, "Oil Privatization by the Back Door," *Global Policy Forum*, 6.26.06; available from http://www.globalpolicy.org/security/oil/2006/0626door.htm; accessed 25 August 2006

2 Basav Sen & Hope Chu, "Operation Corporate Freedom: The IMF and the World Bank in Iraq," *50 Years is Enough*, 9.2006; available from http://www.50years.org/cms/updates/story/320; accessed 5 September 2006

3 Greg Muttitt, "Crude Designs: The rip-off of Iraq's Oil Wealth" *Global Policy Forum*, 11.22.05; available from www.globalpolicy.org/security/oil/irqindx.htm; accessed 12 September 2006

4 Muttitt, "Back Door," 6.26.06

to conservation efforts that might require sacrifice and undermine their political support in the US Sunbelt, the heart of the GOP majority, they simply have no other choice.

> The war may be going badly, but the primary consideration is that there is still a tremendous amount of oil at stake, the second-largest reserves on the planet. And neocon fantasies aside, the global competition for the planet's finite oil reserves intensifies by the hour. . . . There is no real withdrawal plan. The fighting and the dying will continue indefinitely.[1]

EXPANDING THE NETWORK OF MILITARY BASES

The most visible aspect of the American empire is its network of military bases. From the beginning of the debate over invading Iraq, the usefulness of military bases in Iraq was obvious. "Invading Iraq put US power in a vitally important part of the world, positioned neatly over abundant energy reserves and between Iran, Syria, and Saudi Arabia."[2] In the heady early days of the occupation of Iraq, military leaders and civilian decision makers spoke openly of developing a close working relationship with the new government of Iraq that would allow the US to have permanent bases in the country. They identified four bases, three of them with air fields already built by the Iraqi air force, that the military believed would facilitate their ability to rapidly send air and ground forces to any problem spot in the Middle East.[3] Ironically, the four locations mentioned in the *New York Times* article were neatly divided up into the now familiar ethnic divisions of the country, with one air base near Baghdad, another in Shiite southern Iraq, one in the western desert in the Sunni part of Iraq, and another in the Kurdish north.

These bases were expected to anchor American dominance in Iraq and allow the US to intimidate other Middle Eastern countries. The N.Y. Times reported, "Senior administration officials make no secret that the American presence at those bases near Syria and Iran and long-term access to them 'will make them nervous.'"[4] Thomas Donnelly, a military expert at the American Enterprise Institute in Washington (a leading neo-conservative think tank) pointed out in the fall of 2003, in an article in the neo-conservative *Weekly Standard*, that Iraqi airfields "are ideally located for deployments throughout

---

1 Bob Herbert, "Oil and Blood," *New York Times*, 7.28.05; available from http://www.truthout.org/cgi-bin/artman/exec/view.cgi/38/12945; accessed 17 July 2006

2 Daniel Widome, "Are we there to stay? It sure seems that way." *SFGate.com*, 9.29.06; available from http://sfgate.com/cgi-bin/article.cgi?file=/chronicle/archive/2006/09/29/EDG6PKDUAJ1.DTL; accessed 28 August 2006

3 Tom Shanker & Eric Schmitt, "Pentagon Expects Long-Term Access to Four Key Bases in Iraq," *New York Times*, 4.19.03; available from http://www.truthout.org/docs_03/042103B.shtml; access 20 July 2007

4 Shanker & Schmitt, "Pentagon Expects," 4.19.03

the region . . . and they are enough removed from Mesopotamia that they would not be imperial irritants to the majority of Iraqis."[1]

The model for the long-term presence of American forces in Iraq is the occupations of Germany and Japan after World War II. More than 60 years after the war, thousands of American troops are still based in those countries. In February of 2004, neo-conservative stalwart and Deputy Secretary of Defense Paul Wolfowitz had Major General Karl Eikenberry put together a report suggesting that the US should fund Iraqi police and civil defense forces while discouraging the development of an Iraqi army.[2] Limiting funds for a new Iraqi military would leave Iraq dependent on a large-scale deployment of US troops. Andrew Krepinevich, Executive Director of the Center for Strategic and Budgetary Assessments, which consults with the Pentagon on defense issues, told the Boston Globe that:

> If you build up an Iraqi army to the point where it could contend with a foreign threat, then the Iraqis would have a strong incentive to ask us to leave. And if that happens in the foreseeable future, it could create instability.[3]

By March of 2004, the military's appetite for large, secure launching pads had led to an expansion of the number of major bases in Iraq to fourteen. Military spokesmen shunned the word permanent, saying instead that they were "enduring bases" built to serve American soldiers and airmen for the two or three years that the US was projected to keep more than 100,000 troops in Iraq.[4] The creation of enduring bases also allowed the US to move soldiers and airmen out of Saudi Arabia, removing a major source of controversy in that country. Brigadier General Robert Pollman, chief engineer for base construction in Iraq told the Chicago Tribune, "When we talk about enduring bases here, we're talking about the present operation, not in terms of America's global strategic base. But this makes sense. It makes a lot of logical sense."[5]

Consultants from think tanks that provide the Pentagon with policy advice thought permanent US bases would play a positive role in Iraq. In the fall of 2004, John Pike, Director of Global Securities.org, told the *Christian Science Monitor* that the bases would provide stability in Iraq. "To avoid these risks [of civil war] an Iraq government will accept a US military presence despite popular disapproval, Pike says. 'An indefinite American presence

1 Jim Lobe, "Are U.S. Intentions more Base than Honorable?" *Anti-War.Com*, 6.16.06; available from http://www.antiwar.com/lobe/?articleid=8754; accessed 16 June 2006

2 Stephen J. Glain, "Pentagon Said to Favor Prolonged Role for U.S. Forces in Iraq," *Boston Globe*, 3.06.04

3 Glain, "Prolonged Role," 3.06.04

4 Christine Spolar, "14 Enduring Bases Set in Iraq," *Chicago Tribune*, 3.23.04; available from http://www.globalsecurity.org/org/news/2004/040323-enduring-bases.htm access 23 July 2006

5 Spolar, "Enduring Bases," 3.23.04

in Iraq is the ultimate guarantor of some quasi-pluralistic government."[1] Thomas Donnelly, from the American Enterprise Institute, told *CSM* that a withdrawal of US forces from the newly constructed network of bases would be seen as a victory by Iraqi insurgents, giving them an incentive to kill more Americans.

The construction of permanent bases that would allow the US to station large numbers of troops and aircraft in Iraq was a vital link in the new strategy for locating military bases devised by Donald Rumsfeld and Pentagon planners. In a 2004 article titled "The Next American Empire," *The Economist* revealed Pentagon plans to move troops and equipment out of Germany, Japan, and Korea and place them in new bases in the Middle East and Central Asia. According to *The Economist*, along with traditional concerns about China, North Korea, and India vs. Pakistan, military planners are worried about "international terrorism and an arc of post-cold-war instability that stretches from the Balkans to the Caucasus and around the Asian shore."[2] The potentially controversial nature of military action in these regions means that:

> America will need to rely on new allies in hitherto neglected regions, and avoid depending on bases in countries that might prove squeamish about pre-emption or prevention. Douglas Feith, a Pentagon official who is helping conduct the review, says that there is no point in having forces in places from which they can't be moved to the fight.[3]

To help the reader visualize the connection between military bases and empires, *The Economist* printed maps showing where the US had significant bases in 2004, where British imperial bases were located in 1898, and where the Roman Empire placed its major bases in 117 CE. Andrew Krepinevich, of the Centre for Strategic and Budgetary Assessments, extended the analogy by comparing the frontier posts of the Roman Empire, which were rapidly reinforced in periods of conflict, with the new, lightly manned, forward bases the Pentagon is creating in the so-called "arc of instability."

The bases being built in Iraq will certainly be large enough to act as the Middle East anchor for the new arc of military installations. For example, there is Camp Anaconda, which includes Balad Air Base and is about 40 miles northeast of Baghdad. The camp covers 15 square miles and is the largest logistical support center for the army in Iraq. When finished, the camp

---

1 David Francis, "U.S. Bases in Iraq: Sticky Politics, Hard Math," *Christian Science Monitor*, 9.30.04; available from http://www.csmonitor.com/2004/0930/p17s02-cogn.html; accessed 24 July 2006

2 *The Economist*, "The Next American Empire," 3.18.04; available from http://www.economist.com/world/na/displayStory.cfm?story_id=2517421 (premium access article) accessed 15 July 2006

3 *The Economist*, "The Next American Empire," 3.18.04

will accommodate 20,000 soldiers.[1] Balad Air Base, formerly the site of Iraq's air academy, is the largest US airfield in Iraq. There are 250 aircraft based at Balad, 188 helicopters and 70 fixed-wing aircraft. Pilots interviewed by reporters compared landing at Balad to the complex approach procedures used at busy American airports like Atlanta or Phoenix.

At al-Asad, the largest marine base in Iraq, located in the western desert, there are American fast food stores, plus a cinema that shows the latest films from America. For those who dislike dusty military vehicles there is a Hertz car rental place that has automobiles with bulletproof windows.[2] The 2006 supplemental budget for Iraq operations provided $7.4 million to expand the base to cover 19 square miles and build a permanent security fence around the perimeter.[3] At the Tallil military base, located south of Baghdad, there is a new $14 million dining facility, able to seat 6,000 hungry servicemen when lunchtime rolls around.[4] The camp's air base, called Ali Air Base, has a $22 million double perimeter security fence with guard towers and a moat — perhaps the signature aspect of these new castles of the Middle East.

The most elaborate sign that the US is planning for a long presence in Iraq is being built in the capital city. The new American Embassy is located on 104 acres inside the city's "green zone" and will cost approximately $600 million once all of the restaurants, gym facilities, and movie theaters are completed.[5] For security reasons the enormous project, illuminated by flood-lights day and night to speed completion, is being carried out by a company from Kuwait using 900 Asian workers who live on the site. More than 1,000 government officials will live and work in the 21 buildings that will be part of the complex.[6] They will reside in 619 apartments connected to their own water, electricity, and sewage treatment plants so they will not have to depend on Baghdad's deteriorating infrastructure.[7] Inside the embassy's 15-foot thick walls, hundreds of marines will be able to maintain security no matter how desperate the situation in the city outside. From this modern palace, equipped with the most advanced communication systems on the planet,

1 Thomas Ricks, "Biggest Base in Iraq has Small-Town Feel," *Washington Post*, 2.4.06; available from http://www.washingtonpost.com/wp-dyn/content/article/2006/02/03/AR2006020302994_pf.html; accessed 20 August 2006

2 Oliver Poole, "Football and Pizza Point to U.S. Staying for Long Haul," *Telegraph.co.uk*, 2.11.06; available from http://www.telegraph.co.uk/news/main.jhtml?xml=/news/2006/02/11/wirq11.xml; accessed 27 August 2006

3 Charles Hanley, "Huge Bases Raise Question: Is U.S. in Iraq to Stay? *Associated Press*, 3.21.06; available from http://www.azstarnet.com/news/120996; accessed 26 June 2006

4 Hanley, "Huge Bases," 3.21.06

5 Nicholas von Hoffman, "Bush's Baghdad Palace," *The Nation*, 6.20.06; available from http://www.commondreams.org/views06/0621-28.htm; accessed 23 June 2006

6 Dahr Jamail, "Iraq: Permanent U.S. Colony," *Truthout*, 3.14.06; available from http://www.truthout.org/cgi-bin/artman/exec/view.cgi/58/18340; accessed 23 June 2006

7 Jamail, "Permanent Colony," 3.14.06

the US ambassador and his staff will be positioned to oversee the American presence in Iraq — a fitting headquarters for an American proconsul.

Once again, we find that the Bush Administration, far from having no plan for how to manage Iraq after the invasion, had a perfectly logical and understandable plan. The Pentagon proceeded to implement that plan with admirable efficiency and attention to detail. The plan was not discussed very much in the US press because it was so obviously a tactic of empire building that no one cared to bring up such a tactless topic. The question to be raised is: will the US ever leave these bases? The answer is that these bases imply some sort of permanent occupation of Iraq, entailing American troops "guarding" an Iraqi government too intimidated to request that we leave. Unfortunately, this answer guarantees that the American empire will continue to generate conflict in the Middle East and terrorist threats to the American homeland.

Conclusion. Breaking the Bonds of Empire

> Now watch what you say,
> Or they'll be calling you a radical,
> A liberal, oh fanatical, criminal...
> —Supertramp, "The Logical Song"

While we might search the Internet each day for the latest trend, real changes in the tide of human affairs often require a decade or even a generation to take hold. In 63 BCE, Cicero was the senior consul of the Roman Republic, chief spokesman for the nobility and an orator who could sway the minds of juries and crowds. A generation later, in 43 BCE, he was a hunted man, proscribed by Antony and Octavian while the Republic collapsed into monarchy. In 1774, Louis XVI, at the age of 20, became the King of France, the exalted ruler of the largest and most powerful country in continental Europe, rivaled only by the English Empire. A generation later, in 1793, he was found guilty of treason and executed by the revolutionary National Convention. In 1900, Queen Victoria presided over a lavish centennial celebration, secure in the notion that the sun never set on the British Empire. A generation later, in 1926, a few years after the First World War left two and a half million young Englishmen dead or wounded, the country was paralyzed by a general strike. Two million workers from the coal, railroad, printing, docks, and steel industries defied the government for nine days, a sign of England's declining economic vitality and a harbinger of her inability to hold together the world's largest empire.

These sharp changes of fortune in seemingly invincible nations lead us to the question, where will the United States be in 20 years? What kind of country will today's young adults and school children live in? The dire examples in the previous paragraph ring a bell with us because people in this country are concerned and pessimistic about the future. Since Hurricane Katrina battered New Orleans in September of 2005, between 60 and 70 percent of the people responding to the *Newsweek* poll question, "Are you satisfied or dissatisfied with the way things are going in the United States at this time?" have said they are dissatisfied.[1] The Gallup poll has tracked similar findings of unhappiness.

We should not be surprised that the percentage of Americans who are dissatisfied went up after Katrina. For many people, the events surrounding the disaster were a clear signal that first, global warming will mean more than extra time at the swimming pool, and second, that the Bush administration's failures in Iraq might be as deep and long lasting as the bungled response to the plight of New Orleans. The concern is not just about the severity of these problems but the deep roots they have in the American way of life and the American empire.

Global warming is just one threat to the energy intensive, petroleum based economy that is the dominant feature of American life. The prosperity and long-term growth of the US economy has been based on inexpensive oil since Theodore Roosevelt was president. At the beginning of the 20th century, booming domestic oil production fueled the initial wave of automobile, steel, and rubber industry growth that made the United States the largest economy in the world by the 1920s. After the Second World War, as US production peaked, inexpensive foreign oil became essential to the energy intensive growth symbolized by the development of suburbs, strip malls, and inter-state highways. Because of this domestic demand for inexpensive fuel, a powerful dimension of the American quest for empire since the 1940s has been the desire to secure long-term control over supplies of oil.

The search for oil brought United States corporate and political leaders to the Middle East. America's relationships with Arab nations have always been based on our preoccupation with securing inexpensive supplies of oil for the US economy. As we have seen, the quest for cheap oil eventually led to the invasion of Iraq. This bold attempt to make the one last, great source of oil a reliable part of the American empire has failed. That failure has both driven up the price of oil and called into question the United States' ability to secure inexpensive oil in the future.

---

1 *PollingReport.com*, "Direction of the Country," available from www.pollingreport.com/right. htm; accessed 5 July 2007

THE ROOTS OF TERRORISM

Less obvious to most Americans is the way in which roping oil-producing Arab nations and pulling them into the empire has alienated large segments of the Moslem world and spawned the al-Qaeda terrorist movement. The claim that America is the object of terrorist attacks because Osama bin Laden and his allies hate American freedoms and the American way of life is wrong. As a former CIA analyst puts it, "There is no record of a Muslim leader urging his brethren to wage jihad to destroy participatory democracy, the National Association of Credit Unions, or the coed Ivy League universities."[1] He goes on to say:

> The focused and lethal threat posed to US national security arises not from Muslims being offended by what America is, but rather from their plausible perception that the things they most love and value — God, Islam, their brethren, and Muslim lands — are being attacked by America. What we as a nation do, then, is the key causal factor in our confrontation with Islam.[2]

The US military presence in the Middle East and our support over the years for dictatorships in Saudi Arabia, Egypt, Kuwait, Iran, and the United Arab Emirates leads to the perception that "we control the Muslim world's oil production" and impose undemocratic, faithless governments on the residents of those countries.[3] In the Wall Street Journal, Bernard Lewis reported "The overwhelming evidence is that the majority of our terrorist enemies come from purportedly friendly countries and their main grievance against us is that, in their eyes, we are responsible for maintaining the tyrannical regimes that rule over them — an accusation that has, to say the very least, some plausibility."[4]

Rage at American actions in the Middle East has intensified and spread through the Muslim world as a result of the American invasion and occupation of Iraq. Before Iraq, only small number of Muslims supported al-Qaeda. Many were skeptical of the organization's claim that the United States was controlling Muslim countries in order to take their oil supplies at below market prices. The premeditated invasion of Iraq changed that view. Iraq is now a holy beacon, radicalizing Muslims of all types. For example, a study of 154 foreign fighters killed in Iraq, conducted by an Israeli think tank in 2005, found that there were a few senior al-Qaeda operatives involved in training and coordinating activities, but "the vast majority of [non-Iraqi] Arabs killed

---

1 Scheuer, Michael, *Imperial Hubris: Why the West is Losing the War on Terror*, (Wash. D.C., Brassey's, Inc., 2004) p. 9, originally published as writing by "Anonymous."

2 Scheuer, *Imperial Hubris*, p. 9

3 Sliverstein, Ken, "Six Questions for Michael Scheuer on National Security," *Harpers Magazine*, 8.23.06; available from http://www.harpers.org/archive/2006/08/sb-seven-michael-scheuer-1156277744; accessed 27 August 2006

4 Lewis, Bernard, *The Crisis of Islam: Holy War and Unholy Terror*, (New York, Modern Library, 2003) p. 17; quoted in Scheuer, *Imperial Hubris*, p. 12

in Iraq have never taken part in any terrorist activity prior to their arrival in Iraq."[1] The study found that these mostly young men "are part of a new generation of terrorists responding to calls to defend their fellow Muslims from 'crusaders' and 'infidels.' "[2]

In turn, the terrorist threat, made vividly real by the events of 9/11, and continuing with attacks on allies like England and Spain that sent troops to Iraq, has led to a serious erosion of cherished American civil liberties. In the name of protecting Americans from terrorist attacks, the Bush administration set up an interrogation center at Guantanamo Bay, in Cuba, where defendants have almost no legal rights and are subject to harsh interview tactics. Former leaders of the Defense Department's Criminal Investigation Task Force told reporters that they warned senior Pentagon officials in 2002 that the methods used there "could constitute war crimes" and would "embarrass the nation" if they were exposed.[3] The prison at Guantanamo Bay turned out to be just the most visible of a network of "black sites," illegal CIA prisons in Eastern European countries and Afghanistan, where "war on terror" detainees are taken in secret, presumably to be tortured.[4] In addition to people captured on battlefields or at other sites of armed conflict, the CIA fills these prisons with suspects it kidnaps off the streets of their communities.[5]

The international furor over Guantanamo and the CIA's secret prisons is fueled by the abuses at the Abu Ghraib prison in Iraq. While the specific torture methods used in Abu Ghraib seem to have been devised by poorly supervised prison guards who were prosecuted for their crimes, the use of torture was encouraged by a range of policies formulated by senior Pentagon officials, including Secretary of Defense Rumsfeld. These policy makers are clearly not being prosecuted for the crimes at Abu Ghraib prison. In general, the Bush administration has encouraged the use of interrogation tactics that are condemned as torture by most civilized nations. For example, Dick Cheney, the Vice-President of the United States, told a radio audience in October of 2006 that allowing the use of "water boarding" on terrorist suspects is "a no-brainer for me."[6]

His remarks came shortly after the administration was able to get the Republican-led Congress to pass the Military Commissions Act of 2006,

---

1 Bender, Bryan, "War Radicalized most Iraq Foreign Fighters, Studies Find," *The Boston Globe*, 7.17.05

2 Bender, "War Radicalized," *The Boston Globe*, 7.17.05

3 Dedman, Bill, "Gitmo Interrogations Spark Battle over Tactics," *MSNBC*, 10.23.06; available from www.msnbc.com/id/15361458; accessed 23 October 2006

4 Priest, Dana, "CIA Allegedly has Secret Prisons," *The Boston Globe*, 11.2.05

5 Nickerson, Colin, "CIA Abduction Case Ignites Controversy," *The Boston Globe*, 12.7.05

6 Sevastopulo, Demetri, "Cheney Endorses Simulated Drowning," *Financial Times*, 10.26.06; available from www.msnbc.msn.com/id/15433467/; accessed 27 October 2006

which authorizes the continued use of aggressive interrogation tactics on suspected terrorist subjects. The desire to use torture is so strong in the Bush administration that the President himself visited Congress on September 14, 2006 to specifically ask for legislation making it legal for the CIA to put people in secret prisons and use "an alternative set of procedures" for interrogating them.[1]

While several Senate Republicans delayed the Military Commissions Act for a week, it ultimately passed by a 65 to 34 vote, with one Republican voting no and 12 Democrats voting in favor. The vote shows that this is not a purely Republican tendency and a significant bloc of Democrats supporting the use of torture. As a result, the Democratic majority elected in November of 2006 was unable to enact any meaningful restrictions on CIA interrogations in 2007.

Are You an Enemy Combatant?

The Military Commissions Act of 2006 also takes away the right of noncitizens in US military prisons to use a writ of *habeas corpus* to challenge their detention in federal courts. *Habeas corpus* (you have the body) simply means that people who have been put in prison can challenge the legality or appropriateness of their imprisonment by asking a federal judge to review the evidence to see if the government has a reasonable case against the defendant. The right of *habeas corpus*, which is enshrined in the US Constitution, prevents the government from taking perceived enemies and holding them in jail without trial forever.

Going one step further, the Military Commissions Act also authorizes the president and his designated federal officials to seize people, including US citizens, whom they believe have "purposefully and materially supported hostilities against the United States." These individuals can then be labeled "enemy combatants," put in military prisons, and held there indefinitely, with no right of *habeas corpus*.[2]

> We are not dealing with hypothetical abuses. The president has already subjected a citizen to military confinement. Consider the case of Jose Padilla. A few months after 9/11, he was seized by the Bush administration as an "enemy combatant" upon his arrival at Chicago's O'Hare International Airport. He was wearing civilian clothes and had no weapons. Despite his American citizenship, he was held for more than three years in a military

---

1 *The Washington Post* editorial, "A Defining Moment for America," 9.15.06; available from http://www.washingtonpost.com/wp-dyn/content/article/2006/09/14/AR2006091401587.html; accessed 17 September 2006

2 Ackerman, Bruce, "The White House Warden," *Los Angeles Times*, 9.28.06; available from www.latimes.com/news/opinion/la-oe-ackerman28sep28,0,619852.story?coll=la-opinion-right-rail; accessed 28 September 2006

brig, without any chance to challenge his detention before a military or civilian tribunal.[1]

Why would the Bush administration want the power to label people "enemy combatants" and detain them indefinitely? Part of the answer was given by the President's former legal advisor and later Attorney General Alberto Gonzales who said before a Senate Committee, "There is no expressed grant of *habeas* [*corpus*] in the Constitution," a statement that is particularly chilling since the passage of the Military Commissions Act.[2] The Bush administration and its supporters believe that procedural rights like *habeas corpus* are no longer important in a world dominated by their war on terrorism.

This provision allowing detention of people the president thinks are "purposefully and materially supporting hostilities against the United States" is a "ticking time-bomb" that could explode during a future crisis — for example, another terrorist attack on American soil.[3] Given the nature of political debate in the US since 9/11, it is not hard to envision a time when hostility expressed against a president and his policies might be considered a treasonous act. For example, in June of 2006, the *New York Times* ran a story exposing a CIA/Treasury Department program to monitor financial transactions between individuals and 7,800 international financial institutions.[4] President Bush and Vice-President Cheney complained bitterly about the disclosure and White House spokesman Tony Snow implied that criticizing a government spying program would get people killed when he said, "The *New York Times* and other news organizations ought to think long and hard about whether a public's right to know in some cases might override somebody's right to live."[5] Staunch Republican loyalist Representative Peter King of Long Island urged the Bush administration to prosecute the newspaper saying, "We're at war, and for the Times to release information about secret operations and methods is treasonous."[6] As in the case of legislation restricting the use of torture, the Democratic majority elected in November of 2006 was unable to enact any meaningful changes to the Military Commissions Act during 2007.

The Bush administration's is also working hard to develop data profiles on thousands of American citizens through wiretaps. In December of 2005, the *New York Times* revealed that, shortly after 9/11, the National Security

1 Ackerman, "White House Warden," 9.28.06

2 Parry, Robert, "Gonzales Questions Habeas Corpus," *Consortium News*, 1.19.07; available from www.truthout.org/docs_2006/011907D.shtml; accessed 19 January 2007

3 Raimondo, Justin, "Are You an Unlawful Combatant?" Anti-War.Com, 10.2.06; available from www.antiwar; accessed 2 October 2006

4 *NBC News*, "Bush, Cheney Condemn Terror Financing Reports," 6.26.06; available from www.msnbc.msn.com/id/13554907; accessed 26 June 2006

5 *NBC News*, "Bush, Cheney Condemn," 6.26.06

6 *NBC News*, "Bush, Cheney Condemn," 6.26.06

Agency was authorized by President Bush to eavesdrop on American citizens inside the United States without the court approved warrants that are required by law for instances of domestic spying.[1] Legislation passed in the 1970s requires the N.S.A. to get permission from a special court, the Foreign Intelligence Surveillance Court (FISC), before placing a wiretap, but the Bush administration did not want any kind of restraint on who or what could be wiretapped. There was an initial outcry when the surveillance program was revealed, but after a few rounds of speeches in February of 2006, the Republican-led Congress declined to investigate the illegal program.

President Bush said the program was necessary and added, "We're at war, and as commander-in-chief, I've got to use the resources at my disposal, within the law, to protect the American people."[2] This claim, that a president can ignore laws during wartime, is an ominous development. In the past, wars have had clear beginnings and endings, but the "war on terrorism" is different.

> This power will lie around like a loaded weapon for any future incumbent to use when he wants to override a law," said Bruce Fein, a former Justice Department official in the Reagan administration. "There will be terrorism forever, so it will become a permanent fixture on our legal landscape.[3]

In January of 2006, David Rivkin, a former associate White House counsel for President George H.W. Bush, who thinks critics of the president do not believe that the war on terrorism is a real war, rejected Fein's argument. "The rules in war are harsh rules, because the stakes are so high."[4]

> Rivkin also rejected Fein's contention that if Bush's legal theory is correct, a president also could authorize internment camps. He said the president can do things that are normal parts of war, including conducting military surveillance. But it would still be illegal to detain citizens who aren't *enemy combatants*, he said (italics added).[5]

Now, with passage of the Military Commissions Act of 2006, that restriction on a wartime president has been greatly weakened.

It is not hard to imagine how the creation of security profiles might be used in a time of crisis. For example, in 1950, at the beginning of the Korean War, FBI Director Herbert Hoover told President Harry Truman that the bureau had identified 12,000 potential subversives.[6] He recommended that they all be locked up in American military prisons by using "a master warrant"

---

1 Risen, James & Lichtblau, Eric, "Bush Lets U.S. Spy on Callers Without Courts," *The New York Times*, 12.16.05; available from http://www.nytimes.com/2005/12/16/politics/16program.htm l?ex=1292389200&en=e32070e08c623ac1&ei=5089; accessed 12 July 2006

2 Roche, Jr., Walter, & Chen, Edwin, "Bush Defends His Internal Spying Program," *The Boston Globe*, 1.2.06

3 Savage, Charlie, "Bush Launches a Bid to Justify Domestic Spying," *The Boston Globe*, 1.24.06

4 Savage, Charlie, "On eve of Hearing, Split on Spying," *The Boston Globe*, 2.5.06

5 Savage, Charlie, "Split on Spying," 2.5.06

6 Weiner, Tim, "Document shows Hoover sought to Detain 12,000," *The Boston Globe*, 12.23.07

and that their right of *habeas corpus* be suspended in order to "protect the country against treason, espionage and sabotage."[1] Truman ignored Hoover, but a future president, strengthened by the Military Commissions Act, may not be so conscious of the need to preserve civil liberties.

THE PERILS OF EMPIRE

We come then, to the end of the Roman Republic and the future of the American Republic. In Rome, the endless wars and enormous social changes generated by the empire destabilized a political system designed for a small city-state. Efforts by the *optimates* and the *populares* to return to earlier periods of stability or to reform the system by redistributing the empire's wealth often backfired, increasing the level and intensity of social conflict. In the end, vital political questions could not be answered without resorting to military force, a situation that led to the end of the Republic and the creation of an authoritarian government better suited to manage an unruly empire.

In the 21st century, the American Republic has acquired an "open" empire that spans the globe, with military bases and unequal economic relationships on every continent. One prominent aspect of the empire has been the pursuit of cheap oil, with the tentacles of empire ensnaring a number of Islamic countries in the Middle East. Attempts to tighten our grip on these resources have led to the disastrous war in Iraq and strengthened a deadly terrorist movement, which is pledged to kill our citizens and the citizens of our allies. In an effort to protect the United States from terrorist attacks, there have already been significant increases in the power of the federal government to intrude on long standing civil liberties.

We stand on the precipice of disaster. Not because the Bush administration wants to create a police state, but because our continuing attempts to secure inexpensive oil through expansion of our empire is provoking Muslims to resist through the use of terrorism. Former CIA analyst Michael Scheuer puts it this way:

> At the core of the debate is oil. As long as we and our allies are dependent on Gulf oil, we can't do anything about the perception that we support Arab tyranny — the Saudis, the Kuwaitis, and other regimes in the region . . . If we solved the oil problem, we could back away from the contradiction of being democracy promoters and tyranny protectors. . . As it stands, we are going to have to fight wars if anything endangers the oil supply in the Middle East.[2]

Like citizens during the era of the late Roman Republic, we will not have the luxury of fighting "wars" only on foreign battlefields. With the cloud of war and terrorism hanging over our country, there will continue to be nasty disagreements on the home front about the use and abuse of government

---

1 Weiner, "Document," 12.23.07
2 Silverstein, "Six Questions," 8.23.06

power. In this contentious environment, a successful terrorist attack on an American subway system, sports complex, or public building could trigger irreversible changes in civil liberties and political freedoms that have long been cherished parts of the American Republic.

In the last few years, there have been many instances of leaders indicating that they would prefer a more authoritarian approach to defending the United States from terrorism. For example, in September of 2005, Republican presidential candidate Mitt Romney advocated for the US to conduct surveillance on foreign students and to monitor public gatherings of Moslems:

> "How about people who are in settings — mosques, for instance — that may be teaching doctrines of hate and terror," Romney continued. "Are we monitoring that? Are we wiretapping? Are we following what's going on?"[1]

Former Attorney General John Ashcroft, within days of leaving his position, complained that judges are jeopardizing national security by interfering with the president's decisions about how to wage the war on terrorism.

> The danger I see here is that intrusive judicial oversight and second-guessing of presidential determinations in these critical areas can put at risk the very security of our nation in a time of war . . . Courts are not equipped to execute the law. They are not accountable to the people.[2]

When the House of Representatives approved a bill that would make it legal for the Bush administration to wiretap American citizens without a warrant (the Senate did not pass the legislation), Republican Speaker of the House Dennis Hastert questioned the patriotism of those who opposed the bill:

> "Democratic minority leader Nancy Pelosi and 159 of her Democrat colleagues voted in favor of more rights for terrorists," Hastert said, "So the same terrorists who plan to harm innocent Americans and their freedom worldwide would be coddled, if we followed the Democrat plan."[3]

Republican presidential candidate Rudy Giuliani echoed this sentiment. He told a New Hampshire audience that the Democratic presidential candidates were too concerned with civil liberties and soft in their approach to fighting the war on terror:

> "If one of them gets elected, it sounds to me like we're going on the defense," he said. "We've got a timetable for withdrawal from Iraq. We're going to wave the white flag there. We're going to try to cut back on the Patriot Act. We're going to cut back on electronic surveillance. We're going to cut back on interrogation. We're going to cut back, cut back, cut back, and we'll be back in our pre-September 11 mentality of being on defense."[4]

---

1 Helman, Scott, "Wiretap Mosques, Romney Suggests," *The Boston Globe*, 9.15.05

2 Anderson, Curt, "Ashcroft says Judges Undermine Bush," *The Boston Globe*, 11.13.04

3 Kellman, Laurie, "House Votes to Approve President's Warrantless Wiretap Bill," *The Boston Globe*, 9.29.06

4 Balz, Dan, "Giuliani Speech on Terror Fight Decried," *The Washington Post*, 4.26.07; available from http://www.washingtonpost.com/wp-dyn/content/article/2007/04/24/

During the 2008 presidential campaign, fear and resentment of immigrants mingled with the fear of terrorism. One chilling example of the country's mood was a campaign ad shown in Iowa in November of 2007 by Republican Presidential candidate Tom Tancredo. The ad began with a man in a hooded sweatshirt wearing a backpack walking through a crowded shopping mall. The screen went dark at the sound of an explosion then showed scenes from the aftermath of terrorist attacks in Europe.[1] The narrator begins, while the man in the sweatshirt walks through the crowd, "There are consequences to open borders beyond the 20 million aliens who have come to take our jobs."[2] No candidate from either party stepped up to condemn this senselessly provocative ad, showing how responsive they are to the wildest of public fears.

Pop culture also provides a window into the thoughts of many journalists about civil liberties. Once a week, on the Fox Television series *24*, Jack Bauer leads the way in fighting the war on terror with an almost deliberate disregard for civil liberties. Nominated for 12 Emmys in 2006, it won four and the season premiere in the fall of 2006 drew 16 million viewers.[3] Neoconservatives love the show. In January of 2007, columnist Ben Shapiro said, "If torturing a particular terrorist is useful — if we engage in the complicated calculus that tells us that the benefits outweigh the harms — torture is not only justified, it is morally right." The title of this ode to torture was, "Where's Jack Bauer When You Need Him?"[4] On the HBO show "Real Time with Bill Maher," economist Stephen Moore spoke approvingly of the Military Commissions Act of 2006, saying it was "Jack Bauer justice." Moore went on to say, "He should run the CIA . . . This guy knows how to interrogate guys. He takes them in, shoots them in the leg, 'Tell me where the bomb is.' . . ."[5]

A successful terrorist attack on American soil would provide Mitt Romney, Rudi Giuliani, the Republicans in the House of Representatives, Tom Tancredo, and neoconservative journalists with the perfect opening to call for far reaching changes in the way we balance civil liberties and the apparatus of the police state. In the panic and anger following a successful terrorist attack, the likelihood that the Democrats in Congress or even a Democratic president would resist the call for more intrusive measures is very small. We

---

AR2007042402241.html accessed 26 April 2007

1 *CBS News*, "Republican Tom Tancredo Abandons White House Bid," 12.20.07; available from http://cbs2chicago.com/politics/Tom.Tancredo.presidency.2.614720.html; accessed 26 December 2007

2 CBS News, "Republican Tom Tancredo," 12.20.07

3 Dougherty, Michael Brendan, "Why Can't Bush Be more like Bauer?" *The American Conservative*, 3.12.07; available from http://www.amconmag.com/2007/2007_03_12/cover.html; accessed 14 March 2007

4 Dougherty, "Why Can't Bush?" 3.12.07

5 Dougherty, "Why Can't Bush?" 3.12.07

have a clear historical analogy; a full year after the 9/11 attacks, a majority of Democrats in the Congress were afraid to vote against an invasion of Iraq that was clearly unrelated to the chase for Osama bin Laden. The polling constituency for civil liberties in the days of anguish after America suffered another tragic explosion would be much smaller than the number of Americans who opposed the invasion of Iraq.

It is unlikely that the American Republic will collapse as rival generals invade Washington D.C. to support political factions. However, the Republic could be eaten away from within by authoritarian measures designed to protect the citizenry from the turmoil generated by the empire. Of course, we can comfort ourselves with the thought that "it can't happen here," but human history shows that authoritarian rule is far more common than Republican government. History also tells us that in periods of turmoil and fear, people turn to strong leaders who are happy to do away with irritating dissenters and with the messy, noisy, inefficient process that is free, open, democratic government. If and when that happens, then the bright shining light that is the American Republic would go out, just as surely as the Roman Republic and *libertas* did two millennia ago.

To avoid that fate, we must do what the Romans could not bring themselves to do: give up the empire and build a new place in the world. In this new place, energy efficiency and international law will be treasured ahead of hummers, mcmansions, and shock and awe military adventures. There is still reason to hope because, unlike in Rome's final days, the United States is still able to generate an anti-war movement that rejects empire building, and there is still space for critical minds that can help shape public opinion. In addition, the series of natural catastrophes that showcase the growing threat of global warming will provide us with opportunities to initiate public discussions about the uses and abuses of petroleum energy.

To make this break with the past a reality, the anti-war movement will need to expand its horizons beyond the war in Iraq by linking it to the whole vicious cycle of energy inefficiency, the militarization of oil, terrorism, the network of military bases, global warming, and eroding civil liberties that now plagues the American empire. Political work that only focuses on one element of our multi-dimensional dilemma will get lost in the rush of events. Political talk that presents one public policy as the cure all will find itself lost in a maze of conflicting claims. Political action that relies on one leader or one party will bog down in the dreary search for 51% of the vote.

Daunting as this task may seem, the alternative is a dark, confined future, if not for the baby boom generation, then for the next generation, our children and grandchildren. As we strive to create a better world, we should draw strength and resolution by remembering the sad fate of the citizens of the Roman Republic. Their *libertas* was washed away in a swirl of cataclys-mic events — but we do not have to follow their path of imperial misadven-ture. It is our turn to challenge history, and the future is unwritten. When we do save the Republic, when we do restore balance to an unstable world, somewhere in the mists of time, their spirits will be cheering for us.

BIBLIOGRAPHY

SOURCES ON THE ROMAN REPUBLIC

Alfoldy, Geza. *The Social History of Rome.* Baltimore: John Hopkins University Press, 1975.

Appian of Alexandria, *Roman History: Wars in Hispania*; available from www.livius.org/ap-ark/appian/appian_spain_00.html; accessed 22 July 2007.

Appian of Alexandria, *Roman History: The Gaelic Wars*; available from www.livius.org/ap-ark/appian/appian_gallic_1.html; accessed 22 July 2007.

Appian of Alexandria, *Roman History: The Samnite Wars*; available from www.livius.org/ap-ark/appian/appian_samnite_1.html; accessed 22 July 2007.

Astin, A.E., *Scipio Aemilianus.* Oxford: Oxbow Books Limited, 1967.

Aubert, Jean-Jacques, "The Republican Economy and Roman Law," in Flower, Harriet, ed. *The Cambridge Companion to the Roman Republic.* Cambridge: Cambridge University Press, 2004. pp. 160-178.

Beard, Mary and Crawford, Michael. *Rome in the Late Republic.* Ithaca: Cornell University Press, 1985

Bell, Andrew J.E., "Cicero and the Spectacle of Power," *Journal of Roman Studies*, V.87, 1997, pp. 1-22.

Bernstein, Alvin, *Tiberius Sempronius Gracchus: Tradition and Apostasy.* Ithaca: Cornell University Press, 1978.

Boatwright, Mary, Gargola, Daniel and Talbert, Richard. *The Romans: From Village to Empire.* New York: Oxford University Press, 2004.

Boren, Henry. *The Gracchi.* Woodbridge, CT: Twayne, 1968.

Brennan, Corey T. "Power and Process under the Republican Constitution" in Harriet Flower, *The Cambridge Companion to the Roman Republic*, Cambridge: Cambridge University Press, 2004, pp. 31-65.

Brunt, P.A. *The Fall of the Roman Republic and Related Essays.* Oxford: Oxford University Press, 1988.

Cary, M. "An Accidental War," in Erich Gruen, ed. *Imperialism in the Roman Republic.* New York: Holt, Rinehart, Winston, 1970, pp. 31-33

Cornell, Timothy and Matthews, John. *Atlas of the Roman World.* Oxford: Equinox Limited, 1982.

Everitt, Anthony. *Cicero: The Life and Times of Rome's Greatest Politician.* New York: Random House, 2001.

Fagan, Garrett G. *Great Battles of the Ancient World.* Chantilly, VA: The Teaching Company, 2005.

Flower, Harriet I., "Spectacle and Political Culture in Republican Rome," in Flower, Harriet, ed. *The Cambridge Companion to the Roman Republic.* Cambridge: Cambridge University Press, 2004. pp. 322-343.

Grant, Michael. *The Ancient Historians.* New York: Barnes and Noble Books, 1970.

Green, Peter. *Alexander to Actium: The Historical Evolution of the Hellenistic Age.* Berkeley: University of California Press, 1990.

Gruen, Erich S. *The Last Generation of the Roman Republic.* Berkeley: University of California Press, 1974.

Gruen, Erich S. "Introduction," in Erich Gruen, ed. *Imperialism in the Roman Republic.* New York: Holt, Rinehart, Winston, 1970, pp. 1-9

Holland, Tom. *Rubicon: The Last Years of the Roman Republic.* New York: Doubleday, 2003.

Holleauz, Maurice, "Preventive Warfare," in Erich Gruen, ed. *Imperialism in the Roman Republic.* New York: Holt, Rinehart, Winston, 1970, pp. 40-47

Hutchinson, Lester. *The Conspiracy of Catiline.* New York: Barnes and Noble Inc., 1967.

Kahn, Arthur D. *The Education of Julius Caesar.* Lincoln, NE: iUniverse.com, 1986.

LeGlay, Marcel, Voisin, Jean-Louis, and Le Bohec, Yann. *A History of Rome.* Malden, MA: Blackwell Publishers, 1996.

Liberati, Anna Maria and Bourbon, Fabio. *Ancient Rome.* New York: Barnes and Noble Publishing, 2004.

Livius, Titus (Livy), *History of Rome, Book VI*; available from livius.org/rome/ text translated at: http://mcadams.posc.mu.edu/txt/ah/livy/livey06.html; accessed 22 July 2007.

Matyszak, Phillip. *Chronicle of the Roman Republic.* London: Thames & Hudson Ltd, 2003.

McCullough, Colleen. *The First Man in Rome.* New York: Avon, 1990.

Meadows, Andrew and Williams, Jonathan, "Moneta and the Monuments: Coinage and Politics in Republican Rome," *Journal of Roman Studies*, V.91, 2001, pp. 27-49.

Meier, Christian. *Caesar: A Biography.* New York: Basic Books, 1982.

Millar, Fergus. *The Crowd in Rome in the Late Republic.* Ann Arbor: University of Michigan Press, 1998.

Millar, Fergus, "A Critique of the Cambridge History of the Roman Republic," *Journal of Roman Studies*, V.85, 1995, pp. 236-243.

Millar, Fergus, "The Political Character of the Classical Roman Republic 200-151 B.C.," *Journal of Roman Studies*, V.74, 1984, pp. 1-19.

Mommsen, Theodore, *History of Rome*, 1855, Book II, Chapter VI, "Struggle of the Italians Against Rome," available from www.Italian.classic-literature.co.uk/history-of-rome/; accessed 29 December 2007.

Morkot, Robert. *The Penguin Historical Atlas of Ancient Greece.* London: Penguin Books, 1996.

Mouritsen, Henrik. *Plebs and Politics in the Late Roman Republic.* Cambridge: Cambridge University Press, 2001.

Nippel, Wilfred, "Policing Rome" *Journal of Roman Studies*, V.74, 1984. pp. 20-29.

Potter, David, "The Roman Army and Navy," in Flower, Harriet, ed. *The Cambridge Companion to the Roman Republic.* Cambridge: Cambridge University Press, 2004. pp. 66-88.

Rupke, Jorg, "Roman Religion," in Flower, Harriet, ed. *The Cambridge Companion to the Roman Republic.* Cambridge: Cambridge University Press, 2004. pp. 179-195.

Schulten, A., "Roman Cruelty and Extortion" in Erich Gruen, ed. *Imperialism in the Roman Republic.* New York: Holt, Rinehart, Winston, 1970, pp. 60-66.

Scullard, H.H. *A History of the Roman World.* New York: Routledge, 1935.

Seager, Robin. *Pompey the Great.* Malden, MA: Blackwell Publishing, 1979.

Sellers, Mortimer, N. "The Roman Republic and the French and American Revolutions," in Flower, Harriet, ed. *The Cambridge Companion to the Roman Republic.* Cambridge: Cambridge University Press, 2004. pp. 347-364.

Smith, R.E., "City-State Unable to Act as World Power," in Erich Gruen, ed. *Imperialism in the Roman Republic.* New York: Holt, Rinehart, Winston, 1970, pp. 95-101.

Southern, Pat. *Pompey the Great.* Charleston, S.C.: Tempus Publishing, 2002.

Stapleton, Michael. *The Illustrated Dictionary of Greek & Roman Mythology.* New York: Peter Bedrick Books, 1978.

Stockton, David. *The Gracchi.* Oxford: Oxford University Press, 1979

Tatum, W. Jeffrey. *The Patrician Tribune.* Chapel Hill: University of North Carolina Press, 1999.

Taylor, Lily Ross. *Party Politics in the Age of Caesar.* Berkeley: University of California Press, 1949.

Taylor, Lily Ross, "Forerunners of the Gracchi," *Journal of Roman Studies*, #52, 1962. pp. 17-27.

Thiel, J.H., "Roman War Guilt," in Erich Gruen, ed. *Imperialism in the Roman Republic.* New York: Holt, Rinehart, Winston, 1970, pp. 22-30.

Veyne, Paul, "Work & Leisure" in Veyne, Paul editor, *A History of Private Life: From Pagan Rome to Byzantium.* Cambridge, MA: Belknap Press: 1987.

Vishnia, Rachel Feig. *State, Society, and Popular Leaders in Mid-Republican Rome 241-167 B.C.* New York: Taylor & Francis, Inc. 1996.

Warry, John. *Warfare in the Classical World.* New York: St. Martin's Press, 1980.

Yakobson, Alexander, "Popular Participation in the Centuriate Assembly of the Late Republic," *Journal of Roman Studies*, V.82, 1992, pp. 32-52.

Sources on the American Republic

For essays on topics such as oil politics in the 21st century, the impact of open markets on small countries, and the guerrilla war in the Phillipines please go to the author's web site at: www.perilsofempire.com

Bacevich, Andrew J. *American Empire: The Realities & Consequences of U.S. Diplomacy.* Cambridge: Harvard University Press, 2002.

Baran, Paul and Sweezy, Paul. *Monopoly Capital.* New York: Monthly Review Press, 1966.

Chace, James. 1912: *Wilson, Roosevelt, Taft & Debs — The Election that Changed the Country.* New York: Simon & Schuster, 2004.

Eland, Ivan. *The Empire Has No Clothes: U.S. Foreign Policy Exposed.* Oakland, CA: The Independent Institute, 2004.

Fenno, Richard F. *Congressmen in Committees.* Boston: Little Brown and Company, 1973.

Fukuyama, Francis. *America at the Crossroads: Democracy, power, and the Neoconservative Legacy.* New Haven: Yale University Press, 2006.

Goodwyn, Lawrence. *The Populist Moment.* Oxford: Oxford University Press, 1978.

Hansen, Bradley. "Bankruptcy Law in the United States," *EH.Net*; available from http://eh.net/encyclopedia/article/Hansen.bankruptcy.law.us; accessed 22 July 2007.

Hersh, Seymour M. *The Price of Power: Kissinger in the Nixon White House.* New York: Simon and Schuster, 1983.

Johnson, Chalmers. *The Sorrows of Empire: Militarism, Secrecy, and the End of the Republic.* New York: Metropolitan Books, 2004.

Kennedy, Paul M. *The Rise and Fall of British Naval Mastery.* London: Ashfield Press, 1976.

Kennedy, Paul M. *The Rise and Fall of the Great Powers.* New York: Random House, 1987.

Kinzer, Stephen. *Overthrow: America's Century of Regime Change from Hawaii to Iraq.* New York: Henry Holt and Company, 2004.

Klare, Michael T. *Blood and Oil: The Dangers and Consequences of America's Growing Dependency on Imported Petroleum.* New York: Henry Holt and Company, 2004.

Klein, Naomi. *Fences and Windows: Dispatches from the Front Lines of the Globalization Debate.* New York: Picador, 2002.

Mann, Bruce H. Republic of Debtors: Bankruptcy in the Age of American Independence. Cambridge: Harvard University Press, 2002.

Open Collections Program, Harvard University Library, http://ocp.hul.harvard.edu/immigration/dates.html

Parkin, Frank. *Class Inequality and Social Order.* New York: Praeger Publishers, 1971.

Peterson, Merrill D. *The Great Triumvirate: Webster, Clay, and Calhoun.* New York: Oxford University Press, 1987.

Phillips, Kevin. American *Theology: The Peril and Politics of Radical Religion, Oil, and Borrowed Money in the 21st Century.* London: Viking Penguin, 2006.

Scheuer, Michael. *Imperial Hubris: Why the West is Losing the War on Terror.* Washington, D.C.: Brassey's, 2004.

Trefousse, Hans. *Thaddeus Stevens: 19th Century Egalitarian.* Mechanicsburg, PA: Stackpole Books, 2001.

Tritch, Teresa, "The Rise of the Super Rich," *The New York Times*, 7.19.06

Williams, William Appleman. *The Tragedy of American Diplomacy.* New York: W.W. Norton and Company, 1959.

Zimmermann, Warren. *First Great Triumph: How Five Americans Made their Country a World Power.* New York: Farrar, Straus, and Giroux, 2002.

Zinn, Howard. *The Twentieth Century: A People's History.* Cambridge: Harper and Row, Publishers, 1984.

INDEX

Manufactured By: RR Donnelley
                     Breinigsville, PA USA
                     October, 2010